Reason
Faithful and True

Essays in Honour of Dr. George Karuvelil SJ

JDV Philosophy Series - 13

Reason Faithful and True

Essays in Honour of Dr. George Karuvelil SJ

Edited by
Thomas Karimundackal SJ
Dolichan Kollareth SJ

Jnana-Deepa Vidyapeeth

&

Christian World Imprints

First Published in 2020 by

Jnana-Deepa Vidyapeeth
Ramwadi, Nagar Road, **Pune-411014**
jdvoffice@jdv.edu.in
www.jdv.edu.in
Phone: +91 20 41036111

&

Christian World Imprints
Christian Publishing & Books from India
C-3, Wazirpur Industrial Area
Delhi-110052
cwidelhi2017@gmail.com
www.ChristianWorldImprints.com
Phone: +91 11 41526079

ISBN: 978-93-5148-429-5

"Published with the help of the Institute of Missiology – Germany"

Printed in India.

CONTENTS

JDV PHILOSOPHY SERIES - 13

Since 1893 Jnana-Deepa Vidyapeeth has been pioneering philosophy discussion and debate inspired by prominent personalities like Richard De Smet, Jean de Marneffe, Salvino Azzopardi, Cyril Desbruslais, Noel Sheth, John Vattanky, etc. It has been in the forefront of promoting Indian philosophy and making philosophical thinking relevant for contemporary times. In its effort to reach out to like-minded scholars, JDV Philosophy Series has been visualized as a catalyst for interdisciplinary thinking and contemporary exploration on social issues fostering holistic liberation, integral development and creative engagement.

JDV Philosophy Series

1. Salvino Azzopardi: ***Epistemology and Phenomenology of Religions*** (2018)
2. Kuruvilla Pandikattu & Thomas Karimundackal (eds): ***Melodies from the Flute***: For Prof Noel Sheth SJ (2018)
3. Kurien Kunnumpuram: ***Freedom and Joy*** (2018)
4. Cyril Desbruslais SJ: ***Postmodernity: An Indian Christian Philosophical Appraisal*** (2019)
5. Cyril Desbruslais SJ: ***Metaphysics Philosophy of Be-ing for Today*** (2019)
6. John Peter Vallabadoss: ***Indian Thinkers: Modern and Contemporary Period*** (2019)
7. Thomas Karimundackal & Kuruvilla Pandikattu (eds): ***Logic and Love***: For Prof John Vattanky SJ (2019)
8. Fabian Jose UMI: ***Relevance of Thomas Merton's Spirituality for the Consecrated Life in India*** (2019)
9. Kuruvilla Pandikattu & PT Mathew (eds): ***Committed to the Church and the Country***: For Prof Kurien Kunnumpuam SJ (2019)
10. Cyril Desbruslais SJ: ***The Philosophy of God*** (2019)
11. Thomas Karimundackal & Kuruvilla Pandikattu (eds): ***Fully Spiritual, Fully Human***: For Dr Stephen Chundamthadam SJ (2019)
12. Kuruvilla Pandikattu (ed) ***Fully Human and Fully Alive: Essays on Being Human Today in Honour of Dr Cyril Desbruslais SJ*** (2020)
13. Thomas Karimundackal SJ & Dolichan Kollareth SJ (eds) ***Reason: Faithful and True***: For Dr. George Karuvelil SJ (2020)

FOREWORD

To think through issues and concerns and articulate the underlying assumptions and emerging perspectives is the work of a true thinker. That distinguishes him from a routine teacher. For Heidegger poet is one who listens to Being. One could say that a thinker is one who deciphers the arguments and formulates the emerging newness.

Prof. George Karuvelil SJ has been teaching philosophy for many years at JDV, Pune. As a philosopher he dwelt on the domain of reason. Rightly so. The questions of faith however remained with him. He allowed them to intersect and fecund one another. It is faith seeking understanding, distinguishing faith from belief system. The former refers to the quest for the ultimate, while the latter refers to the articulated form of that quest. In that sense, the thrust of fundamental theology to network with philosophical search remained one of the passions of Prof. George.

As part of team teaching, students had occasions to listen to his lectures during our lessons on 'faith and revelation' and 'theology of religions'. On both occasions we were impressed and enlightened by his efforts on eliciting the nuances of faith and reason dialogue. Now we learn that he has elaborated on those questions and ready to publish it in book form for the benefit of many.

Dr. Karimundackal has organized an impressive collection of essays on marginal questions related to science, faith, reason, scripture and philosophy in honour of Prof. George. This is a fitting homage to Prof. George who dared to walk consistently on border questions and formulate its implications for the quest for the Ultimate. I am happy to learn that this volume is a worthy, addition to the already existing collections in 'JDV-Philosophy Series, thanks to the initiative of Prof. Kuruvilla Pandikattu.

May the quest ever continue; may the findings ever find light of the day.

Prof. Dr. George Pattery SJ
President, Jesuit conference of South Asia, and
Vice-Chancellor of Jnana-Deepa Vidyapeeth, Pune

EDITORIAL

Henry David Thoreau once said: "To be a philosopher is not merely to have subtle thoughts, not even to found a school, but so to love wisdom as to live according to its dictates, a life of simplicity, independence, magnanimity and trust." This is quite true with Dr. George Karuvelil. For Karuvelil, philosophy is something not concerned exclusively with words and books, nor is it something to be confined to the ivory tower, but something to be lived: philosophy is a way of life, a practice of immersing his own whole being to the mysteries of God, human and society. Karuvelil is a creative philosopher who is original in his thinking and not a mere, pedantic, derivative, academic scholar. Being passionate about living a life of reason and faith has enabled him to make his own synthesis of on faith and reason by not condemning the perspectives of others, but rather by seeking the truth of those perspectives.

Karuvelil loves wisdom and truth so deeply that he lives according to the truth, which goes back to the original etymology of philosophy: *philo-sophia* (love of wisdom). And this is, really, a practice of devotion - devotion to the truth - that refuses to let the truth be rusting ideas stored in our heads, instead manifesting it as embodied insight: a devotion to the truth that confronts us, challenges us and changes us.

To be a philosopher is to ask and try to answer the questions that we ordinarily do not ask in our everyday lives. Karuvelil is something of a skeptic with metaphysical truths as he kept on asking questions related to them and tried to answer them with a creative mind, because to philosophize is to seek in oneself the courage to ask painful questions. He asked questions that no one else wants to ask, not about having all the answers, but learning all he can along the way.

Aristotle once said, "all philosophy begins in wonder." As a true philosopher, Karuvelil used to wonder about life: about right, wrong, love, freedom, truth, beauty, time, and many other things. As a true philosopher, he raised profound questions relating to the nature of being and truth, and rejected any conventional wisdom related to them. As a true philosopher he condemned ignorance, but sought after truth, wisdom, enlightenment. In short, as a true philosopher he used to take a critical view of life in its many aspects, inwardly and outwardly, leaving the biases for further exploration.

Karuvelil's life long academic commitment was to find a way to integrate faith and reason to see the truth in its totality. How can a Christian unite faith and reason? This was the heart of his epistemological and hermeneutical quest. He firmly believed that faith and reason are integral to understand the truth revealed in the religion since "each without the other is enfeebled" (Fides et Ratio # 48). He was convinced that the truth conferred by revelation is a truth to be understood in the light of reason.

In short, Karuvelil is a philosopher with a difference: one who differs and inspires with a philosophical vision; a philosopher who tries to integrate faith and reason in his philosophical and theological thinking; a philosopher who offers views and clarity on profound questions in metaphysics, hermeneutics, logic, and other related fields; a philosopher who is passionately involved in teaching epistemology and hermeneutics; a philosopher who is committed to bring transformation in the young minds by being a mentor and guide; a philosopher who seeks and speaks the truth at all costs; a philosopher who keenly motivates the others.

This special volume is a token of our gratitude to Dr. George Karuvelil. Through this book, we acknowledge his contribution not only to Philosophy and the Church but also at the personal level. He has personally touched and inspired us. Seeking good reasons to answer our deepest questions and not accepting "easy answers" to those questions constitute the subject matter of philosophizing in the context. Therefore the book is titled as '*Reason: Faithful and True*' and it is meant to convey the idea that reason is always in a context (perspective, worldview, faith, etc.), but it is not a matter of clinging on to the context. Reason can go beyond different perspectives in as much as truth is not merely a matter of perspectives and faith commitments. Thus, the title brings together hermeneutics (different perspectives) and epistemology (truth seeking), and religious faith. The title, in a way, summarizes his life.

This book, which we humbly offer to him, is divided into four parts, reflecting Karuvelil's own philosophical and theological vision and concerns. In the *prologue* Karuvelil himself vividly narrates his own journey in the academic pursuit. A close reading of his academic journey will unravel his journey towards a "maverick philosopher-theologian." In the 'purview' section we have two articles: in the first article Michael Devin Coonghe, a research scholar at JDV, Pune makes a journey through the articles of Karuvelil and shows the task of philosophy according to the mind of Karuvelil. He ably shows that the task of philosophy is a call and a vocation rooted in human living conditions rather than on speculative thinking. In the second article, Thomas Karimundackal, a student of Karuvelil and the Professor of Old Testament at the Faculty of Theology, JDV, Pune makes an attempt to draw the inherent relationship between faith and reason as it is elicited in the *Fides et Ratio*, the lifelong academic goal of Karuvelil to integrate faith and reason to understand the truth in its totality.

The first part titled "*Philo-Sophia-* Reason Meeting with Wisdom" has seven scholarly articles that basically deal with metaphysical questions. In the first article of this section, Gerald O'Collins, a close friend of Karuvelil and emeritus Professor of Theology at the Gregorian University, Rome and adjunct Professor of the University of Divinity, Melbourne, and a research fellow of Australian Catholic University, deals with Aristotle's category of substance, and non-existence as a subject of the ontological criterion. In the second article, Jojo Varakukalayil, the President of the Little Flower Institute of Philosophy & Religion, Aluva, Kerala, reflects upon Hegel's philosophy of free will, and shows that will, for Hegel, is objectively manifested as right in a rational society and accordingly the structures of the society are structures of the will. In the next article, V. Sebastian, Professor of Philosophy and Theology at JDV, Pune, seeks to explore dialectics of history and human intentionality through Bernard Lonergan's philosophy of history. In the next paper, Keith D'Souza, the Rector of St. Xavier's College, Mumbai, and the President of the Association of Christian Philosophers of India (ACPI), elaborates the hermeneutical principles governing science and religion. He argues that as meaning-making interpretive systems, science and religion are subject to common hermeneutical principles, or common principles pertaining to the art and science of interpretation. In the next paper, Clement Jesudoss Santhanam, a student of Karuvelil and a research scholar at the University of Innsbruck, Austria reflects upon the concept of 'ignorance' and he argues that 'ignorance' must be defined in terms of three doxastic attitudes, namely belief, disbelief and suspension of belief and disbelief. In the next article, Dolichan Kollareth, a student of Karuvelil and Professor of Psychology at JDV, Pune and a research associate Professor at Boston College, USA, argues in favor of the role of concepts and categories in constituting human experiences taking the example of the emotional experience of shame. In the last article of this section, Dolreich Pereira, the Dean of Philosophy at St. Pius X College, Goregaon - the Archdiocesan Seminary and also Professor of Systematic Theology, deals with the question about the beginning of modernity by considering the contributions of Nicholas of Cusa and Giordano Bruno, and shows that they - Nicholas of Cusa and Giordano Bruno - constitute two sides of the threshold of an epoch.

The second part titled "*Theo-Sophia*: Faith Meeting with Wisdom" has five discussions on how faith interacts with reason in a meaningful way. In the first article of this section, Thomas Kalary, Professor of philosophy at Suvidya College, Bangalore and an Associate Editor of Heidegger Studies, Germany, deals elaborately on the three Heideggerian foundational notions, such as onto-theology, ontological and theological difference, and 'the last god.' In the second paper, Jose Nandhikkara, Professor of Philosophy, at Dharmaram Vidya Kshetram and Christ (Deemed to be University), Bangalore, and the Chief Editor of the Journal of Dharma, argues that Wittgenstein's way of doing philosophy and his thoughts on aesthetic, ethical, and religious values can be fruitfully applied to throw light on understanding the nature and meaning of religious epistemology. In the next essay, Isaac Parackal, Professor of Philosophy at JDV, Pune, elaborates the nature of theology for a scientific age by considering A. R. Peacocke's vision of God, human and world. In the next paper, Savio Martires, a student of Karuvelil and a post-graduate fellow at the Pontifical Urban University, Rome, discusses the mystery of God and the dialectics of evil by examining the manner in which St. Augustine and St. Ireneaus attempt a justification of God in the face of evil in their theodicies. In the final article in this section, Arun Philip, a student of Karuvelil who currently pursues his theological studies at Centre Sèvres, Paris, attempts to integrate Christian philosophy and the ideas of Gilles Deleuze and Gianni Vattimo by arguing that the multifaceted religious faith needs to interact with various dimensions of reason.

The third part titled "*Religio-Sophia*: Religion Meeting with Wisdom" has four scholarly discussion on how religion to be understood today, especially in a pluri-religious context. In the first article, Maxim Pinto, Professor and head of the Department of Philosophy at Holy Trinity Regional Major Seminary, Jalandhar, Punjab, shows how can the Wilberian parameter of "All Quadrant – All Level" (AQAL) can become a meaningful tool to understand religious diversity. He argues that the AQAL is one of the key factors to understand growing religious intolerance, and this method invites everyone to deepen one's own religious experience by learning to integrate that of others. In the second article, Doni Raja, a student of Karuvelil who currently pursues his theological studies at Vidyajyoti College, Delhi, explores the multiple understanding of religious experience, and he argues that there are no convincing and persuasive reasons to show that religious experiences should not be trusted. Therefore, it is rational to believe them. In the next essay, Sathya Balan, a student of Karuvelil and a research scholar at JDV, Pune tries to see convergence between Wittgenstein's concept of "family resemblance" and George Karuvelil's ideas of the distinct roles of fundamental theology and theology of religions from a communication perspective for a pluralistic society. In the final article of this section Subhash Anand, emeritus Professor of Indian Philosophy and Religions at JDV, Pune, emphasizes the need for the critical reflection of our religious experience to interpret it meaningfully and articulate it intelligibly for our times. According to him "enlightened religion would mean a shift from belief to faith, from rituals to values, from law to discernment, from prayers to contemplation, from religiosity to humanity."

The fourth part titled "*Indo-Sophia*: Indology Meeting with Wisdom" has three scholarly contributions. In the first article Henry D'Almeida, Professor of Logic, Indian Philosophy, Sanskrit, Pali and Bhagavadgita at JDV, Pune, focuses on Madhva's interpretation of the *mahavakya tat-tvam-asi* in the Chandogya Upanishad in order to highlight his contribution to shruti Hermeneutics. In the next article, Joseph Kaipayil, Professor of Philosophy at Jeevalaya Institute of Philosophy, Bengaluru, discusses the contemporary interpretations of Shankara's Advaita and the affirmation of the world by four contemporary thinkers, such as K.C. Bhattacharyya, S. Radhakrishnan, P.T. Raju, and Richard De Smet. The final article by Victor Ferrao, the Dean of Philosophy at Rachol Seminary, Goa, shows how Hindutva has emerged as an offshoot of colonization, and he argues that "as a colonization of our minds, it has become a hauntology that haunts all Indians."

In the Epilogue, John Karuvelil, brother of George Karuvelil and Professor of Moral Theology at JDV, Pune gives a personal account of George Karuvelil whom he has encountered as a brother, a Jesuit companion and a good friend. His sentiments can be summarized in his concluding words: "it was God's special favour that even as Jesuits and, that too from two different provinces, we could be in the same place working in the same institution and, therefore, also as colleagues and companions on the same mission of the Lord."

We are grateful to the three campus houses in Pune, which made this book possible. To Prof. Dr. Selva Rathinam SJ, the President, Jnana-Deepa Vidyapeeth, Pune and Prof. Dr. Jose Thayil SJ, the Registrar, Jnana-Deepa Vidyapeeth, Pune, where the three of us, including Dr. George Karuvelil taught, to Rev. Fr. Edward Mudavassery SJ, the Rector, Rev. Fr. Jacob Kulangara SJ, the Minister, and community, De Nobili College, where the three of us stayed. Our sincere gratitude goes to the Papal Seminary community, Pune especially to Rev. Fr. Bhausaheb Sansare SJ, the Rector and Rev. Fr. Vincent Crasta SJ, the Minister, where Dr. George Karuvelil and Thomas Karimundackal are currently residing. We thank these communities for the opportunities given to us for our academic and spiritual fulfillment. We also thank Rev. Dr. George Pattery SJ, the President of Jesuit Conference of South Asia, and Vice-Chancellor of Jnana-Deepa Vidyapeeth, Pune for writing a fitting forward to this Festschrift to honour Dr. George Karuvelil.

Thomas Karimundackal SJ
Dolichan Kollareth SJ

PROLOGUE

My Intellectual Journey: Recollections of a Maverick Philosopher-Theologian

George Karuvelil SJ

A statement that is attributed to Mark Twain says that the two most important days of your life are the day you are born and the day you find out why. Unfortunately, the second day may not be a single date like the birthday; it may involve a process of gradual realization. But once the realization sets in, you have no choice but to live it. Such has been the story of my academic life.

Early Years

The journey of coming to know why I was born was a long and slow process. It began at a relatively young age. I joined the Jesuits in the enthusiastic, revolutionary days after the Second Vatican Council that boldly declared that salvation was not the monopoly of Christians, much less of Catholics. And here I was, a youth of 18, hailing from a traditional Catholic family that valued missionary work, and now wanting to be a Jesuit missionary. When I had an occasion to meet the director of candidates, a senior Jesuit, I placed my problem before him. If salvation is available to all, why be a Christian missionary? He responded that I will find the answer while doing philosophy and theology. It is a different matter that neither philosophy nor theology helped me find answers to my question. But before that I must say something about how my novitiate played a role in shaping my sense of mission.

I began my novitiate in 1975, immediately after the 32nd General Congregation of the Society of Jesus. As novices we were expected to study the documents put out by the Congregation, and in that process I discovered that in pursuit of the special Jesuit vow of obedience to the Pope with regard to missions, the Pope renewed the mandate given earlier (1966) to confront atheism. Atheism was not of much pastoral significance in my province; rather than confront them, atheists were often our friends in the field in their stand for the poor. Although such was the case in the field, atheism posed an intellectual challenge to me as a religious believer. And meeting that challenge was very much a mission entrusted to the Society by the Pope.

Philosophy Studies

Philosophical and theological studies only worsened my puzzlement about missionary work I had raised as candidate. I say 'worsened' because besides the issue of religious diversity, now I was also introduced to the problem of God's existence. During my ecclesiastical baccalaureate in philosophy I realised that the Thomistic tradition of arguing for God's existence had come under severe strain during the modern period.[1] Ignoring this, the First Vatican Council had made the St. Thomas's teaching that we can have some knowledge of God by using our natural reason the official teaching of the Church. And thus arose the need to reconcile the tension between modern thought and the Church teaching. A brilliant Belgian Jesuit by the name of Joseph Maréchal took up this challenge. Combining the Aristotelian dictum that 'All men, by nature desire to know' (Meta. Book1) with the Kantian teaching that knowledge is the result of an active pursuit, he became the founder of what is known as Transcendental Thomism. His argument for an Absolute Being or Unlimited Existence was the mainstay of metaphysics and philosophy of God in the Jesuit circles in India those days, and Marechal also influenced giants of Catholic theology such as Karl Rahner and Bernard Lonergan. Faced with the failure of traditional arguments for God's existence, although I tried to convince myself of the validity of the argument for Unlimited Existence/God, somehow I did not feel comfortable with it. Looking back today, I know the reason for my discomfort. It has to do with the motivation that makes human beings seek knowledge. In the Aristotelian scheme of things, it is curiosity that drives the human search for knowledge. The Kantian twist to Aristotle meant that we are never satisfied with what we know; having gained knowledge of one thing we seek to know something more and this seeking is an endless process. This is intellectual dynamism. It tends toward knowledge of Unlimited Being. While curiosity may be the driving force of our knowledge of the environment, including the most advanced scientific knowledge, I am convinced today that this cannot be said of all knowledge. I am sure that the question I had asked my candidate director was not prompted by curiosity. It was prompted by a concern for personal integrity and wholeness.

A second memory that has remained with me from my undergraduate study in philosophy is the symposium on 'Theology and Falsification'.[2]

1 Michael Buckley, S.J., *At the Origins of Modern Atheism* (New Haven: Yale University Press, 1990).

2 Antony Flew, R.M. Hare, and Basil Mitchell, "Theology and Falsification," in *New Essays in Philosophical Theology*, ed. Antony Flew and Alasdair MacIntyre (London: S.C.M

Probably because it rekindled in me my novitiate memories of the mission toward atheists given to the Jesuits by the Pope. The original symposium took place at Oxford in 1950 and was introduced to us by Lisbert D'Souza as part of the course on Philosophy of God. I found the interaction between Antony Flew (representing atheism), R.M. Hare and Basil Mitchell (representing believers) very enlightening. Although originally posed in terms of the logical positivist theory of meaning, it raised issues that far outlived the demise of positivism and continues to be relevant today. Using simple parables, the three symposiasts lucidly presented their case against and for the existence of God. The response of Mitchell convinced me that theological language does not suffer from any logical deficiency as Flew had argued. This point was further elaborated by I.M. Crombie. Another thing I learned from Mitchell's conduct of the believers' case is that unlike Flew who can rely only on sense experience, Mitchell subtly brings a different kind of experience into the conversation. This convinced me about the need to bring in religious experience into discussions about God, rather than detached observation of the world and arguments from the observed world to prove the existence of God as done in traditional natural theology.[3] However, I had absolutely no chance to follow this insight for many years. Later this would prompt me to take up 'Possibility of Religious Knowledge' for my doctoral dissertation. But here I am jumping ahead. Let me keep to the chronological development of my intellectual journey.

In spite of my dissatisfaction with the state of philosophy in the Church I still did not see it as having any personal bearing on my vocation. It is for this reason that when Fr. Salvino Azzopardi, the then dean of the Faculty of philosophy, asked me to consider joining the faculty, I was not enthusiastic. Seeing my hesitation, he said 'You can decide later but do not decline straightway'. Although I was not enthusiastic about joining the faculty, I wanted to pursue the questions that had troubled me during my philosophy studies. Not being very hopeful of finding answers in JDV itself with its neo-Thomistic orientation, I decided to do a secular M.A. in philosophy. It is thus that I joined the University of Pune in 1984, after a year of regency required for Jesuit scholastics. Other than increasing my analytic skills, those two years did not help in any way for finding answers to my religious questions, as the orientation of studies in the university was completely different.

Theology Studies

After the Masters it was time for undertaking theology studies. As part of a thrust towards 'Formation in Mission', many Jesuit provinces in India had

Press, 1955), 96-130.

3 Mitchell's own thinking would develop in a different way. He came to advocate a cumulative case argument for God's existence rather than simple traditional arguments.

started what was known as Regional Theology Centres. The idea was that theological formation must take place in the context where one was going to do one's ministry. There would be sufficient exposure to the ground realities of the place, especially to poverty the caste realities of society. Since the issues bugging me were more global than local, I requested my Jesuit authorities if I could do theology at one of the two national centres of theology, since they were academically much better equipped than the regional centres. But authorities did not grant me that permission.

As a result, not only did I carry my unsettled questions from philosophy into theology, but they remained unsettled during theology. My initial question about diverse religions was expected to be handled in theology of religions. After Vatican II my Jesuit teachers wanted to make sure that they sided with the most 'progressive' thinking in philosophy and theology. Most progressive in theology of religions at that time was John Hick, with his classification of theologies into the categories of exclusivism, inclusivism and pluralism. But my own attitude to Hick was mixed. On the one hand I loved the clarity of his thinking and on the other I felt that something is not right in his handling of theology. Though he called it theology of religions, and no one questioned him on this matter, I felt deep down that Hick was not doing theology. But neither I nor my teachers knew any better and I could do nothing about the confusions raging within me. In order to clarify things for myself I began to move into uncharted waters. I wrote on the need for a 'metatheology' along the lines of metaphilosophy so that metatheology could function as a bridge between philosophy and theology. I am grateful to the members of the faculty for their openness to exploring this idea. It would take me another two decades to find that the need for the kind of discipline I called 'metatheology' was widely felt in the Church and that the proper name for that discipline was 'fundamental theology'.

Higher Studies

The unresolved problems I encountered in the course of my philosophical and theological studies put an end to my wavering about joining JDV and I decided that this was the best way to work on those issues. Thus, after my ordination and a brief period in a parish, I joined the University of Delhi for higher studies. The first memory that stands out from this period is that I became aware of the study of mysticism done in an academic setting for the first time. This came as a surprise because mysticism was not even mentioned during my ecclesiastical studies of philosophy and theology. This fitted into the post-conciliar mood of replacing traditional Catholic topics like mysticism with social activism. And here I was being introduced to mysticism as an academic topic in a secular university! Although the required reading was only a chapter from William

James, I realized for the first time that study of religious experience is a respectable academic subject.

Another memory of the period is a growing sense of confidence in my philosophical abilities. It was a matter of pride for me to get published in a prestigious journal like *Journal of Indian Council of Philosophical Research* (*JICPR*), the first to get a national recognition after stalwarts like Richard De Smet who had made a name in the Indian philosophical circles. This was in 1993.[4] A second article played a special role in boosting my self-confidence. Prepared as a chapter of my dissertation, I presented it at the annual conference of the Association of Christian Philosophers of India in 1992. Professor Srinivas Rao of Mysore University (later, of Bangalore University) was an invitee for the conference and he missed my presentation as he arrived late. But on the way back he read through it and was so impressed as to write a personal note of appreciation and post it to me soon after. This was great encouragement indeed! JICPR published it in 1994.[5]

My third memory of this period is the realization that religious experience raised far too many problems than could be handled in any single dissertation of reasonable length. That prompted me (on the advice of my supervisor, Professor V.K. Bhardwaja) not to seek solution to all the problems connected to religious knowledge within one doctoral dissertation, but keep much of it for the future. Still I dealt with the major problems confronting epistemology of religious experience proposed by the like of Richard Swinburne, William Alston, and Alvin Plantinga. (This was before Plantinga' major works on epistemology and Christian belief were published). I ended my dissertation by suggesting some solutions to those problems. I would eventually spend a life time working on the insights gained then.

Key to that solution was the insight that discussing any kind of knowledge (whether empirical or religious) requires that we take into account the kind of consciousness in which cognition takes place. This content of my 1993 article titled 'Knowledge and Religious Consciousness'. If this article showed my dissatisfaction for ignoring the state of consciousness in epistemology, my next article (1994) concerned the manner in which epistemology of empirical knowledge is done. Repudiating the tendency to do epistemology in a monadic manner, I argued that justification must be based on evidence that is inter personal (public). Both these articles are significant, as they provide early signs of the direction I would take in epistemology of religious experience. If epistemology needs to take into account the state of consciousness in which

4 George Karuvelil, "Knowledge and Religious Conciousness," *Journal of Indian Council of Philosophical Research* XI, no. 1 (1993): 37-58.

5 "Epistemic Justification and the Possibility of Empirical Evidence," *Journal of Indian Council of Philosophical Research* 12, no. 1 (1994): 29-48.

cognition takes place, since religious/mystical consciousness is an entirely different state of consciousness than the ordinary perceptual consciousness, it makes room for religious experience as an independent source of knowledge, different from empirical experience. Eventually it would become one of my chief claims that science and religion are autonomous disciplines and neither should colonize the other. The second one did not touch upon religion at all. But my treatment of empirical knowledge arose from my conviction religion does not have any epistemology of its own, but follows the general epistemology. But general epistemology needed serious re-working, and it would take me decades to do that.

Teaching at JDV

If the experience in Delhi had boosted my academic confidence and I had hoped to continue with scholarly research, joining JDV proved to be the ultimate dampener. By the time I joined JDV in 1996, stalwarts who had established themselves at the national and international circles were no longer active. The generation after that was more interested in sciences (sociology, psychology, cosmology) than in philosophy or religion. It is only much later that I would find out the reason for this anomaly of full-fledged members of a philosophical establishment showing such antipathy towards philosophy! This had to do with the rigours of the anti-modernist movement in the Church and its strict adherence to neo-Thomism that was out of touch with the modern world, and the abrupt end to those rigours with the Second Vatican Council. But an ecclesiastical faculty needed some of systematic philosophy and not having any other alternative, the old neo-Thomistic scheme continued to be used for this purpose. In the meanwhile, the effect of deemphasizing philosophy studies was beginning to be felt in theology, with theologians being 'swayed uncritically' by the cultural fashion of the day. This prompted Pope John Paul II's encyclical *Fides et Ratio*, some 35 years after the Council. It emphasized the need for philosophy in the Church, without saying what philosophy to follow. But some outer boundaries were visible, such as caution against consensus theory of truth (56), not being content with hermeneutics without getting to truth (84), and above all, agnosticism and relativism that reduces everything to an opinion (5).

As a new member of the faculty, I was tasked with teaching epistemology, with the mandate to integrate it with hermeneutics. While picking up the basics of hermeneutics was not a problem, integrating it with epistemology was a different matter. I divided the course into three parts: (1) basic concepts of epistemology as was done in the past, only with minor innovations based on my own studies; (2) basic ideas of hermeneutics, not only from a historical perspective but also a thematic treatment of some key ideas; (3) a more tentative 'post-hermeneutic epistemology' where I was sure about the dangers of stopping with hermeneutics, but less sure about how to integrate interpretation with the search for truth. It would take me years of work and reflection to arrive at a satisfactory integration of the two. What was worse is that while the generation before me at least saw the need integration, those who came later and got accustomed to the postmodern fragmentation, wanted to separate the two subjects, with different teachers handling them. Only upon my stubborn refusal to separate the two was I allowed to treat them together.

In the midst of the barrenness of creative scholarship I found in JDV, I kept alive my initial passion for exploring the rationality of faith. I tried to find an alternative venue in the annual meetings of the Association of Christian Philosophers of India only to give up it after a few years. Within JDV, I continued to seek ways of pursuing research into issues that were close to my heart. Accordingly, not only did I use insights from my doctoral dissertation to help interested students to arrive at a comprehensive view of their philosophy studies (course: Epistemology, Metaphysics, and God) but also prepared other courses conducive to it. One was "Philosophical Roots of Modern Atheism" where I dwelt on how neglect of religious experience and focussing solely on arguments for God's existence helped the growth of modern atheism. The insight of Michael Buckley helped me in this matter. Next was a course on "Religious Experience" where I dealt with the various classical theories of religious experience, such as those of Schleiermacher, William James, Rudolf Otto, and the newer ones like Walter Stace and Steven Katz. These labours would eventually help me to find satisfactory answers to my long standing quest.

The Breakthroughs

The first major breakthrough in answering my manifold questions came during my sabbatical in 2009-10 at Woodstock Theological Center at Georgetown University. I had decided to focus on religious pluralism –one of my major concerns—and Mark Heim's critique of Hick and others had given me the clue as to where pluralists like Hick went wrong. I explored this further with the help of the well-furnished library of the university that was not available to me at JDV. I laid bare the necessarily existential dimension of theology with the help of Kierkegaard and classical Indian theological traditions (with which I was already familiar but was also helped by my senior colleague Noel Sheth of happy memory). Hick's epistemology, I showed, was typically modern inasmuch as he wanted to base his theology on data that is 'neutral' to different religions (called 'science of religions'). My study of Heidegger, Gadamer and others had convinced me that such neutral data is a myth. Getting it published in *Theological Studies* was a major achievement.

If Hick's reliance on science of religions helped me to uncover the weakness of his thoroughly modern epistemology, it also helped to enter into the wider arena of science and religion interactions because the alleged irredeemable conflict between science and religion was based on the same epistemology as Hick's science of religions. As Providence would have it, *Zygon*, the prestigious international journal of religion and science, accepted it for publication without even a revision.

A third achievement of these articles is the clarity regarding the distinctive nature of theology and science, without immunizing them from the influence of each other. The same was done for philosophy and theology in 2013. This clarity was a major achievement as syllabi of our faculties in the post-Conciliar period tended to be a hotchpotch of materials drawn from philosophy, theology, and different sciences without being able to distinguish or relate them to each other. (It is a different matter that the syllabus of our philosophy faculty continues to be a hotchpotch of fragments from different disciplines without an overarching vision demanded by the Church). Knowing this, irrespective of the course involved, I begin my engagement with the students with the idea of philosophy and how it is similar and yet different from theology.

Another thing which happened during this period is that I had found the correct name for the kind of inquiry I was involved in from the time of my theology studies. I realized it was called fundamental theology. While reading about fundamental theology, I also became aware that this discipline was on the verge of dying a premature death. I began to sense that the reason why fundamental theology had not taken off the ground is for lack of sufficient distinction between fundamental theology (expected to deal with the rationality of faith) and systematic theology (dealing with the content of faith). Failure to make this distinction led Hick to call his *attempted* fundamental theology of religious diversity as *theology* of religious pluralism. Having read Hick extensively I became increasingly convinced that the important distinction between systematic theology and fundamental theology concerns the addressee of communication. But communication was considered a specialized field and I was not into it. Yet, convinced of the need to deal with it, I approached Jacob Srampical of happy memory (teaching at Gregorian University, Rome, at that time) and he referred me to Wilbur Schramm. That was helpful. Eventually I also found other useful material on communication and relating it to some standard ideas in hermeneutics I formulated a theory of communication. Using this theory I drew a principled distinction between these disciplines and the various tasks of fundamental theology. However, being neither a theologian nor a communication theorist, and having none to consult in the matter, I let the material remain with me for four years before finally deciding ed to take the chance by sending it as an article to *Theological Studies*. To my great happiness and satisfaction, the referees gave a very favourable opinion and it was published in 2015.

Besides the satisfaction it gave, this article also brought me the greatest gift of my life, the friendship senior Jesuit colleague Gerald O'Collins. Though retired from Gregorian University, he had had published widely in theology and fundamental theology. Impressed by my treatment of fundamental theology, he made arrangements for me to go and work with him for some time and carry out the task of fundamental theology I had outlined. I consider it the greatest blessing of my life because in him I found a perfect conversation partner, friend and mentor. He shared my passion to seek the truth of Christian faith, and not just believing and teaching it. With his help and encouragement I worked at a hectic pace to put into words my incipient ideas into a well-researched book.

These ideas were mainly in the twin fields of religion and theology on the one hand, and epistemology and hermeneutics, on the other. In the field of religion, the ideas included (1) my long held conviction that arguments for the existence of God cannot make much headway in the contemporary world, (2) adopting the Rahnerian teaching that the "Christian of the future would be either a mystic… or he will cease to be anything at all"[6] and (3) finding that experiences of nature mysticism can be an alternative avenue to explicate the theistic concept of God in place of traditional arguments for God's existence, (4) and that the foundational Christian experience is one of experiencing the divine in another human person (Jesus of Nazareth) in the background of the humanistic tradition of Judaism.

Among the epistemological ideas, while I shared the view of *Fides et Ratio* that hermeneutics cannot substitute for the epistemological concern with truth, I struggled for decades with how to make room for both meaning and truth. When a final solution emerged, it combined some ideas that were brewing in my mind for long and some new insights. Among the former were the following: (1) the conviction that the so-called theory-laden observations traded on an ambiguity that conflated the idea that the search for observational evidence being guided by prior theories (which is as it should be) and such evidence being determined by prior theories (which was baseless), (2) that traditional empiricist epistemology did not make the needed distinction between perception (general term) and observation (that class of perception which is guided by prior theories) that provides empirical evidence. The most important insight that helped me to overcome the relativism of the postmodern trends is (3) the realization that though nature and culture are inseparable from one another, they are still distinguishable. I called it the NaC-Di-NoS (Natural-and Cultural-are-Distinguishable-but-not-Separable) principle. This was contrary to the modern trend that focussed exclusively on the natural to the exclusion of the cultural and postmodern trend of dissolving the natural

6 Karl Rahner, *Theological Investigations* VII, trans. David Moreland (London: Darton, Longman & Todd, 1979), 15.

into the cultural. This helped me to bring together the perspectival character of interpretations with the absolutist character of truth.

These epistemological breakthroughs were important for my religious quest regarding the rationality of faith. I realized that the exile of religion from the intellectual arena and modern universities was built on modern epistemology and its antagonism to human interpretations and perspectives (involving culture). I also learned that the postmodern dissolution of epistemology was based the one-sided emphasis on culture to the exclusion of the natural. These are brought together in my forthcoming book titled *Faith, Reason and Culture: An Essay in Fundamental Theology*. Falling in between philosophy and theology, this book provides 'a fresh balance [between philosophy and theology], grounded in attention to contemporary intellectual movements and concerns, such as atheism, secularization, and postmodernism, along with new science and religion configurations, and of course religious pluralism', as one perceptive reviewer put it. In place of the old balance between philosophy and theology provided by Thomas Aquinas in the 13th century, this new balance addresses the problems of the 'world in which we actually live' now.

Let me explain: theology, whether Eastern or Western, has always needed a philosophy as its basis. The link between them is sometimes so strong that it is often impossible to distinguish philosophy from theology, as we find in most systems of Indian thought. A special feature of Christian theology has been its ability to adapt itself to different philosophies, depending on the changed cultural conditions. This dynamism was best seen in the 13th century when Aquinas managed to change the philosophical basis of Christian theology from the previously dominant Platonism to Aristotelianism that was becoming dominant at that time. However, when faced with the most drastic cultural change during the modern period, this adaptability was no longer in sight. Either the Church attempted to return to Aquinas (Neo-scholasticism prior to Vatican II) or did away with the philosophical basis of theology itself (after Vatican II). My work attempts to restore this dynamic link between philosophy and theology.

It recognizes that while there is much to learn from the past (views of Stoics, Aquinas, etc.) we are called to address the issues of our times, not theirs. With this book, I have laid the groundwork for a systematic philosophy that is hospitable to religion and theology in place of the dominant naturalism and secular humanism that has suffocated theology for the last three centuries. I am delighted that a reputed international publisher like Palgrave Macmillan has 'enthusiastically' taken up its publication. In the meanwhile I have been teaching this material both at the graduate and postgraduate levels. Most recently I have provided samples of this material to students at Windhoek, Namibia, and Harare, Zimbabwe. The African exploration has also helped to broaden my horizons beyond the Indian and the Western.

Conclusion

There is no doubt that a lot more remains to be done, but I have the satisfaction of having lived (so far) the mission that was entrusted to me. The mission began to get identified with the tentative hints during my novitiate but took more and more concrete shape with the disarray I experienced during my philosophy and theology studies.

It has indeed been a long journey, although not an easy one. But I have reason to be profoundly grateful to God who has guided me in mysterious ways. I am also grateful to each and every one, especially those colleagues who have supported me in my journey. A special word of thanks to my students who have been my strength; I thank them for their direct or indirect support to my intellectual adventure.

PURVIEW: PHILOSOPHICAL AND THEOLOGICAL CONCERNS OF DR. GEORGE KARUVELIL SJ

1

Philosophy with Higher Goal: The Task of Philosophy According to George Karuvelil

Michael Devin Coonghe IVD

Abstract

This article analyses the task of philosophy according to George Karuvelil and the carrying of this task through his writings and teaching. The task of philosophy is a call and a vocation rooted in human living conditions and existential factors rather than on speculative thinking.

Keywords

Task of philosophy, fundamental theology, wisdom, way of life, communication and fusion of horizons, higher goal, experiential.

Introduction

The inspiration to write this paper is nothing other than the twofold encounter with the person Fr. George Karuvelil, SJ. The encounter is twofold because, one is to encounter his teaching in the classroom of M. Ph. and the other is the philosophical discussion (a friendly chats concerning philosophy) with him outside the classroom, namely in the refectory during the tea-breaks. For me, from the first class itself, he inspired me in the sense that I felt that it is not just a mere academic teaching of some content, but something more than that is taking place. He is a person who differs and inspires with his own philosophical content. It could be said that he was instilling systematically the philosophizing journey of his life, which was like re-living the moments of his thinking-journey.

Generally, when we begin a course, we get the introduction about the course, but this was different that we had a genesis of the course as it began in Karuvelil's life as a student. The journey of his search and his reflections had become the present course on Faith and Reason. It concentrates on the need of a new face to fundamental theology to make Reality and Faith accessible through reflecting on human experience. Looking into the content of this course, I saw they were mainly his methodological presentations of his philosophical contributions related to a higher-goal and task of philosophy. Those classes made me to realize that he has lived with philosophical questions, thirst, and the search. His life is an existential search to communicate the truth of faith and possibility of religious knowledge with foundation of reason accessible for all, believers, non-believers, fellow believers, and believers of other faith and ideologies. It was studying under a philosopher whose philosophical writings made up the content. This experience did not remain as a feeling but became true and reality as time went on.

Therefore, with all that I had studied under him in the classes, listening to him during the class breaks and read from his writings, I volunteered to pen this article. I shall divide it into two sections. In the first section, I shall consider the task of philosophy as he has conceived it and in the second section, how he has systematically carried this out.

1. Problem: What is Philosophy?

Defining anything is the first and fundamental problem of everything, and I do not find George Karuvelil entering into this issue neither in his writing nor in his teaching. He says "We cannot begin with definitions because that would pre-judge the matter of their identities."[1] Does it mean that he neglects and escapes defining the theme? Actually, it is not so, rather in the process of writing and teaching at the appropriate moment, he places the position of definition meaningfully. He knows that without clarifying the issues that could arise in any definition, defining something will not be helpful in any way. Thus, his writing on philosophy does not begin with definition, but he establishes it perfectly at proper time in the article. He has his reasons to do so. His answer for not defining philosophy is very beautiful that "Neither philosophy nor theology is a natural category, like gold, water and dog,"[2] and he while discussing the love-hate relationship of philosophy and theology explores the identity of these two important disciplines of his teaching.

1 George Karuvelil, "Philosophy and Theology," *Divyadaan* 24.2 (2013), 218.

2 George Karuvelil, "Philosophy and Theology," 218.

Down through the history of philosophy, there are numerous answers and expressions to what philosophy is. For George Karuvelil, it is neither mere speculation of a concept nor a specific content or subject matter; rather, it is a call for rational thought necessitated in the existential context of human life. Once in answering my question, he said that philosophy does not possess any determinate content for itself and the history of philosophy should not be taken as a subject matter of philosophy. I picked up some important elements for what philosophy is from his article "Philosophy and Theology."

1.1. Philosophy as Existential

I used to teach in 'Introduction to Philosophy,' that philosophy was born when human being began to think without being victim to the mythological and religious explanations for their fundamental questions of wonder. Here, George Karuvelil argues "philosophy was born with an existential orientation of offering guidance to life, [though] it got severed from its existential roots to become a theoretical and academic pursuit."[3] But the "original vocation of philosophy was existential."[4] For him, this is an important feature of the true nature of philosophy. Using the etymological meaning of philosophy as 'Love of Wisdom' he states, "Wisdom is always rooted in concrete, existential situations of life, enabling one to take practical decisions in such situations."[5] He also points that a good part of modern philosophy cannot be considered as wisdom. This is one of the reasons that makes defining philosophy a problem. Another is lack of any identifiable subject matter or its status as purely a reflective discipline.

1.2. Philosophy as a Pure Second Order Discipline

For Karuvelil, philosophy is not only a reflective discipline but also a pure second order discipline. He begins the distinction of first and second order reflection with an analysis of an example, 'John is a good person.' If one reflects the goodness of John that is first order reflection, if one reflects what the idea or concept of what 'goodness' means then it is second order reflection. He continues explaining it and its objection and the responses to the objection.

That "philosophy is a pure second order discipline does not mean that philosophy is unmixed with the empirical...; it means that philosophy as philosophy cannot lay claim to any identifiable first order material as its

---

3 George Karuvelil, "Philosophy and Theology", 217. To know how he establishes the argument of the journey of philosophy from existential orientation to academic pursuit, the article needs to be read. He explains it how in the modern time the existential dimension got separated from philosophy.

4 George Karuvelil, "Philosophy and Theology," 230.

5 George Karuvelil, "Philosophy and Theology," 224.

own."[6] He contrasts it with first order disciplines like biology, physics, and even theology, all of which can be defined by their subject matter. In fact at this point he explores the varied subject matter that philosophy discusses, namely, matter, non-matter, language, ethics, metaphysics, politics, art, literature, logic, mathematics and says precisely, "Given such diversity, it is hard to see how philosophy could be defined in terms of its subject matter."[7] Many authors have expressed that philosophy cannot be defined, but he is one among such who gives the best explanation why it cannot be defined. In doing it, he helps us to understand philosophy as a pure second order discipline.

1.3. What About Truth?

Considering philosophy as a pure second order discipline would seem to undermine truth-seeking that has always been considered the task of philosophy. Andrzej Szahaj says, "Since the time of Parmenides and Plato the task of philosophy has been the pursuit of Truth and the attempt to provide certain knowledge (*episteme*), thus distinguishing itself as a specific kind of human activity in opposition to the rule of prejudice and mere opinion (*doxa*)."[8] How should we respond when some of our basic beliefs are put into question? What makes a human body distinctively human? Why is truth an important good? These are among the questions explored in his collection of essays by Alasdair MacIntyre.[9] Pope John Paul II says, "Philosophy must remain faithful to its own principles and methods. Otherwise there would be no guarantee that it would remain oriented to truth and that it was moving towards truth by way of a process governed by reason"[10]

Does Karuvelil neglect this task of philosophy? On the one hand, epistemology is central to his philosophy; it is his concern with truth that makes him approach his course on faith and reason as 'applied epistemology'. On the other hand, philosophy as a second-order discipline deals with ideas or concepts. How does he reconcile this idea of philosophy with truth? After all, truth is not a matter of ideas, but a matter of ideas as they relate to reality. My interaction with Karuvelil in the course of writing this paper clarified this matter.

---

6 George Karuvelil, "*Philosophy and Theology*," 231.

7 George Karuvelil, "*Philosophy and Theology*," 231.

8 Andrzej Szahaj, "*Task of Philosophy*," History of European Ideas, Vol. 20. Noo 1 3 (Great Britain: Elsevier Science Ltd, 1995) 559

9 See Alasdair Macintyre, "Tasks of Philosophy: Selected Essays" Vol I, (UK: Cambridge University Press, 2006).

10 Pope John Paul II, *Fides et Ratio,* 49.

1.4. Philosophy as Way of Life

Truths are numerous. They come from a variety of sources: from empirical sciences, from our everyday interactions with the world and one another, and from Religion. No matter how numerous, they cannot but enter into philosophy when philosophy is considered in existential terms. Using quotations of Wittgenstein and Mary Midgley who speaks of a good map by which we find our way around. A map that is not based on truth would mislead us. He says, "It is the task of philosophy to offer such a guide map for human living. Rooted in one's lived conditions, philosophy seeks to offer a sense of unity, direction and passion for life."[11] This is very much important not just for the understanding of task of philosophy but also in the act of philosophizing and writing philosophy. This is where philosophy gets itself closer to the sense of a way of life. Philosophy as a way of life is an important and essential feature Karuvelil's discussion of the nature of philosophy.

1.5. Philosophy, Theology, and Change

The existential character of philosophy makes room for change. Karuvelil holds that as culture and life situations change, philosophy must change; only then can it offer guidance to life. He shows that such has been the case in the history of philosophy-theology relations. He says,

> As long as philosophy maintained its existential roots and sought to offer guidance to life, it had a sense of direction: it was a way of life...whether it be the Platonic Good or the Aristotelian *Eudaimonia* (happiness) or the Stoic indifference, a philosophy with existential roots has a sense of vocation.[12]

Because of this existential character of philosophy, Christians could introduce their message to the Greco-Roman world as a philosophy.[13] This meant that there existed no distinction between philosophy and theology at this stage. This early philosophy-theology arose from the fusion of the Gospel's way of life and the Neo-Platonic Philosophy.[14] However, "Already in the Middle Ages, philosophy had lost its life-guiding character and had become 'largely an academic study,' ....'Philo' and 'Sophia' of 'philosophy' had been divorced for many centuries in the West... [This is due to the] triumph of

11 George Karuvelil, "Philosophy and Theology," 223.

12 George Karuvelil, "Philosophy and Theology," 233.

13 George Karuvelil, "Christian Faith, Philosophy, and Culture: The Triumphs and Failures of Wisdom," *Jnanadeepa: Pune Journal of Religious Studies* (JPJRS) 17/1 January 2014: 105.

14 Pope John Paul II, *Fides et Ratio,* 39.

Christendom ..[which] resulted in the transfer of the life-guiding function of philosophy to theology."[15]

Karuvelil traces the next major change in philosophy-theology relations to the 13th century, when the lost works of Aristotle re-emerged and began to gain popularity. Under these changed circumstances, Thomas Aquinas was faced with the task of Christianizing Aristotle's philosophy, just as the Early Fathers had Christianized Platonism. This was not an easy task because unlike the other-worldly philosophy of Plato, Aristotle's philosophy was very much a this-worldly one. Since Christian theology could not function as philosophy under these circumstances, a new role had to be found for philosophy. Using Aristotle's arguments for a Prime Mover, First Cause, etc., Aquinas gave a new role for philosophy. Philosophy was now to function "as preambles or prolegomena to theology."[16] The result is a drastic re-configuration of the manner in which Christian faith related to culture. Rather than directly engage culture, faith related to culture indirectly through the mediation of philosophy.

Even this re-configuration did not alter the life-guiding function of the philosophy-theology complex as theology continued to provide orientation to life in Christendom. This situation changed with the breakup of Christendom and the forceful arrival of modernity, with its attendant secularization of Western society. Thus, philosophy that had already become a theoretical enterprise without any life-guiding role got divorced from theology that maintained its existential roots. It is thus that even the indirect support for providing orientation to life (as handmaid of theology) is undermined during the modern period. It is under these conditions that Karuvelil takes the call of *Fides et Ratio* seriously. This encyclical asks Christian thinkers to adopt Aquinas as the "guide and model" for relating faith and reason.[17]

1.6. The Contemporary Task

It is Karuvelil's conviction that philosophy should respond to the issues of the time. Therefore, while taking the call of *Fides et Ratio* seriously, he is also aware that repeating the teachings of Aquinas cannot succeed in our times, as the contemporary life-situation is very different from the cultural situation of the thirteenth century. If his culture was theistic, ours is secular. Presently, we face the challenges of post-modern relativistic tendencies, where there is no belief on any objective reality and truth as such, the scientistic monopoly in the field of knowledge, rationality of religious faith in the midst of pluralism,

15 George Karuvelil, "*Philosophy and Theology*," 225.

16 George Karuvelil, "Christian Faith, Philosophy, and Culture: The Triumphs and Failures of Wisdom," 112.

17 Pope John Paul II, *Fides et Ratio,* 78.

relativism, secularism, materialism, atheism of different formats and so on. Discussing the rationality of faith in such a situation is not an easy task.

But he finds that Aquinas can still become an exemplar for our times on account of the manner in which he synthesized philosophy and theology, the secularity of Aristotelian science and the faith of the Gospels. He achieved this by making philosophy as preambles to theology. The need for preambles assumes a gap between Christian faith and culture, between what can be communicated to all in a culture and those Christian doctrines that cannot be directly communicated. He says, "it was the task of philosophy to bridge this gap."[18] Therefore, "to imitate Aquinas today is to build a tightrope to contemporary culture as he did to his culture."[19]

Given that unlike the times of Aquinas we live in a secular culture, we cannot expect theology to perform the life-guiding function. Therefore, philosophy needs to recover that function. Only then can it become the tight rope bridging the Christian Faith and culture. Thus, the task of philosophy according to George Karuvelil is that of setting a higher goal in the lived context of human life and thereby providing the guide-map for human living; it would offer a sense of unity, direction and passion for life. More specifically, he wants to restore the role of religion in one's conduct of life. He identifies such faith-inspired philosophy as fundamental theology. Now I want to summarize how Karuvelil executed this task in his course of faith and reason. Awareness of the contemporary issues and his manner of dealing with them prepares the students to practice philosophizing on the existential issues of today's world.

2. Tasks Executed

Karuvelil's works are not the re-works of the others, but taking the contributions of others when necessary, he has established his own positions in diverse areas. As far as I know, he is the first one to develop an experiential model of rationality as the base in fundamental theology to provide the accessibility of religious truths in the postmodern society where we are all faced with immense diversity, relativistic tendencies, religious fundamentalism, deism and denial of religious truths and knowledge. It is for this reason that I want to point out how he has executed the tasks he set for philosophy.

Sometimes, if we do not know the philosophical character of fundamental theology as faith-inspired philosophy, we may tend to think that he is a theologian than a philosopher. But acquaintance with his teaching and reading his articles, will tell us how systematic a philosopher he is. Realizing that the core philosophical challenge to religious faith has been epistemological,

18 George Karuvelil, *"Christian Faith, Philosophy, and Culture: The Triumphs and Failures of Wisdom,"* 112.

19 George Karuvelil, *"Christian Faith, Philosophy, and Culture: The Triumphs and Failures of Wisdom,"* 114.

he takes the bull by the horns by executing the difficult task of developing an alternative epistemology and considers his approach to examining the rationality of faith a matter of 'applied epistemology'.

2.1. Parable of the Boat: A Comprehensive Picture of Epistemology

Epistemology, which is commonly defined as the scientific study of knowledge, its nature, features, different theories, is one of the conceptual studies and quite difficult one to comprehend. But he knew that epistemology is essential in any effort to understand the rationality of faith. Therefore, to enable the students to understand his applied epistemology and provide an epistemological foundation for discussing the rationality of faith he summarized the history of modern and contemporary epistemology in an extended parable of a boat tethered in the port. He spoke of seven stages of the situation of the boat, namely the tethered boat, boat in the sea, dispute in the boat, awareness of the other boats, inability to communicate with others, rumors of piracy, alleged death and mushrooming of diverse epistemologies. He connected these stages with theories of epistemology from the modern era to the present. They are respectively, foundationalism (rationalism and empiricism) represented by the tethered boat, Coherntism (result of the Existentialist revolution) represented by the Neurath's imagery of boat in the middle of the sea, Internalism and Externalism represented by the dispute in the boat about the possibility and admissibility of external help, Social Epistemology (attempts to communicate to other boats), Relativistic tendencies arising from failures to find objective grounds for deciding truth (represented by alleged impossibility of help from the shore) and finally numerous epistemologies existing side by side. The explanation of this parable and its application will make the students to remember the details and the journey of the epistemological theories properly and their challenges. This parable is one of the many things he taught that inspired me and many other students.

2.2. The Question of Antony Flew

Applying the parable to discuss the rationality of religious faith, he begins with the symposium on 'Theology and Falsification' about the meaningful communication of religious experience and language. Antony Flew opened the symposium by challenging the meaningfulness of religious statements. The logical positivist background of this challenge makes it an application of foundationalist epistemology represented by the tethered boat. Flew was followed by the responses of R. M. Hare and Basil Mitchell. The symposium raised so much interest that many others like I. M. Crombie, John Hick, Mitchell Tooley joined the discussions later on through their writings.

Antony Flew began by stating that religious statements are so greatly qualified that on logical grounds they cannot be considered assertions. He uses the criteria of falsifiability for the purpose. R.M Hare tried to answer that religion is not science; so scientific verification cannot be applicable (parable of lunatic student). Basil Mitchell contributed that religious statements have their own reason (parable of partisan). I. M Crombie contributes by saying that no crucial experiment can be conducted to falsify religious statements. John Hick takes the argument to the next level by talking about eschatological verification of religious statements. Michael Tooley counters it by saying that such talk cannot communicate theological meaning to non-believers, as 'eschaton' is a theological term. This realization prompts Flew to demand that believers explain what they mean by 'God' without using other theological terms. I have given this summary in my words; for a better clarification one will have to refer the text.

The most important element here is the question of Antony Flew challenging the meaningfulness, rationality, and the accessibility of religious language to non-believers and atheists. George Karuvelil takes up the task of meeting this challenge. Meeting Flew's challenge of explaining the concept of 'God' in a manner that is accessiblc to non-believers is at the heart of his fundamental theology.

For Karuvelil, "...fundamental theology is a 20th century successor to the older traditions of natural theology and apologetics; its task is to provide a propaedeutic path to faith."[20] He goes on to spell out the three-fold task of fundamental theology, namely in propaedeutic, apologetic and inter-faith dialogue. This manner of conceiving fundamental theology owns up the task of *Fides et Ratio* to hold faith and reason together. By doing so, it attempts to make the call of Pope John Paul II a reality. He has executed this task consistently, methodologically and systematically. This makes him an original thinker who stands out from many, and it make us to understand the task of philosophy and theology in today's context.

In the process of showing the rationality of faith he refers to the epistemological views of many current thinkers. One crucial move is repudiating the scientism of modern epistemology and showing the need for existentializing epistemology after the manner of Heidegger, Gadamer, and Wittgenstein.

2.3. Repudiating Scientism

His awareness of the harm inflicted by the science of religion on traditional theology looks to me a pioneering attempt. In that process, he explores four different models of relating science and religion. The first model is the Standard view according to which science and religion are in conflict with each other.

20 George Karuvelil, "To whom I am speaking? Communication, Culture, and Fundamental Theology," *Theological Studies*, vol. 76(4), 2015, 682.

Many are aware that this is a false picture of science-religion relations and have attempted to refute it but the model continues to persist. According to Karuvelil, this is due to the fact that at certain level, such conflict is a matter of experience. He goes on to say that "theories can be refuted; facts and experiences call for explanation, not refutation. It is the task of theories of science-religion relations to explain ... irrefutable facts and experiences."[21] With this understanding, he goes on to explore the epistemological basis of science-religion relations, the only one who has done so to the best of my knowledge. He says, "As an epistemological thesis, the standard view tells us that the conflict between the empirical sciences and theology is built into the methodological genes of these disciplines."[22] The second model is that of natural theology. As it argues from the world to God, he calls the Holy Science Model. Since it is based on the same assumptions as the Standard view, he treats them together and shows why they are not viable. Using Gould's NOMA theory as an example of the third model (the Autonomy view) he states, "Gould does not see anything in the genes of the either discipline to suggest that they are necessarily at war with each other."[23] He goes on to establish that the real conflict is not between science and religion, but between the naturalistic horizon of science and the religious orientation of different theological horizons. This is done, first, by establishing that science of religion is not a neutral enterprise without any horizon of its own, and second, by showing that the horizon of the scientific study of religion is naturalism. In other words, naturalism and atheism are as much matters of faith as theism. This existentialization of epistemology or the recognition that every philosophical position involves a definite perspective with its attendant commitment and passionate involvement "helps us to explain the conflict between the scientific study of religion and theology."[24]

2.4. A New Epistemology

Existentialization of epistemology with its diverse perspectives corresponds, in the parable, to the boat being rocked by the waves in the middle of the sea. This situation raises the problem of incommensurability or the alleged inability to communicate and understand those whose perspectives differ from one's own. This is the problem of disagreement, an important topic in social epistemology. The problem of disagreement becomes acute when the concerned horizons or perspectives are so radically different that they may be opposed to each other, as with naturalistic or atheistic faith on the one hand and theistic faith on the other. He calls it deep disagreement.

21 George Karuvelil, "Science of Religion and Theology," *Zygon*, vol. 47, no.2, (2012) 418.

22 George Karuvelil, "Science of Religion and Theology," 418

23 George Karuvelil, "Science of Religion and Theology," 418.

24 George Karuvelil, "Science of Religion and Theology," 429.

The reality of deep disagreement makes the epistemological task of truth-seeking difficult. Modern epistemology, because of its neglect of the perspectival character of knowing, could glibly talk about establishing truth and rationality in terms of foundational justification. Recognition of deep disagreements makes such justification impossible. In its place Karuvelil proposes a two-stage epistemology where justification is preceded by efforts to communicate and understand each other. The question arises at this point as to whether is possible at all to understand another person whose existential commitments are diametrically opposed to one's own.

In order to solve this problem he deals with a communication theory and shows that communication is possible as long as there is some commonality between the horizons of the communicator and the addressee. The real question is whether there is anything common to the horizons of those involved in deep disagreements. It is at this point that he, with the help of W.V. Quine, uses the idea of natural perception as common to different inter-locutors. The reality of certain natural abilities like perception that are universal to human beings makes it possible for anyone to begin a process of communicating and understanding another though that person is from an entirely different cultural background. Though such initial communication would lack the finer nuances, communication theory shows that through an inter-locutionary process they can attain a fusion of horizons. This is one of the important tasks he has executed to solve incommensurability between different disciplines and horizons.

Having attained adequate understanding of the other's claim, one can proceed to raise the question of truth and justification of the other's claim. Adapting a version of Michael Williams's Wittgenstein-inspired contextual epistemology, and combining it with insights from philosophy of science, Karuvelil shows how people journeying in entirely different existential boats can obtain evidence from the common shore of reality such that truth can be established. Key to obtaining such evidence is the distinction between perception and observation, where observation is understood as that class of perception that is guided by some theory or hypothesis.

While this procedure seems eminently sensible in science, it also raises difficulties for the justification of natural perception where it is hard to talk about theory-guided perception. Karuvelil overcomes this difficulty by showing that the "theory" that guides the search for observational evidence for resolving disputed perceptual claims is the very idea of perception. Exploring various theories of perception that are prevalent today, he shows how they could be held together by using Wittgenstein's idea of "grammar". Grammar of perception is then used for obtaining evidence for resolving disputed perceptual claims.

2.5. Rationality of Religious Faith

Having shown how truth might be obtained in the midst of diverse perspectives without succumbing to relativism, Karuvelil turns to its application to religion. In keeping with the experiential approach he has adopted he explores studies in mysticism and finds that parallel to natural perception in empirical knowledge, nature mysticism is natural to human beings. By using the same method he adopted for arriving at the grammar of perception, he explores the grammar of mysticism, taking it to be the core of religion. It so happens that the grammar of religion coincides with many of the attributes of theistic God. In that process, not only does he respond to Flew's demand to explain the concept of God without using other religious concepts but also performs the first task of fundamental theology. A third function of the grammar of 'God' is they provide the rules by which genuine religious claims can be distinguished from those that are not genuine.

Finally, Karuvelil brings empirical knowledge and religious knowledge together to provide an integral map for human living. There are many other tasks that he has executed in his teaching and writing but I have written only a few that I could get from my encounter with him.

Conclusion

There are two major challenges facing philosophy today. Firstly, philosophy has come to be understood as an abstract theoretical exercise unrelated to life. As against this, Karuvelil insists that philosophy must recover its original task of providing a way of life. This feature of wisdom should not be compromised and the task of philosophy should be to give right direction for life. Secondly, it is said that we live in a post-truth world. We are faced with so much of schisms in all the fields; it has come to a point that there is no objectivity of truth, belief, knowledge and reality. Guidance for life would be impossible without concern for truth as one would be living in the air. For this reason Karuvelil insists that any guide-map for life must be built on truth and not make-believe. Irrespective of whether they are truths of science or theology, they must be brought together into an integral map that offers guidance to life.

This is the higher goal of philosophy that I found in George Karuvelil. Not only has he conceived the task in this manner but also carried it out systematically. I am really thankful to what he has taught and written and happy of writing this paper too

Response of Karuvelil

It is not an easy task to absorb and summarize an almost entirely new way of thinking with a short course lasting three weeks, especially when it involves complex issues in epistemology and religion. And yet, this is exactly what

Devin Coonghe has tried to do in this article. I admire his enthusiasm for doing it, and I am grateful to him for undertaking this task, and carrying it out more or less successfully.

I say "more or less" because there is more to the systematic philosophy I have developed than what is done in this paper, as he himself acknowledges. For example, given the map-building character of philosophy in concrete existential situations that I advocate, I have also dealt with the live issues of secularism, the specific character of Indian secularism, the liberative potential of Indian philosophy, ecological concerns, and the like, besides rationality of religion. Even in treating rationality of religion, he has not said anything about religious diversity, which has been one of my abiding concerns. This observation is not meant to be a criticism of what Coonghe has done but meant to place his achievement within the larger canvass.

He has taken my understanding of philosophy as his main theme and successfully shown how I have accomplished that task. In that process he has implicitly raised the criticism that my treatment of philosophy ignores its truth-seeking character. I agree. I thank Coonghe for pointing this out. Having done that, let me also say this in my defense that the purpose of my article "Philosophy and Theology" was not to define philosophy but to show how these two disciplines are confused with each other by the likes of John Hick and John Caputo, a confusion that is still prevalent in the academic circles.

2

Faith and Reason: Revisiting *Fides et Ratio* from the Perspective of Karuvelil

Thomas Karimundackal SJ

Abstract

Faith and reason are integral to understand the truth revealed in the religion since "each without the other is enfeebled." The truth conferred by revelation is a truth to be understood in the light of reason. It is this mutuality which allows us to specify correctly the relationship between revealed truth and philosophical learning. Reason lays the foundation for faith and makes revelation "credible." Faith without reason withers into myth or superstition. Deprived of reason, faith is left with only feelings and experience. *Fides et Ratio*, the 13th Encyclical Letter of Late Pope John Paul II explores the relationship between faith and reason. The complementarity of faith and reason is stressed in *Fides et Ratio* when the Pope explains the dialogical character of philosophy and theology in seeking and explaining the universal metaphysical truths. This paper is an attempt to draw the inherent relationship between faith and reason as it is elicited in the *Fides et Ratio*.

Keywords

Faith, reason, rationalism, fideism, revealed truth, metaphysical reasoning, *intellectus fidei, auditus fidei.*

Introduction

"Faith and reason are like two wings on which the human spirit rises to the contemplation of truth; and God has placed in the human heart the desire to know the truth - in a word, to know himself - so that by knowing and loving God, men and women can come to the fullness of the truth about themselves" (*FR* 1). With these words Pope John Paul II, the former philosophy professor begins the encyclical, *Fides et Ratio*.[1] It is the first encyclical on the relationship between faith and reason since Pope Leo XIII issued *Aeterni Patris* in 1879, and it resulted much reflection on the relationship between faith and reason. Shortly after the encyclical was published, Pope John Paul II provided his own summary of some of its key elements in an address to a group of American bishops who were visiting Rome. He said that he "wished to defend the capacity of human reason to know the truth. This confidence in reason is an integral part of the Catholic intellectual tradition, but it needs reaffirming today in the face of widespread and doctrinaire doubt about our ability to answer the fundamental questions: Who am I? Where have I come from and where am I going? Why is there evil? What is there after this life?"[2] Thus, Pope John Paul II himself believed that truth is known through a combination of faith and reason. The absence of either one will diminish human being's ability to know himself/herself, the world and God (cf. *FR* 16). In *Fides et Ratio,* Pope John Paul II first attempts to explain the proper roles of faith and reason on human being's path to truth, and then he explains how they complement and support one another with complete compatibility.

Dr. George Karuvelil's lifelong academic commitment was to find a way to integrate faith and reason to see the truth in its totality. How can a Christian unite faith and reason? This was, as far as my knowledge about Dr. George Karuvelil goes, the basis of his quest for the epistemological and hermeneutical understanding of human being and God. Therefore, I see a lot of resonance between Pope John Paul II's encyclical *Fides et Ratio* and Dr. George Karuvelil's academic journey. Along with Pope John Paul II, Dr. George Karuvelil too believes that human reason can seek the truth, but the ultimate truth about the meaning of life cannot be found by reason alone (cf. *FR* 42); "with the light of reason human beings can know which path to take, but they can follow that path to its end, quickly and unhindered, only if with a rightly tuned spirit they search for it within the horizon of faith" (*FR* 16). Therefore, to my mind, both are convinced that "reason and faith cannot be separated without diminishing the capacity of men and women to know

1 Fides et Ratio is Pope John Paul II's 13th Encyclical Letter dated September 14, 1998, feast of the Triumph of the Cross, is addressed to his fellow bishops to address the relationship between faith and reason.

2 Ad Limina Address of October 24, 1998, n. 5

themselves, the world and God in an appropriate way" (*FR* 16). This paper is an attempt to draw the mutuality of faith and reason as it is elicited in the *Fides et Ratio,* and thus to show that the academic path taken by Dr. George Karuvelil is in tune with the Church's attempt to integrate faith and reason in seeking the truth.

1. The Two Wings: Integrating Faith and Reason

Fides et Ratio begins by claiming that faith and reason are needed for the human spirit to ascend to the truth, and it is metaphorically compared with two wings of a flying creature or an object: "Faith and reason are like two wings on which the human spirit rises to the contemplation of truth" (*FR* 1). Trying to fly with only the wing of faith is what the philosophers call "fideism"; trying to fly with only the wing of reason is what they term "rationalism". One-winged flying, to extend the analogy, is to live a maimed existence. One way of understanding philosophy, which stands for the "reason" aspect of our existence, is to see in it man's search for God. And, drawing on a famous title by Heschel, we can see revelation as an expression of God's search for man.[3] So the task of integrating reason and faith may be understood in terms of the convergence of these two quests. We need not faith alone or reason alone, but for their reintegration.

The modern culture, however, reveals a gradual and 'fateful separation' of faith and reason (cf. *FR* 45), resulting in a changed role for philosophy to the point where it became "instrumental reason directed towards the promotion of utilitarian ends, towards enjoyment or power" (cf. *FR* 47). This brought an impoverishment of both faith and reason, since "each without the other is enfeebled" (cf. *FR* 48).

For John Paul II, the relationship between faith and reason "is best construed as a circle" (cf. *FR* 73), by which he means that theology's source and starting-point must always be the word of God revealed in history, while its final goal will be an understanding of that word which increases with each passing generation' (cf. *FR* 74). Faith needs reason strengthened by the truth in order to explain why it acts with full freedom. In *FR* 28 the Pope considers different 'faces' of the truth, leading to the claim that "one may define the human being as the one who seeks the truth" (*FR* 28). He further explains how the genuine search for truth with proper reasoning leads to the absolute:

> It is the nature of the human being to seek the truth. This search looks not only to the attainment of truths which are partial, empirical or scientific; nor is it only in individual acts of decision-making that people seek the true good. Their search looks towards an ulterior truth which would explain the

3 Abraham Joshua Heschel, God in Search of Man: A Philosophy of Judaism (New York: Noonday, 1976)

> meaning of life. And it is therefore a search which can reach its end only in reaching the absolute. ... Such a truth is attained not only by way of reason but also through trusting acquiescence to other persons who can guarantee the authenticity and certainty of the truth itself (*FR* 33).

According to John Paul II, reason is nothing but the capacity to know by relying on one's own resources (cf. *FR* 53). The natural knowability of God's existence is presumed by revelation itself. There can be no divergence between these two orders of knowledge because it is the same God who reveals the mysteries and bestows the gift of faith, and who places the light of reason in the human spirit: he cannot deny himself, nor can the truth contradict the truth (cf. *FR* 53). Therefore, the Pope believes that the message of salvation, communicated through revelation, is a message of truth itself. By its very nature it is addressed to reason and thus implies the recognition of its prerogatives (cf. *FR* 53). For this reason, the Pope says repeatedly: "reason is able to arrive at universal and absolute truth, to acquire the certitude of truth and of its absolute value; man is a being in search of truth. Faith has trust in reason" (*FR* 43).

The reason for integrating the faith and reason, according to the Pope, is to avoid the possible errors, such as rationalism and fideism (cf. *FR* 55). If faith is to require the debasement and humiliation of reason as its condition of possibility, it would be turned against itself. On the contrary, "faith ... becomes the convinced and convincing advocate of reason": "it is necessary not to abandon the passion for ultimate truth, the eagerness to search for it or the audacity to forge new paths in the search. It is faith which stirs reason to move beyond all isolation and willingly to run risks so that it may attain whatever is beautiful, good and true" *(FR* 56). "Faith asks that its object be understood with the help of reason; and at the summit of its searching reason acknowledges that it cannot do without what faith presents" (FR 42). That is, faith gives reason a higher goal to shoot for and spurs it on.

Theology as the *intellectus fidei* seeks to respond through speculative inquiry "to the specific demands of disciplined thought" (*FR* 65). This means that theology, beginning with the *auditus fidei*, must by its nature seek the sort of completeness and comprehensiveness that any philosophical system demands. In other words, the formal properties of wisdom as delineated by classical philosophy are requirements for complete understanding which serve as ideals for theology as well. This does not exhaust theology, which has other sides as well, just as metaphysics and moral theory do not exhaust philosophy broadly construed.

Dogmatic theology, the Pope says, would be impossible without philosophy, since it must articulate the faith "through concepts formulated in a critical and universally communicable way" (*FR* 66). The same holds for moral theology, which needs philosophical concepts such as law, conscience, freedom, etc., "which are in part defined by philosophical ethics." This is even more obvious with respect to fundamental theology, which aims to "expound the relationship between faith and philosophical thought" (cf. *FR* 67). Therefore, what is necessary is to have the complementarity between faith and reason, theology and philosophy.

The Pope, then draws our attention to the circularity of relationship between faith and reason revealed in the Word of God, and he shows how the study of the Word of God can be mutually enhancing for the revealed truths in the Scripture and the truths constructed by the natural reason:

> Yet, since God's word is Truth (cf. Jn 17:17), the human search for truth-philosophy, pursued in keeping with its own rules-can only help to understand God's word better. It is not just a question of theological discourse using this or that concept or element of a philosophical construct; what matters most is that the believer's reason use its powers of reflection in the search for truth which moves from the word of God towards a better understanding of it. It is as if, moving between the twin poles of God's word and a better understanding of it, reason is offered guidance and is warned against paths which would lead it to stray from revealed Truth and to stray in the end from the truth pure and simple. Instead, reason is stirred to explore paths which of itself it would not even have suspected it could take. This circular relationship with the word of God leaves philosophy enriched, because reason discovers new and unsuspected horizons (*FR* 73).

The complementarity of philosophy and theology is further stressed when the Pope explains the dialogical character of philosophy and theology in seeking and explaining the universal metaphysical truths:

> As a work of critical reason in the light of faith, theology presupposes and requires in all its research a reason formed and educated to concept and argument. Moreover, theology needs philosophy as a partner in dialogue in order to confirm the intelligibility and universal truth of its claims. It was not by accident that the Fathers of the Church and the medieval theologians adopted non-Christian philosophies. This historical fact confirms the value of philosophy's autonomy, which remains unimpaired when theology calls upon it; but it shows as well the profound transformations which philosophy itself must undergo (*FR* 77).

This complementary of faith and reason can be seen in the mutual support and interfacing of philosophy and theology. Reason supports the faith and theology in the following ways:

- "There is a path which the human being may choose to take, a path which begins with reason's capacity to rise beyond what is contingent and set out towards the infinite" (*FR* 24). So the same deep desire for truth which has led to philosophical and scientific achievement leads us toward self-transcendence.

- "The truth conferred by Revelation is a truth to be understood in the light of reason. It is this duality alone which allows us to specify correctly the relationship between revealed truth and philosophical learning" (*FR* 35).
- Reason prepares the way to faith, for example, St. Justin and the apologists used philosophy as a "preamble" to the faith (cf. *FR* 38). Moreover, Philosophical logic shows how the Catholic faith is not contrary to reason, and it can demonstrate the errors of arguments against the faith. Thus, St. Clement of Alexandria called philosophy a "stepping stone to the faith" (*FR* 38).
- Reason lays the foundation for faith and makes revelation "credible." Reason is thus the common ground between believers and unbelievers. Faith without reason withers into myth or superstition. Deprived of reason, faith is left with only feelings and experience. It loses its universality (cf. *FR* 48).
- Philosophy provides a language for theology. Its concepts and patterns of thought permit theology to have a logical structure and to be a true science (cf. *FR* 65). For example, while the Real Presence in the Holy Eucharist is to be believed as a matter of faith, theology attempts to make it more understandable in terms of substance, accidents, transubstantiation, etc. Philosophical language permits theology to speak about God, the personal relations within the Trinity, God's creative activity in the world, the relationship between man and God, and Christ's identity as true God and true man, to take a few examples (cf. *FR* 66).
- Philosophy can inspire people to discover "both their capacity to know the truth and their yearning for the ultimate and definitive meaning of life" (*FR* 102).

Faith supports reason and philosophy in the following ways:

- Human reason is inherently weak and inclined to error. Deprived of revelation, reason can go off course and miss its destination (cf. *FR* 48). Faith warns reason against the paths that will lead it astray (cf. *FR* 73). It shines light on the true paths (cf. *FR* 79).
- Faith stirs reason to explore paths that it would not otherwise have suspected it could take (cf. *FR* 56). It proposes truths that might never have been discovered by unaided reason. For example, the notions of free will and a personal God who is the Creator of the world have been crucial for the development of a philosophy of

being. The Christian proclamation of human dignity, equality and freedom is reflected in modern philosophical thought (cf. *FR* 76).

- Faith gives the philosopher the courage to tackle difficult questions such as the problem of evil and suffering, the personal nature of God and the metaphysical question "Why is there something rather than nothing?" (*FR* 76). Faith gives the conviction that reason will find solutions.
- Faith, strengthened by love, facilitates the intellectual grasp of the truth about human being and his/her real needs (cf. *FR* 76).
- Faith asks that its object be understood with the help of reason; and at the summit of its searching, reason acknowledges that it cannot do without what faith presents (cf. *FR* 42). As St. Thomas Aquinas argued, because the light of reason and the light of faith both come from God, there can be no contradiction between them (cf. *FR* 43).

The affinity of faith and reason is further echoed in the concluding verses of the chapter v:

> In short, Christian Revelation becomes the true point of encounter and engagement between philosophical and theological thinking in their reciprocal relationship. It is to be hoped therefore that theologians and philosophers will let themselves be guided by the authority of truth alone so that there will emerge a philosophy consonant with the word of God. Such a philosophy will be a place where Christian faith and human cultures may meet, a point of understanding between believer and non-believer. It will help lead believers to a stronger conviction that faith grows deeper and more authentic when it is wedded to thought and does not reject it (*FR* 79).

2. Mutuality of Faith and Reason

Faith needs reason, because "our vision of the face of God is always fragmentary and impaired by the limits of our understanding" (*FR*13). Faith as an obedient response to God "alone makes it possible to penetrate the mystery in a way that allows us to understand it coherently" (*FR*13). The Pope says that faith 'surrounds' reason with two reference points, the meaning of human life and the mystery of God, both of which are revealed in their fullness by Christ. And it is within the realm defined by these points of reference that reason operates (cf. *FR* 15).

Faith as the context for natural *scientia* and consonant with it:

> What is distinctive in the biblical text is the conviction that there is a profound and indissoluble unity between the knowledge (cognitio) of reason and the knowledge of faith. The world and all that happens within

> it, including history and the fate of peoples, are realities to be observed, analysed and assessed with all the resources of reason, but without faith ever being foreign to the process. Faith intervenes not to abolish reason's autonomy nor to reduce its scope for action, but solely to bring the human being to understand that in these events it is the God of Israel who acts. Thus the world and the events of history cannot be understood in depth without professing faith in the God who is at work in them. Faith sharpens the inner eye, opening the mind to discover in the flux of events the workings of Providence (*FR* 16).

Faith as the context for natural *scientia* and necessary for it:

> On the basis of this deeper form of knowledge, the Chosen People understood that, if reason were to be fully true to itself, then it must respect certain basic rules. The first of these is that reason must realize that human knowledge is a journey which allows no rest; the second stems from the awareness that such a path is not for the proud who think that everything is the fruit of personal conquest; a third rule is grounded in the "fear of God" whose transcendent sovereignty and provident love in the governance of the world reason must recognize (*FR*18).

Faith as the basis for metaphysical reasoning and part of it:

> If the *intellectus fidei* wishes to integrate all the wealth of the theological tradition, it must turn to the philosophy of being, which should be able to propose anew the problem of being, and this in harmony with the demands and insights of the entire philosophical tradition, including philosophy of more recent times, without lapsing into sterile repetition of antiquated formulas. ... In theology, which draws its principles from Revelation as a new source of knowledge, this perspective is confirmed by the intimate relationship which exists between faith and metaphysical reasoning (*FR* 97).

Conclusion

Human being's ability to reason and to think in abstract terms is a great gift. They can acquire true knowledge about himself/herself, God and the world. As *FR* 27 says, human being is born with a desire to know the truth about himself/herself. No one can avoid the need to address life's ultimate questions (cf. *FR* 27). In fact man can be defined as "the one who seeks the truth" (*FR* 28). Therefore, we can say that it is the nature of human being to seek the truth. This search looks not only to the attainment of truths which are partial, empirical or scientific, but also looks towards an ulterior truth which would explain the meaning of life. It is here the link between faith and reason stands in need of close examination because "each without the other is impoverished and enfeebled. Deprived of what Revelation offers, reason has taken sidetracks which expose it to the danger of losing sight of its final goal. Deprived of reason, faith has stressed feeling and experience, and so run the risk of no longer being a universal proposition" (*FR* 48).

Truth is discovered through the interaction of faith and reason together. Both are necessary to know God, human person and world. Faith and reason alone cannot result in the ultimate truth. The rise of rationalism has led some to believe in the separation of faith and reason but the result has been disastrous for the promotion of life. Why should faith be concerned with reason and why does reason need faith's contribution? Because they are in fact deeply related to life because they determine how people act. The ultimate purpose of personal existence, then, is the theme of philosophy and theology alike. For all their difference of method and content, both disciplines point to that "path of life" (Ps 16:11) which, as faith tells us, leads in the end to the full and lasting joy of the contemplation of the Triune God (*FR*15). "This means that the human being – the one who seeks the truth – is also the one who lives by belief" (*FR* 31).

As John Paul II articulated in Fides et Ratio Dr. George Karuvelil also believed that theology without a metaphysical horizon could not move beyond an analysis of religious experience, nor would it allow the *intellectus fidei* to give a coherent account of the universal and transcendent value of revealed truth (cf. *FR* 83). He also believed that if were theologians to refuse the help of philosophy, they would run the risk of doing philosophy unwittingly and locking themselves within thought-structures poorly adapted to the understanding of faith (cf. *FR* 77). Likewise, he is also convinced that Philosophy must transcend empirical data and consider the sapiential dimension of life, that is, it must renew its search for wisdom and the ultimate meaning of life (cf. *FR* 83). In short, Both John Paul II and Dr. George Karuvelil believed that "faith and philosophy should recover the profound unity which allows them to stand in harmony with their nature without compromising their mutual autonomy. The *parrhesia* (*boldness*) of faith must be matched by the boldness of reason" (*FR* 48).

PART I

PHILO-SOPHIA: REASON MEETING WITH WISDOM

3

Aristotle's Concept of Substance

Gerald O'Collins SJ

Abstract

For Aristotle's category of substance, non-existence in a subject is the ontological criterion, and non-predictability of a subject is the logical criterion. The basic difference between substance and all other categories comes from its separate or independent existence. It is the 'substratum' for other categories such as quality or quantity. Ontologically substance does not exist in a subject and hence, logically, substance is not predicated of another subject. While sometimes ready to call species 'secondary substances', actually existing, individual substances remain the only real substances for Aristotle. He can be defended against the much later criticisms of Berkeley, Locke, and Hume. Their objections to substance illustrate the shift towards epistemology that has characterized Western philosophy.

Keywords

Aristotle, Berkeley, Hume, Locke, Species, Substance, Substratum

Introduction

As the first of his categories, the primary and irreducible divisions of the data of reality, Aristotle places substance. He gives the following account of it: 'a substance—that which is called a substance most strictly, primarily, and most of all—is that which is neither said of a subject nor in a subject: e.g. the individual man or the individual horse.'[1] The two criteria used here are the ontological criterion, non-existence in a subject, and the logical criterion, non-predictability of a subject.

1. Ontological Criterion

Aristotle distinguishes substance from all other things on the grounds that it alone does not exist in a subject. He explains what he means by existence in a subject: 'by "in a subject" I mean what is in something, not as a part [in a whole], and cannot exist separately from what it is in'.[2]

This criterion centres on the notion of separate or independent existence. If a thing can exist separately and in its own right, Aristotle will call it a substance. Whatever cannot enjoy such existence does not qualify for the name of substance. As he states in the *Metaphysics*, the basic difference between substance and all other categories is established by the notion of separate or independent existence: none of the other categories is 'self-sufficient or capable of being separated from substance'. Substance is 'primary in every sense'.[3]

It follows that what cannot exist independently must exist in dependence on substance, which can exist independently. This is the second (ontological) feature of substance: while remaining one, it acts as the subject or substratum for other categories. Aristotle writes: 'it seems most distinctive of substance that what is numerically one and the same is able to receive contraries'.[4] Thus substance is that in which and by which the other categories (the accidents) are.

2. The Name 'Substance'

It is this latter notion of subject or substratum for accidents that has given substance its name (*substantia, quod substat accidentibus* (what underlies accidents)). This is a somewhat unhappy choice, as it highlights the secondary and ontologically derived aspect of substance. Aristotle's own special name for substance, *ousia*, which we could translate as 'the existent', reflects the basic feature of his doctrine of substance. It is 'being' in the highest sense, the most real of all things, since it is what can exist separately.

1 *Categories*, 5; in Jonathan Barnes (ed.), *The Complete Works of Aristotle: The Revised Oxford Translation*, vol. 1 (Princeton, NJ: Princeton University Press, 1984), 4; hereafter Barnes. For a summary of the issues concerning Aristotle on substance, see S. Marc Cohen, 'Substances', in Georgios Anagnostopoulos (ed.), *A Companion to Aristotle* (Malden, MA: Wiley-Blackwell, 2009), 197–211.

2 *Categories*, 2, Barnes, vol. 1, 3.

3 *Metaphysics*, book VII, ch. 1, Barnes, vol. 2, 1623–24.

4 *Categories*, 5, Barnes, vol 1, 7.

The fact that substance supports in existence what cannot so exist is not only a secondary consideration, but is also a dispensable mark of substances. Aristotle holds that there exist substances such as God, which do not serve as substrata for changing and contrary accidents.

3. Substratum for Accidents

When we speak of substance as the substratum for accidents, that is, as underlying or standing under them, we use a spatial metaphor. However, the philosophical principle involved is simply the very general notion of dependence in existence, whatever that dependence may be. We could imagine a corporeal substance that is coloured in red throughout. By calling this substance the substratum of redness, we mean no more than this colour cannot exist independently. Disembodied redness seems impossible. We do not mean that the substance literally stands under or underpins the redness in the way in which foundations stand under a building and support it.

To make this point more strikingly, we have imagined a substance which is completely penetrated and permeated with redness. In no spatial sense can it be said to 'stand under' the redness.

4. Logical Criterion

From the ontological fact that substance does not exist in a subject follows the logical fact that 'substance alone is not predicated of another subject, but everything else of substance'.[5]

Unless the relations between the ontological and logical aspects of Aristotle's doctrine of substance are grasped, various difficulties will arise. In a classical article entitled 'Substance', J. D. Mabbott, for example, begins by offering as Aristotle's account of substance 'that which has predicates and is not predicated of anything else'.[6] He then proceeds to speak of the confusion 'between being a substance and being independent of other things'.[7] This confusion would be avoided by accepting that the ontological power of separate existence is the essential feature of substance. From this feature derives the notion that substance has predicates but is not predicated of anything else.

5. Species as Substance

Where Aristotle's notion of substance does become complicated is in his discussion as to whether the individual substance (for instance, the individual man) enjoys the sole claim to the title of substance. What of matter, form, and species? Are they also truc substanccs?

5 *Physics*, book I, ch. 7, Barnes, 325.

6 'Substance', *Philosophy* 10 (1935), 186.

7 'Substance', 186.

As his inquiry (in the *Metaphysics*) about matter and form presupposes that the theory of hylomorphism has already been established, let us limit ourselves here to Aristotle's position on specific natures, the *infimae species*: for example, man or horse in general.

In the *Categories* Aristotle proposes that the specific nature, although truly predicated of many individuals, is not actually present *as such*, that is *qua* a universal species in singular, individual subjects. He writes: 'Man is said of a subject, the individual man, but is not in any subject.'[8] The mind has seized on the formal nature of the individual subject, and, conceiving it in a universal way, can now apply the concept to many individuals who share the same nature. Although we can truly predicate this nature of them, we cannot, however, also predicate of them the universal way in which the given nature is conceived by the mind. It is in an individual way that the nature exists in the individual substances. But in the *Categories* Aristotle is willing to assign to the specific natures (and also to the genera such as 'animal') the title of 'secondary substances' in contrast to the 'primary substances', the actually existing individual substances which, in the strict sense, are the only real substances.[9]

In the *Metaphysics* where he is preoccupied with rival theories of substance, Aristotle will not call the genera and species 'substances', even if previously he had been ready to call them substance in a secondary and derived sense. The claims of the genus to the title of substance are ruled out in the later chapters of Book VII: for instance, in Chapter 13. The specific essence is described in the *Metaphysics* as a material universal, the combination of 'this' form with 'this' matter taken as a universal. Aristotle flatly denies that it is a substance.[10] In the *Metaphysics* the individual substance rather than the species is the real substance for Aristotle. Yet in the context of some discussion, where his remarks could apply to both, he does bother to distinguish species from individuals.

To sum up Aristotle's doctrine of substance. Ontologically, substance has a separate existence and supports in existence whatever cannot exist independently. Logically, substance is not predicated of anything else, while other things are predicated of it.

6. Criticisms of Aristotelian Substance

What sort of criticisms have faced Aristotle's category of substance? Some of his categories were unacceptable to major philosophers in the ancient world. The Atomists denied the category of quality, above all sensible qualities.

8 *Categories*, 2, Barnes, vol. 1., 3.

9 *Categories*, 5, Barnes, vol. 1, 4–5.

10 10 *Metaphysics*, Book VII, ch. 13, Barnes, vol. 2, 1640.

As they reduced all reality to matter, this involved rejecting completely the Aristotelian category of quality.[11]

The case was different, however, with the category of substance. Among ancient philosophers we find, either explicitly or by implication, the doctrine of a being which exists independently. This being may be realised in many instances, as in the infinite multitude of atoms postulated by Leucippus and Democritus. Or it may be verified only once, as with the Parmenidean One. Heraclitus is the only major philosopher among Aristotle's predecessors and contemporaries whose teaching may be interpreted as rejecting substantialist philosophies. The interpretation of Heraclitus is notoriously difficult and controversial. Even if we felt sure that Heraclitus denied the concept of substance, his reasons for this denial would remain a matter of conjecture. What remains of his writings is a series of enigmatic pronouncements. It is not until Parmenides that we have a reasoned series of premises and conclusions.

Leaving aside the problematic case of Heraclitus, we find in later philosophy numerous criticisms of Aristotle's notion of substance. These criticisms do not necessarily involve such drastic doctrines as universal change and a denial of the principle of contradiction, doctrines which may be involved in Heraclitus's rejection of earlier substantialist philosophies. We will outline several classic arguments against Aristotelian substance and suggest some replies that can be found in Aristotle's work.

Probably the most significant critic of substance is David Hume (1711–76). To a degree, John Locke (1632–1704) had initiated a criticism of Aristotelian substance, which was taken up by George Berkeley (1685–1753), and proved even more destructive in the challenges coming from Hume. In saying this, we are not, however, alleging that Hume, either on the issue of substance or in his general philosophical position, is a logical third in a neat trio.

In Locke's view, substance is the unknown substratum, which we suppose to exist under the qualitative data of experience, and to act as their support. Substances, both material and spiritual, exist, albeit unknown:

> The idea, then, we have, to which we give the general name 'substance', being nothing but the supposed, but unknown, support of those qualities we find existing, which we imagine cannot subsist *sine re substante*, 'without something to support them'. We call that support *substantia*, which, according to the true import of the word, is in plain English 'standing under' or 'upholding'.[12]

---

11 See Democritus, fragments 9 and 11, in G. S. Kirk, J. E. Raven and M. Schofield, *The Presocratics*, second edn. (Cambridge: Cambridge University Press, 1983), 410.

12 *An Essay Concerning Human Understanding*, book II, ch. 23, par. 2, ed. A. S. Pringle-Pattison (Oxford: Oxford University Press, 1924), 156.

Berkeley denied substantiality to material things, which he declared to be mere subjective representations produced by minds. 'Their *esse*', he wrote, 'is *percepi* nor is it possible they should have any existence, out of the minds or thinking things which perceive them.'[13] He held, however, that there are spiritual substances which we encounter in our own personal consciousness.

Hume rejected substance completely, both on the level of matter and in the world of spirit. There is simply no intelligible content in the concept of substance, he argued. We cannot distinguish the substance of things from the immediate data with which these things furnish us. There is nothing 'over and above' these data. Take them away and there is nothing left to know. First, as regards material substances, Hume claimed that nowhere in our sense experience can we detect substance. The senses reveal to us different qualities, which our imagination groups into various collections, to each of which we attach the name of 'substance'. The qualities we experience are thus 'commonly refer'd to an unknown something in which they are supposed to inhere'.[14] Second, Hume also denied the reality of the thinking, soul-substance, which is postulated as a permanent substratum for the changing data of consciousness. There exists for Hume only a flux of impressions and feelings, which through memory we gather into a unity:

> But setting aside some metaphysicians of this kind, I may venture to affirm of the rest of mankind that they are nothing but a bundle or collection of different perceptions, which succeed each other with an unconceivable reality, and are in perpetual flux and movement.[15]

To sum up Hume's position: both the concept of external, material substance and that of internal soul-substances are mere fictions. In neither case can we derive the concept of substance directly from experience. In both cases the concept is an illusion produced by the imagination. It combines what are frequently found together into one idea and gives that idea one name. The unity is merely nominal; substance remains an empty term, one of the fictions of 'ancient philosophy'.[16]

7. Aristotle's Defence

Hume's rejection of substance as a meaningless fiction can be answered by an argument drawn form the contrast Aristotle made between being a substance and being anything else. Substance is unique in that it can exist

13 *Principles of Human Knowledge*, 3, in *Berkeley's Philosophical Writings*, ed. David M. Armstrong (London: Collier-Macmillan, 1965), 62.

14 *A Treatise of Human Nature,* book I, part 1, sect. 6, ed. Ernest G. Mossner (London: Penguin, 1969), 63.

15 *A Treatise on Human Nature*, book I, part 4, sect. 6, Mossner, 300.

16 *Treatise of Human Nature*, book I, part 4, sect. 3, Mossner, 268–74.

'independently'.[17] In conjunction with this dichotomy between substances and non-substances, we can take up a principle recognized by Aristotle: an infinite regress in a chain of things or events, each of which in producing its effect intrinsically depends on its predecessor, is impossible.

Aristotle needs, however, a little supplementing here. He recognizes that an infinite 'linear' regress is impossible. Thus in the *Physics* he argues against a 'change of change' and a 'coming-to-be of coming-to-be' on the grounds that this would involve an infinite regress or series that would make change impossible. 'Since in an infinite series', he states, 'there is no first term, here there will be no first stage and, therefore, no following stage either. On this hypothesis, then, nothing can become or be moved or change.'[18] But we could also imagine closed or 'circular' series of things or events dependent on one another, and infinite in the sense that there would be no first term. A, for instance, is asserted to depend on B, B on C, C on D, and D on A. In this hypothesis, however, the same thing in the same respect would be both prior and posterior—which is unintelligible. For A exists only insofar as (through the mediation of B and C) it depends on D. Thus A is posterior to D. Yet D exists only insofar as it depends on A. Therefore, A is prior to D. Thus A is both prior and posterior to D—which is unintelligible.

Taking up then both the impossibility of an infinite regress and Aristotle's notion of substance, we might fashion the following argument. What is given in experience either exists independently, or it does not. If it exists independently, it is a substance. If it does not, we can ask the same question about that on which it depends for its existence. Eventually, we must either admit that there is something which exists independently or else postulate an infinite regress: that is, an unending series of things, none of which exists independently but each of which depends on its predecessor. Such an infinite regress leaves the whole series unintelligible, since, *ex hypothesi*, it never reaches a first term which exists independently and can thus account for the existence of all the things that depend on it. Thus the data of experience involves the existence of at least one thing which is independent in its existence. This argument can be summed up in Aristotle's words: 'if the primary substances did not exist, it would be impossible for any of the other things to exist'.[19]

8. Further Objection by Hume

Hume is willing to admit that in a sense we can allow some reality to the concept of substance. Taking as a definition of substance 'something which may exist by itself', he argues as follows:

17 *Physics*, book I, part 2, Barnes, vol. 1, 316.

18 *Physics*, book V, part 2, Barnes, vol. 1, 382.

19 *Categories*, 5, Barnes, vol. 1, 5.

> This definition agrees to everything that can possibly be conceiv'd and never will serve to distinguish substance from accident, or the soul from its perceptions. For thus I reason. Whatever is clearly conceiv'd may exist; and whatever is clearly conceiv'd, after any manner, may exist after the same manner...all our perceptions...may be consider'd as separately existent, and may exist separately, and have no need of anything else to support their existence. They are, therefore, substances, as far as this definition explains a substance.[20]

By thus extending the application of substance to 'everything that can possibly be conceiv'd', Hume has deprived of meaning any distinction between the first category and other things.

However, as Aristotle points out, it is impossible to reduce all things to substance. There cannot be, for instance, disembodied, independently existing whiteness. Aristotle observes: 'heat and straightness can be present in every part of a thing, but it is impossible that the thing should be nothing but hot or white or straight'.[21] The example of colour is particularly telling. How could we have instances of colour without something coloured? On this point at least, we can question the success of Hume's attempt to destroy the distinction between things which can exist independently and those which cannot so exist. With this, we conclude the brief confrontation between Hume and Aristotle, noting that, since their opposition in the matter of substance connects with their differing views on the nature and formation of ideas, a full-scale treatment would call for an examination of their respective theories of knowledge.

What happened to Aristotle's view of substance at the hands of Hume exemplifies a change that George Karuvelil, SJ, has explored significantly: the move to epistemology which has characterized much Western philosophy. We cannot adequately assess Aristotle's long dominant notion of substance without being brought to face epistemological questions.

---

20 *Treatise of Human Nature*, book I, part 4, sect. 5, Mossner, 282.

21 *Length or Shortness of Life*, 3, Barnes, vol. 1, 741.

4

Will As Freedom: Hegel's Philosophy of Free Will

Jojo Varakukalayil CST

Abstract

George Wilhelm Friedrich Hegel, in his Encyclopaedia of the Philosophical Sciences, deals with the concept of the Geist, and discusses the concept of the 'Objective Spirit' as elaborated as Philosophy of Right dealing with the concept of the 'Wille', i.e., 'will as freedom' as manifested in the realm of the 'Die Sittlichkeit," 'Ethical Life'. 'Spirit,' argues Hegel, has an objective dimension in social structures as the objective spirit. The concept of the Will in Hegel's Philosophy of Right remains as formal, for the Will has its own purpose; and thus, the unity of subjective and objective. The Will is initially abstract and, immediately, it is its determinate existence that constitutes the sphere of abstract right; and these two moments of the Will, in its concept and in its determinate existence, break apart into independent extremes; i.e., it is the third moment of the concept of the Will as the actual free Will. The concept of the Will, for Hegel, as indeterminate and determinate is without contradicting each other. The free will depend on the membership in a rational state that results in the development of civil rights and property rights of law and morality, and of social institutions, such as, the family and the state. This article, in delineating the concept of the Will, argues that the Will, for Hegel, is objectively manifested as right in a rational society; accordingly, the structures of the society are structures of the Will.

Keywords

Spirit, mind, will, freedom, right, and Society.

Introduction

George Wilhelm Friedrich Hegel (1770-1831) in his *Encyclopaedia of the Philosophical Sciences*[1] deals with the concept of the *Geist,* the Spirit. He discusses the concept of the 'Objective Spirit', 'Mind' which is further elaborated as *Philosophy of Right* that deals with the concept of the '*Wille',* 'will as freedom' which is manifested in the realm of the '*Die Sittlichkeit*", 'Ethical Life'. 'Spirit' or 'Mind' has an objective dimension in social structures, and this system of philosophy is objective mind, or spirit.

The *Philosophy of Right* analyses the concept of the will (*PR* §§ 4-7). The will as a concept is merely formal, for the will is its own purpose, and we have here the unity of subjective and objective. The will is free and, by implication, it is the principle of the structures of the social world that are structures of freedom. The science of right has the free will as its principle and starting point. The external/objective world constitutes the material for the embodiment of the will (*EPS* § 483). The free will is initially abstract and immediately, as is its determinate existence or realisation; this constitutes the sphere of abstract right. The second sphere is where these two moments of the will, in its concept and in its determinate existence, break apart into independent extremes. It is the third moment of the concept of the will that discusses the actual free will (*EPS* § 481, *PR* § 7). This is the concrete understanding of the freedom of the will. This is the unity of the preceding moments. The concept of right is the way the will interacts with the external world.[2] The will is to will freedom. Hegel argues that the conditions for free actions enormously depend on the membership in a rational state. This results in the development of civil rights and property rights of law and morality, and of social institutions, such as, the family and the sate. Hence, Hegel argues that the structure of the society is the

1 Fredrich Hegel, *Philosophy of Mind Being Part Three of the Encyclopaedia of the Philosophical Sciences* (1830), trans. William Wallace (Oxford: Clarendon Press, 1971), §§ 483-552. Further citations from this book will be abbreviated with their corresponding page numbers as *EPS.* This is elaborated in G. W. F. Hegel, *Hegel's Philosophy of Right*, trans. T. M. Knox (Oxford: Clarendon Press, 1952). Further citations from this book will be abbreviated with their corresponding page numbers as *PR*. Hegel gives an explanation to show how *Geist*, Spirit goes through three stages of its development. Spirit is always Idea, but at the beginning, it is only the Concept of the Idea, in its indeterminate and abstract mode of being. Spirit is universal, undeveloped and not yet particular unless it passes from itself to nature and then posits this nature as its presupposition. Hegel speaks of the spirit as (a) Subjective Spirit, (b) Objective Spirit, and (c) Absolute Spirit.

2 Howard P. Kainz, *Hegel's Philosophy of Right with Marx's Commentary: A Handbook for Students* (Netherlands: Martinus Nijhoff, 1974), p. 14. Further citations from this book will be cited as Kainz, *Hegel's Philosophy of Right with Marx's Commentary.*

structure of the will. These social structures are necessary structures for the will to will its freedom objectively.

This article aims at analysing Hegel's concept of the *wille*, its structure and the will as freedom. The will is to achieve its freedom. In order to achieve this freedom the will need to primarily achieve its goals and engage in voluntary actions. The most basic end of the human will is to act free. Thus, in delineating the concept of the will, its structure, and its content the article argues that the will, for Hegel, is objectively manifested as right in a rational society. Hence, the structures of the society are structures of the will.

1. Hegel's Concept of the Will

Hegel's *Philosophy of Right* deals with the concept of the will.[3] The main thrust of the will is to achieve its freedom.[4] Speaking about the will, Hegel would say that human will is free.[5] According to him, "[t]he will is free, so that freedom is both the substance of right and its goal, while the system of right is the realm of freedom made actual, the world of mind brought forth of itself like a second

---

3 Michael Inwood, *A Hegel Dictionary* (Oxford: Blackwell Publishers, 1992), p. 311. Further citations from this book will be abbreviated with their corresponding page numbers as Inwood, *A Hegel Dictionary.* Inwood gives a clear explanation of the will and will fullness. "*Wollen* means 'to wish, want intend, be about to', etc. This gave rise to *(der) Wille* ('(the will'). (*Whal*, choice and *wählen*, 'to choose', are also cognate with *wollen*). A now obsolete verb, *kissen (*'to check, inspect, choose, (after checking)'), gave rise to *Kür* ('choice'). (*Kür* now occurs only in the sense of 'free, optional exercise (in sport)'. This is an abbreviation of *Kürübung* 'optional exercise'). *Wille* combined with Kür to give *WillKür,* which thus originally meant a 'decision, resolve of the will'. *Willkür* developed a derogatory sense: 'caprice, acting as one pleases with no regard for others'. In the late eighteenth century this became its predominant sense in the ordinary usage, and it now commonly means 'arbitrariness'. The adjective *willkürlich* means 'arbitrary, high handed' but its negation, *unwillkürlich*, still means 'involuntary, automatic'... Hegel's main accounts of *wille* and *Willkur* occur at *Enc.* III §§ 473-82 and especially at *PR* §§ 4-28. The *wille* is essentially free, but it has three main phases, each involving a different phase of freedom:"

4 Inwood, *A Hegel Dictionary*, p. 110. Inwood explains the notion of freedom in Hegel: "*Freiheit* and *frei* correspond closely to 'freedom' and 'free'. They refer both to freedom of the WILL and to freedom in all its social and political senses. Thus 'freedom' contrasts with 'slavery', 'dependence', 'compulsion', 'NECESSITY', ETC. Hegel attempts to interconnect this variety of senses into a single theory of freedom. The core notion of freedom is this: something, especially a person, is free if, and only if, it is independent and self-DETERMEINING, not determined by or dependant on something other than itself."

5 *PR*, pp. 225-226. Hegel explains it in his additions to *PR* § 4. "The freedom of the will is best explained by a reference to the physical world. Freedom, I mean is just as fundamental a character of the will as weight is of bodies. If we say: matter is 'heavy', we might mean that this predicate is only contingent; but it is nothing of that kind, for nothing in matter is without weight. Matter is rather weight itself. Heaviness constitutes the body and is the body. The same is the case with freedom and the will, since the free entity is the will. Will without freedom is an empty word, while freedom is actually only as will, as subject."

nature."[6] The will as freedom, speaks of the realm of the actualised freedom. In order to speak about the free will, one has to ask how does Hegel explain the concept of the will or the structure of the will? He says; "[t]he basis of right is, in general, mind [spirit]; its precise place and point of origin is the will" (*PR* § 4). The will is manifested in articulating human goodness in self - actualization of its spirit as freedom in the society.

The main issue here is what is required for the will to achieve its freedom. The most basic end of the human will is to act freely (*PR* § 27). Freedom is not arbitrariness (*PR* § 15), but acting objectively in accordance with the concept of the will. It states about two basic requirements for achieving freedom, namely, achieving one's ends and engaging its voluntary actions. According to Hegel, voluntary actions requires both achieving one's ends and matching one's intentions with the consequences of one's acts (*PR* §§10, 22, 23, 28, 39). The end of the will, the purposive action, is the realization of freedom in the world outside (*EPS* § 484). Hegel holds that obligations are generated by commitment to the basic end of calling to be free and by the consequent commitment to the necessary legitimate means or conditions for achieving freedom. Correlatively rights are generated and justified by showing that a right secures some necessary legitimate means or condition for achieving freedom (*PR* §§ 4, 29, 30). Principles, practices and institutions are justified by showing that they play a necessary and irreplaceable role in achieving freedom. Free will has existence and it is the law. Free will exists as duties and its temper and habits are manners. He calls it second nature (*PR* § 151). Accordingly "what is a right is also a duty, and what is a duty, is also a right."[7] This is understood by the subjective consciousness as duty and the finite nature of the objective will that shows the distinction between rights and duties. In the phenomenal range these are correlated. My right is somebody else's duty. In the light of the concept of my right a thing is not merely a possession but a possession of a property or legal possession and it is a duty to possess things as property, i.e., to be a person. When this is viewed from the phenomenal relationship, relation to another person grows to be a duty of someone else to respect my right. In morality my duty is in me. The rights of the individuals

6 *PR*, p. 21. Hegel explains that: "In considering the freedom of the will, we may recall the old method of cognition. The procedure was to presuppose the idea of the will and to attempt to establish a definition of the will by deriving it from that idea; then the so called 'proof' of the will's freedom was extracted, in the manner of the old empirical psychology, from the various feelings and phenomena of the ordinary consciousness, such as remorse, guilt, and the like, by maintaining that they were to be explained only in the light of a will that was free. But it is more convenient of course to arrive at the same point by taking the shortcut of supposing that freedom is given as a fact of consciousness and that we must simply believe in it!"

7 *EPS*, p. 242.

come back to them as their duties towards and through that it appear both different and remain intrinsically the same. Those who have no rights have no duties either (*EPS* § 486).

The introduction to Hegel's *Philosophy of Right* deals with Hegel's social idealism. This is well articulated in his discussion of the social institutions, political establishments, economic organizations, domestic arrangements, religious movements and social units. These are to be understood as structures of the mind and the will. The structures of the will comprise the normative life of the society and they are the structures of freedom.[8] The spirit in itself manifests the sphere of the objective spirit. The "objective" means the rational self organization of an immediate actuality. The person as the individual, who is conscious of his/her freedom, gives external expression to his/her nature as free spirit, and s/he actualizes his/her freedom as free spirit in the external sphere. The manifestation of the will as freedom is brought to express itself in the realm of *sache,* material things.[9] One expresses his/her free will by appropriating or owning things whereby things become property. The material things as material things do not have a right of its own but it is the instance or moment for the will to express its freedom upon the *sache*. Thus they are the instrument for the expression of the rational will.

In *PR* §4, Hegel says that the basis of right is the realm of spirit and it is the point of the origin of the will. He means that social life is the sphere of the actualized freedom. The system of rights speaks about this idea of the freedom of the will thus manifested in this realm of the actualized freedom. The meaning of freedom can be found only in the life of the individual namely the subjective spirit and in the ethical living of the individual in a society. Here freedom does not mean the possibility to do as one wishes, rather it is acting according to the concept of the will. Thus freedom does not mean 'arbitrariness' *Willkur;* at the same time we find that Hegel does not speak of the mind and will as distinct. He is rather averted to, for these might be discrete

---

8 Cf. Dudley Knowles, *Hegel and the Philosophy of Right*, Rutledge Philosophy Guide Books (London and New York: Rutledge, 2002), pp. 25-26. Further citations from this book will be cited as Knowles, *Hegel and the Philosophy of Right.* "It is distinctive of Hegel's thought in these areas that we can act freely only in the context of a form of social life that sustains and protects that freedom; a free society is necessary if freedom of the will is to be a real feature of citizens' life."

9 *PR*, p. 40 "Thing', like 'the objective', has two opposed meanings. If we say 'that's the thing' or the thing is what matters, not the person', 'thing' means what is substantive. On the other hand, when 'thing' is contrasted with 'person' as such, not with the particular subject, it means the opposite of what is substantive, i.e., that whose determinate character lies in its pure externality. From the point of view of free mind, which must, of course, be distinguished from mere consciousness, the external is external absolutely, and it is for this reason that the determinate character assigned to nature by the concept is inherent externality."

faculties of the mind. Hence, they are inseparable. All subject object models of knowledge is rejected and replaced by knowledge as self-knowledge, as the knowledge of the maker available to the spirit.[10]

2. Structure of the Will

In elaborating the very concept of the will Hegel proceeds with his own argument from the very structure of the will. The will is said to have two elements. In *PR* §5, Hegel speaks of one side of the will, i.e., the unrestricted possibility of abstraction from every determinate state of mind, which I find in myself. It proceeds to a negative freedom.[11] This is idealization and this thinking is universal. This is the moment of absolute indeterminacy. From this utter indeterminacy, he moves on to the second moment, the moment of determination. This is analysed in *PR* § 6, where he speaks of the will of a particular subject with a determinate object. The will of the particular subject also has the capacity to determine its object of determination. Hence, it is determinate and concrete. The first element of the will is indeterminate and the second element of the will is determinate, hence, particular. The second element cancels the abstract negativity of the first element.[12] It seems as opposed to the first but it has to be taken in its general form, it belongs to freedom but does not constitute the whole of it. The indefinite will is one sided as the will that continues merely in the definite. But the actual will, for Hegel, is the unity of both these elements namely the indeterminate infinite and the determinate finite. This is expressed in the thought where the essence of freedom of the will is self-determination. Hegel writes:

> The will is the unity of both these moments. It is particularly reflected into itself and so brought back to universality, i.e., it is individuality. It is the self-determination of the ego, which means that at one and the same time

10 Cf. Knowles, *Hegel and the Philosophy of Right*, pp. 27-28.

11 Cf. *PR*, p. 22. In his explanation to *PR* § 5, Hegel says that: "When the will's self-determination consists in his alone, or when representative thinking regards this side by itself as freedom and clings fast to it, then we have negative freedom or freedom as the Understanding conceives it. This is the freedom of the void which rises to a passion and takes shape in the world; while still remaining theoretical, it takes hope in religion as Hindu fanaticism of pure contemplation, but when it turns to actual practice, it takes shape in religion and politics alike as the fanaticism of destruction - the destruction of the whole subsisting social order - as the elimination of individuals who are objects of suspicion to any social order, and the annihilation of any organization which tries to rise anew from the ruins."

12 *PR*, p. 22. Hegel explains that: "The first moment, I mean - because by itself is only the first - is not true infinity or concrete universality, not the concept, but only something determinate, one-sided; i.e., being abstraction from all determinacy, it is itself not without determinacy; and to be something abstract and one sided constitutes its determinacy, its defectiveness, and its finitude."

> the ego posits itself as its own negative, i.e., as restricted and determinate, and yet remains by itself, i.e., in its self-identity and universality. It determines itself and yet at the same time binds itself together with itself. The ego determines itself in so far as it is the relating of negativity to itself.[13]

The I, ego, as such is pure activity itself, universal; and this universal determines itself, in so far as no longer by itself, but establishes itself as another, and ceases to be the universal. The will is by itself, while it limits itself; it yet remains with itself and does not lose its hold on the universal. This is then the conception of freedom as concrete, while the other two elements have been thoroughly abstract and one-sided. But this concrete freedom we already have in the form of perception. Free will consists in willing a definite or particular concrete object. Self as other is necessary to view self-determination as part of the freedom. For Hegel, the will becomes will by self-mediating activity and return to itself. One needs to be free to determine the particular and he is not determined by the indeterminacy alone. The will goes beyond restriction and can actualize its freedom. Hence, "freedom is to will something determinate, yet in this determinacy to be by oneself and to revert once more to the universal."[14] Hegel elaborates the concept of the will in accordance with the triadic moments of the logical concepts of the will, namely, abstract universality, particularity and singularity.[15] Hence we analyse these three moments of the will accordingly.

2.1. The Universal Will

The universal will[16]appears in pure abstract form, and it appears negative. This shows an abstract conception of human will and freedom, but it corresponds to something essential. It is the human ability or capacity to abstract from

---

13 *PR*, p. 23. Hegel adds further: "Every self-consciousness knows itself (i) as universal, as the potentiality of abstracting from everything determinate, and (ii) as particular, with a determinate object, content, and aim. Still both these moments are only subtractions; what is concrete and true (and everything true is concrete) is the universality which has the particular as its opposite, but the particular which by its reflection into itself has been equalized with the universal. This unity is individuality, not individuality in its immediacy as a unit, our first idea of individuality, but individuality in accordance with its concept; indeed, individuality in this sense is just precisely the concept itself."

14 *PR*, p. 229.

15 Paul Franco, *Hegel's Philosophy of Freedom* (New Haven and London: Yale University Press, 1999), 156. Further citations from this book will be abbreviated with their corresponding page numbers as Franco, *Hegel's Philosophy of Freedom.*

16 Cf. Inwood, *A Hegel Dictionary*, pp. 312-313. Inwood explains that "[t]he UNIVERSAL *Wille* is our capacity to abstract from all our desires, impulses, etc., and to satisfy none of them. This type of freedom is wholly negative and appears, in a pure form, only in such unsatisfactory enterprises as suicide, oriental mysticism and the destructiveness of

every determination and it is the specific character that distinguishes humans from other beings.[17] The rational subject can abstract the content of his/her thinking from the act of thinking itself; in other words, humans are capable of reflexive thinking. I know my knowing. This is the self-conscious self. Hence, he argues:

> The element of pure indeterminacy or that pure reflection of the ego into itself which involves the dissipation of every restriction and every content either immediately presented by nature, by needs, desires and impulses, or given and determined by means whatever. This is the unrestricted infinity of absolute abstraction or universality, the pure thought of oneself.[18]

Hegel speaks of the will that thinks of itself. There has been a thinking that self has the capacity to think its thinking, hence, self as self-conscious of it. The thinking subject can abstract its thinking from its very thinking or willing itself. This has been traditionally explained as; 'Man is a being which can think of its own thinking'. It has been one of the trade marks to distinguish human beings from other animals and to define him/her as "rational animal". The thinking of man is a self-conscious thinking as pure thought thinking itself. This pure thought thinking itself doesn't have any specific content as this or that. It cannot be understood by the thought itself since we have used our thinking to think of it. This is the universal will in all its respects.[19] The abstraction from all content and determinateness is a "negative freedom".[20] It intends the will a kind of ruin or destruction. There is nothing as in itself. The individuals are suspected by a given order where the negative freedom is characterised as universal and absolute.[21] In its extremes it is individualism of a negativistic kind and can ruin. From the absolute indeterminacy of the will

---

the French revolutionary terror. But the ability to abstract from one's desires is an essential ingredient of higher types of freedom."

17 Paul Franco, *Hegel's Philosophy of Freedom*, pp. 159-160.

18 *PR*, pp. 64-73. See also in G.W.F. Hegel, *Lectures on Natural Right and political Science, The First Philosophy of Right*, trans. J. Michael Stewart and Peter C. Hodgson (Berkeley Los Angeles London: University of California Press), p. 53. Further citations from this book will be cited as, Hegel, *Lectures on Natural Right and Political Science, The First Philosophy of Right*.

19 Cf. Dudley Knowles, *Hegel and the Philosophy of Right*, pp. 28-33.

20 Franco, *Hegel's Philosophy of Freedom*, p. 160. Paul explains that for Hegel the most frightening example of the actualization of the negative freedom is the French Revolution. The absolute freedom embodied led to the fury of destruction.

21 Cf. Knowles, *Hegel and the Philosophy of Right*, pp. 27-28. See also in G.W.F. Hegel, *Hegel's Phenomenology of Spirit*, Trans A.V. Miller (Oxford: Oxford University Press, 1977), pp. 359-360, §590. Further citations from this book will be abbreviated with their corresponding page numbers as *PS*.

Hegel moves now to the determinate, particular moment of the will which is "the negation of the previous negation."[22]

2.2. The Particular Will

The particular will[23] discussed here is in terms of its form and content. In other words the will must will something. Hence, it is determinate. The content of the will is its own purpose or its end. Kainz says that "[t]hrough volitional processes of decision-making, consent, action, and creativity, the will gives determination not only to the external world but also to itself."[24] Hegel states:

> If the will's determinate character lies in the abstract opposition of its subjectivity to objectivity of external immediate existence, then this is the formal will of mere self-consciousness, which finds an external world confronting it. As individuality returning in its determinacy into itself, it is the process of translating the subjective purpose into objectivity through the use of its own activity and some external means. Once mind developed its potentialities to actuality (*wie er an und fur sich ist*), its determinate character is true and simply its own.[25]

The will is determined both in its content and in its form. The desiring subject has the formal consciousness as it identifies himself through the desiring consciousness. The formal self-consciousness brings itself to an experience of the external world. If my purpose is to eat a particular fruit, I find myself identified to this particular act of fulfilling my desire. Here the subjective desire for a fruit is actualised objectively through the self mediation. The self-consciousness is not mediated through any other third via medium but by the self itself. Its determinate character is its own. "The desiring conseiousness of the particular will introduce the moment of self-consciousness. It is the most primitive sense of ourselves that we have acquired."[26] The other aspect

---

22 Kainz, *Hegel's Philosophy of Right with Marx's Commentary*, p. 15.

23 Inwood, *A Hegel Dictionary*, p. 313. Inwood explains: "The PARTICULAR *wille* reflects on its desires and impulses to see which of them it will opt for in order to DETERMINE itself to a particular course of action. Since it can abstract from all its desires, it is not bound, like an animal, to act on any one of them, even the strongest of them and is thus free to pick and choose between them. This is the freedom of the *willkur*, the IMMEDIATE or natural will and it is, Hegel argues, what is usually meant by freedom of the will. But it is unsatisfactory, because (a) the will is dependant for its CONTENT on a range of options that are simply *given* to it – I am free to choose which of my desires to fulfil, but I do not choose what desires I have – and (b) none of the options is an appropriate object (*Gegensatnd*) of the will, since, while the will is universal, each of its potential objects is merely particular: if it rests content with one of them, the *Wille* will not fulfil its CONCEPT."

24 Kainz, *Hegel's Philosophy of Right with Marx's Commentary*, p. 15.

25 *PR*, p. 24.

26 Knowles, *Hegel and the Philosophy of Right*, p. 34.

of particularity which we can find in the particular will is the moment of its content. This is mostly nothing other than the very purpose or end. This shows that the will's content is always its goal. Hegel writes:

> In so far as the specific determinations of the will are its own or, in general, its particularization reflected into itself, they are its content. This content, as content of the will, is, in accordance with the form of will described in (a), its purpose, either its inward or subjective purpose when the will merely images its object, or else its purpose actualized and achieved by means of its activity of translating its subjective purpose into objectivity.[27]

The content of the will is manifested in its very end. However, he says that the content as content of the will is manifested in accordance with the form of the will. The will of the person is expressed as freewill, it is not like the will of animals, and the content of the will is the very purpose of the will, the will in its willing. End or purposes takes the content of the will. "[P]urpose may be evinced in the activity of the will which formulates and acts out a plan – which may be or may not be successful."[28] This is the determinacy of the form of the will and fulfilment of its purpose. The purpose though internal and subjective has to be objectively realized in its externality. The particular will subjectively felt expresses itself externally through the medium of self's activity. Thus the will's potentialities are actualised and its determinateness is simply its own. The will wills something, and this something must be concrete, which is the third moment of the will. This is the individual will.

---

27 *PR*, p. 24.

28 Knowles, *Hegel and the Philosophy of Right*, p. 34. Hegel makes a very clear presentation on the purpose of the will in the sub-section 'I and Morality', 'Purpose and Responsibility' *PR* §§ 115-118. The background of the external world makes the finitude of the subjective will. My action sets up on change in this state of affairs and my will has responsibility for effecting actions. I can be held responsible for those actions that my will is responsible – the right knowledge (§ 115). I can be made responsible for whatever was contained in my purpose and this is the chief consideration as far as crime is concerned. But responsibility involves only the wholly external judgement as to whether I have done something or not; and the fact that I am responsible for something does not mean that the thing (*sache)* can be imputed to me. The damage caused by things of my possession is chargeable to me for they are mine in principle and belongs to my control and supervision (§ 116). The freely acting will has an idea of the attendant circumstances. The will right however is to recognise as its action, and to accept responsibility for (§ 117). I can be made *accountable* for a deed only *if my will was responsible for it* – the right of knowledge. The action has various consequences in reference to the external existence. The actions are as end in reference to the external world. The will has the right to accept responsibility only for the first set of consequences, having the actions were part of its purposes (§ 118). One can be held responsible for only what he or she is aware of. One has to foresee those consequences that might be checked. I need to be aware of not only the individual but also the universal action associated with it. This involves a shifting from purpose to intention. The universal is what I have willed, i.e., my intention.

2.3. The Individual Will

This individual will[29]is the unity of the first and second moment of the will. Hegel discusses the activity of the finite spirit or mind in the *Philosophy of Right*. The spirit or mind is studied both from its theoretical and practical aspects. The actual free will is the unity of both the theoretical and practical spirit. He says: "Actual free will is the unity of theoretical and practical mind: a free will, which realizes its own freedom of will, ... the will is the immediate individuality self-instituted-an individuality, ... i.e., with freedom itself."[30] The will is conscious of its freedom as intelligence. Thus, "the concept of the Spirit in itself is the concept of the rational will, *der vernkünftige Wille,*[31] individual will. "This unity is individuality, not individuality in its immediacy as a unit, our first idea of individuality, but individuality in accordance with its concept; indeed, individuality in this sense is just precisely the concept itself."[32] Hence, Hegel would mean that the "will proper is the unity of these moments, individuality."[33] The individual will expresses itself as conscious of his/her freedom and gives external expression to his/her nature as free spirit. This is expressed in the realm of *sache, material* things. This externalization of the will as freedom consists in will's taking possession of material things and in the proper use of it. He says "[a] person must translate his freedom into an external sphere in order to exist as Idea. Personality is the first, still wholly abstract, determination of the absolute and infinite will, and therefore this sphere distinct from the person, the sphere capable of embodying his freedom, is likewise determined as what is immediately different and separable from him."[34] Possessing something means that one becomes owner of a thing not by the internal act of the will but by embodying his/her will upon it (*PR* § 53). Thus

---

29 Inwood, *A Hegel Dictionary*, p. 313. Inwood, in speaking about the Individual will, writes that "[t]he INDIVIDUAL will overcomes these problems by willing itself or willing freedom as such, thus generating from its own resources an object that is, like itself, universal. The individual will is conceived as a combination of 1 and 2, as a restoration of universality out of particularity. Since the will now has itself as its object and is wholly self-contained, it is entirely free (and also INFINITE)."

30 *EPS*, p. 238.

31 Frederick Copleston, *A History of Philosophy 18th and 19th Century German Philosophy* (London, New York: Continuum, 1963, 2003), p. 203. Further citations from this book will be cited as Copleston, *A History of Philosophy 18th and 19th Century German Philosophy.*

32 *PR*, pp. 23-24.

33 Knowles, *Hegel and the Philosophy of Right*, p. 33.

34 *PR*, p. 40. Hegel adds "[t]he rationale of property is to be found not in the satisfaction of needs but in the suppression of the pure subjectivity of personality. In his property a person exists for the first time as reason. Even if my freedom is here realized first of all in an external thing, and so falsely realized, nevertheless abstract personality in its immediacy can have no other embodiment save one characterized by immediacy."

the will of the person as a single will becomes objective to him in property (*PR* § 46). Therefore "[t]he will is not a will until it is this self-mediating activity, this return into itself."[35] The will is a will in its concrete manifestation as free will. The free will, as conscious of its freedom, gives external expression to its nature as free spirit. It expresses one's free will in the realm of material things. Hence, we have a discussion on *The Philosophy of Right*.[36]

3. Will in itself and for itself

The will is free in itself, and for itself. The will free in itself has the will as its object. Hence, the will becomes for itself what is in itself. He says: "This content, or the will's determination on something specific, is in the first place immediate. Consequently, the will is then free only *in* itself or *for* an external observer, or, to speak generally, it is the will in its concept. It is not until it has itself as its object that the will is for *itself* what it is in itself."[37] The will as in itself is in accordance with its concept and is that which exist in its own way. But the idea that the will exists as for itself means existing in a different way. Hegel gives the example of the child and the plant in itself.[38] This implies that person has reason as his essence and nature that is to be explicitly expressed. As Hegel states "The will which is a will only in accordance with its concept is implicitly free but at the same time it is also unfree, for it would first become truly free as truly determinate content. At that point it is free in its own eyes, has freedom as its object, and *is* freedom."[39] It would simply mean that the child is a man implicit. It is only when man actualizes his freedom,[40] one's

35 *PR*, p. 24.

36 Cf. *PR*, p. 24. See also in Copleston, *A History of Philosophy 18th and 19th Century German Philosophy*, pp. 203-205. A person becomes owner of a thing not by a mere internal act of the will but by embodying his/her will in it (*PR* §§ 41-47). In taking possession of a thing my will is directly present in it (*PR* § 54). One can also withdraw his/her will from it thereby alienating it. There is an opposition between the particular will and the universal will in wrong (*PR* § 83). The particular will negates right, and in doing so it negates the conception of the notion of the will, that is universal, the rational free will as such.

37 *PR*, pp. 24-25.

38 *PR*, p. 312. Knox in his 'Translator's Note' to *PR*, explains that: "For itself and in itself '– in itself or in its essential nature a child is a man, a rational being. The child exemplifies the generic essence of manhood, and it is only if we know this that we can understand what a child is at all. But this generic essence is only implicit in the child; in itself the child is a man, but *for* itself or in its own eyes it is a child and a child only. Childhood is the mode of *existence* correlative to the *concept* of manhood while that concept is still only *implicit*, or, to use Hegel's terminology, in the child, manhood is 'in its concept' or is a concept only or is 'in accordance with its concept'."

39 *PR*, p. 229.

40 In speaking about the nature of man as reason and freedom that has to be worked out in concrete living is expressed in Hegel's treatises on education at the section on Ethical Life.

potentialities become true to its concept. Freedom is the self-conscious act of the humans. "Only human can be in-and-for-themselves on this account, since for-itself is a reflexive perspective which only consciousness admits of."[41] One has to actualize himself/herself in rationally articulating[42] his/her freedom in the rational society as free agents, not as objects or things. Dudley Knowles observes: "Freedom is the prize of transparent self-awareness. Beginning with the simplest elements of free action, Hegel concludes the *Philosophy of Right* with the description of actuality (*Wirklichkeit*) which is nothing less than a portrait of the modern soul as a display of will in the full dress of freedom."[43] Thus the will which is in itself and for itself is the will that wills its own freedom which is right. Hence we analyse next how the concept of will as freedom is right.

4. Will, Freedom and Right

The concept of will as freedom speaks of right, *recht*.[44] The basis of right is the sphere of spirit and its proper locus and departing point is the will. Hegel says that right is any existence in general which is the existence of the free will (*PR* § 29). The immediate and most fundamental purpose or goal of the will is to act free. This would mean that the will has its concept as its freedom which is both its form, here determination means subjective end (*PR* § 8), and content, that means what is specifically willed (*PR* § 9). Hegel in his *Philosophy of Right* speaks about the freedom of the will and its relation to right. This is clearly discussed in his elaboration of the first part on abstract rights. Hegel says that "[t]he definition of the concept of the will in abstraction from the idea of the will is 'the free will which wills the free will'."[45] It would mean to say that free will is that which looks for free human actions in a society. One wills in terms of the good or true. This is in terms of the social institutions. One does

---

The very purpose of education itself is gaining liberation.

41 Knowles, *Hegel and the Philosophy of Right*, p. 36.

42 Franco, *Hegel's Philosophy of Freedom*, pp. 178-179. Franco argues that "Only the rational will is genuinely free because only the rational will has itself, its freedom and its universality, for its content; only the rational will is for itself what it is in itself."

43 Knowles, *Hegel and the Philosophy of Right*, p. 36.

44 Knowles, *Hegel and the Philosophy of Right*, p. 83. Knowles speaks about the meaning of right in Hegel following "In translation, 'right' as used broadly is probably best understood as 'ethics' or perhaps even 'morality', so long as we are aware that Hegel himself uses the term 'morality' for a distinctive and limited conception of ethics. Ethical rules or prescriptions as these are studied in Part 3, 'Ethical Life', include both rules of morality and laws. 'Right' also has the narrower meaning, in 'Abstract Right', of a specific claim, as when we speak of natural rights and designate a limited segment of ethics."

45 *PR*, p. 32.

will what the concept of the will has as its purpose, namely freedom.[46] The will is in-itself. The will is spoken in terms of its relation to the right. The will wills the free will. It means to act knowingly which is according to the true and the good. Hegel says: "It is only because right is the embodiment of the absolute concept or of self-conscious freedom that it is something sacrosanct."[47] This is to act in terms of moral precepts or rules that govern the social institutions taken in the universal principles of right that manifests externally, objectively in the social, which is the manifestation of the spirit. The will actualizes itself as objective freedom, which speaks of the very purpose of the will which is the content of the will itself.

5. Objective Freedom

According to Hegel, right means actualized freedom. Reason is the governing principle of the spirit and which is concretized in the structures of the will. It constitutes the social world; thus the structures of the social world are structures of freedom. Understanding social world as rational means to conceive the ethical precepts of the society upon the individual and identifying with itself and its principles constitute objective freedom. The freedom that is gained or actualized through ethical life is objective. The actualization of freedom is in terms of the right. Here the right has the claim of freedom. For Hegel the essence of the will, objective spirit, is the freedom. This is freedom understood in its subjective realm but the objective realm of freedom is the freedom expressed as a right. Hence the notion of right is the technical use of the idea of freedom in terms of its objectivity (*PR* § 29). In speaking about the right Knowles states:

> [t]he idea of right, which is the topic of investigation in the Philosophy of right, is the concept of right, the totality of our ethical beliefs systematized in accordance with its dialectical character, together with its actualization, the fact of its constituting personal and social moral reality. Thus the

---

46 *PR*, p. 317. In his 'Translator's Notes' Knox clarifies that; "The ultimate destiny of mind which, *qua* rational, is free, is that it shall find in its object nothing but itself and its own freedom. The process whereby this goal is achieved is described in Paragraph 28. Thereafter, mind is at peace with the world; it has fully developed its potentialities and exists as Idea, the unity of subject and object. Such a unity is achieved in a sense when 'the free will wills the free will', but this is only an abstract identity; a genuine content is lacking. Kant's ethics, in Hegel's view, never rises above this abstraction. What is required further is that the object willed shall take a form apparently the opposite of freedom itself (because the concrete is not an abstract identity but a unity of opposites), i.e., the form of the concrete laws. Hence, concrete freedom is the will willing, not simply itself, but what is in accordance with laws embodying the intelligence and so the will of the people who live under them, and the Idea of the will is the synthesis of the subjective volition with the system of objective institutions which give content to that volition."

47 *PR*, p. 33.

subject matter of the philosophical science of right is the Idea of right – the concept of right and its actualization.[48]

The idea of right is fully manifested in the idea of the will realizing or actualizing itself in the world. The understanding of freedom as arbitrariness, do as you like, is not true according to Hegel. He distinguishes his notion of freedom from its everyday notion as the ability to do as you like it. Freedom, according to Hegel, is subjective freedom and the self-actualization of the sprit in and through the rational society. Hence freedom for him consists in being with oneself in the other.[49] When the other which I distinguish from myself does not limit but expresses my self, then it is not a hindrance on me, but is in fact the very actualization of my freedom.[50] The social institutions constitute the realm of the actualization of will's freedom.

The state becomes the actuality of concrete freedom (*PR* § 260). It safeguards the personal freedom and particular interest of its citizens. It provides universal or rational way of life which they willingly acknowledge. The subjective freedom is developed through the sate that its right is recognised, for, the state respects and safeguards the individual choices of family, civil society. It is the individual who decides for him the how, what, and why of the matters in life. But at the same time the individual also acknowledges the state as the one which universally guarantee this subjective freedom.[51]

In speaking about the freedom actualized, he speaks about the 'Abstract Right' (*EPS* §§488-502, *PR* §§ 34-104), 'Morality' (*EPS* §§ 503-512, *PR* §§ 105-141), and 'Ethical Life' (*EPS* §§513-552, *PR* §§ 142-360). Abstract right corresponds to the image of the self as a person. Hence, the idea of person here would simply mean to have rights and one's exercise of the arbitrary choice. This is the sphere of property; this is the external dimension of a person which cannot be taken away from one's life, which is inseparable from personal life itself.

There is a dialectical structure of the will as shown by Hegel. First, the will as stages in the development of the idea of the will which is free in and for itself (*PR* § 33); it is the stage of immediacy; next, the stage of morality which goes beyond this immediacy to a reflective mode, a mode of subjectivity; and

48 Knowles, *Hegel and the Philosophy of Right*, p. 61.

49 *PR*, pp. 30-31. Hegel says: "The will is then true, or rather truth itself, because its self-determination consists in a correspondence between what it is in its existence (i.e. what it is as objective to itself) and its concept; or in other words, the pure concept of the will has the intuition of itself for its goal and its reality."

50 Cf. Frederick C. Beiser (ed.), *The Cambridge Companion to Hegel* (Cambridge: Cambridge University Press, 1993), p. 219. Further citations from this book will be cited as Frederick C. Beiser (ed.), *The Cambridge Companion to Hegel.*

51 Alan Patten, *Hegel's Idea of Freedom* (Oxford: Oxford University Press, 1999), pp. 190-193. Further citations from this book will be cited as Patten, *Hegel's Idea of Freedom.*

finally, the ethical life becomes the unitary moment of the above two stages, which is actualized in concrete living.[52] The purpose of the freewill is to will freedom as its object. Thus freedom becomes objective. The question is, does it mean to say that freedom becomes objective? The purpose of the will is to will itself because the will to be fully free means in and for itself. Hence, freedom becomes its own object (*PR* § 23). Freedom is the rational system of the mind in its objective understanding. The rational system of the spirit is the world of immediate relation. The actualization of freedom objectively is the content of the *Philosophy of Right*. The rational system becomes the objective manifestation of the subjective freedom which is the concept and content of the will. The objective freedom is also realized in the state, for the actions of the individual will are guided by reason. This objective freedom is the "substantial freedom."[53] It means it is based on his/her true and rational nature of human. The objective freedom relates to its particular content (*PR* § 26). This demand duties and virtues of everyday in the *Sittlichkeit*. This represents the particular content of the will. Thus, the will in willing its own content become manifested as objective. "The freedom which is attained objectively within the substantial norms of ethical life is objective."[54] The freedom of the will to will itself does not point to an everyday conception of freedom as, doing as one likes, but "the distinguishing feature of the modern state is the way in which its institutions allow for what Hegel calls 'subjective freedom', including personal arbitrariness and private self-satisfaction (PR§§ 124, 185R, 206R), the sanctity of individual moral and religious conscience (PR §139), and the universal status for all individuals of personhood and abstract right (PR § 209)."[55]

In speaking about the stages of the development of the idea of free will, Hegel would say that the will is immediate which stands for its concept. The section on abstract right speaks about this idea of the subject as person[56] who has the nature and essence of freedom and reason. Hence, it would speak of the arbitrary character of the person who can make choices. "Abstract right corresponds to the image of the self as person."[57] The person is externally embodied spirit, an embodiment into itself which is the subjective individuality of the person. The individuality of the person is considered as a volitional agent.

52 Knowles, *Hegel and the Philosophy of Right*, p. 61.

53 Patten, *Hegel's Idea of Freedom*, p. 45.

54 Knowles, *Hegel and the Philosophy of Right*, p. 75.

55 Beiser (ed.), *The Cambridge Companion to Hegel*, p. 219.

56 *PR*, p. 37. "Hegel speaks of the person as: "Personality essentially involves the capacity for rights and constitutes the concept and the basis (itself abstract) of the system of abstract and therefore formal right."

57 Beiser (ed.), *The Cambridge Companion to Hegel*, p. 220.

The subject has to make the particular will confirmed to the universal will. The opposite of which is "wrong."[58] Morality delves into the very subject as moral agent who is accountable for its own actions which are not according to one's consciousness alone but in conformity with the universal will. It would simply state that morality cannot be subjective.[59] In speaking about the actualization of the free will Hegel states that "When the free will is the substantial will, made actual in the subject and conformable to its concept and rendered a totality of necessity-it is the ethics of actual life in family, civil society, and State."[60] Ethics becomes fundamental to Hegel's concept of practical philosophy. The idea of freedom in its concept is the abstract right which is objectified in the ethical life[61] of the society where the self-conscious moral subject actualizes freedom. He adds, "...ethical life is the concept of freedom developed into the existing world and the nature of self-consciousness."[62] Thus, he says that the subjective spirit is realized in objective spirit. Here the concept of freedom is a reality of real freedom, namely freedom in its objectivity. "Subjective freedom is attained when the individual recognizes the validity of substantial ethical norms identifying with those institutions and their constitutive ethical

58 *PR*, pp. 64-73. "If the particular will is explicitly at variance with the universal, it assumes a way of looking at things and a volition which are capricious and fortuitous and comes on the scene in opposition to the principle of rightness. This is wrong." The will in contract, one not universal as such, they are only relatively universal; hence they are particular will. In contract the will contracted by particular individuals can retain their particular wills, where the contract does not go beyond the individual arbitrariness, hence remains susceptible to wrong. Hegel makes this clearer in *EPS*, p. 246. "The will may just as well not be conformable to law (right), and, in that case, produces a wrong: by which, however, the absolute law (right) is not superseded, but only a relationship originated of right and wrong."

59 Beiser (ed.), *The Cambridge Companion to Hegel*, p. 224. "Hegel strongly criticizes an extreme error aberrant of subjectivism to which he thinks the morality of conscience is prone: the ethics of conviction' that he associates with the moral philosophy of Jakob Friedrich Fries (1773-1843). This is the view what no act can be morally condemned as long as the agent followed his own conscience or moral convictions (no matter how wrong and misguided those convictions might be)."

60 *EPS*, p. 243.

61 *PR*, p. 103. Ethical life is a harmonious and coherent structure of will, a realm of freedom. Hegel says that: "The identity of the good with the subjective will, an identity which therefore is concrete and the truth of them both, is Ethical Life." See also in Beiser (ed.), *The Cambridge Companion to Hegel*, p. 219. "The term "ethical life" is coined to describe a state of the human will in which reason and sense are in harmony. Accordingly, "ethical life" originally refers to an ethics of character, emphasising rational dispositions and practical judgement in concrete situations, in contrast to a morality of norms, where the emphasis is on deriving particular actions from general rules."

62 *PR*, p. 104.

principles which compose a realm of objective freedom."[63] This concretization of the concept of freedom through the self-conscious willing of the particular will be manifested in the institutions of the society namely family, civil society and State. Therefore, these institutions are the moment of the concrete and spiritual unity of the universal and the particular.

Conclusion

Our exploration of Hegel's concepts of 'will as freedom' and *Philosophy of Right* enable us to answer our initial question, namely what is the concept of 'the will'; what does it mean to say 'will as freedom', and its triple moments; where does it actualize its freedom objectively, etc. Hegel argues that the concept of the will as indeterminate and determinate is without contradicting each other. Free will is the unity of both these moments of the will as reflective will. But free will is in willing the particular, and in doing so, it returns again to the universal. The notion of self-determination seems puzzling. How can one make something of oneself what one is not? Hegel seems to argue that the modern political state is the realm where the *Sittlichkeit* of the spirit as freedom is manifested. The human will flourish as freedom and subjectivity in the modern state. Freedom presents itself under the shape of necessity in this world. Hence the objective spirit as a person who has reality of freedom in property is achieved in the state in which spirit develops its freedom into the ethical world.

Bibliography

Hegel, G. W. F. *Philosophy of Mind Being Part Three of the Encyclopaedia of the Philosophical Sciences,*1830. Trans. William Wallace. Oxford: Clarendon Press, 1971.

__________. *Hegel's Phenomenology of Spirit.* Trans A.V. Miller. Oxford: Oxford University Press, 1977.

__________. *Lectures on Natural Right and political Science, The First Philosophy of Right.* Trans. J. Michael Stewart and Peter C. Hodgson. Berkeley Los Angeles London: University of California Press, 1995.

__________. *Hegel's Philosophy of Right.* Trans. T. M. Knox. Oxford: Clarendon Press, 1952.

Beiser, C. Frederick. (ed.), *The Cambridge Companion to Hegel.* Cambridge: Cambridge University Press, 1993.

Copleston, Frederick. *A History of Philosophy 18th and 19th Centaury German Philosophy.* London, New York: Continuum, 2003.

Franco, Paul. *Hegel's Philosophy of Freedom.* New Haven and London: Yale University Press, 1999.

63 Knowles, *Hegel and the Philosophy of Right*, p. 74.

Inwood, Michael. *A Hegel Dictionary*. Oxford: Blackwell Publishers, 1992.

Kainz, P. Howard. *Hegel's Philosophy of Right with Marx's Commentary: A Handbook for Students*. Netherlands: Martinus Nijhoff, 1974.

Knowles, Dudley. *Hegel and the Philosophy of Right*, Rutledge Philosophy Guide Books. London and New York: Rutledge, 2002.

Patten, Alan. *Hegel's Idea of Freedom*. Oxford: Oxford University Press, 1999.

5

Interfaces between Dialectics of History and Human Intentionality: Philosophical Perspectives from Bernard Lonergan

V. Sebastian SJ

Abstract

Often the dynamics and process of history might look somewhat obscure and incomprehensible. In this context we need to ask: Is it possible to understand the fundamental dynamics which generate historical process? Can we understand at least in some measure the unevenness, disruptions, and anomalies of historical processes? And does human intentionality play any role in generating the dynamics of history? This article seeks to explore answers to these questions through Bernard Lonergan's philosophy of history.

Keywords

History, Philosophy of history, Lonergan, probability, intentionality, authenticity.

Introduction

This article focuses on the philosophical interpretation of historical processes and the role of human intentionality within that process. Philosophy of history focuses, among other things, on the philosophical dimensions of interpreting history, meaning of history, historical processes, patterns and laws of historical development, dynamics of growth and decline of cultures, and attempts to delineate overarching theories of historical processes. Very specifically, this article intends to explore the relationship between historical processes and human intentionality from the philosophical perspective of Bernard Lonergan (1904-1984).

In order to focus our inquiry we may raise the following questions: is there a fundamental process that generates historical process? If there is such a process, then what is its nature? Are there schemes and patterns which can be discerned in the historical process? Is history merely a product of blind forces acting upon human beings? Is history a sum total of cause-effect principle? Can we understand at least in some measure the unevenness, disruptions, and anomalies of historical processes? This article is divided into two parts: the first part deals with the philosophical principles involved in understanding the dynamics of history in terms of probability schemes and patterns. The second part focuses on human intentionality embedded in history and its relation to emergent probability.

1. Historical Process and Emergent Probability

This section delineates the philosophical dimensions of history and therefore, here we are not directly focusing on the 'content' and the interpretations of historical events. Our interest here is the underlying dynamics and processes of history. To begin with, we understand historical process as a series of complex phenomena which involves various sequences, patterns and schemes. The underlying dynamics and processes of history which involves sequences, patterns and schemes are interpreted by the Jesuit philosopher Bernard Lonergan within the framework of probability and philosophy. Lonergan, who was also a gifted mathematician, used probability theory to enunciate the sequences, patterns and schemes which are embedded in the dynamics of history.

1.1. Dynamics of Probability

As historian Arnold Toynbee has noted, historical process 'proceed from wider causes, which operate upon each of the parts and are not intelligible in their partial operation unless a comprehensive view is taken of their operation throughout the society.'[1] From the perspective of philosophy, historical processes entail cumulative schemes, patterns and variations. Toynbee notes the collective and cumulative nature of historical process in the following manner:

> A society, we may say, is confronted in the course of its life by a succession of problems which each member has to solve for itself as best it may...

1 Arnold J. Toynbee, *A Study of History*, Vol. 1 (New York: Dell Publishing Co., 1965), 18.

> Throughout, it is impossible to grasp the significance of any particular member's behaviour under a particular ordeal without taking some account of the similar or dissimilar behaviour of its fellows and without viewing the successive ordeals as a series of events in the life of the whole society.[2]

To the mathematician, probability is the frequency with which one phenomenon takes place in relation to possible alternatives. When combined, the probabilities of particular events can be used to evaluate the chances of chain events. To deal with such combinations, certain basic rules have been formulated; it is these rules which have come to be known as the laws of chance. Taken individually, the random movement of the tiniest molecules in nature is not predictable. But they act in such great numbers that their aggregate combined behaviour is predictable. Thus, millions of gas molecules in a jar and a population of millions of drivers behind the wheel are predictable in the same way. Indeed, it is almost impossible to predict whether molecule A will bump into molecule B or that driver X will collide into driver Y. Nonetheless, it is possible to say *about* how many molecules collide in a second or *about* how many drivers in a month. And the forecast will be exact enough to allow the scientists reach a reasonable conclusion or to let an insurance company establish its premium rates.[3]

Two fundamental laws are at the basis of probability: (1) a *both-and* law, to calculate the probability of two events both happening, and (2) an *either-or* law, to calculate the probability of one or the other of two events happening. The both-and law states that the chance of two independent events both happening is equal to the probability of one happening multiplied by the probability of the other happening. The either-or law states that the chance of either one or the other of two mutually exclusive possibilities coming true equals the sum- the addition- of the separate chances of each coming true individually.[4]

It is not suggested here that all historical phenomena are reducible to statistical probability. We are more concerned about patterns, sequences and schemes of history. Indeed it is suggested here that to comprehend the patterns, sequences and schemes of history probability can mediate as a tool of correlation. It is important to note that modern scientific methods do not speak not so much in terms of absolute certitude rather it terms of correlation and probabilities. If we are interested in understanding the unfolding patterns and sequences in the historical process then such dynamics can make sense within the framework of probability.

---

2 Arnold J. Toynbee, *A Study of History*, Vol. 1 (New York: Dell Publishing Co., 1965), 18.

3 David Bergami and the Editors of Life, "Figuring the Odds in an uncertain World," in *Life Science Library Mathematics* (New York: Ime Inc., 1963), 127-28.

4 David Bergami and the Editors of Life, "Figuring the Odds in an uncertain World," in *Life Science Library Mathematics* (New York: Ime Inc., 1963), 130.

1.2. Historical Process and Probability

Historical phenomena involve a number of schemes, systems and seriation. Lonergan engages probability principles to understand the cumulative process and the dialectics of history. According to Lonergan, there are basically three generating principles of history, namely, progress, decline, and recovery and the point is how to understand the underlying dynamics behind these generating principles. Though these are three distinct generating principles the actual human history is what results from their simultaneous operation.[5] Here, generating principles denote those conditions and factors which initiate, propel and create events in human history. Now, let us clarify further the dialectics of history in terms of probability schemes.

The first type of scheme is the *scheme of recurrence*. In concrete terms, schemes of recurrence begin, continue, and cease to function according to statistical probabilities. If A occurs, B will occur; if B, then C…, A will occur. This type of scheme may be indefinitely complex, and excludes disruptive elements. Let us name such an element F. in such a case, if F occurs, then G will occur, if G, H; and H will disrupt the recurrence of F. Examples of this scheme of recurrence include planetary systems, rhythms of animal life, and biological defensive cycles. These schemes are part and parcel of what is known as the 'world-process.'[6] Some of the historical processes entail this scheme of recurrence. For example, in a country there may be an ongoing democratic system which is disrupted at a given point in time by civil unrest which in turn, may give rise to a military dictatorship. Here, the democratic system had been an ongoing process until a disruptive element in the form of civil unrest brings a mutation in the historical process and gives rise to military rule. The civil unrest itself may have been caused, let us say, by prolonged corrupt practices of politicians in the democratic set up.

Another type of scheme is known as a *conditioned series*. Schemes P, Q, and R constitute a conditioned series, when P can function though neither Q nor R exists, but Q cannot function unless P exists, nor R unless Q exists. The dietary schemes of animals are examples of a conditioned series. All carnivorous animals cannot live off other carnivorous animals; some animals must be herbivorous. But inversely, there could be herbivorous animals without any carnivorous animals. Again, plants cannot live off animals; their survival involves chemical process and that scheme can function apart from animals. Finally, chemical cycles are not independent of physical laws, yet inversely,

---

5 Joseph A. Komonchak, "The Church," *The Desires of the Human heart: An Introduction to the Theology of Bernard Lonergan*, ed., Vernon Gregson (New York: Paulist Press, 1988), 223.

6 Bernard Lonergan, *Insight: A Study of Human Understanding* (London: Darton, Longman and Todd, 1983), 118.

the laws of physics can be combined into schemes that are independent of chemical processes.[7] To take another simpler example, we can say that internet functions in relation to satellites and computer technologies. In this conditioned scheme, internet cannot function unless there are satellites and computers. In other words, satellites and computers are the 'condition for the possibility' of internet. Technology might bring changes in the functioning of internet in the future, but as it is now, internet functions in conjunction with satellites and computers. But satellites and computers can function, as of now, without internet. However, computers depend on a host of other elements such as hardware, software, and computer languages.

Some historical processes involve such conditioned series. For instance, in the evolutionary process, human beings developed language. This perhaps went on for several thousands of years in the form of oral communication; they did not know how to write and read since alphabets and writing systems had not been invented. The emergence of alphabetization and writing which occurred around 3000 BCE, were indeed significant steps in the development of human communication.[8] It took several thousands of years before one of the major steps in human development occurred in the form of printing, first in China, and then in Germany. As historians point out printing marks a significant stage in the history of human development, since storage, retrieval and dissemination of knowledge became now easier, thus paving the way for the emergence of modern science. What we have just described in a nutshell is an example of a conditioned series of development in history. Modern science would not have been possible without the discovery of printing; printing would not have been possible without alphabetization and writing; and writing and alphabets would not have been possible without language, thus making the complex process of a conditioned series. But language does not necessarily depend intrinsically on alphabets, or on writing or on print. There are perhaps thousands of languages which do not yet have alphabets or writing system. They depend primarily on oral communication in which speech and hearing are predominant.

Further, Lonergan distinguishes between the *possible*, *probable* and the *actual* seriation. The *actual* seriation is unique and it consists of the schemes that actually were, are, or will be functioning in our universe along with precise specifications of their places, their duration, and their relations to one another.

---

7 Bernard Lonergan, *Insight: A Study of Human Understanding* (London: Darton, Longman and Todd, 1983), 118-19.

8 We do not know the exact date when the script arrived, but evidences suggest it might have arrived with Neolithic populations. The approximate appearances according to Diringer's calculations in his book *Writing* are: Minoan pictographs around 2000 BC; Indus valley script around 3000-2400 BC, and Chinese script around 1500 BC. Cf., Walter Ong, S.J., *Presence of the Word: Some Prolegomena for Cultural and Religious History* (New haven: Yale University Press, 1967), 36.

The *probable* seriation differs from the actual. The actual is the factual. But the probable seriation has to exhibit the cumulative ramifications of probable alternatives. Hence, the probable seriation is not a single series, but a manifold of series. At each stage of world process, there is a set of probable next stages, of which some are more probable than others. The actual consists of only the stage that occurs. Finally, the *possible* seriation is even more remote from actuality.[9]

Out of the three seriation outlined, the possible exhibits the greatest variety and complexity. The probable seriation depends on statistical laws that arise from the initial or basic situation of our world. Each moment of world history, it assigns the most probable future course. That which is probable, sooner or later occurs; when that happens, probability of occurrence is replaced by the probability of survival. It follows that as long as the scheme survives, it fulfills the conditions for the possibility of later or further schemes. This is in short, the general notion of emergent probability. The emergent probability results from the combination of the conditioned series of schemes with their respective probabilities of emergence and survival. To put it briefly, the probability of emergence of a scheme of recurrence consists in the sum of the respective probabilities of all the events included in the scheme, and it arises as soon as the prior conditions for the functioning of the scheme are satisfied.[10]

Now let us come back to our original question of history. How is the notion of emergent probability related to history? Lonergan explains the relation between the two in the following manner:

> Generically, the course of human history is in accord with emergent probability; it is the cumulative realization of concretely possible schemes of recurrence, in accord with successive schedules of probabilities. The specific difference of human history is that among the probable possibilities is a sequence of operative insights by which men grasp possible schemes of recurrence and take the initiative in bringing about the material and social conditions that make these schemes concretely possible, probable, and actual.[11]

In this manner human beings become the agent of the emergent probability of human affairs. Human being is not a passive spectator in the unfolding of events in history. Human remain under the exigency of emergent probability

9 Bernard Lonergan, *Insight: A Study of Human Understanding* (London: Darton, Longman and Todd, 1983), 119.

10 See, Bernard Lonergan, *Insight: A Study of Human Understanding* (London: Darton, Longman and Todd, 1983), 120-22. See also, Kenneth R. Melchin, *History, Ethics and Emergent Probability: Ethics, Society and History in the Work of Bernard Lonergan* (Lanham: University Press of America, 1987), 108-111.

11 Bernard Lonergan, *Insight: A Study of Human Understanding* (London: Darton, Longman and Todd, 1983), 226-27.

to the extent their insights and decisions remain probable realizations of concrete possibilities and the extent earlier insights and decisions determine later possibilities and probabilities of insights and decisions.[12] Thus, on the one hand, history is not an aggregate of some predetermined blind forces. On the other hand, as it can be inferred, human history does not run in straight line either. History is a complex network of schemes and conditioned seriation which involve further complex variations – like complex variations in the game of chess. It is important to note that the dynamics that underpin history in terms of emergent probability remain invariant and trans-cultural.

2. Human Intentionality and Emergent Probability

In Lonergan's analysis of historical process, human intentionality plays a key role. Here, intentionality denotes the intrinsic dynamism which propels humans to inquire, understand, decide, and to act. As far as human history is concerned, the subjection to emergent probability differs from the subjection of other evolving species. Lonergan points out two such differences: (1) Insight is an anticipation of possible schemes, and decision to bring about the concrete conditions of their functioning instead of merely waiting for such condition to happen. Moreover, the greater the human being's development, the greater their control over circumstances and so the greater their capacity to realize possible schemes by deciding to bring about such conditions.[13] (2) Human beings can discover emergent probability. In other words, humans can work out the manner in which prior insights and decisions determine the possibilities and probabilities of later insights and decisions. Present decisions can be guided in the light of their influence on future decisions. This control of the emergent probability can be exercised by individual and collective decisions taken in a responsible, reasonable and intelligent manner.[14]

2.1. Dynamics of Human Knowing and Authentic Existence

What Lonergan says about human insight and its relation to the emergent probability needs to be understood within the framework of his comprehensive philosophical theory of human knowing. According to Lonergan, human knowing is a dynamic whole which has distinct parts. This dynamic whole is related to each of the parts, and each of these parts is related to other parts and to the whole. Human knowing involves many distinct and irreducible operations and activities such as seeing, hearing, inquiring, understanding,

12 Bernard Lonergan, *Insight: A Study of Human Understanding* (London: Darton, Longman and Todd, 1983), 227.

13 Bernard Lonergan, *Insight: A Study of Human Understanding* (London: Darton, Longman and Todd, 1983), 227.

14 Bernard Lonergan, *Insight: A Study of Human Understanding* (London: Darton, Longman and Todd, 1983), 227.

reflecting, weighing the evidence and judging. Each part of these activities is absolutely necessary to constitute the whole, and therefore, when one of the parts is missing, the whole remains incomplete. Lonergan maintains that no one of these operations by itself may be named human knowing. Various parts are potential components in knowing but in itself they are not human knowing.[15] According to Lonergan, human knowing is a dynamic structured process which involves experience,[16] understanding,[17] judgment,[18] and acting.[19]

Lonergan's philosophic position on human knowing may be summarized in the following manner: When we come to know anything- be it in common sense, or in natural sciences or in social sciences – we attend to data, produce explanations and theories to account for the data, and then we judge that on of

---

15 Bernard Lonergan, "Cognitional Structure," *Collected Works of Bernard Lonergan*, Vol. 4, ed. Frederick E. Crowe and Robert M. Doran (Toronto: University of Toronto Press, 1988), 205-21.

16 The process of inquiry and of knowing is set in motion by a given experience. What experience gives us is not knowledge but data, the raw material. It evokes a sense of wonder and we want to know the meaning of our experience. Human beings constantly ask the question "why?" see, Bernard Lonergan, *Insight: A Study of Human Understanding* (London: Darton, Longman and Todd, 1983), 252 and 636-38.

17 In the process of inquiry we take hints and clues and then we tend to formulate possible connections and explanations. This is the level of understanding. The act of apprehending the connections and clues related to our experience or data, Lonergan terms as "insight," and this is a common experience which all of us have experienced some time or the other in our lives. The story of Archimedes running through the streets of Syracuse shouting eureka ("I have discovered") is a good example of the occurrence of an insights. But at this level of understanding, the explanations are only provisional and tentative. These explanations may be true or in many cases, it may prove to be not true. See, Bernard Lonergan, *Insight: A Study of Human Understanding* (London: Darton, Longman and Todd, 1983), 3-6 and 279ff.

18 The process of knowing becomes complete when we are in a position to affirm what we have understood, and this takes place at the level of judgment. We need to ask whether we have considered relevant questions in the process of enquiry. In other words, we need to ask that little question: "Is it so?" to reach the truthfulness of our affirmation. If there are further questions to be considered, the process of inquiry remains incomplete. If we form a judgment without sufficient evidences, we may be jumping into conclusions which are questionable. But if we are in a position to affirm on the basis of reasonable evidence, then the process of knowing becomes complete. See, Bernard Lonergan, *Insight: A Study of Human Understanding* (London: Darton, Longman and Todd, 1983), 271-339.

19 The fourth level is the level of deciding and acting and this is the level of morality. Here we deliberate and decide our actions in accordance with our knowing. Here the questions involved are related to human values: Is it worthwhile? Is it only apparently good or truly good? In short, these are the various operations that take place within us when we are engaged in the process of inquiry and the process of knowing. See, Bernard Lonergan, *Insight: A Study of Human Understanding* (London: Darton, Longman and Todd, 1983), 559-60.

these explanations or set of explanations to be probably correct. In a similar manner, when we decide to do something, we act according to what we have judged to be the case. Both knowing the truth and doing what is "good" are attained by what Lonergan terms as the 'four transcendental precepts.' These transcendental precepts are: "Be attentive, Be intelligent, Be reasonable, Be responsible."[20] On any given subject we tend to arrive at truth to the extent we exercise the first three precepts. The fourth precept is to do with our actions based on values. These transcendental precepts point to the very core of Lonergan's account of human knowing. According to Lonergan, it is by being attentive, being intelligent, being reasonable and by being responsible that we gradually learn to become more and more authentic human beings.[21] Human authenticity is intrinsically connected with truth; one has to 'appropriate' the truth or personalize the truth of one's knowing. As Lonergan puts it, to appropriate a truth is to make it one's own. It demands consistency between what we *know* and what *do*.[22] On the contrary, to the extent human beings live their lives inattentively, unintelligently, unreasonably and irresponsibly, they exclude the possibility of arriving at truth. Lonergan calls such human propensity 'flight from understanding,' which leads to untruth and inauthentic existence.

2.2. Human Authenticity and Historical Patterns

Human authenticity and inauthenticity are not abstract but concrete realities; they affect the very process of historical patterns. In Lonergan's perspective, dynamics of history and its emergent patterns and schemes are intrinsically related to human pursuit of truth or negation of truth. It is our reasonable and responsible pursuits and actions embedded in human knowing that make us truthful and authentic humans. Such individual and collective pursuits will have an effect on our lives, actions and ultimately on the course of history. Gandhi and Martin Luther King did make a positive difference in history; so do countless unsung heroes continue to make positive difference through their authenticity and self-transcendence.

On the other hand, human beings also have tendency to turn away from the pursuit of truth or engage in 'flight from understanding' as Lonergan prefers to call it. When we live our lives in non-attentive, unreasonable, and irresponsible ways, we engage in what is termed as 'flight from understanding,' which blocks insights and understanding. Such unreasonable and irresponsible

---

20 Bernard Lonergan, *Method in Theology* (New York: Herder and Herder, 1972), 231. Transcendentals (such as truth, goodness, and love) are trans-cultural and are rooted in the very human dynamism.

21 Bernard Lonergan, *Method in Theology* (New York: Herder and Herder, 1972), 53.

22 Bernard Lonergan, *Insight: A Study of Human Understanding* (London: Darton, Longman and Todd, 1983), 558.

ways of acting will have an effect on our lives and in the lives of others and ultimately in the process of history itself. Hitler did make such a negative impact on history, so do countless others continue to have negative influence on history through their inauthenticity rooted in hatred and falsehood.

Now we shall briefly delineate how human intentionality affects the process of history. We have noted that history is not a victim of blind forces. On the one hand human beings have the capacity and freedom to effect changes in history to the extent they exercise intelligence, reasonableness and responsibility. On the other hand, it is also true that due to a host of reasons humans do not always exercise the freedom in intelligent, reasonable and responsible ways. According to Lonergan, human intentionality contributes to the dynamics of historical process and the emergent probability. More to the point, human intentionality contributes to historical progress, decline and recovery. In other words, the generating principles of historical progress, decline and recovery are embedded in human intentionality.

Within the framework of the emergent probability, the first generating principle of history is progress. According to Lonergan, when human beings live out their lives intelligently and pursue the common good, there are fair chances of these societies and cultures experiencing progress. Insights can build further insights, thus providing the conditions for the possibility of progress in these groups and societies, here, progress should not be understood in a narrow sense of material and economic progress. Rather, it needs to be understood as growth, development, well being, common good and welfare of people. Such progress becomes a possibility only when narrow interests and selfishness of individuals and groups are set aside in favour of common good. Lonergan notes: "Progress, of course, is not some single improvement but a continuous flow of them."[23]

The second generating principle of history within the scheme of emergent probability is decline. In the emergent probabilities there can be blind alleys too. These blind alleys emerge from what Lonergan calls 'general bias' which results in the cycle of deterioration and self-destruction in societies. If human are capable of acting intelligently, they are also capable of acting egoistically. The problem with egoism is that it conflicts 'with the good of order.'[24] In each stage of the historical process, just as practical intelligence grasps the concrete intelligibility, general bias involves the disregard of timely and fruitful ideas. Such disregard of general bias not only excludes the implementation these insights and ideas, but also excludes subsequent stages both of further ideas and the possibility of the implementation of correction. Lonergan writes:

23 Bernard Lonergan, *Method in Theology* (New York: Herder and Herder, 1972), 53.

24 Bernard Lonergan, *Method in Theology* (New York: Herder and Herder, 1972), 54.

"Corrupt minds have a flair for picking the mistaken solution and insisting that is alone is intelligent, reasonable, good."[25]

If human history knows progress and development, it also knows decline in terms of tragedies, wars, injustices, and crimes. Conflicts, hatred and oppression are not generated in the thin air; they originate from concrete individuals and groups and contribute to decline. Under such circumstances, the social situation deteriorates cumulatively. This is because just as progress entails the realization of some ideas which lead to the realization of others till a whole coherent set is concretely operative, so the repeated exclusion of timely and fruitful ideas involve a cumulative departure from coherence. The cumulative effect of general bias is incoherence and increased unintelligibility into the emerging social and cultural situation. Lonergan calls such unintelligibility generated by general bias, 'social surd.' [26] Basically, bias is the negation of one's own drive for rationality and the possibility of insight.

The third generating principle within the framework of emergent probability is recovery. Though societies and groups experience decline, they cannot withstand prolonged periods of decline. If unchecked, prolonged decline would result in the fragmentation and the ultimate decline of cultures and groups. History testifies to the fact that while some empires, religions, cultures and civilizations have declined and become extinct, others have recovered and regenerated in different forms. Such recovery is initiated by human intelligence which seeks to restore balance and harmony. Such recovery could take shape in various forms. Reform movements could be an example of efforts by individuals and groups to arrest the process of decay and decline in a given society. Struggle for justice and equality can be seen as instances of historical efforts to correct past bias and mistakes, thus reversing the process of decline. Often the process of recovery may lead to a gradual process of transformation. The implicit retrieval and recovery involved in such transformation are examples of human interventions and intelligence at work in the process of emergent probability.

Conclusion

Emergent probability is not some sort of prediction about historical events (like weather forecast) following the laws of probability, rather an aid to understand the dynamics and patterns of historical processes. Patterns and schemes of history are open-ended with innumerable possibilities waiting to be actualized. What Lonergan seems to be suggesting is that the dynamics of human history and world-process are intrinsically bound up with human intentionality which

25 Bernard Lonergan, *Method in Theology* (New York: Herder and Herder, 1972), 55.

26 Bernard Lonergan, *Insight: A Study of Human Understanding* (London: Darton, Longman and Todd, 1983), 229-30.

is indeed a complex affair. Though human societies do have structures which can assume a life of its own, they are products of human decisions and actions which ultimately mould and shape the patterns of history. Just as authentic human existence affect the schemes of history in a positive way, inauthentic existence affects historical process in a negative way. If individual and collective authenticity paves the way for cumulative progress, inauthenticity leads to cumulative decline, deterioration and diminishment in the long run. Preventing historical decline requires a return to individual and collective authenticity by being attentive, reasonable and responsible.

6

Hermeneutical Principles Governing Science and Religion

Keith D'Souza SJ

Abstract

Scientific and religious claims and worldviews exemplify unique interpretations of the world. As meaning-making interpretive systems, science and religion are subject to common hermeneutical principles, or common principles pertaining to the art and science of interpretation. Both science and religion make cognitive claims, operate from unique presuppositions and assumptions, and are subject to a surplus of meaning in terms of possible interpretations. Besides these phenomenological conditions which they fulfill, they also need to adhere to common normative principles—communicative, ethical and social. They need to be cognitively meaningful and coherent—at least to their adherents. This also entails the need for contemporary reinterpretation of traditional thought and practice. They need to be based on truthful claims by their proponents. This principle has to do with transparency and ethical responsibility. They need to be as objective or truth-oriented as possible, even though the approximation towards the truth may be expressed via diverse symbolic and narrative means. Finally, they need to be communicated and operationalized in an ethically appropriate manner—demonstrating intentional as well as practical sensitivity and non-violence. When these normative conditions are fulfilled, there is more scope for mutual understanding rather than conflict between science and religion.

Keywords

Science, religion, interpretation, understanding, critical, meaning, truth.

Introduction

Science and religion are both mediating systems which help to make sense of the data of the world.[1] While science is relatively more cognitively-based, religion also has a significantly affective and voluntarist dimension to it. Both science and religion attempt to make sense of a world that may otherwise be considered to be meaningless, unpredictable and even hostile. Both take rationality seriously, though the understanding of rationality and the explanatory mechanisms within both these worlds of meaning may differ in various ways. This paper is an attempt to outline primary governing principles of interpretation that apply to both science and religion as meaning-making systems. These principles need explication in order to arrive at better clarity concerning the nature, scope and function of religion and science. These mediating or interpretive systems of meaning need to be complemented and governed by normative or ethical constraints, if they are to function well. These normative constraints have to do with the important areas of the social significance and responsibility of both science and religion.

The paper will accordingly be divided into two parts. The first part—the descriptive part—will outline basic *hermeneutical features* governing science and religion, while the second part—the normative part—will outline basic *hermeneutical and critical imperatives* governing science and religion. In the first part I will attempt to show how both science and religion share features of textuality which are interpretive in nature. The second part of the paper will deal with more normative considerations and proposals, keeping in mind both internal constraints which ensure a healthy functioning and growth of science and religion, as well as external challenges and obligations necessary towards the building up of a more humane and wholesome life for the human family and the wellbeing of the environment.

1. Hermeneutical Features Governing Science and Religion

Hermeneutics in the narrow sense is the theory of the interpretation of texts. However, textuality may be interpreted in a broad sense to include any dimension of reality which is cognitively engaged with and appropriated. The world itself may be considered to be a text which is read by both science

1 In Sandra Harding, *Objectivity and Diversity: Another Logic of Scientific Research* (Chicago: University of Chicago Press, 2015), 105, the author argues that, "the world is full of sciences." Even though in practice there are indeed many sciences—and more obviously, numerous religions—for the sake of simplicity of presentation and argumentation from a hermeneutical perspective, I have classified these two realms of meaning into cluster concepts of "science" and "religion."

and religion. The human sciences have given rise to various interpretations of human behavior, while the natural sciences have interpreted their specific objects of inquiry (e.g., animal life in biology, natural forces in physics, and elemental compositions in chemistry) according to diverse schema. Different religions too have given rise to diverse interpretations concerning the major metaphysical questions of life, i.e., "*Who am I? Where have I come from and where am I going? Why is there evil? What is there after this life?*"[2] These questions address a broader canvas of textuality which includes originary, evolutionary and eschatological aspects of reality. We will now outline the major hermeneutical features which govern both these realms of science and religion in their attempts to make sense of the world and all of the data it offers for experience and investigation.

1.1. The World is a Text which can be Understood Rationally

This thesis has to do with the cognitive validity of discourse as a means of communication in general. Any form of discourse—even discourse which severely critiques the possibility and the grounds of valid discourse, as manifested in different forms of philosophical skepticism—presupposes a cognitive intent on the part of the communicator and the receptor. In this regard, both science and religion can easily be recognized to constitute attempts to talk meaningfully about the world.

However, the understanding of 'world' may differ between science and religion. Science largely restricts itself to an investigation of empirical data by way of a postulation of theoretical frameworks and causal relations which help us to understand how such data may best be comprehended.[3] For religion such a world also includes intuitive *personal* experiences as well as the recognition of *transcendent* and *transcendental* dimensions of being (ontology), truth (epistemology), goodness (ethics) and beauty (aesthetics).[4]

Besides this differentiation between the nature and scope of the object of study, i.e., divergent and specific aspects of the 'world' or 'reality,' the understanding of what constitutes a valid *means* of investigation may also differ between and within science and religion. There are primarily two forms of argumentation, based upon the nature of the evidence provided. One form of argumentation is based upon or primarily concerned with empirical features.

2 Pope John Paul II, *Fides et Ratio* (Libreria Editrice Vaticana: Rome, 1998), No. 2, original italics.

3 See Sundar Sarukkai, *What is Science?* (New Delhi: National Book Trust, 2012), for a basic introduction to the nature of science and to basic questions stemming from the philosophy of science.

4 The term "transcendent" has to do with the depth or ultimate dimension of reality: that which is beyond the phenomenal world. The term "transcendental" entails that which is common to human consciousness: the conditions for the possibility of human experience.

The other is based upon or primarily concerned with rational or logical connections between propositions. However, it is very difficult in practice to employ only one of these means of argumentation, for most arguments—whether scientific or religious—employ a combination of both of these forms of evidence, i.e., empirical as well as rational. This was the stark realization that challenged one of the most scientifically-oriented philosophical schools, viz., logical positivism, to reexamine the rigorous presuppositions of its philosophy limiting rational discourse to purely empirically-based propositions, in favour of more a reasonable philosophical approach based on the nature and functions of ordinary language.[5]

Besides this disjunction between the worlds of the empirical and the rational, there is also the disjunction between the worlds of the secular and the sacred. Some scientists and believers assume a methodological disjunction when it comes to a meaningful investigation of these two worlds, while for others there is an overlap between these worlds of meaning. For some religions like Catholicism, there is a continuum between the realms of the secular and the sacred, while in other religions—especially some Eastern religions—there is an epistemological and even ontological disjunct or separation between these two realms. When such a disjunct or separation is operative, there is typically no conflict between the claims of science and religion, because each realm of meaning literally belongs to a different world. Yet other schools of thought consider both science and religion to be on the same plane of argumentative rationality, with some preferring the domination of scientific rationality and others preferring the domination of religious rationality. This is a cause of much of the religious and even scientific fundamentalism we see today. Religious fundamentalists assume that scientific claims and discoveries need to be warranted by religious belief, e.g., those who hold that evolutionism must cede to creationism in scientific discourse. Scientific fundamentalists, on the other hand, assume that religious claims need to meet scientific criteria of investigation, e.g., the attitude manifested in some of the writings of Richard Dawkins and others of his ilk.[6]

Both science and religion use narrative forms as explanatory devices in order to make sense of reality. Religion is concerned with ultimate narratives,

---

5 See Oswald Hanfling, *Philosophy and Ordinary Language: The Bent and Genius of our Tongue* (London: Routledge, 2000), for a defense of the engagement with, and use of ordinary language in philosophical discourse, as opposed to the use of more technical language presupposed by the logical positivists.

6 See Richard Dawkins, *The God Delusion* (London: Bantam Press, 2006), for a representative scientific fundamentalist argumentation. Also see John Haught, *God and the New Atheism: A Critical Response to Dawkins, Harris and Hitchens* (Louisville: Westminster John Knox Press, Louisville, KY, 2008), for a critical response to such versions of scientific fundamentalism and reductionism.

in which teleology or an ultimate final cause is presupposed, while science pays attention largely to shorter or smaller narratives in which causal connectedness is linked to a simple plot. However, science on occasion also ventures into the formulation of grand narratives, with the 'big bang' theory as a prime example. How one looks at time and the unfolding of narratives makes a difference with regard to how history and developmental projects are evaluated. When time matters, then human intervention in history becomes even more committed. A linear understanding of time as found in the religions of West Asian origin—as compared to a cyclic understanding of time in many East Asian religions—gives rise to a relatively more serious appraisal of the realm of the secular, and of personal and collective secular projects.

In both discovery and invention, science often uses methods which ostensibly go beyond what is regular and legitimate within the field, and includes features such as imagination, intuition, guesswork and simple luck, especially in the areas of problem solving or devising advanced or new theories. On the other hand, religion too uses scientific or empirical methods, e.g., in historical-critical and archeological studies of the Bible. Besides this, some religions have also developed a long tradition of rich philosophical reflection which is related to but not directly dependent upon the data of revelation or sacred scripture.

The terminology and the claims of both science and religion may sometimes seem rationally incomprehensible, unacceptable and even absurd to the uninitiated or unsympathetic, but one cannot deny that the products of science in terms of relevant technology and that of religion in terms of committed and fulfilling lives prove to be very tangible results stemming from the operations of both of these systems of meaning.

Finally, even contemporary scientific skepticism about methodological certitude, driven by the uncertainty principle, probability theory and fuzzy logic, does not result in the abandonment of scientific projects, but in fact the spirit of hypothesizing and experimentation towards greater certitude about aspects of reality still continues.

1.2. Understanding is Based Upon a Set of Presuppositions and Assumptions

Having argued that both science and religion take rationality seriously, it must also be accepted that human rationality comes with its own limits. Human beings do not and cannot grasp the nature of reality in itself, except via the mediation of specific concepts, terms of expression and their underlying operating systems. These concepts, terms and systems are themselves embedded within limited and limiting socio-cultural forms of life-experience. This realization of human finitude when it comes to knowledge claims has been especially enhanced over the last two centuries. It has affected philosophical discourse to the point of severe skepticism about metaphysical claims, and has led to the gradual abandonment of knowledge regarding the transcendent in favour of philosophical investigation largely restricted to the human horizon dominated by cultural and linguistic parameters. It has also contributed to the growth of a relativistic mindset with regard to faith and morals, especially in more secular cultures.

Any understanding of the world is ultimately based upon foundational beliefs that are intuitively accepted rather than epistemologically validated. In effect, the presuppositions and assumptions of a cultural or theoretical or ideological system constitute the hermeneutical *foundations* of the system. Be it in science, religion, philosophy or any dimension of human culture, these presuppositions and assumptions are composed of at least some belief statements that cannot be epistemologically justified, but are rather presupposed on faith or adopted by collective inclination or practice. That every religion is based on culturally embedded spiritual and metaphysical claims that are *sui generis* does not need much elaboration. But even in the realm of science, it has become increasingly accepted that data are heavily dependent upon theory, and furthermore, that there is a general underdetermination of theory by any given data or set of evidence. This is true not only for more radical assessments of underdetermination as argued by thinkers like Thomas Kuhn[7] and Paul Feyerabend, but even by those who have taken a less radical and a more linear approach with regard to scientific development such as Imre Lakatos.[8]

However, this has not proved disconcerting for those who are more practically minded in the field of science, as a major part of the scientific enterprise is not as much concerned with ultimate causes or consequences, as it is with more pragmatic goals focused on productive results stemming from innovative thinking and experimentation. Rather than busying itself with the examination of the metaphysical or epistemological worthiness of these innovative schemes or paradigms being projected and experimented with, science and technology for the most part are concerned with the short-term utility of such projects and goals. It is rather the field of religion—which is more serious about the validity of its ultimate claims—which has to cope with the underdetermination of its own theology by similar data which is processed and theorized quite differently by other religions. The theological challenge before each religion would be to continually provide better and more relevant interpretations of reality, without sacrificing the core beliefs and values of the

7 See William Devlin and Alisa Bokulich, eds. *Kuhn's Structure of Scientific Revolutions – 50 Years On* (Cham: Springer, 2015), for an appraisal of the influence of the thought of Thomas Kuhn over half a decade.

8 See Joseph Agassi, *Popper and his Popular Critics: Thomas Kuhn, Paul Feyerabend and Imre Lakatos* (Cham: Springer, 2014), for a good overview of the theories of these radical theorists of the philosophy of science.

tradition and without minimizing the commitment of its adherents. Another challenge that faces theology is to engage in a process of mutual learning from other systems of belief and practice—an issue which will be highlighted in the normative section of this paper.

1.3. Every Understanding of the World is an Interpretation of the World

This thesis follows from the two theses above. The first thesis about the rationality involved in scientific and religious claims adopts an anti-skeptical stance, and asserts a realistic foundationalism for knowledge enterprises. However, the second thesis somewhat softens this ostensibly hard-nosed epistemological position in favour of a critical, and even further, a pluralistic form of realism. This pluralistic or perspectival disposition towards knowledge is based on a hermeneutical rather than an epistemological orientation. An epistemological orientation would concern itself with truth and validity, whereas a hermeneutical orientation is more concerned about meaning, significance and relevance.

Especially since the late nineteenth century, the historically, culturally and linguistically conditioned nature of human knowledge has been consistently recognized and reinforced. It is not easy today to make claims based on total objectivity, as human beings simply do not possess a God's eye view or an Archimedean point of view from which to neutrally scrutinize any aspect of reality. This is certainly true of the human sciences—in which personal and community-based differences resist easy standardization—and especially the humanities, in which personal creativity and genius is given more significance. That is why Wilhelm Dilthey's attempt to give history the same explanatory precision of the sciences was met with failure. Religious claims often find their articulation from within religious matrixes which are culturally determined, and sometimes founded on the genius of the individual founders or gurus of the different religions. But even within any given religion, and indeed, even within the canon of foundational religious texts one finds scope for interpretation. This has made it possible for four Gospels rather than only one to be considered as authoritative within the Christian tradition. This is because the same phenomena of the 'Jesus-event' gradually gave rise to four valid testimonies that were and are still accepted as canonical by believing Christian communities. The same logic applies to subsequent formulations of dogmatic statements. Each statement itself is an interpretation of a foundation text in terms of relevant and prevailing theological formulations.

This thesis of the interpretive nature of any system or specific understanding of an aspect of reality is tacitly accepted by the scientific guild, as every hypothesis or even widely accepted theoretical position, however sound and well-founded it may appear at any given time, is subject to revision and even rejection as time goes by. The history of science is testimony to this series of worldviews or paradigms which all had their 'sell-by' date. In the scientific realm there is no theory that is in principle not subject to revision, and in practice we have seen that different theories, however certain they may have seemed at the time, have been replaced with superior theories which have had better explanatory value.

Even axiomatic or self-definitional systems are clearly interpretive formulations in themselves, and thus we may have different systems of enumeration (e.g., decimal or binary), calculation, and higher-end abstract mathematics. If we have debates between mathematical theorists—maths being considered one of the purest of the sciences or meta-sciences—then one can imagine the multiplicity of interpretations when it comes to the natural sciences, certainly the social sciences, and most certainly the humanities and the wide variety of subject-areas which come under the humanities, including cultural and religious products of an intellectual nature. Indeed, the words 'science' and 'religion' are mere cluster concepts useful for argumentative purposes, but in reality they designate a wide variety of phenomena and undergirding theoretical frameworks. For example, the terms 'Hindu' and 'Christian' in real life refer to a broad spectrum of religious thought and social phenomena that may only loosely be united via these cluster concepts.

1.4. An interpretation of the World Possesses a Surplus of Meaning

One of the main features of textuality is the possibility for a variety of interpretations to spring from the same text. This "surplus of meaning," in the words of Paul Ricoeur, is to be found in both, the formulation of any text arising from interaction with an aspect of reality—as we have demonstrated in the previous thesis—and the reception or rereading of any text which has been formulated.[9] Texts range from axiomatic systems on the one hand to fictional or poetic works of literature on the other. One may think that the former does not possess a surplus of meaning, while it is only the latter which gives rise to various readings. However, a simple computational exercise may be seen to have quite different ways of being processed, even though the final answer arrived at is expected to be the same. This is because even in an apparently straightforward exercise such as counting, human beings choose to employ quite divergent cognitive processes.

That there is a surplus of meaning in both science and religion is obvious. The same theoretical framework—both in science and religion—can give rise to different applications or tangential achievements in science and religion. It is

9 See Paul Ricoeur, *Interpretation Theory: Discourse and the Surplus of Meaning* (Fort Worth: The Texas Christian University Press, 1976), where Ricoeur deals extensively with the notion of the "surplus of meaning" in the theory and practice of interpretation.

not often that scientists and theologians give explicit credit to their theoretical predecessors—those upon whose shoulders they stand, and those who have provided the fundamental interpretive frameworks within which they operate. Rather, more attention is paid to the creative offsprings which stem from these originary ideas and systems. This happens in terms of the credit demanded by way of patenting processes, scholarly recognition, a heightened social status and monetary benefits which often accompany these ostensibly new 'discoveries' or 'inventions.' The East has a comparatively more traditional and less individualistic perspective when it comes to these matters, and hence less credit is endowed upon personal creativity, because it is assumed to be related to the past and is not considered to be entirely new or entirely personal.

The consequences of the acceptance of this thesis are manifold. First of all, reality cannot easily be reduced to only one system of meaning. Secondly, it becomes very difficult to fix or close the meaning of the text, apart from juridical or administrative processes in legal or governmental action. Apart from these administrative measures, attempts to fix or control truth have met with serious repercussions. Thus it is that almost every major religion has had ruptures within it, precisely because of this feature of rationality. This can be seen when a new religious movement emerges from a greater tradition: some features are retained while others are modified or rejected. In Buddhism, much of Brahmanic ritualism was rejected, but not the karma theory and the notion of rebirth. In Christianity, the primary Jewish Scriptures were retained, but reinterpreted and developed in the form of a New Testament. Protestantism opted for a rejection of clericalism and sacramentalism, but retained the sacred texts of the tradition, for the most part.

This thesis of the surplus of meaning of any text is significant for religion, especially when confronted with newer scientific evidence which may fly in the face of religious claims as found in foundational texts. Instead of being threatened by this evidence, it is hoped that aspects of foundational religious texts are considered to be rich enough to be bestowed with new forms of meaning and significance in the light of validated and commonly accepted empirical data and the theories which support such data.

2. Hermeneutical and Critical Imperatives Governing Science and Religion

The basic normative challenge posed to science is that the 'is' does not entail the 'ought.' What this means is that scientific and technological inventions do not by themselves constitute a validation of their social implementation. Just because it is possible to do something new and efficient and practical, it does not follow that it should be done. On the other hand, the basic normative challenge to religion is that the 'ought' does not entail the 'is.' Metaphysical claims and moral strictures embedded in foundational texts and discourses are to be considered as exhortative prescriptions rather than historical and scientific descriptions. This means that revelatory religious texts are not to be read as if they are intended to be historically or scientifically authoritative: they are rather to be treated as inspirational and morally directive by nature, focusing on the spiritual and moral nature of life.

Besides these basic normative challenges, a comprehensive and useful normative framework would run along the lines of one provided by Apel and Habermas in their reflections on communicative action.[10] These critical theorists highlight four ideal constraints of communication which provide a useful normative basis in order to govern interpretations within scientific and religious discourse. Every communicative act, according to Apel and Habermas, ought to be meaningful, true, truthful and right. The first criterion has to do with linguistic and culture-specific clarity; the second with epistemological objectivity; the third with subjective morality and the fourth with inter-personal and social propriety. We shall now explore how these critical criteria may be applied to scientific and religious interpretations.

2.1. Scientific and Religious Interpretations Need to be Meaningful

This normative constraint has to do with the reasonable nature of scientific and religious interpretations. If such interpretive claims are rational—as was attested in the very first thesis of the paper—then these claims need to be as understandable and hearer-friendly or reader-friendly as possible. We live in an age of sound-bites and video clips, an age which demands clarity and simplicity of communication, an age which expects transparency rather than obscurantist—or worse, esoteric—formulations.

The purpose here is to overcome misunderstanding, keeping in mind of course the unique nature of the realm of discourse under consideration. But more than being meaningful, this normative constraint can be extended to include the need to be relevant and non-anachronistic in one's intent and discourse—a theme which will be further addressed while elucidating the fourth hermeneutical imperative. Both science and religion need to engage in a process of continually raising pertinent questions, addressing pressing problems, and finding appropriate solutions to these questions and problems. Science needs to provide more meaningful solutions to contemporary problems stemming from newer theories which prove to be better explanatory devices. Religion on the other hand needs to provide solutions stemming from a better anthropological and moral assessment of human existence. If science and religion do not come up with relevant answers and solutions, then they may

10 See Karl-Otto Apel, "Regulative Ideas or Truth-Happening?: An Attempt to Answer the Question of the Conditions of the Possibility of Valid Understanding," in *The Philosophy of Hans-Georg Gadamer*, ed. Lewis Edwin Hahn (Chicago: Open Court, 1997), 87, where ideal criteria of communicative action are proposed.

soon appear to be anachronistic and may lose their adherents as well as gain opponents who demand better scientific theories, technological products and religious teaching and practices.

2.2. Scientific and Religious Interpretations Need to be True or Objective

Scientific and religious interpretations need to be subjected to rational scrutiny. This scrutiny will entail the employment of explanatory and validating procedures in service of a better understanding of the interpretive claims being made. The focus on truth or objectivity here does not imply the possession of a bird's eye view—or even better, a God's eye view—of any given situation, but rather the offering of the best possible evidence and argumentation with regard to the issue or facts under discussion or investigation. One is here no doubt concerned about the nature of the object under consideration, but sometimes arriving at this may be difficult, e.g., the origins of the universe in science or the nature and the functioning of divine beings in religion. Thus, more than being concerned about whether one arrives at the truth about these issues, this normative constraint ensures the employment of a process involving the best available validating mechanisms, so that one can make the best sense of the object under consideration, given one's limitations within a spacio-temporal framework. In the words of Paul Ricoeur, we need to "explain more in order to understand better."[11]

There are usually high standards and procedures of validation followed in science, but not all scientific procedures and claims are as epistemologically sophisticated as one imagines them or would like them to be. Too often we find research driven by economic and political interests, with a small sample taken as evidence, and which sometimes results in an embarrassing reversal of conclusions and recommendations. This is especially evident in the health-care sector which is given ample media coverage, but it is quite possible that insufficient and inadequate processes may be employed in many other areas of specialized scientific research, either on account of a lack of education and vision, a lack of resources, a lack of trained personnel, or perhaps from a baser desire to ensure a hefty profit margin even at the expense of truth and social wellbeing.

If in the scientific realm there may be inadequate measures being employed towards truth and objectivity, then this is perhaps even more rampant in the religious realm. Religion has had its fair share of charlatans and the superstitions which they have generated in the name of God and faith. As a result of this, religious belief and practice has sometimes led to tragic consequences in terms

11 Paul Ricoeur, "Interpretation and/or Argumentation" in *The Just*, trans. David Pellauer (Chicago: University of Chicago Press, 2000), 125.

of human wellbeing and life itself. However, whenever religions have allowed for the use of scientific methodology in the investigation of religious data, the tools of the human sciences and the humanities have often been used to good effect. In mainstream Christian denominations today, there is a wide variety of scripture commentaries using the latest exegetical and historical-critical methods, and in theology, procedures which explain the historical conditions within which dogmatic formulations and basic faith-stances were arrived at and developed. This position of affirming and even embracing the usefulness of these methods, alas, has not been a part of the religious mindset in general, as faith has too often been unnecessarily opposed to reason in different religions and in different epochs within any given religion.

2.3. Scientific and Religious Interpretations Need to be Undertaken Truthfully

This normative constraint has to do with the presupposition of honesty or integrity on the part of scientists and theologians, so that what they say matches what they know to be true and what they have in their minds. More than this, truthfulness entails a transparency which overcomes the need for games and manipulative strategies in communication. This entails an overcoming of personal and collective biases while dealing with others. This further entails the need to operate from a sense of security rather than a desire to protect one's own or one's community's interests.

If one is a religious zealot and adopts not just a fundamentalist standpoint, but even a strategic rather than an open, transparent or communicative rationality when dealing with the 'other'—and even with the 'self,' or fellow-believers within the tradition—then it is extremely difficult for this interpretive constraint to be operative. Similarly, if one is a scientific zealot—like Richard Dawkins—then too it is futile to hope for a neutral, reasonable and just—indeed a socially scientific—assessment of religious beliefs and practices.

Truthfulness also entails the cultivation of the virtue of humility. In the intellectual field, this entails the recognition of human finitude and consequently the recognition that the interpretive products of the human intellect—be it in science or religion—will always be limited from a larger perspective. Truthfulness thus entails the recognition of the limits of the nature, scope, sources and uses of the human knowledge enterprise.

2.4. Scientific and Religious Interpretations Need to be Ethically Appropriate

This normative constraint has to do with the social propriety of communicative action. It is not enough to have strong linguistic, epistemological and personal ethical propriety. One also has to take into cognizance the social appropriateness of interpretive claims. This constraint has two dimensions to it. On the one hand, one has to consider what needs to be avoided in the pursuit of scientific and religious interpretations, i.e., how science and religion *ought not* to interpret reality. On the other hand, one has to consider the issues that need to be addressed in the pursuit of scientific and religious interpretations, i.e., how science and religion *ought* to interpret reality.

2.4.1. Ethically *Inappropriate* Scientific and Religious Interpretations

Scientific and religious interpretations need to avoid both sins of omission as well as sins of commission. Sins of omission may seem the lesser evil, but they involve serious obligations such as the avoidance of the development of scientific interpretations which lead to a technology that is environmentally friendly, and the avoidance of the development of theological interpretations that take into account those who live on the margins of society, or those who constitute the 'other,' whoever the 'other' may be: gender, race, nation, caste, religion. Sins of commission are more serious, as they entail conscious decision-making and strategic planning in the interpretive process in order to inflict some form of violence on another person or community. In science, these include the development of covert technology that is specifically oriented towards human destruction, or the manipulation of data in order to justify an ideological position such as racial supremacy. In religion, sins of commission would include the development of a theology that generates a warped understanding of the 'other,' or spiritual and theological interpretations which justify social inequality, marginalization and domination.

In general, scientific and religious interpretations need to be processed in such a manner that they avoid causing personal, interpersonal or social harm. Such interpretations must also be free from personal and social biases, to the best of one's ability and the ability of the scientific or theological guild within which one works. Finally, it would be inappropriate for both scientific and religious interpretations to be undertaken only for the sake of profit, at the expense of other common goods such as harmony, health, environmental concerns, etc.

2.4.2. Ethically *Appropriate* Scientific and Religious Interpretations

Scientific and religious interpretations need to be socially significant. For this to happen, they would need to consider the prevailing social context and specific needs and interests of the community of stakeholders, including those who will be affected in some way or the other by the interpretation undertaken. Too often both scientific and religious theorizing has taken place in isolation from the needs of this larger community of the stakeholders and others affected by scientific and religious offerings. The positivistic, naturalistic and idealistic presuppositions of scientific methodology do not typically consider the human and social dimensions of life, which include the realms of culture, religion and socio-political reality. Perhaps the most well-known critique of such a methodology was made by Edmund Husserl in the *Crisis of European Sciences*, and his "Vienna Lecture."[12] Husserl argued that such a crisis had arisen in the West because science and subsequently technology had developed without consciously relating themselves to the social context in which research had originated and without considering practical human—and not just technical—problems which formed the original context within which science was born. This critique of science and especially of technology has been echoed by a wide variety of philosophers in the West. Gabriel Marcel argued that the mode of 'having' was slowly overtaking the mode of 'being.'[13] Martin Heidegger argued that Western civilization had engaged in a 'forgetfulness of being' in favour of the obsession with 'beings' and their technological usefulness—an instrumental approach which had also crept into theological discourse, so that God too became another object of methodological inquiry and alienated worship.[14] Hans-Georg Gadamer wrote in favour of an orientation towards and an appropriation of 'truth' versus a raw adoption of methodological inquiry in the human sciences.[15] The critical theorist Herbert Marcuse critiqued the positivist, consumerist and instrumentalist culture which arose from an industrially driven society.[16] In fine, all of these writers critique any interpretation of reality—be it in science or religion—which does not consider the holistic, affective and socially beneficial nature of the process of interpretation. Scientific 'praxis' must be thus guided by 'phronesis' or practical wisdom, which in turn must be guided by 'sophia' or wisdom, and not just 'scientia' (knowledge) and 'techne' (skills).

It would appear that the realm of religion would be more directly oriented towards the resolution of social problems. But this has unfortunately not always been true. Too often, human beings have been sacrificed at the altar of a false understanding of the divine which has been propagated by vested interests. Also, not all religions give importance to the historical and social reality in which we live, justifying to an extent Marx's palliative assessment

---

12 See Edmund Husserl, *The Crisis of European Sciences and Transcendental Phenomenology: An Introduction to Phenomenological Philosophy*, trans. David Carr (Evanston, IL: Northwestern University Press, 1970).

13 See Gabriel Marcel, *Being and Having* (NY: Harper and Row, 1965).

14 See Martin Heidegger, *Being and Time*, trans., John Macquarrie & Edward Robinson, 3rd ed., (Oxford: Basil Blackwell, 2001), 1.3 of the Introduction, "*The Ontological Priority of the Question of Being*." On p. 31, Heidegger states: "Ontological inquiry is indeed more primordial, as over against the ontical inquiry of the positive sciences."

15 See Hans-Georg Gadamer, *Truth and Method*, 2nd rev. ed., trans. revised by Joel Weinsheimer and Donald G. Marshall (New York: Continuum Publishing Company, 1989).

16 See Herbert Marcuse, *One-Dimensional Man: Studies in the Ideology of Advanced Industrial Society* (London: Routledge, 2006).

of religious belief as "an opium for the people." Today, the 'me-generation' takes recourse to new age spiritualities to attain an elusive peace, but again at the cost of a deeper spiritual recognition of a social imperative of solidarity towards the attainment of the common good and equitable social welfare. When science and religion consciously relate themselves to the social context, then we will have better solutions for the more pressing problems which affect a vast swath of humanity. An elitist agenda within scientific and religious interpretive projects needs to be corrected or at least complemented by more socially-sensitive and socially-productive programmes.

We have reached a time in human history when we are better able to know more about and communicate with others. This knowledge and communication needs to take place not only within and between the different sciences and the different religions, but in the spaces where the different sciences and the different religions meet. Panikkar's model of a framework of cosmotheandric harmony could serve as a good working model for this mutual interaction and 'mutual fecundity' or mutual productivity of meaning and purpose between science and religion and within the different sciences and the different religions.[17] The natural sciences tend to focus on the cosmic dimension of reality, while the social sciences tend to focus on the human. Religions tend to focus on the divine or depth dimension of reality. What is urgently called for today is an interactive and less fragmented mindset that considers all of these dimensions of reality, in spite of our different specializations. We need one another's different perspectives to provide a somewhat different and complementary lens through which reality can be understood even better. Albert Einstein is reported to have stated that "Religion without science is blind, science without religion is lame."[18] Saint Pope John Paul II elucidates this relationship between science and religion even further when he claims that, "science can purify religion from error and superstition; religion can purify science from idolatry and false absolutes. Each can draw the other into a wider world, a world in which both can flourish."[19]

Conclusion

The age of the religious guru of earlier times has been replaced by the age of the scientific guru in contemporary times. However, in this democratic and increasingly educated age, whoever is the guru and whatever be his or her

17 See Raimundo Panikkar, *The Cosmotheandric Experience: Emerging Religious Consciousness* (Maryknoll, NY: Orbis, 1993).

18 Albert Einstein, "Science and Religion," in *Science, Philosophy, and Religion: A Symposium* (New York: The Conference on Science, Philosophy, and Religion in Their Relation to the Democratic Way of Life, Inc., 1941), 211.

19 Pope John Paul II, *Origins* 18 (November 17, 1988): 378, in a letter to George Coyne, S.J., the Director of the Vatican Observatory.

affiliation, the guru will need to provide evidence of personal authenticity. Mere testimony and an appeal to authority and tradition will not suffice. Both scientific and religious practitioners cannot expect their claims and the claims of their ancestors to be taken for granted. Both of them will need to have the interpretations of the past and the present reasonably validated, as well as to come up with continuous reinterpretations of their inherited frameworks, in the light of new data and new problems.

Science and religion share similar features of interpretive activity in the process of meaning-making. Both of these realms of meaning engage in the production of rational claims which are embedded in particular linguistic, cultural and ideational frameworks. Each of these frameworks may be considered to be interpretive windows through which one has an opening into the nature of different aspects of reality. Each of these frameworks also constitutes a wide canvas upon which creative ventures of meaning-making can be entertained, some of which are directly intended for human welfare, and many of which bear fruit in innovative technology in the scientific realm and peaceful and harmonious lives in the religious realm.

Keeping in mind the expected fruitfulness of both science and religion, hermeneutical and critical imperatives or constraints which govern both of these fields need to be taken into consideration. Scientific and religious interpretations need to be meaningful and relevant, to be oriented towards the truth, to be produced in a truthful and integrated manner and to be expressed in a socially appropriate and socially productive manner. Both science and religion independently serve human interests and needs. When this service is engaged in collaboratively between scientists and religious experts, the social benefits for both of these disciplines and for humankind in general will be enormous. The challenge that lies before us is to abandon lines of suspicion and opposition between science and religion, and instead adopt more collaborative and beneficial interpretations of reality. In the long run, it is these approaches which will facilitate human solidarity, serve the common good, and enable a more harmonious relationship between the human, cosmic and divine dimensions of reality.

7

Defining Ignorance

Clement Jesudoss Santhanam SJ

Abstract

The conditions of knowledge – JTB, along with Gettier-type counter examples – make an epistemic agent to *know* a proposition in question. The Standard View defines ignorance as the *lack of knowledge*. However, the rival view – the New View – defines ignorance as the *lack of true belief.* This paper analyses both the views and argues that ignorance must be defined in terms of three doxastic attitudes: belief, disbelief and suspension of belief and disbelief.

Keywords

Ignorance, true belief, standard view, new view, doxastic attitudes, belief, disbelief, suspension of belief and disbelief.

Introduction

We often claim that knowledge is power, but the knowledge of ignorance can make us more powerful. Whether it is politics or religion or society, knowledge of one's ignorance can empower a person. And so, it is also important to know what one is ignorant of. However, in order to know what one is ignorant of, the fundamental notion 'what ignorance is' needs to be clarified and defined well. This paper aims at defining ignorance. The traditional view defines ignorance as *the lack or absence of knowledge* and the New View defines ignorance as *the lack or absence of true belief.* According to the New View, an epistemic agent is ignorant of the proposition in question, only when she lacks true belief. The other conditions such as lack of justification or warrant do not make an epistemic agent ignorant. Though I endorse the New View, I extend my arguments further to define ignorance in terms of three doxastic attitudes[1], such as belief, disbelief and suspension of belief and disbelief.

In the first section, I spell out both the Standard View and the New View in detail. In order to build my arguments, I take up negations of the tripartite conditions of knowledge, along with Gettier-type counterexamples, and analyse each of them. Then, I distinguish *ignorance* from *not-knowing* and argue for the New View that among the negations of the four conditions of knowledge, only the lack of true belief qualifies as the case of ignorance. Then, I extend my arguments to the third doxastic attitude: *suspension of belief and disbelief* and argue that suspension of belief and disbelief is also a case of ignorance. To do this, I draw on the work of Sylvain Bromberger (1988), René van Woudenberg (2009), Rik Peels (2010, 2016), Martijn Blaauw (2016) and Pierre Le Morvan (2016). Finally, I conclude that ignorance can be defined in terms of doxastic attitudes, because it is not only *disbelief* that makes a person ignorant of a proposition but also *suspension of belief and disbelief.*

1. What is Ignorance?

There are two rival views regarding ignorance. Both are well developed and defended based on various arguments. On the first view – called the Standard View – ignorance is the lack or absence of *knowledge*, whereas on the second view – called the New View – ignorance is the lack or absence of *true belief.* Among the adherents of the Standard View are Lloyd Fields, Susan Haack, Pierre Le Morvan, and Michael Zimmerman. The New View is embraced, among others, by Alvin Goldman, Alexander Guerrero, Rik Peels, and René van Woudenberg.[2]

Before going to the main debate whether ignorance is the lack of knowledge or the lack of true belief, I make a few preliminary comments on different kinds of knowledge and its tripartite conditions. My aim is to anchor our focus on propositional knowledge and propositional ignorance.

1 'Doxastic attitudes' means 'belief-like attitudes. Though many philosophers posit that there are only three doxastic attitudes such as belief, disbelief and suspension of belief and disbelief, we cannot ignore the difference of opinion regarding doxastic attitudes. The Bayesian understanding of doxastic attitudes differ from the mainstream understanding of doxastic attitudes. They are degree of belief and degree of confidence or credence. However, I fix my focus only on the three standard doxastic attitudes: belief, disbelief and suspension of belief and disbelief.

2 Pierre Le Morvan and Rik Peels, "The Nature of Ignorance: Two Views," in *Epistemic Dimensions of Ignorance*, 12-32, ed. Rik Peels and Martijn Blaauw (Cambridge: Cambridge University Press, 2016), 12.

There are different classifications regarding the kinds of knowledge. *Knowledge-that and knowledge-how* is one such classification. *Factual or factive knowledge*, *objectual knowledge*, and *procedural knowledge*[3] is another one. Though there are different kinds of classifications, epistemologists are mainly concerned about factual or factive (propositional) knowledge. Knowledge *that some specific proposition is true* is called factual or factive (propositional) knowledge.[4] *For our further discussion the term 'knowledge' refers only to factual or factive (propositional) knowledge.*

2. Ignorance According to the Standard View

The adherents of the Standard view define ignorance as the lack or absence of *knowledge*. In many languages, ignorance is used as the *antonym* of knowledge.[5] Two well-known examples for such a claim could be from two ancient languages in India: Sanskrit and Tamil. In Sanskrit the words *Vidya* and *Avidya* refer to knowledge and ignorance respectively. The word *Vidya* means to know, to perceive and to understand, and the word *Avidya* (*A-vidya*) means not to know, not to perceive and not to understand. Similarly, in Tamil the words *Arivu* or *Arithal* and *Ariyaamai* refer to knowledge and ignorance respectively. The word *Arithal* means to know, and the word *Ariyaamai* means not to know. Thus, in many languages, ignorance is defined as the lack or absence of knowledge. When ignorance is defined as the lack or absence of knowledge on the Standard View, then the negation of the conditions of knowledge must also qualify as conditions of ignorance. And so, we shall take up the conditions of *knowledge* first, and then formulate the conditions of *ignorance* by negating them. So that we can analyse them on both the Standard View and the New View.

Traditionally knowledge is defined as *justified true belief* (JTB). However, the Gettier-type counter examples also qualify as a condition of knowledge.[6] Thus, knowledge has four necessary and sufficient conditions.

---

3 Le Morvan and Peels define objectual knowledge as *knowing a certain object, where that object can but need not be a person* and procedural knowledge as *knowledge of how to do something and how to perform some task.* See Le Morvan and Peels, "The Nature of Ignorance: Two Views," 13.

Le Morvan and Peels argue that the negation of *objectual and procedural knowledge* can be termed as *objectual and procedural ignorance*. See Le Morvan and Peels, "The Nature of Ignorance: Two Views," 30-31.

4 Le Morvan and Peels, "The Nature of Ignorance: Two Views," 13.

5 The etymology of the word 'ignorance' comes from the Latin term *ignorantia*. The prefix *in* means 'not' and the old Latin term *gnarus* means 'aware of, acquainted with'.

6 Though JTB has been a traditional standard definition of knowledge, it has been challenged by the Gettier-type counterexamples. These counterexamples prove that there are also some possible cases in which S has a JTB regarding *p*, yet fails to know that *p*. In order to avoid Gettier-type counterexamples, I have added it along with the other three conditions (JTB).

The first condition for knowledge is that *the belief in question is true*.[7] We will hold this condition fixed and focus on the additional conditions that pertain to the epistemic agent's (S's) propositional attitude.

A person S is ignorant of the proposition p iff at least one of the following conditions holds:

(i) S *believes* that *p*, while *p* is true; and
(ii) S's belief that *p* is *justified*, while *p* is true, and
(iii) S's justified belief that *p* withstands Gettier-type counterexamples, while *p* is true.

(i)-(iii) conjunctively qualify as conditions of knowledge. Ignorance, on the Standard View, is defined as the lack or absence of knowledge, so that all that it takes for a person to be ignorant is that she fails to meet one of the conditions (i)-(iii) for knowledge. And so, according to the adherents of the Standard View, ignorance can be defined as,

S is ignorant of the proposition *p* if

(i*) S *disbelieves* that *p,* while *p* is true; or
(ii*) S's belief that *p* is *not justified*, while *p* is true, or
(iii*) S's justified belief that *p* *fails* to withstand Gettier-type counterexamples, while *p* is true.

According to the adherents of the Standard View, (i*)-(iii*) disjunctively qualify as conditions of ignorance, because if any one of the conditions (i*)-(iii*) is met, then we have a case of ignorance. We shall take up each condition and analyse – on the Standard View – whether each condition amounts to ignorance or not.

The adherents of the Standard View argue that (i*) is a case of ignorance, because when a person disbelieves a true proposition, then naturally she fails to know it. Consider the following true proposition that Vienna is the capital of Austria. When Barbara disbelieves that Vienna is the capital of Austria, then naturally she fails to know that it is. And so, in this case, Barbara is ignorant of the true proposition that Vienna is the capital of Austria, because she fails to know it. Thus, (i*) qualifies as a case of ignorance according to the adherents of the Standard View.

---

7 The reason why I hold the first condition (*that the belief in question is true*) fixed and continue with the other conditions is that the negation of the first and second conditions mean the same. The negation of these conditions can be written as: (a) S believes that *p,* while *p* is *false*; and (b) S *disbelieves* that *p,* while *p* is true. It is clear that (a) belongs to the not-*p* world, where not-*p* is true (while *p* is false) and (b) belongs to the *p* world, where *p* is true. However, both (a) and (b) mean the same, because (b) implies that S believes that not-*p*, while not-*p* is false, which is none other than (a). And so, in order to avoid the repetition, I hold the first condition fixed and continue with the other conditions.

The adherents of the Standard View argue that (ii*) is also a case of ignorance. That S's belief that *p* is not justified – while *p* is true – makes S be ignorant of the proposition *p*. Look at this example: Anna, the mother of Mary is suffering from a terminal illness for last three months. On one evening, the doctors tell Mary that Anna may not survive more than 24 hours, because all clinical reports say that her health condition is sinking significantly. On hearing this news, Mary cries so bitterly that she goes to a semi-unconscious state. When she wakes up, she rushes to the doctor and says that her mother is all right now, because she had a dream in which Anna came to her and said, "Mary, look, I am all right, we can go home now." Mary's belief is so strong that she persuades the doctor to go and check the health condition of her mother. When the doctor goes to the ICU, he is surprised to see that Anna's pulse rate and other readings are back to normal. The doctor exclaims that it is a medical miracle. After a few days Anna returns home hale and hearty.

In this case, Mary's belief – that her mother's health condition is all right – is not justified, because her belief is based on her dream. Moreover, her belief happens to be true by luck. Even if we try to argue that Mary had a sort of extra sensory perception (ESP) which helped her to form her belief that Anna was all right, this claim does not seem to have any evidence. And so, Mary does not come to know that *p*. Thus, the adherents of the Standard View argue that (ii*) is a clear case of ignorance.

That (ii*) is a case of ignorance on the Standard View, leads us to similar cases where S's belief that *p* lacks the *warrant* that is necessary for knowledge.[8] Alvin Plantinga says that it is warrant that distinguishes knowledge from mere true belief.[9] Swinburne writes that Plantinga defines warrant as that characteristic which is enough to turn a true belief into knowledge.[10] Thus, S cannot come to know that *p*, when S's true belief that *p* lacks the warrant that is necessary for knowledge. And so, we have another case of ignorance on the Standard View now.

(iv*) S has the true belief that *p*, but S's belief that *p* lacks *the warrant necessary for knowledge*.

The adherents of the Standard View claim that (iv*) is a case of ignorance, because the lack of warrant yields to the lack of knowledge.

---

8 Warrant, according to Alvin Plantinga, is an externalist account of the property of belief that converts true belief to knowledge. Justification is an internalist account of the property of a person, who has the belief. For example: S is justified in believing that Vienna is the capital of Austria. S's belief that Vienna is the capital of Austria is warranted. See Alvin Plantinga, *Warrant and Proper Function* (Oxford: Oxford University Press, 1993).

9 Plantinga, Alvin. *Warrant and Proper Function, v.*

10 Richard Swinburne, "Plantinga on Warrant," Religious Studies, Vol 37, No. 2 (June 2001): 203.

So far, I have argued that (i*), (ii*) and (iv*) qualify as cases of ignorance on the Standard View. Then, how about (iii*) where *S's justified belief that p fails to withstand Gettier-type counterexamples, while p is true*? Gettier-cases are the ones that just fall short of knowledge. In Gettier-type counterexamples, S's belief happens to be true *by luck* and the justification or warrant also arise *by luck*. Therefore, the adherents of the Standard View argue that when S's belief that *p* fails to withstand the Gettier-type counterexamples, then it is a case of ignorance as well.

Thus, if at least one of the conditions (i*)-(iv*) is met, then we have a case of ignorance. However, the adherents of the New View disagree with the Standard View and argue that only (i*) is necessary and sufficient for S to be ignorant of the proposition *p*.

3. Ignorance According to the New View

The adherents of the New View define ignorance as the *lack or absence of true belief*. I also endorse the same view. When we look at (i*)-(iv*) in the light of the New View, then it becomes easy to understand that only (i*) suffices as the case of *ignorance* and the rest fall under the category of *not-knowing*.[11] That is to say, (i*) S is *ignorant* of a proposition *p* if S *disbelieves* that *p,* while *p* is true is the necessary and sufficient condition of ignorance. Now I shall take up (i*)-(iv*) and defend the New View by analysing how and why conditions (ii*), (iii*) and (iv*) don't suffice as the conditions of ignorance and how only (i*) suffices as the condition of ignorance. I also do it by differentiating ignorance from not-knowing.

We shall analyse (ii*) and (iv*) first. It is clear that (ii*) and (iv*) are cases of not-knowing, because when S fails to have justification or warrant then S fails to know that *p*. However, according to the New View, S is *not* ignorant of the proposition *p,* mainly because S *has a true belief*. In the case of Mary, she is not justified in believing that her mother's health condition is all right, because her belief is based on her dream and her justification happens to be true by luck. However, her *belief is true*. And so, on the New View, *that she has a true belief* is sufficient to argue that she is not ignorant of the proposition 'that her mother's condition is all right.' In other words, Mary does not lack true belief, and so, (ii*) cannot be a case of ignorance.

Similarly (iv*) cannot also be a case of ignorance. Plantinga's definition of warrant – as the characteristic which is enough to turn a true belief into knowledge – can help us argue that (iv*) is a case of not-knowing. However, the adherents of the New View argue that (iv*) is not a case of ignorance either, merely because S's belief is *true*. Look at the following example: Lucy

11 See Rik Peels, "What is Ignorance?" *Philosophia*, 38(1) (2010): 57-67 and René Van Woudenberg, "Ignorance and Force: Two Existing Conditions for False Beliefs," *American Philosophical Quarterly*, Vol 46. No. 4 (October 2009): 373-386.

and her friend Nancy travel by train from Innsbruck to Vienna. They have a connecting train at Salzburg, and they have just ten minutes to catch the next train. Unfortunately, their train from Innsbruck gets delayed by five minutes. Lucy looks really panicked due to the delay. Nancy pacifies her saying that in most cases, connecting trains will wait when there is a delay for a short period of time. As the delay is just five minutes, Lucy believes that she can catch the connecting train. When they reach Salzburg, Lucy sees the connecting train and they board the train happily.

In this case, Lucy has a true belief – that the connecting train will wait, when the delay is for a short period of time – but her belief has no warrant. Why do we say that Lucy's belief has no warrant? The very fact that Lucy is still on board and that she is unable to verify her belief with an evidence – that the connecting train will wait – make her belief unwarranted. Moreover, Lucy's belief remains unwarranted till she sees the connecting train. However, her belief is also not false because the connecting train has been waiting, when her train reached Salzburg. Thus, though it qualifies as a case of mere not-knowing, it does not qualify as a case of ignorance. Van Woudenberg affirms it in his writing that "someone having the true but unwarranted belief that *p* doesn't know that *p* but can hardly be said to be ignorant of *p*."[12] So, both (ii*) and (iv*) fail to be the cases of ignorance on the New View, because both Mary and Lucy don't lack true belief.

Condition (iii*) – *S's justified belief that p fails to withstand Gettier-type counterexamples, while p is true* – is also not a case of ignorance on the New View, because S's belief that *p* happens to be true and justified by luck. In the fake barn case of Goldman (1976), even though Henry looks at a genuine barn, he *doesn't* come to know it, because the region is full of papier-mâché facsimiles of barns,[13] moreover, his warrant or justification also happens to be true by luck. So, it is a merely a case of not-knowing. However, the adherents of the New View argue that the fake barn case doesn't make Henry ignorant because Henry's belief is true, although it is by mere luck. They also argue that Henry may be ignorant of other propositions such as 'the district is full of papier-mâché facsimiles of barns' or 'Henry happens to see a true barn by luck' or 'Henry's belief happens to be justified merely by luck' etc. However, of the truth of the proposition that it is a genuine barn, *itself*, Henry doesn't seem to be ignorant.[14] That S does not lack true belief qualifies (iii*) to be not a case of ignorance on the New View.

12 Van Woudenberg, "Ignorance and Force: Two Existing Conditions for False Beliefs," 373.

13 Alvin I Goldman, "Discrimination and Perceptual Knowledge," *The Journal of Philosophy*, Vol. 73, No. 20 (November 1976): 773.

14 Le Morvan and Peels, "The Nature of Ignorance: Two Views," 13.

Now we are left only with (i*), which states that *S disbelieves that p, while p is true*. The adherents of both the Standard View and the New View agree that (i*) is a case of ignorance. When S disbelieves that Vienna is the capital of Austria, then S lacks the true belief that it is. As a result, S does not know that Vienna is the capital of Austria. Thus, (i*) qualifies as a case of ignorance on the Standard View. Moreover, that S *lacks the true belief* – that Vienna is the capital of Austria – makes S is ignorant on the New View as well. Thus, (i*) – S *disbelieves* that *p,* while *p* is true – qualifies as the case of ignorance.

(i*) can lead us to two sub-cases of ignorance: *rational ignorance*[15] and *deep ignorance.*[16] Bromberger, the proponent of rational ignorance says, when S knows that there exists a question; and that S doesn't know the answer to this question, and thus, S disbelieves it, then, S's ignorance is called rational ignorance.[17]

We shall take up the following case. Joe takes a great interest in space research and is fascinated by the question whether there is a green planet like the Earth other than solar system. However, he finds that most of the evidence is inconclusive. So, when Joe disbelieves that there exists a green planet like the Earth, then Joe is rationally ignorant. In this case, Joe knows the question – whether there is another green planet like the Earth – and also knows that he does not know the answer, because he finds the evidence inconclusive. That Joe knows the question; and that he knows that he does not know the answer to this question, makes him rationally ignorant, when he disbelieves that there exists another green planet like the Earth. According to Bromberger, it is both the knowledge of the question and the knowledge that S does not know the answer that make S to be rationally ignorant, when S disbelieves it.[18]

However, there is another case where S disbelieves that *p* without even knowing that there is a question. Van Woudenberg calls this type of ignorance as deep ignorance, because, he claims that in this case there seems to be more ignorance than rational ignorance.[19] We shall look at the following case. Hans has never been interested in cricket, and accordingly has never heard of Duckworth-Lewis method in cricket. So, he has no awareness of the question, "What will happen when rain interrupts a T20 cricket match?" Accordingly, he doesn't believe the proposition that Duckworth-Lewis method can be used

15 See Sylvain Bromberger, "Rational Ignorance," *Synthese*, Vol. 74, No. 1, (January 1988): 47-64.

16 See Van Woudenberg, "Ignorance and Force: Two Existing Conditions for False Beliefs," 373-386.

17 Bromberger, "Rational Ignorance," 47.

18 Bromberger, "Rational Ignorance," 48.

19 Van Woudenberg, "Ignorance and Force: Two Existing Conditions for False Beliefs," 374.

when rain interrupts a T20 cricket match; but neither does he disbelieve it. When Hans neither believes nor disbelieves a proposition, then he is obviously ignorant of the proposition. As there is more ignorance than rational ignorance in this case, it is called deep ignorance.[20]

Whether S knows the question (rational ignorance) or does not know the question (deep ignorance), the very fact that *S disbelieves that p* makes S ignorant of the true proposition *p*. Thus, (i*) is a clear case of ignorance on the New View.

Therefore, according to the New View, it is the lack of true belief that makes a person ignorance of the true proposition. Now, we are encountered with a question, "What about a person, who neither beliefs nor disbelieves a true proposition instead suspends both her belief and disbelief?" In order to answer this question, I extend my discussion to the third doxastic attitude: *suspension of belief and disbelief* and analyse whether suspension of belief and disbelief can also be a case of ignorance.

4. Ignorance as the Lack of Doxastic Attuites

The New View confines its definition of ignorance only to belief and disbelief because it defines ignorance as the lack of true belief. In the previous section, we have analysed the New View and have come out with a case of ignorance of ignorance as,

(i*) S is *ignorant* of a proposition *p* iff S *disbelieves* that *p*, while *p* is true.

However, I claim that though (i*) is a case of ignorance, it is not a sufficient one, because the New View has omitted the third doxastic attitude: suspension of belief and disbelief. And so, I extend my analysis to the third doxastic attitude in this section and argue that it is not only *disbelief* but also *suspension of belief and disbelief* that can make a person ignorant. I also argue that both become necessary and sufficient conditions of ignorance.

Many philosophers posit that there are three doxastic attitudes: belief, disbelief and suspension of belief and disbelief. When S concludes that a proposition is *true*, then S's attitude towards that proposition is called *belief*. When S concludes that a proposition is *false*, then S's attitude towards that proposition is called *disbelief*. When S is *unable to conclude* whether a proposition is true or false, then S's attitude towards that proposition is called *suspension of belief and disbelief*.[21]

There are mainly three possibilities for a person to suspend her belief and disbelief.

(a) when S's evidence may be equally balanced in favour of and against a proposition; or

20 Van Woudenberg, "Ignorance and Force: Two Existing Conditions for False Beliefs," 375.

21 Peels, "What is Ignorance?" 58.

(b) when S may not have any evidence that is relevant to the claim, or
(c) when S may not be in a position to assess the weight of evidence.

All the three possibilities (a), (b) and (c) for suspending one's belief and disbelief can be rational. (a) is a case of rational suspension. In this case, though S has evidence, they are equally balanced in favour of and against the proposition. Thus, S is unable to conclude anything based on the evidence that she has. And so, S suspends her belief and disbelief till she gets further evidence. That S *knows* – that the evidences are inconclusive – makes S's suspension rational. In order to explain this notion, we shall consider the proposition that 'Even light does not escape from black hole.' Michell, an astronomer does research on black holes and collects evidence regarding this proposition. However, he finds that the evidence is equally balanced in favour of and against the proposition. He is unable to conclude, and so he would naturally suspend his belief and disbelief – about whether light escapes from black hole or not – till he gets further evidence. In this case, Michell's suspension of his belief and disbelief is rational because he *knows* that all his evidence is inconclusive, and he also knows that based on inconclusive evidence he cannot form his belief or disbelief.

(b) is also a case of rational suspension of belief and disbelief. In this case, S suspends her belief and disbelief towards a proposition because S *knows* that S does not have any evidence at all. When John, a junior astronomer – who has just joined as an assistant to Michell – happens to read a note written by Michell that "I need more evidence to conclude whether light escapes from black hole or not," then he would naturally suspend his belief or disbelief towards the proposition, for the simple reason that he does not have any evidence at all. Thus, (b) is a case of rational suspension, because John suspends his belief and disbelief *with the knowledge* that he does not have any evidence at all regarding the proposition.

(c) is also a case of rational suspension, because S *knows* that she is not in a position to assess the weight of evidence and so she suspends her belief and disbelief. Tom, the nephew of Michell, is a medical student and he is not at all interested in astronomy. When Michell meets Tom at a dinner, he explains about black holes and narrates all the evidence that he has collected. He also shares with him his question whether light can escape from black hole or not. In this case, Tom would naturally suspend his belief and disbelief rationally, because he *knows* that he does not know anything about black holes, and he also knows that he is not in a position to assess the weight of all the evidence that Michell has told him. Thus, (c) is also a case of rational suspension.

We shall come back to our question now – *whether S can be ignorant of a proposition p when S suspends her belief or disbelief on p, while p is true.* Suspension seems to be a case of both not-knowing and ignorance. We shall take up the following example. Marco suspends his belief and disbelief about whether Vasco da Gama landed in India on May 20, 1498. That Marco suspends his belief and disbelief about a true proposition, hinders him from knowing that it is. And so, *that Marco lacks knowledge* makes it a clear case of not-knowing. Moreover, it is also a case of ignorance on the New View. When Marco suspends his belief and disbelief towards a true proposition – that Vasco da Gama landed in India on May 20, 1498 – then he naturally *lacks true belief* that it is. And thus, Marco's suspension of belief and disbelief makes him ignorant of the true proposition that Vasco da Gama landed in India on May 20, 1498. And so, that S suspends her belief and disbelief towards a true proposition makes her be ignorant of it. Thus, suspension of belief and disbelief is also a necessary condition of ignorance on the New View. And so, we write, S is ignorant of a proposition that *p*, if (v*) S *suspends* her belief or disbelief on *p*, while *p* is true.

Though (v*) is a case of ignorance on the New View, (v*) alone cannot qualify as a necessary condition of ignorance, because both (i*) and (v*) disjunctively qualify as necessary and sufficient conditions of ignorance on the New View. That is to say, when at least one two conditions is met, then we have a case of ignorance. (i*) and (v*) qualify as cases of ignorance disjunctively, because the doxastic attitudes are mutually exclusive. That *S believes that p* implies that S *neither disbelieves nor suspends* her belief and disbelief and the vice versa. Therefore, (i*) and (v*) are disjunctive.

And so, the definition of ignorance can be written as, S is ignorant of a proposition p, iff at least one of the following conditions holds:

(i*) S *disbelieves* that *p*, while *p* is true; or
(v*) S *suspends* her belief or disbelief on *p*, while *p* is true.

From all the arguments and analyses, I now conclude that only (i*) and (v*) disjunctively qualify as cases of ignorance. And so, on the New View, it is not only disbelief that *p* that makes a person ignorant of the true proposition *p*, but suspension of belief and disbelief that *p* also makes a person ignorant of the true proposition *p*. Now, I conclude that the definition of ignorance on the New View can be complete, only when it is defined in terms of all three doxastic attitudes.

Conclusion

Traditionally knowledge is defined as justified true belief. Thus, JTB, along with Gettier-type counterexamples, make an epistemic agent to *know* a proposition in question. When the Standard View defines ignorance as the lack of knowledge, then it implies that each of these conditions disjunctively qualifies as a case of ignorance. That is to say, on the Standard View, when an epistemic agent lacks at least one of these conditions, then she fails to have knowledge, and this lack of knowledge makes her ignorant of the true proposition. On the contrary, the rival New View defines ignorance as the lack of true belief. I have analysed both the views by distinguishing not-knowing from ignorance, and finally, I came out with the necessary condition of ignorance on the New View. In the last section, I extended my arguments to the third doxastic attitude: suspension of belief and disbelief, and argued that the definition of ignorance on the New View can be complete as necessary and sufficient, only when it is defined in terms of all the three doxastic attitudes.

Bibliography

Audi, Robert. "The Place of Testimony in the Fabric of Knowledge and Justification." *American Philosophical Quarterly*, Vol. 34, No. 4 (October 1997): 405-422.

Audi, Robert. *Rational Belief: Structure, Grounds, and Intellectual Virtue*. Oxford: Oxford University Press, 2015.

Bromberger, Sylvain. "Rational Ignorance." *Synthese*, Vol. 74, No. 1, (January 1988): 47-64.

Gelfert, Axel. *A Critical Introduction to Testimony*. London: Bloomsbury, 2014.

Goldman, Alvin I. "Discrimination and Perceptual Knowledge." *The Journal of Philosophy*, Vol. 73, No. 20 (November 1976): 771-791.

Guerrero, Alexander A. "Living with Ignorance in a World of Experts." In *Perspectives on Ignorance from Moral and Social Philosophy*, edited by Rik Peels, 156-185. New York: Routledge, 2017.

Le Morvan, Pierre and Peels, Rik. "The Nature of Ignorance: Two Views." In *Epistemic Dimensions of Ignorance*, edited by Peels, Rik and Blaauw, Martijn, 12-32. Cambridge: Cambridge University Press, 2016.

Peels, Rik and Blaauw, Martijn, eds. *Epistemic Dimensions of Ignorance*. Cambridge: Cambridge University Press, 2016. A

Peels, Rik. "What is Ignorance?" *Philosophia,* 38(1) (2010): 57-67.

Plantinga, Alvin. *Warrant and Proper Function*. Oxford: Oxford University Press, 1993.

Swinburne, Richard. "Plantinga on Warrant." *Religious Studies*, Vol 37, No. 2 (June 2001), 203-214.

Van Woudenberg, René. "Ignorance and Force: Two Existing Conditions for False Beliefs." *American Philosophical Quarterly*, Vol 46. No. 4 (October 2009): 373-386.

8

Concepts and Experience: The Case of Shame

Dolichan Kollareth SJ

Abstract

Concepts mediate human experiences. This article argues in favor of the role of concepts and categories in constituting human experiences taking the example of the emotional experience of shame. If we regard emotions to be evolved biological mechanisms, an emotional experience becomes a matter of an external stimulus triggering an internal mechanism. However, this traditional view has received little empirical support. In the emerging alternative view, emotions are constructions out of biological reactions as well as conceptual categorizations. Thus, an emotional experience depends not merely on biology but also on the conceptual categorization. Research on shame supports this alternative view: theories on shame differs markedly, empirical studies do not find any consensual features for the emotion, translation words for shame in other languages differ in the details of meaning, and there is no fixed meaning for the word shame in history. Depending on the underlying conceptual structure, words such as shame may have different meanings in different subcultures and historical periods and even in different individuals in the same culture.

Keywords

Concepts, experience, categorization, lexical, shame, construction, evolved mechanism.

Introduction

Emotions are intimate human experiences. We feel angry, happy, sad, fear and so on. How do we experience an emotion? Theoretical views differ: For one group of theorists, an emotional experience is when an eliciting event triggers a relevant (evolutionarily determined) affect program, which in turn causes autonomic nervous system activity, expressive behavior, and a subjective state. The other group, however, do not consider emotions to be neural modules that trigger sets of patterned responses. According to one such view, discrete emotions arise from a combination of affective biological responses with culture-specific categories. Thus, emotional experiences are dependent on the conceptual categories that go into the making of those experiences. Consistent with this latter view, this article highlights the role of concepts in human experience taking an example of an emotional experience that in English is labeled "shame".

1. Concepts, Language and Emotion

Language is inherently conceptual. The inherent conceptual nature of language becomes clear in an attempt to translate a word. The Sanskrit word for philosophy is *darsana*, which literally, in English, means seeing. The German word *Schadenfreude* can be translated into English using a sentence (pleasure derived from another's displeasure). The Ilongot *liget* might take a paragraph to be translated. Literal translations become difficult, because of the difficulty in translating a cultural concept.

Concepts mediate psychological experiences. Concepts are not biological entities but structures dynamically formed by contextual factors. Culture influences the way emotion is categorized.[1] Quantity and quality of emotions differ with age, culture, gender, expectations etc.[2]

The incompatibility of the conceptual worlds of two cultural communities reflects in the meaning incompatibility of words. Therefore achieving translation equivalence might be harder for complex concepts like anger and fear compared to concrete concepts like table and chair. Because of the socio-cultural embeddedness of complex concepts, word alone becomes a poor representative of the concept. Similarly, a language community may use one word for different concepts. The same word will have different meanings depending on its conceptual context. In other words, a word derives its meaning from the fact of it being part of an underlying concept. The meaning

1 J. A. Russell, J. A., "Natural language concepts of emotion," in *Perspectives in Personality: Self and Emotion,* by D. J. Ozer, J. M. Healy, Jr. and A. J. Stewart (eds.), (London: Jessica Kingsley Publishers, 1991).

2 B. Mesquita and M. Boiger, "Emotions in context: A socio-dynamic model of emotions," *Emotion Review,* (2013) 1-14.

of "windows" differs when used in the context of a building and a computer. The meanings of "hunger" differ from each other when used in the context of food, love and justice. Thus within a language, it is possible for the same word to be extended to include different concepts.

Conceptual nature of the language alerts us to the possibility of using an emotion word in relation to different concepts. Analyzing emotion sentences from counselling sessions and newspaper texts, Edwards concludes that the use of emotion words in everyday life is highly variable.[3] Gee shows that the meaning of emotion words are context specific.[4] Some of the contexts in which emotion words regularly features are physical, aesthetic, religious, and moral. These contexts may vary across cultures, as contexts are culturally dependent. The physical context may vary across cultures to a lesser degree whereas the other three contexts to higher degrees. Each of these cultural contexts brings unique concepts in mediating experiences relevant to that context. Thus, physical, aesthetic, religious, and moral contexts involve unique concepts. It is interesting to see how emotion words used in these contexts differ in meaning. Happiness, fear, anger, sadness etc. used in physical, aesthetic, religious, and moral contexts may not align, in meaning or experience, neatly with each other. The following examples illustrates how the meaning of emotional experiences differ from aesthetic to religious contexts.

Menon and Shweder shows how an ancient Indian theory of aesthetic appreciation differentiates *bhava* (discrete emotions) from *rasa* (emotional experience).[5] Theory proposes eight stable emotions (*sthai bhava*). Each *bhava* has its own *rasa*. An actor, in drama, combines facial expressions, hand gestures, body movements, and music to express appropriate *bhava*, which is supposed to evoke the corresponding *rasa* in the audience. As per the theory, the *bhava* and *rasa* are incommensurable. The non-identical relationship postulated between *bhava* and *rasa* acknowledges the uniqueness of an emotional experience in an aesthetic context. Similarly some of the emotions (or lack of emotions) experienced in a religious context are mediated through appropriate cultural concepts and are evaluated as unique. Tears in the life of Christian saints are often valued as signs of religious perfection. Aghori sadhus in India use human skulls as jewels and drinking bowls, and not being disgusted or fearful is a sign of spiritual perfection. The Indian concept of Samadhi (the state of final liberation) may cognitively be a neutral state but experienced as absolute bliss.

---

3 D. Edwards, "Emotion discourse," *Culture & Psychology,* (1999) 271-291

4 J. P. Gee, "Mind and society: A response to Derek Edwards' "emotion discourse". *Culture and Psychology,* (1999) 305-312.

5 U. Menon and R. A. Shweder, "Dominating Kali: Hindu family values and Tantric power," in *Encountering Kali: In the Margins, at the Center, in the West,* by R. F. McDermott and J. J. Kripal (eds.), (Berkeley: University of California Press, 2003).

2. The Case of Shame

In this part, I argue that shame is not an entity with essential features that make it distinct from other emotions. Perhaps "shame" refers to a heterogeneous cluster of events. Here I diverge from a traditional approach in emotion research that assumes emotions in general to be distinct entities with essential features.[6] As indicated above, in that tradition, an emotion is presupposed to be a mechanism within the person that can be identified by and assessed in terms of its causes and consequences. That is, the emotion cannot be observed but is inferred from the specific kind of situations or appraisals that trigger the emotion, from the underlying brain circuitry, and from its manifestations in conscious subjective experience, peripheral physiological changes, expressive signals, and behavioral reactions. A coherent and predictable pattern of manifestations is predicted for each occurrence of a particular emotion because they stem from a single cause, the emotion. Thus, for example, every instance of the emotion "shame" would be invariably associated with a coherent set of features. One account of shame might be that it is triggered by exposure to a specifiable type of event and that it leads to a specifiable conscious subjective experience and to a nonverbal signal and instrumental behavior. However, researchers have not still fond any such consistent pattern.

Views on shame differs markedly. If shame is indeed a distinct entity, then one might expect a convergence on a clear conceptualization of shame. However, theoretical views have not converged. In one theory, shame is caused by public exposure;[7] whereas, in another, shame is caused by violating internal private standards rather than by public exposure;[8] and, in yet another theory, shame is caused not by any external event per se, but by a focus on the self as flawed.[9] One theory assumes a unique combination of bodily and behavioral display associated with shame,[10] another theory has no expressive signal that is

6 P. Ekman and D. Cordaro 2011. "What is meant by calling emotions basic." *Emotion Review,* (2011) 364-370.

7 D. P. Ausubel, "Relationships between shame and guilt in the socializing process," in *Psychological Review* (1955), 378-390.

8 R.J. Edelmann, "Embarrassment: The state of research." *Current Psychological Reviews,* (1981) 125-137.

9 J.P. Tangney and R. L. Dearing, *Shame and Guilt,* (New York: Guilford Press, 2002).

10 M.E. Kemeny, T. L. Gruenewald and S. S. Dickerson, "Shame as the emotional response to threat to the social self: Implications for behavior, physiology, and health," *Psychological Inquiry,* (2004) 153-160.

unique to shame.[11] In one theory, shame leads to maladaptive and pathological reactions,[12] whereas in another shame leads to adaptive reactions.[13]

Empirical studies also do not agree on the features of shame. In support of the view that shame is caused by public exposure, participants reported more shame for transgressions discovered by another person than when the same transgressions were done in private.[14] In other studies, participants reported more shame than embarrassment for violation of important personal standards, whereas they reported more embarrassment than shame for flaws exposed to the public.[15] Still in other studies, shame was caused by both public exposure and private events.[16] Participants recalled rather an equal number of public exposure events for both shame and guilt, they also recalled, again, an equal number of solitary events for both shame and guilt.[17] The view that shame is caused by a negative evaluation of self rather than specific behavior also did not have unanimous support: Some studies found that the shamed participants tended to change their flawed self more often than their specific behavior.[18] However, in other studies, shamed participants attempted to alter specific behaviors more often than the whole self.[19]

A more convincing evidence in support of the conceptual nature of shame comes from the translation equivalence of the English word shame in other languages. Other languages lack an exact equivalent, although some languages have similar (albeit not identical) concepts. Shame is often translated into other languages by referring dictionaries or using the method of translation-back-translations. However, these methods yield the most similar

---

11 J. L. Tracy, and R. W. Robins, "Putting the self into self-conscious emotions: A theoretical model. *Psychological Inquiry,* (2004) 103-125.

12 Tangney and Dearing, *Shame and Guilt.*

13 P. Gilbert, "What is shame? Some core issues and controversies," in *Shame: Interpersonal Behavior, Psychopathology, and Culture,* by P. Gilbert and B. Andrews (eds.), (New York: Oxford University Press, 1998).

14 R.H. Smith, J. M. Webster, W. G. Parrott and H. L. Eyre, "The role of public exposure in moral and nonmoral shame and guilt," *Journal of Personality and Social Psychology,* (2002) 138-159.

15 M.K. Babcock and J. Sabini, "On differentiating embarrassment from shame," in *European Journal of Social Psychology,* (1990), 151-169.

16 D. Keltner and B. N. Buswell, "Evidence for the distinctness of embarrassment, shame, and guilt: A study of recalled antecedents and facial expressions of emotion," *Cognition and Emotion,* (1996) 155-171.

17 Tangney and Dearing, *Shame and Guilt.*

18 P.M. Niedenthal, J. P. Tangney and I. Gavanski,"'If only I weren't' versus 'If only I hadn't': Distinguishing shame and guilt in counterfactual thinking," *Journal of Personality and Social Psychology,* (1994) 585-595.

19 I.E. De Hooge, M. Zeelenberg and S. M. Breugelmans. 2010. "Restore and protect motivations following shame," *Cognition and Emotion,* (2010) 111-127.

term, not necessarily an equivalent term. More demanding standards indicate that lexical terms in other languages for shame often did not have the exact meaning of the "shame". There were cross-cultural variations in the typical causes, consequences, and non-verbal expressions associated with the emotion experiences denoted by "shame or its translations".[20] The following table summarizes lexical studies on shame not reported by Edelstein and Shaver.

Table: Lexical Studies on Shame

Publication	Language	Word/s for shame	The way the word differs (in meaning or its similarity to other emotions) from English *shame*
Abu-Lughod 1999	Bedouin of western Egypt	*Hasham*	An emotion used to pay deference to people of higher status
Al Jallad 2002	Arabic Javanese	*xajal, fadiHa, 9ar, isin, isan-isin, ngisin-isini*	Can be translated as shame, embarrassment, and humiliation
Alonso-Arbiol et al. 2006	Basque	*Lotsa*	When categorizing emotions, *lotsa* falls within the realm of fear and anxiety
Bedford 2004	Mandarin from Taiwanese	*can kui, xiu kui*; and *diu lian, xiu chi*	Two types of shame: *can kui, xiu kui* – internal private shame; and *diu lian, xiu chi* – external public shame
Crozier 2014	Welsh	*cywilydd* and *gwarth*	*cywilydd* can be translated as shame and embarrassment; *gwarth,* as shame, reproach, and disgrace.
De Mendoza, Fernandez-Dols, Parrot and Carrera 2010	Spanish	*Vergüuenza*	*shame* (U.S.) and *vergüenza* do not share the cluster of central features
Fessler 2004	Begkulu	*Malu*	*shame* (U.S.) is more guilt-like compared to *malu*
Fischer, Manstead and Rodriguez Mosquera 1999	Netherlands and Spain	*schaamate* and *verguenza*	The prototypical cause of *schaamate* is loss of self-esteem, whereas *verguenza* is being the focus of others' attention
Fontaine, Poortinga, Setiadi and Markam 2002	Netherlands and Indonesia	*schaamte* and *Malu*	*schaamte* is more like anger, and *malu* is more like fear

20 R.S. Edelstein, and P. R. Shaver, "A cross-cultural examination of lexical studies of self-conscious emotions," in *The Self-conscious Emotions: Theory and Research,* by J. L. Tracy, R. W. Robins and J. P. Tangney (Eds.), (New York: Guilford Press, 2007).

Geertz C. 1973	Balinese	*Lek*	*lek* is more like stage fright
Keeler 1983	Javanese	*Isin*	Can be translated as shame, shyness, embarrassment, guilt. It is a value praised by parents in their children
Menon and Shweder 2003	Many South Asian languages	*lajya/lajja*	Can be translated as shame, shyness, embarrassment, modesty. It is a desirable quality that people display in their interactions with significant others
Ogarkova, Soriano and Lehr 2012	Russian	*Styd*	Can be translated as shame, guilt, and embarrassment
Rosaldo 1980	Illongot	*Betang*	Can be translated as shame, humility, respect, and sometimes even fear.
Rusch 2004	Japanese	*Hazukashii*	Can be translated as shame and embarrassment

Note. For details of the publications, see the bibliography

There are also cultural differences. French speakers from Quebec and Gabon could be distinguished by idiosyncratic facial muscle movements and differential use of head movements respectively for "honte".[21] For English speakers recollecting "shame" events, European Americans remembered mostly those events experienced by themselves, whereas first generation Asian Americans remembered events experienced by self as well as parents or family.[22]

Yet another evidence in favor of shame being a concept is the history of this word. The meaning of "shame" as an English language concept is not fixed. The view that shame is a distinct biologically founded emotion would favor a constant word use over a historical period. However, the word did not have a fixed meaning over a historical period in English. Research in the historical linguistics of the English word "shame" showed change in the meaning and frequency of the word use. The word meaning of "shame" depended on historical time periods and the kind of texts in which the word was used. The word was used more frequently and in increasingly diverse contexts in later English.

There was a change in the meaning of "shame" from being more of an experience in the social context to being more of an experience in the

21 H.A. Elfenbein, M. Beaupré, M. Lévesque and U. Hess, "Toward a dialect theory: Cultural differences in the expression and recognition of posed facial expressions," *Emotion,* (2007) 131-146.

22 R. Liem, "Shame and guilt among first- and second-generation Asian Americans and European Americans," *Journal of Cross-Cultural Psychology,* (1997) 365-392.

individual or moral context. Over a period in Old English (before 950 to 1150), meaning of "shame" changed from being considered more of an experience related to social status such as loss of reputation or dishonor to more of an internal negative evaluation of oneself.[23] In the writings in the early modern to the present day English (from a period of 1418 to 1991), there is a shift of emphasis in the meaning of "shame" from being an experience in the religious and social duties context to an experience in the individual and moral context.[24]

"Shame" had diverse meanings depending on the context of the word use. Shame words in the English translation of the Psalms—translated from Latin to English from 8th to 11th centuries—communicated conversion and repentance in a religious context.[25] In the late medieval English texts (14th- and 15th-century), "shame" in religious texts meant evil; in texts describing chivalry, failure; in texts describing romantic love, a desirable quality; and in advisory text, a restraint on undesirable behavior.[26]

The frequency of the word use was not constant over a history period. The word was used increasingly in diverse contexts and there was also an increase in the use of shame-specific metaphors: There was very little use of "shame" before 850, between 850 and 950, "shame" occurred only in religious and philosophical texts, between 950 and 1050, the word occurred in religious and philosophical texts, and in fiction and private letters, and between 1050 and 1150, the word began occurred in legal texts.[27] Similarly, there was an increase in the number of metaphors for shame from Old English to the present day English, such that some of the present day shame-specific metaphors such as "shame is having no clothes on, shame is decrease in size, an ashamed person is small, and to be ashamed is to block out the world" could not be observed in Old English.

Conclusion

The word, such as "shame", may have different meanings in different subcultures and historical periods and even in different individuals in the same

23 J. Díaz-Vera, "From cognitive linguistics to historical sociolinguistics: The evolution of Old English expressions of shame and guilt," *Cognitive Linguistic Studies*, (2014) 55-83.

24 H. Tissari, "Conceptualizing shame: Investigating uses of the English word shame," in *Selected Proceedings of the 2005 Symposium on New Approaches in English Historical Lexis,* (Somerville: Cascadilla Proceedings Project, 2006), 1418–1991.

25 T. Birnbaum, "Naming shame: Translating emotion in the Old English Psalter Glosses" in *Anglo-Saxon Emotions* by A. Jorgensen, F. McCormack and J. Wilcox (Eds.), (Burlington: Ashgate Publishing Company, 2015).

26 M.C. Flannery, "The concept of shame in late-Medieval English literature," *Literature Compass*, (2012) 166-182.

27 M. Fabiszak and A. Hebda, "Emotions of control in Old English: Shame and guilt," *Poetica: An International Journal of Linguistic-Literary Studies,* (2006) 1-35.

culture. As a descriptive concept, shame is used widely by English speakers in their everyday discussions. However, unlike figures in geometry, the descriptive concept of shame seems not well defined, and instead refers to a cluster of events that share overlapping features. This view of shame, or any other emotion, as a cluster of events is consistent with an emerging alternative to the traditional perspective on emotion. Traditionally, each emotion was considered distinct; however, in the emerging alternative, allegedly discrete emotions (such as fear, guilt, and shame) are viewed as overlapping vaguely defined clusters with varying conceptual structures. Concepts color one's experiences.

Bibliography

Abu-Lughod, L. 1999. *Veiled Sentiments: Honor and Poetry in a Bedouin Society*. Berkeley, CA: University of California Press.

Al Jallad, N. T. 2002. *Shame in English, Arabic, and Javanese: A Comparative Lexical Study* Accessed July 2018. PsycINFO: 619950666; 2002-95013-146.

Alonso-Arbiol, I., P. R. Shaver, R. C. Fraley, B. Oronoz, E. Unzurrunzaga, and R. Urizar. 2006. "Structure of the Basque Emotion Lexicon." *Cognition and Emotion,* vol. 20, no. 6: 836-865.

Ausubel, D. P. 1955. "Relationships Between Shame and Guilt in the Socializing Process." *Psychological Review,* vol. 62, no. 5: 378-390.

Babcock, M. K. and J. Sabini. 1990. "On Differentiating Embarrassment from Shame." *European Journal of Social Psychology,* vol. 20, no. 2: 151-169.

Bedford, O. A. 2004. "The Individual Experience of Guilt and Shame in Chinese Culture." *Culture and Psychology,* vol. 10, no. 1: 29-52.

Birnbaum, T. 2015. "Naming Shame: Translating Emotion in the Old English Psalter Glosses. In *Anglo-Saxon Emotions,* edited by A. Jorgensen, F. McCormack and J. Wilcox, 109-126. Burlington, VT: Ashgate Publishing Company.

Crozier, W. R. 2014. "Differentiating Shame from Embarrassment." *Emotion Review,* vol. 6, no. 3: 269-276.

De Hooge, I. E., M. Zeelenberg and S. M. Breugelmans. 2010. "Restore and Protect Motivations Following Shame." *Cognition and Emotion,* vol. 24, no. 1: 111-127.

De Mendoza, A. H., J. M. Fernández-Dols, W. G. Parrott and P. Carrera. 2010. "Emotion Terms, Category Structure, and the Problem of Translation: The Case of Shame and Vergüenza." *Cognition and Emotion,* vol. 24, no. 4: 661-680.

Díaz-Vera, J. 2014. “From Cognitive Linguistics to Historical Sociolinguistics: The Evolution of Old English Expressions of Shame and Guilt.” *Cognitive Linguistic Studies*, vol. 1, no. 1: 55-83.

Edelmann, R. J. 1981. “Embarrassment: The State of Research.” *Current Psychological Reviews,* vol. 1, no. 2: 125-137.

Edelstein, R. S. and P. R. Shaver. 2007. “A Cross-cultural Examination of Lexical Studies of Self-conscious Emotions.” In *The Self-conscious Emotions: Theory and Research,* edited by J. L. Tracy, R. W. Robins and J. P. Tangney, 194-208. New York, NY: Guilford Press.

Edwards, D. 1999. “Emotion Discourse.” *Culture and Psychology,* vol. 5, no. 3: 271-291.

Ekman, P. and D. Cordaro. 2011. “What is Meant by Calling Emotions Basic.” *Emotion Review,* vol. 3, no. 4: 364-370.

Elfenbein, H. A., M. Beaupré, M. Lévesque and U. Hess. 2007. “Toward a Dialect Theory: Cultural Differences in the Expression and Recognition of Posed Facial Expressions.” *Emotion,* vol. 7, no. 1: 131-146.

Fabiszak, M. and A. Hebda. 2006. “Emotions of Control in Old English: Shame and Guilt.” *Poetica: An International Journal of Linguistic-Literary Studies,* vol. 66: 1-35.

Fessler, D. M. T. 2004. “Shame in Two Cultures: Implications for Evolutionary Approaches.” *Journal of Cognition and Culture,* vol. 4, no. 2: 207-262.

Fischer, A. H., A. S. R. Manstead and P. M. Rodriguez Mosquera. 1999. “The Role of Honour-Related vs. Individualistic Values in Conceptualising Pride, Shame, and Anger: Spanish and Dutch Cultural Prototypes.” *Cognition and Emotion,* vol. 13, no. 2: 149-179.

Flannery, M. C. 2012. “The Concept of Shame in Late-Medieval English Literature.” *Literature Compass*, vol. 9, no. 2: 166-182.

Fontaine, J. R. J., Y. H. Poortinga, B. Setiadi and S. Markam. 2002. “Cognitive Structure of Emotion Terms in Indonesia and the Netherlands.” *Cognition and Emotion,* vol. 16, no. 1: 61-86.

Gee, J. P. 1999. “Mind and Society: A Response to Derek Edwards' "emotion discourse." *Culture and Psychology,* vol. 5, no. 3: 305-312.

Geertz, C. 1973. *The Interpretation of Cultures: Selected Essays.* New York, NY: Basic books.

Gilbert, P. 1998. “What is Shame? Some Core Issues and Controversies.” In *Shame: Interpersonal Behavior, Psychopathology, and Culture,* edited by P. Gilbert and B. Andrews, pp. 3-38. New York, NY: Oxford University Press.

Keeler, W. 1983. “Shame and Stage Fright in Java.” *Ethos,* vol. 11, no. 3: 152-165.

Keltner, D. and B. N. Buswell. 1996. "Evidence for the Distinctness of Embarrassment, Shame, and Guilt: A Study of Recalled Antecedents and Facial Expressions of Emotion." *Cognition and Emotion,* vol. 10, no. 2: 155-171.

Kemeny, M. E., T. L. Gruenewald and S. S. Dickerson. 2004. "Shame as the Emotional Response to Threat to the Social Self: Implications for Behavior, Physiology, and Health." *Psychological Inquiry,* vol. 15, no. 2: 153-160.

Liem, R. 1997. "Shame and Guilt Among First- and Second-Generation Asian Americans and European Americans." *Journal of Cross-Cultural Psychology,* vol. 28, no. 4: 365-392.

Menon, U. and R. A. Shweder. 2003. "Dominating Kali: Hindu Family Values and Tantric Power." In *Encountering Kali: In the Margins, at the Center, in the West,* edited by R. F. McDermott and J. J. Kripal, 80-99. Berkeley, CA: University of California Press.

Mesquita, B. and Boiger M. 2013. "Emotions in Context: A Socio-dynamic Model of Emotions." *Emotion Review*, vol. 6, no. 4: 298-302.

Niedenthal, P. M., J. P. Tangney and I. Gavanski. 1994. "'If Only I weren't' versus 'If Only I hadn't': Distinguishing Shame and Guilt in Conterfactual Thinking." *Journal of Personality and Social Psychology,* vol. 67, no. 4: 585-595.

Ogarkova, A., C. Soriano and C. Lehr. 2012. "Naming Feeling: Exploring the Equivalence of Emotion Terms in Five European Languages." In *Dynamicity in Emotion Concepts*, edited by P. A. Wilson, 247-333. New York, NY: Peter Lang.

Rosaldo, R. 1980. *Ilongot Headhunting, 1883-1974: A Study in Society and History*. Stanford, CA: Stanford University Press.

Rusch, C. D. 2004. "Cross-cultural Variability of the Semantic Domain of Emotion Terms: An Examination of English Shame and Embarrass with Japanese Hazukashii." *Cross-cultural Research*, vol. 38, no. 3: 236-248.

Russell, J. A. 1991. "Natural Language Concepts of Emotion." In *Perspectives in Personality: Self and Emotion,* edited by D. J. Ozer, J. M. Healy, Jr. and A. J. Stewart, 119-137. London, England: Jessica Kingsley Publishers.

Smith, R. H., J. M. Webster, W. G. Parrott and H. L. Eyre. 2002. "The Role of Public Exposure in Moral and Nonmoral Shame and Guilt." *Journal of Personality and Social Psychology*, vol. 83, no. 1: 138-159.

Tangney, J. P. and R. L. Dearing. 2002. *Shame and Guilt.* New York, NY: Guilford Press.

Tissari, H. 2006. "Conceptualizing shame: Investigating Uses of the English Word Shame, 1418–1991." In *Selected Proceedings of the 2005 Symposium on New Approaches in English Historical Lexis,* Vol 143, 154. *Somerville, MA: Cascadilla Proceedings Project.*

Tracy, J. L. and R. W. Robins. 2004. "Putting the Self into Self-Conscious Emotions: A Theoretical Model. *Psychological Inquiry,* vol. 15, no. 2: 103-125.

9

Two Sides of the Threshold of an Epoch: Nicholas of Cusa and Giordano Bruno

Dolreich Pereira

Abstract

The relationship between Nicholas of Cusa and Giordano Bruno deals with the question about the beginning of modernity. According to Hans Blumenberg in the legitimacy of the Modern Age, they belong to the same historical period, they ask the same kind of questions and they attempt to resolve the same kind of problems. Nonetheless, they seem to give very different answers. Whatever has happened, a threshold has probably been crossed. Is it an invisible limit that has been transgressed or is it rather a rupture of an epoch? With the notion of "threshold", Blumenberg re-envisions the possible coexistence of two different epochs. In this way, Nicholas of Cusa and Giordano Bruno themselves become the symbol of the impossibility of conceiving history in terms of "epochs" and, consequently, of interpreting modernity in this way.

Keywords

Hans Blumenberg, Nicholas of Cusa, Giordano Bruno, epoch, incarnation, modernity.

Introduction

The notion of "succession" seems profoundly alien to the modern consciousness, which implies breaking away from the cycle and tradition. What is a "succession"? The dictionary defines it as a replacement. Here, one can give several meanings: replace identically, replace in a function (shift of a team) or performance of a similar task. The interpretation of this notion involves a legacy of thought of history and temporality. Indeed, to consider the so-called "traditional societies", where a legitimacy based on an "eternal yesterday" prevails (Max Weber), the notion of succession can only have a univocal meaning: to perpetuate the immemorial value of what has always been, ensure the permanence of its contents and keep the inheritance intact.

On the other hand, a certain representation of modernity, whose fundamental claim asserts itself as a tearing away from the past and from tradition, rejects this meaning and gets rid of this notion of "succession", understood as being relevant. The modern age that thinks and wants to be a self-founded project implies indeed a radical break and *de facto* abolishes this idea of succession, namely, replacement through continuity. But it is possible, as Hegel does, to give the notion of "succession" a dialectical meaning. "Succession" can then be understood as the German *Aufhebung*, a dialectical surpassing, a sublation. Dialectical development is conceived in such a way that the experience of the subject or the historical experience progresses only through the work of the negative. The contradictions experienced by humans in the mode of opposition are overcome and outdated; but far from being abolished, they are integrated so that suppressed as logical oppositions, they are retained as stages or terms of development.

This final synthesis of the contradictions thus surmounted could be interpreted as a solution to the antinomy of continuity and discontinuity, of rupture and continuity, and thus of the old and the modern. However, the Hegelian approach is inseparable from a teleology of denouement: the various phases of human experience form a whole and this totality is directed towards an end whose predefined meaning determines the whole process. The meaning is revealed through contradictions finally overcome, and the whole human experience is thus assimilated.

It is on this point that this idea of "succession", linked to the Hegelian perspective, is debatable. It is undermined by contemporary experiences that no longer allow us to think of this recapitulation of knowledge and historical experience. Not only is there in the human experience elements that cannot be assimilated (especially evil), but especially the event as it is unique, unforeseen, creates a disconnect, breaks this idea of an "eternal present". It turns out that total mediation is impossible and that contemporary history no longer allows us to reconcile the presence of the tragic in history and the march towards a fullness or plenitude of the meaning of history.

How then do we deal with the issue of "succession", which, as such, is a fundamental question? One could start with the nodal point which is the ratio of the continuum and the discontinuity, rupture and continuity. How does one think of the new, without falling into the fantasy of the *tabula rasa* or an absolute beginning? How can one, without dissolving it, root novelty in an inheritance?

In *The Legitimacy of the Modern Age*,[1] Hans Blumenberg explores these questions with an original and interesting perspective on the origin of modernity. How can one think of the permanence of a world in which humans can renew their experiences without continuity being that of a substance harbouring an intangible nucleus behind transformations or apparent modifications? In other words, how can one think of the notion of succession in such a way that it is neither coextensive with traditional societies nor irreparably attached to the great processes of dialectical totalization? For Blumenberg, if the world is perennial, it does not resemble that of the piece of wax whose qualitative alterations (by heat or cold) do not affect its being. It is precisely a question of thinking of a mode of continuity that allows us to understand the reality and the depth of the ruptures.

One must not believe that the permanence of the world is ensured by a stock of great questions that would persist in the history of humanity: it would be another form of substantial continuity. Surprising and paradoxical as it may seem to be, continuity is more on the side of crises: namely of those moments when the consciousness of humans encounter problems that they can no longer cope with. There is therefore a history of ideas whose continuity is not ensured by a substantial permanence but by the reinvestment of places that have become empty because the traditional responses have proved ineffective. With regard to this reinvestment, we can talk about succession.

The theme elaborated is a “mortgage of questions in excess of the answers”, and this excess requires one to reoccupy precisely the positions that have become vacant. This problematic of the excess of questions is nothing other than a problematic of historical thresholds; by which we can clearly see that the relationship of continuity and discontinuity is at the centre of the problem of succession. The questions, in fact, do not always precede the answers and at certain moments, which one can without doubt describe as crises, the human consciousness meets problems which it is no longer able to solve. We are thus at the antipodes of Marx’s scheme for which humanity poses to itself only the problems it can solve! On the contrary, because the explanatory power of responses has become inoperative or has been exhausted; that, under the pressure of an excess of questions, something new can happen. One can thus approach the question of the succession of (and in) modernity by removing it from the alternative of the repetition of the same or a beginning *ex nihilo* and *tabula rasa*.

1 Hans Blumenberg, *The Legitimacy of the Modern Age*, trans. Robert M. Wallace, (Cambridge Massachusetts: MIT Press, 1985).

Blumenberg proposes four analyses to show that the transition to modernity is not a guilty uprising but a passage from the transcendent to the immanent. The first part, which is theoretical, bases the principle of the analysis through the historical and theoretical use of the notion of secularization and then illuminating it differently. He names it consistently and opposes the value judgments that up to now, in his view, have delegitimized it.[2] In the second part, it is a question of seeing how theological absolutism occurring at the end of the Middle Ages proceeded to a radicalization of transcendence, leading one to think of an immanent absolute. As a result, in the third part, curiosity - vice and passion for St Augustine and all theologians - becomes a full-fledged activity devoted to penetrating the secrets of nature. It is an activity which, first of all, confronts the forbidden, then reduces its field of action by restricting the borders of the unknowable sacred and, finally, gives to itself a human virtue, the ontological attribute of humanity and the essential quality of human dignity. In the fourth part, Blumenberg looks for traces of the transition to modernity using two examples: that of Nicholas of Cusa,[3] who precedes Copernicus, and that of Giordano Bruno,[4] who comes after him. It is here that the idea of philosophical and epistemological threshold is approached, which

2 In Hans Blumenberg's many inquiries into the history of philosophy, the threshold of the late Middle Ages and the early Renaissance provides a focal point (*Legitimacy of the Modern Age* and *The Genesis of the Copernican World*). Blumenberg rejects the substantialism of historical continuity — fundamental to the so-called "theorem of secularization"; the Modern age in his view represents an independent epoch opposed to Antiquity and the Middle Ages by a rehabilitation of human curiosity in reaction to theological absolutism. Blumenberg targets Karl Löwith's argument that progress is the secularization of Hebrew and Christian beliefs and argues to the contrary that the modern age, including its belief in progress, grew out of a new secular self-affirmation of culture against the Christian tradition.

3 Nikolaus Krebs or Nikolaus von Kues was born in 1401 in Cusa. He studied law and mathematics in Padua, then theology in Cologne. As an archdeacon of Liège, he was a member of the Council of Basel (1437) and was sent to Constantinople to try to realize the union of the Eastern and Western Churches; he returned to Germany as legate of the pope (1440). In 1448, he was raised by Pope Nicholas V to the dignity of Cardinal and in 1450 appointed Bishop of Brixen. He died on August 11, 1464.

4 Giordano Bruno was born in Nola, near Naples, in 1548; he became a Dominican in 1566, but ten years later, in 1576, because of some rather heretical ideas he professed about transubstantiation and the Immaculate Conception, he was forced to separate from his order and leave Italy. In 1579, he went to Geneva (where he could not stay), then to Toulouse and Paris (1581) where he did a course on the logical system of Raymond Lulle. In 1583 he went to England where he taught and wrote some of his best works (*La Cena de Ceneri, De la causa, principio and uno*, and *De l'infinito universo e mondi*). From 1585 to 1592 he traveled to Europe and finally, in 1592, he imprudently accepted an invitation to Venice. Denounced and arrested by the Inquisition he was taken to Rome, where he remained imprisoned for seven years, to be finally excommunicated and burned in the public square on February 17, 1600.

allows one to perceive the way in which modernity is founded. This is why it is necessary to examine the notions of threshold and epoch in Blumenberg, before undertaking an analysis of Nicholas of Cusa and Giordano Bruno.

1. The Concepts of "Epoch" and "Threshold" in Blumenberg

The word "epoch" comes from the Greek word *epokhḗ* meaning "to stop" (*innehalten*). It has a specific meaning in astronomy: the point at which a star seems to halt after reaching the highest point, and generally the stopping point (*angehalten wird*), or position of a star in the zodiac which allows to one calculate the respective position of other stars. It thus refers - and it is in this sense that it is known in philosophical literature – to a historical period forming a whole, a totality that can be considered as having a unity. It is generally given the name of a key person or a central event that thus becomes eponymous of the period under consideration. We owe to Condorcet the introduction of the notion of leap or break of epoch, which is obviously linked to the rupture event that was the French Revolution for its contemporaries. The question that arises is to determine how the concept of epoch makes historical events intelligible.

For Blumenberg, epochs are not only considered as separate entities, but are apprehended according to their points of comparison. Their differences can be evaluated. "The quality of the 'epoch' presents itself to begin with, as the summation of those features that protect the historian from levelling off the course of history into the monotony of what is always the same, and thus from the error of thinking that anything can happen at any time."[5]. The question of the dates of the turning points is thus supplanted by that of the circumstances and features of the formations which are merely contiguous at those points.

Blumenberg uses Heinrich Heine's dictum, but reverses it: "every age is a Sphinx which plunges into the abyss the moment one has solved its riddle."[6] For Blumenberg, "eras exhaust themselves more in the transformation of their certainties and unquestionable axioms into riddles and inconsistencies, than in their solution."[7] The change of epoch as caesura has the function of identity maintenance, in that the changes which it authorizes is only the correlate of the constancy of the requirements which it must fulfil. Thus, after the great conception of each epochal project, the historical process produces a "reoccupation" (*Umbesetzung)* as a restoration of its continuity. For Blumenberg, it is only a heuristic principle that provides a criterion of what can still be understood at all in history when that history experiences profound upheavals, revaluations and reversals that affect the entire structure of life.[8]

5 Hans Blumenberg, *The Legitimacy of the Modern Age*, p.460.

6 Hans Blumenberg, *The Legitimacy of the Modern Age*, p.464.

7 Ibid.

8 Ibid.

The problem of epochs must be approached from the perspective of the question of the possibility of experiencing them. Any change, any transformation from old to new is only accessible to us insofar as it can be related to a constant frame of reference by whose means the requirements can be defined that have to be satisfied in an identical "position". What is new in history cannot be arbitrary in each case, but rather is subject to rigorous expectations and needs. The idea of "reoccupation" (*Umbesetzung*) designates the minimum of identity that it must be possible to discover or at least to search for in even the most agitated movement of history.[9]

What should we expect when the question of a change of epoch arises? All history is made up of changes; however, the 'epoch-making' movements must be assumed to be both copious and rapid but also to move in a single unambiguous direction. Whoever speaks of a change of epoch must prove that something definitive has been decided. It must be shown that something is present that cannot be disposed of again, that an irreversible change has been produced.[10]

Blumenberg believes that there are witnesses to changes of epoch. The turning point of an era is an imperceptible boundary not linked to any date or event. From a different point of view, however, a threshold marks itself off, which can be ascertained as something either not yet arrived at or already crossed. That is why it is necessary to examine at least two witnesses, as will be the case here for the threshold of modernity: Nicholas of Cusa, who stands before this threshold, and Giordano Bruno, who has already left it behind. The Cardinal, who relates to this threshold through his concern for the dangers weighing upon his system and the heretic, who is certain, in his triumphant backward glance, of having crossed it.[11] These inquiries, however, could not constitute a 'historical experience' if they did not meet the criteria of the transcendental principle that the alteration of appearances refers us to what is enduring and which, in the eyes of a historian, requires nothing more than this relative extension. This is why one of the conditions for achieving clarity of relations, and therefore of differences, is the possibility of showing that there exists an identical basic system of elementary assertion needs, notions of the world and the self, on both sides of the threshold.[12]

On one side the Cusan tries to grasp reality in a consistently medieval fashion, and on the other side, the Nolan postulates and celebrates the new reality more than he understands it. They can only be brought into confrontation insofar as they allow us to recognize congruent frameworks for their reality,

9 Ibid.p.466.

10 Ibid. p.468.

11 Ibid. p.469.

12 Ibid.

and where they pose homologous questions to which their answers continue to still relate inspite of their mutual opposition. According to Blumenberg, only a differential analysis can show what separates the positions on either side of the threshold of the epoch and reveal what must have happened in order for them to become incompatible.[13] This is what we are going to do now by studying successively the thought of Nicholas of Cusa and Giordano Bruno.

2. Nicholas of Cusa: The World as God's Self-Restriction

The thought of Nicholas of Cusa, according to Blumenberg, is significant in the context of a crisis-laden self-dissolution of the Middle Ages, related to systematic relationships in the metaphysical triangle: man, God, world. The ambivalence of Christian theology is presupposed: it is both anthropocentric and theocentric.[14] The first motif gives coherence to theology, anthropology and cosmology; the second fragments them. The Cusan tries to unite these two motives in an autonomous construction: he attempts to save the Middle Ages by using the spiritual means of the epoch itself. This attempt is "conservative without having any inclination towards restoration. The Cusan does not want to go back to the level of organization [...] of High Scholasticism."[15] Thus, he wants to go beyond the Aristotelian theory of knowledge (a conceptuality taken from the objects themselves) and contribute to the enrichment of the world as an object, to which he gives a new meaning and a new questioning.

To better understand the task of the Cusan, Blumenberg stresses the relationship of intense proximity between a sharper sense of metaphysical transcendence and sceptical resignation to immanence. Apart from the Bible, the roots of the medieval concept of transcendence come from Neoplatonism: this transcendence could be related to a spatial schema in which Ideas are nothing in this world, but separate and apart from it. On the other hand, the biblical transcendence of God is rather temporal: His presence in the world and to humans is exemplary and comforting - from Creation to interventions in the history of His people. The biblical God hides in transcendence to make faith possible as an attitude of submission and at the same time in fact the condition for the lifting of his self-concealment. This type of transcendence can only be related to a process and not to a static system. This conception of transcendence must be considered as allowing the difference between the cosmic and the non-cosmic: "This relating of theological transcendence to the schema of the finite ancient cosmos signifies the vulnerability of this conception in relation to any possibility of a non-finite cosmology."[16]

13 Ibid. p.470.

14 Ibid. p.484.

15 Ibid. p.485.

16 Ibid. p.486.

It is in this context of a speculative projection that breaks the spell of Scholasticism and its binding force, that we must place the cosmology of Cusan, the richest part of the consequences of his thought. Let's summarize now and try to understand the cosmology of Nicholas of Cusa.

2.1. Extract from *De Docta Ignorantia* of Nicholas of Cusa *(1440)*

The ancients did not attain unto the points already made, for they lacked learned ignorance. It has already become evident to us that the earth is indeed moved, even though we do not perceive this to be the case. For we apprehend motion only through a certain comparison with something fixed. For example, if someone did not know that a body of water was flowing and did not see the shore while he was on a ship in the middle of the water, how would he recognize that the ship was being moved? And because of the fact that it would always seem to each person (whether he were on the earth, the sun, or another star) that he was at the "immovable" centre, so to speak, and that all other things were moved: assuredly, it would always be the case that if he were on the sun, he would fix a set of poles in relation to himself; if on the earth, another set; on the moon, another; on Mars, another; and so on. Hence, the world-machine will have its centre everywhere and its circumference nowhere, so to speak; for God, who is everywhere and nowhere, is its circumference and centre. (…)

Therefore, the shape of the earth is noble and spherical, and the motion of the earth is circular; but there could be a more perfect [shape or motion]. And because in the world there is no maximum or minimum with regard to perfections, motions, and shapes (as is evident from what was just said), it is not true that the earth is the lowliest and the lowest. For although [the earth] seems more central with respect to the world, it is also for this same reason nearer to the pole, as was said. Moreover, the earth is not a proportional part, or an aliquot part, of the world. For since the world does not have either a maximum or a minimum, it also does not have a middle point or aliquot parts, just as a man or an animal does not either. (…)

Therefore, the earth is a noble star which has a light and a heat and an influence that are distinct and different from [that of] all other stars, just as each star differs from each other star with respect to its light, its nature, and its influence. And each star communicates its light and influence to the others, though it does not aim to do so, since all stars gleam and are moved only in order to exist in the best way [they can]; as a consequence thereof a sharing arises (just as light shines of its own nature and not in order that I may see; yet, as a consequence, a sharing occurs when I use light for the purpose of seeing). Similarly, Blessed God created all things in such way that when each thing desires to conserve its own existence as a divine work, it conserves it in communion with others.[17]

The world of the Cusan is no longer the medieval cosmos, but it not yet the infinite universe of the moderns.[18] The universe of Nicholas of Cusa is an expression - or a development (*explicatio*)[19] [*explicare*, unfold, unroll, clarify, develop] - inevitably imperfect and inadequate, of God. It is imperfect because it unfolds in the realm of multitude and separation, which, in God, is present in an indissoluble and intimate unity (*complicatio*) [*complicare*: fold, roll up], a unity that embraces not only different, but even the opposite, qualities and determinations of being. In its turn, every concrete and singular being of the universe represents it – the universe - and also represents God, in its own particular and unique way, different from that of all others, by contracting (*contractio*) the wealth and fullness of the universe according to its own individuality.[20]

What does the term "infinite world" mean for the Cusan? The universe of Nicholas of Cusa is not infinite in the positive sense of the term, but unbound (*interminatum*); thus it is not contained in the outer shell of the celestial spheres, which also means that it is not bound in its constituents, but indeterminate.

---

17 Nicholas of Cusa, *De Docta Ignorantia II,11-12.*

18 The distinction that we currently make between the universe and the world is ignored in the Middle Ages and Nicholas of Cusa is no exception to the rule. Certainly, we can detect a small nuance in his words: the universe (*universum*) refers to all that is not God, that is to say the whole of all that has been created. The world (*mundus*) represents an isolated astronomical system, located under the celestial vault, possibly inhabited. World often seems synonymous with Earth. But, in use, this nuance hardly appears.

19 The *complicatio* or envelopment - literally the folding back - is that by which everything is in God. It is a divine name which means simplicity, equality with oneself. God contains in himself all that can exist. The *explicatio* (literally unfolding), which is translated by development in order to avoid confusion with the process of knowledge, is what God is all about. The universe is the development of God in multiplicity and inequality. To illustrate this pair of concepts, the Cusan frequently gives geometric examples. The point is the *complicatio* of all geometric objects. The point develops in the line. The point and the line develop in the circle. The line develops in the surface, and the surface in the bodies. The Creator has united them to constitute a single point. The enveloping of the universe took place in this unique point. We find the same kind of explanation with number, borrowed from Plotinus' theory: number is the principle according to which being is deployed in beings. There is a progression of numbers in beings. The development relationship is not a relation of everything to parts, because then there would simply be a subdivision of the whole according to parts. It is rather a causal relationship, each part being marked by the cause and in turn becoming the principle of other developments. The principle is not only a unit; it is a generative power. *See* Nicholas of Cusa, *Complementum Theologicum, IX.*

20 Alexander Koyre, *From the Closed World to the Infinite Universe*, (Baltimore: The John Hopkins Press, 1957), pp. 8-9.

Hence the use of *Docte Ignorance* (1440) as a means of transcending the limits of our rational knowledge.

A pure and simple "infinite" is an absolute ontological necessity, even if the intelligence cannot represent such a reality. Infinity is the one and only absolute eternity. There is no proportion of infinity to finite. Consequently, infinity is incomprehensible to human thought; it is unknown. "Compared with the infinite there is nothing that is greater or smaller than anything else. The absolute, infinite maximum does not, any more than the absolute, infinite minimum, belong to the series of the great and small. They are outside it, and therefore, as Nicholas of Cusa boldly concludes, they coincide."[21]

2.2. The Coincidence of Opposites *(oppositorum coincidentia)*

Nicholas of Cusa demonstrates the validity of his principle of coinciding the opposites to infinity by the infinitization of geometric figures. The first example, the most famous, is that of the rectification of the circumference of the infinite circle. He first posits a general proposition: if there was an infinite line, it would be a straight line, it would be a triangle, it would be a circle and it would be a sphere. Then he "demonstrates" each proposal.

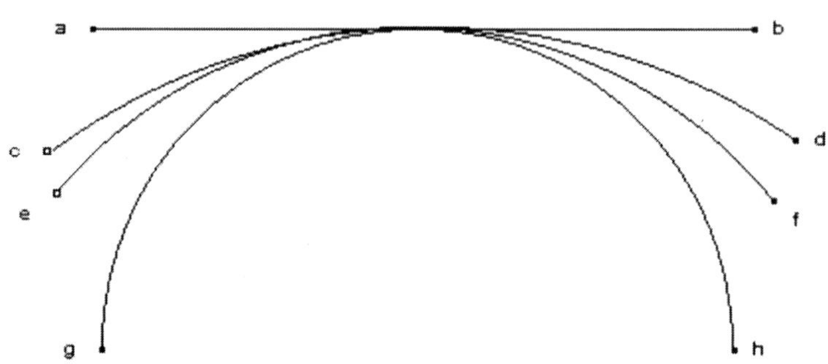

In this figure, an infinite line is a straight line: The larger a circle, the less curved its circumference, and the more it is straight. Conclusion: the maximum curvature of a line is straight. Thus the centre of the world coincides with the circumference. For Nicholas of Cusa, it is a metaphysical centre and not physical, and therefore does not belong to the world. This centre of the world, which is the same as its circumference, that is to say, beginning and end, foundation and limit, the place which contains it, is nothing but the Absolute Being or God.[22]

21 Alexander Koyre, *From the Closed World to the Infinite Universe*, pp.9-10.

22 Ibid. p.11. The "coincidence of opposites" is first an ontological principle. It is the idea that all kinds of multiplicity in the finite world become one in the infinite realm of God. For

As a result, the stars themselves are not fixed. Nothing in this world can be absolutely and completely at rest. Nicholas of Cusa goes even further by drawing as a conclusion from the relativity of the perception of space and movement (nowhere is there any precise circular orb nor rigorously uniform motion): just as the image of the world formed by a certain observer is determined by the place it occupies in the Universe, and as none of these places can claim an absolutely privileged value, we must admit the possibility of the existence of different and equivalent images of the world, the relative character of each of them, and the ultimate impossibility of forming an objective and valid representation of the Universe.

This leads to another aspect of Cusan's cosmology, historically the most important perhaps: the rejection of the hierarchical structure of the Universe and, in particular, its negation of the particularly low and despicable position assigned to the Earth by traditional cosmology, at the same time as its central position. Indeed, in the infinitely rich, diverse and organically bound together universe of the Cusan, there is no centre or perfection which consigns the rest of the universe to a subordinate role. The ontological structure of the world everywhere is expressed in the same temporal manner, that is to say, unstable and changing, and does not have the immutable and eternal perfection of the Creator.

Faithful to the Platonic tradition, Nicholas of Cusa distinguishes the infinite from the creative principle, God, who gives existence to the finite. It is the infinite that gives and the infinity of the created universe which

---

example, if the number of sides of a polygon are increased from a square to a pentagon, to a hexagon, and so on, the polygon will become closer to a circle. If the number of sides are extended to infinite, the polygon coincides with a circle. Take another example: The center of a circle and its circumference are opposites, but if the radius of the circle is made infinitely small, the center and the circumference coincide. A curve and a straight line are opposites, but if the radius of a circle is made infinitely long, its curved circumference coincides with a straight line. Through these examples, Nicholas tried to explain the idea that multiplicity and the many of this finite world are one in the infinite world of God. To put the same idea in a different way, multiplicity and the many in this world are derived from the original oneness of God. This means that the world is enveloped in God, meaning that the finite is potentially in the infinite; and the infinite is in the finite. They are within each other. Every part of the world reflects God, and the totality of the world and numerous individuals exist in harmony. A human being reflects the cosmos through cognition which is divided into three stages: Senses; conceptual understanding; and intellectual intuition, which is mystical unity with God. The individual is thus a microcosm filled with creativity and freedom, and the universe is a macrocosm. Diverse individual beings exist in harmony and unity. Since God resides in every individual being in the cosmos, there is no fixed center of the cosmos. This idea entailed the denial of geocentricism, which made the earth the center of the universe. In his view of the universe, the surrounding universe and its center are one and coincide. His cosmology was also built upon the idea of the "coincidence of opposites."

receives this existence, hence, it is an indefinite or private infinity. This allows Blumenberg to qualify the Cusan's thought of self-restraint of God. The Cusan, however, cannot cross the threshold he seems to have noticed, and he turns to the Aristotelian vocabulary: the infinity of the universe is an infinity of power, by default, whereas the infinity of God is an infinity of action. Therefore, even though in relation to the infinite power of God, which has no limit, the universe may be greater, however, because of the possibility of being or matter is not, in act, extensible to infinity, the universe cannot be greater. The universe as a divine work and as a material composite cannot be greater than God is. It is a maximum, but it is not an absolute maximum. It is only a relative maximum, insofar as it can "potentially" further increase or decrease. The universe cannot be greater than the infinite power of God. Therefore, although the same adjective "infinite" is attributed to both God and the universe, it is not the *same* infinity. God, by his power, could make the universe greater than it is. But the universe, by its material nature, could not be greater than it is. God made the universe as big as it could be. It's a reduced infinity. It is the best that could be depending on its conditions of nature. It is therefore prudent to moderate the enthusiasm of those who would make the Cusan a forerunner of the modern infinite universe.

However, Nicholas of Cusa opens the door to the modern formulation of the question of the link between theology and cosmology in the famous formula on the infinite sphere, inspired by the second sentence of the Hermetic *Book of the XXIV philosophers*: "God is an infinite sphere whose centre is everywhere and whose circumference is nowhere."[23] Nicholas of Cusa is the first to transfer this image of God to the universe: If we read the complete formula, the close link between the world and God is obvious. It is more a theological affirmation than a cosmological assertion. If the world is infinite, it is because God is infinite.

For Blumenberg, if the concept of infinity proves to be the means of representation of the *docta ignorantia* for transcendence, then there are necessary consequences for cosmology and anthropology. The world is not only the appearance of the invisible God, but God is the invisibility of the visible itself: "*quid est mundus nisi invisibilis dei apparitio, quid deus nisi visibilium*

---

23 "*Deus est sphaera infinita cuius centrum est ubique, circumferentia nusquam.*" The *Book of the Twenty-Four Philosophers* is an influential Latin text that began circulating in the twelfth century, but its origins are unknown. Some believe that it derives from a Greek original circulating in Alexandria in the fourth or fifth century AD and transmitted to the Latin West via an Arabic intermediary. A minority opinion holds that the text is a fragment of Aristotle's lost *On Philosophy*, but most scholars believe it to be a product of the Middle Ages.

invisibilitas?".[24] "Such symmetry, derived once again from the Neoplatonic model, means not only that the assertions metaphysical and mystical theology offer points of departure for speculation about the world and man, but also that the propositions of the teaching of faith can provide the considerations that reach downward from the realm of theology."[25]

Did Nicholas of Cusa actually see the physical world as infinite? Does he not speak rather of a certain idea of the world, of a way of representing it in the hands of God? With Nicholas of Cusa, the cosmos begins to crack, but it is only about a *desire* for infinity, unrelated to external experience. This is why, facing the infinite, his serenity contrasts sharply with Blaise Pascal's subsequent anguish. Some even speak of "jubilation" to the extent that the knowledge of the infinite is a path to God. But it is not surprising to see this contrast. The Pascalian world is silent; it is the world of modern science from which God has withdrawn. While the world of Cusan is infinite without being scary; it is filled with the reassuring presence of God. For Nicholas of Cusa, the infinite is the mark of the fullness of being and everything is perfectly ordered.

2.3. Critique by Jean Wenck

We cannot really appreciate the contribution of Nicholas of Cusa without mentioning the hostile reaction of scholasticism in the person of Jean Wenck de Herrenberg, professor of theology at the University of Heidelberg. Going beyond the reproaches of heresy - Nicholas of Cusa seems to have abolished the difference between God and the world and debased the event of the Incarnation - the bottom of the polemic launched by Wenck in the *De Ignota Litteratura* relates to the categories of Aristotelian thought. In fact, by his coincidence of opposites, Nicholas of Cusa completely questions the distinction between genres and species and the principle of non-contradiction. He undermines the principles of rational knowledge as defined by Scholastic tradition. Even if the protagonists did not have a lucid awareness of this issue, it is none the less true that the formulas of Nicholas of Cusa, his new logic, his effort to overcome the principle of non-contradiction had something to frighten his contemporaries. Attempting to square the circle is not only a beautiful problem of geometry but also a challenge to the distinction of genres and species. Whether a circumference of an infinite circle becomes a straight line or a regular polygon of infinite number of sides becomes a circle, is in any case an unnatural production, a transgression of the barrier that separates the species. The controversy with Wenck allows us to measure the importance of

24 "What is the world, if not an appearance of the invisible god; and what is god if not the invisibility of visible things?" Nicholas of Cusa, *De Possest*.

25 Hans Blumenberg, *The Legitimacy of the Modern Age*, p.501

the work of Nicholas of Cusa: it is the rupture that begins to operate on the dominant thought in the Late Middle Ages.

Nicholas of Cusa experienced the internal crises of Christianity very closely. He was able to witness the internal decomposition of the medieval system, and therefore, he could not escape the worry of an end of time. He is trying to save the theological representation of the world. He tries with the intellectual tools of his time to prop up a system which maintains the place of God at the centre of the world. But it is too late. But at the very heart of his endeavour, he gives modernity its first sketches of its main themes.

3. Giordano Bruno: the World as God's Self-Exhaustion

A century later, Giordano Bruno read and pondered *Docte Ignorance*, citing and commenting on whole passages. His appreciation of the Cusan is tantamount to a eulogy. He continues to build on the works of Nicholas of Cusa only to put forward proposals far more risky than those of the Cusan. According to him, if Nicholas of Cusa did not go further in his affirmations, it is because he was prevented from it by his ecclesiastical function. Bruno thinks he could have come closer to the truth:

> Great was the knowledge of this honest Cusan, and great his understanding; he is indeed one of the most remarkably talented men who has lived on this earth. Nevertheless, as to the apprehension of the truth, he was a swimmer struggling with tempestuous waves, sometimes emerging, sometimes sinking, because he did not see continuously, openly and clearly the light, and did not swim in stillness, but always intermittently.[26]

Bruno makes abundant use of the principle of the coincidence of opposites, but while this principle allows him to bypass Aristotelian logic, it does not allow him in reality to pass from one opposite to another. This is why he must go beyond Cusan metaphysics by a passage from the limits of the universe to the divine. The God of Nicholas of Cusa remains the transcendent God of the Church, while the God of Giordano Bruno becomes immanent; God is in every point of the universe. The few traces of transcendentalism that remain in his texts come from the Neoplatonic vocabulary borrowed from Nicholas of Cusa. He also borrows from him other notions such as the link, as in the formula on the infinite sphere, but he goes further in his cosmological audacities: he makes his universe an infinite positive (and not private, as did Nicholas of Cusa). Nicholas of Cusa maintained that no fixed and constant point allows an exact observation of movements in space, but he did not draw from this a purely relativistic conception of space, as Bruno does. Finally, if Bruno was condemned and Nicholas of Cusa acclaimed, it is not only due to the fact that in the meantime the Counter-Reformation took place, but also

26 Giordano Bruno, *On the Infinite Universe and Worlds*, Third Dialogue, Philotheo, 1584.

because Bruno went much further than the Cusan in supporting theses that threatened the established order.

Giordano Bruno was sentenced to death as an "unrepentant, obstinate and obstinate heretic". Blumenberg begins the last chapter of his book by examining the reason why Bruno was executed: he did not die as a doubter or as a heretic with dogmatic deviations, but for an opposition directed against the very centre and substance of Christianity as the organizing system of the world.[27] At this point, we need to clarify the cosmological content of Giordano Bruno's thought. He re-visioned in a different way the Universe, Nature, God, Being and substance, knowledge etc. he had no pretensions about being enlightened, an occultist, a scholar or a politician; he always presented himself as a philosopher. In spite of certain forms of esotericism, he remained very attached to rationality in his search for a philosophy of the infinite.

3.1. The intuition of the infinity of the universe

The Nolan refuses to stick only to the evidence of the senses to establish the truth. Our senses are limited. Our vision of distant objects is weak. We must therefore accept sensory information with caution and provided that it does not contradict our reason. It is the intellect that must judge the validity of sensory data. The world appears to us as enclosed in a sphere simply because we project on it the finitude of our own senses. Aristotelian finitism proceeds from this perceptive illusion.

Like Copernicus, Bruno admits to the movement of the Earth. However, he questions the existence of the eighth sphere, that of fixed stars. With Bruno, the finite sky disappears and infinite space succeeds it. How does one explain the cause of movement of innumerable worlds around their respective suns? Rejecting all external causality, Bruno invokes the action of internal principles, i.e. the motor souls inherent in the worlds. The driving soul is at the same time a kind of intellect and a spontaneous vital principle, the "natural and living tendency of each being to perpetuate itself in being and to regenerate itself".

3.2. From the infinity of the universe to the infinity of God

Giordano Bruno adopts the heliocentric image of the world of Copernicus,[28] but, abandons the fixed spheres which, according to his hypotheses, limit the

27 Hans Blumenberg, *The Legitimacy of the Modern Age*, p.549.

28

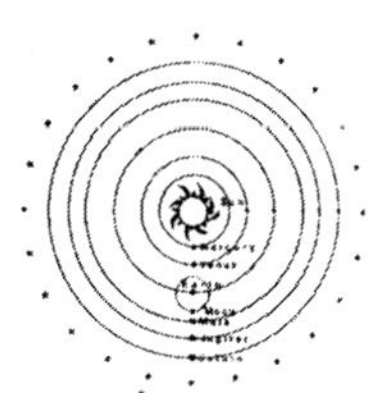

The Universe of Copernicus.

universe. He deduces the idea of an infinite plurality of worlds.[29] The Universe would consist of an infinite number of other earth-like worlds that could be populated like it. The reason invoked by Bruno is that the infinite God could only create something infinite. Like the Cusan, he links the cosmological motif to the theological motif:

> As soon as we have recognized that the apparent world-motion is caused by the real diurnal motion of our earth (which happens similarly to other similar stars), no argument will constrain us to accept the vulgar opinion that the stars are equidistant from us, that they are as though nailed and fixed in an eighth sphere; and no persuasion will hinder us from knowing that the differences are innumerable in the distances from us of these innumerable stars. We shall understand that the orbs and spheres of the universe are not disposed one beyond another, each smaller unit being contained within a greater -- as, for example, the layers of an onion. But throughout the ethereal field, heat and cold, diffused from the bodies wherein they predominate, gradually mingle and temper one another to varied degree, so as to become the proximate origin of the innumerable forms and species of being.[30]
>
> Why should we or could we imagine that divine power were otiose? Divine goodness can indeed be communicated to infinite things and can be infinitely diffused; why then should we wish to assert that it would choose to be scarce and to reduce itself to naught -- for every finite thing is as naught in relation to the infinite? Why do you desire that centre of divinity which can (if one may so express it) extend infinitely to an infinite sphere, why do you desire that it should remain grudgingly sterile rather than extend itself, as a father, fecund, ornate and beautiful? Why should you prefer that it should be less or indeed by no means communicated, rather than that it should fulfil the scheme of its glorious power and being? Why should infinite amplitude be frustrated, the possibility of an infinity of worlds be defrauded? Why should be prejudiced the excellence of

29

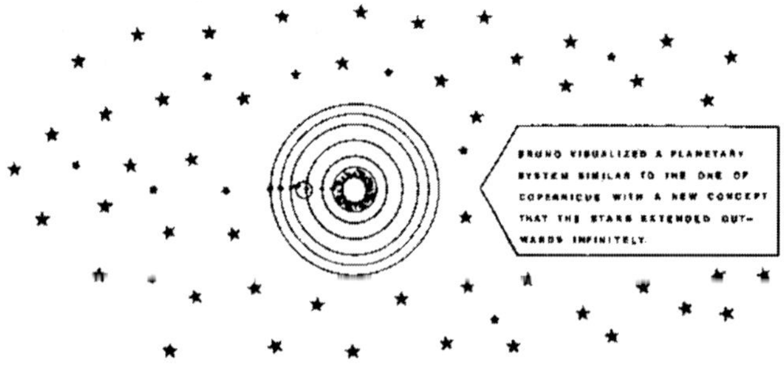

30 Giordano Bruno, *On the Infinite Universe and Worlds*, Fourth Dialogue, Philotheo, 1584.

> the divine image which ought rather to glow in an unrestricted mirror, infinite, immense, according to the law of its being? Why must we affirm this opinion which bear with it so many inconveniences and penalties and, without in any way fostering law, religions, faith or morality, destroys so many philosophical principles? Why wouldst thou that God should in power, in act and in effect (which in him are identical) be determined as the limit of the convexity of a sphere, rather than that he should be as we may say the undetermined limit of the boundless?[31]

Aristotelian theologians defended the finiteness of the world by pointing to the difference of nature between creation and its creator: creation could not be infinite as its creator. Bruno countered this argument by showing that limiting of creation can be considered as an offense against God, as a limit against his omnipotence and infinite goodness. The real contradiction would be that an infinite God would have created only a finite universe. For Bruno, the infinity of God necessarily implies the infinity of the universe. There must be a correspondence between God and his creation, not in nature, certainly, but in greatness. Otherwise, one would arrive at the image of a mean God, holding on to his power and goodness to create only what is limited. The crossing of what was taken as the horizon in previous perceptions of the Universe, shows that we can always cross a limit, since there is always something else behind the limit (starting with what supports it). By this, Giordano Bruno has the intuition - but not yet the demonstration - of an infinite universe in action. The infinity of the universe was the second charge of his trial.

Thus there is presence of the divine in all forms of nature. God is not out of the world, but in it. The cause acting within nature is the soul of the world. The spirit that comes from it is the inner artist who shapes matter from the inside to the outer diversity of nature. But matter is not modelled on the shape of the outside; its contours are in itself and unfold outwards. Matter and all parts of the world are penetrated by the spirit and therefore animated. At the end of his work, Bruno develops the idea that the monads, as the smallest and simplest units, contain the being of things and are the elements of nature.

3.3. Theological Consequences

The divine infinity and infinity of the Universe are not of the same order, as this formula, which is frequent in many of Bruno's texts, states: "God is the whole, comprehensive and complete totality of the infinite, but the universe is the explicit though not the all-comprehensive totality".[32] The Universe is "an infinite sphere whose centre is everywhere and whose circumference nowhere", according to the formula taken from Nicholas of Cusa. Each finite

---

31 Giordano Bruno, *On the Infinite Universe and Worlds*, First Dialogue, Philotheo, 1584.

32 Giordano Bruno, *On the Infinite Universe and Worlds*, First Dialogue, Philotheo, 1584.

world, each atom, each individual expresses respectively one of the infinite aspects of the infinite being; each one is unable to exhaust by itself the infinite variety of the totality of the being.

It is different with God. "And I say that God is all-comprehensive infinity because the whole of him pervades the whole world and every part thereof comprehensively and to infinity. That is unlike the infinity of the universe which is comprehensively in the whole but not comprehensively in those parts which we can distinguish within the whole (if indeed we can use the name parts, since they appertain to an infinite whole)."[33]

Giordano Bruno adopts a resolutely immanent vision of God and vehemently rejects the Creator- creature dualism, where God intervenes to act *from outside* on the Universe: "God is not an external intelligence making the universe spin around in a circular motion; he must be more dignified than to be the internal principle of movement." Giordano Bruno rejects the idea of a primary external motor (*moto immobilis*), whose existence had been posited by Aristotle and some medieval scholastics. Moreover, there is no trace of a personal God having freely created the Universe *ex nihilo*. Not unlike the Aristotelian theologians, the God of Bruno is that of the biblical revelation. He is a God of the philosopher, characterized by his unity and total immanence within the infinite universe: "God is infinite in the infinite, everywhere in all things, neither above nor outside but totally intimate to all things". "There is no craftsman who presides from above, and from the outside who commands and shapes everything."

In reality, Divine Unity shapes the Universe from within. For Bruno, the fiction of divine transcendence stems from a conception placing the craftsman outside of matter that is foreign to him and on which he imposes his art. But nothing can be external to the infinite universe, since its very infinity precisely implies that it has no other. Bruno simply wants to suggest that it is God who revives natural beings from within and connects them in a common order of co-belonging.

The post-Copernican universe no longer holds ready any designated location or distinct substratum for the divine deed of salvation. In this universe, the Divinity has already fully spent Himself in the Creation. Since He did not and could not hold anything back regarding the infinity of the worlds, He was left with nothing to make up in relation to any creature in this world.[34] Hence the expression "self-exhaustion of God". If, for the Nolan, the infinite cosmos is said to represent the incarnation of the deity, it remains impossible to name it as a particular person (the second Person of the Holy Trinity) of this world. Thus, the satire on the

33 Ibid.

34 Cf. Hans Blumenberg, *The Legitimacy of the Modern Age*, p.551.

gods which he writes in the *Expulsion of the Triumphant Beast* (*Spaccia de la bestia trionfante*) implicitly criticizes the fundamental theological representations of Christianity itself. Let us quote, for example, the passage where the expulsion of the Centaur Cheiron, whose double nature is mockingly defined in the theological language of the hypostatic union: "*in cui una persona è fatta di due nature, e due sustanze concorreno in una ipostatica unione*".[35]

To understand Bruno well, everything depends on grasping what is irresistible in his rejection of the theological idea of the union of two natures, of the identity of the divine person in its union with humanity. The incarnation becomes for him the symbol of a theological model: "a system of extraordinary actions conditions, preferences and acts of grace, which is superimposed on a reality that seems to be established as 'order,' as 'nature,' solely to make the extraordinary, the supernatural, definable."[36]

On the other hand, Bruno rejects theocentric and anthropocentric positions by favouring a new metaphysics in which "Divinity bears innumerable names for a transcendent substance that stands behind everything and is no longer the "person" who could choose one nature from the abundance of forms of his creation for his Incarnation, but is rather the divinity that "appears" in all forms, without simply becoming one of them and definitively entering into it."[37]

One can recall the problem with which the Cusan struggled and with which any confrontation with the crisis of the Middle Ages was to have to dealt with: the stabilization of the world in the face of its being put to question by theological absolutism. This is no longer addressed by the metaphorical relationship but rather by means of the congruence between divinity and worldliness. The world as the Creation absolutely "exhausts" the possibilities of the ground of being. It is, therefore, contradictory to think that God could still have realized a new possibility, after Creation and into it, even against it. "If the world as such already credibly represents God's self-extravagance, the He cannot have made Himself once again into the historical fact of an Incarnation in it."[38] Bruno is opposed to the metaphor that represents God as having given many of his treasures in creating the world, but not all.

At the point where the Cusan had stopped on an arbitrary and doubtful construction, Bruno took and was able to take, the decisive step, because in

35 In which one person is made of two natures, and two substances concur in one hypostatic union.

36 Hans Blumenberg, *The Legitimacy of the Modern Age*, p.561.

37 Ibid.

38 Ibid.

the meantime, there had been Copernicus (1473-1543). Copernicus offered the point of departure from which to introduce the infinity of the universe not just as a mere speculative extravagance, but rather by letting the consequence of a scientific insight unfold on the basis of a metaphysical need that had become historically necessary. "Bruno shows the age that the new perspective of the (optically unexpected) immeasurability of the heavens, which followed from the surrender of geocentricism, did not need to be translated into disappointment, into the diminution and annihilation of man with respect to the world. Instead, this could be the price paid for overcoming the distressing consciousness of contingency that man had experienced in himself and the world and that was now removed by a newly characterised world."[39]

The transfer of infinity from the divinity to the universe is not the transformation of a historical doctrine, but the opposition to the consequence of the notion of the *potentia absoluta* that the Middle Ages had elaborated in a more radical way. Blumenberg indicates the precise point where the Nolan goes beyond the Cusan. In *Docta ignorantia* II, 2, Nicholas of Cusa had said that the infinite form is only taken up in a finite manner, so that everything created is a finite infinity or a created God, and consequently could be more perfect than it is, and that with the fiat of Creation, it was only because a God could not come into being that something came into being that could become similar to God: "This sentence designates the limit that is set to the penetration of the omnipotence speculations of theistic religions and their scholasticisms. That limit is in the rejection, which cannot be based on a logical contradiction, of the possibility that omnipotence could become absolute precisely by being able to posit its equivalent, by reproducing itself."[40]

Confronted with the theological consequences of his thought, Bruno insists that his point of departure was only philosophical and unrelated to faith. He did not plan to attack religion but to exalt philosophy. His specific philosophical conception sees the infinity of the universe as the effect of infinite divine power, which he explicitly justifies by the fact that he would have regarded the finite world as unworthy to be the product of divine goodness and power.[41] This infinity relates to the magnitude of the universe and the number of worlds. The earth would be only one star among others. There would be a universal providence, as an omnipresent world soul or nature, but also explicitly as God's essential omnipresence in

39 Ibid. p562.

40 Ibid. p.563.

41 Ibid. p.563.

an inexplicable manner.[42] In evoking the double infinity, Bruno recognized that it could indirectly affect the truth according to faith. But, he did not help his inquisitors understand the connection between this position and his attacks on theology. He was not able to understand the Incarnation with the concepts of philosophy, he doubted and wavered in his faith. A question arises: could it be that Bruno did not know how to explain the decisive relationship between his infinite cosmology and his theological ideas? To be specific, did he not see that his infinite universe had taken precisely the place occupied in theology by the intratrinitarian generation of the second Person? Where Creation exhausts the productive power of God, there can be no place for the Trinitarian process. But, and this is the next step, "if the absolute self-realization of divine omnipotence is the 'world' and not a 'person,' then the character of personhood must also be denied to the ground that reproduces itself."[43] Bruno therefore rejects the concept of "person" as this concept was introduced by Augustine and remained incomprehensible to him. Subsequently, he will declare that the predicate 'person' appeared to him incompatible with divinity.

If Bruno emphasises the fact that he helped to establish the truth of the Copernican system, he did not die for this truth. It obviously had an important function in his mind, but only that of a key that opened access to a space of speculation. Infinity, with its characterization as the *coincidentia oppositurum*, engulfs the finite realities and problems: "Even if an individual world moves in relation to and around another, as the earth does in relation to and around the sun, yet nevertheless no world moves in relation to the universe itself or around it, but only within it."[44]

This is how the Copernican truth gives way to this superior truth which it itself had first made possible. This indifference of systems encompasses all finite beings and their proportions to one another, their places in the hierarchical "scholastic" order and also concerns man and his idea of a God who was supposed to have irrevocably committed himself in human nature, as his favourite creature: "You come no nearer to commensurability, likeness, union and identity with the infinite by being a man than by being an ant, or by being a star than by being a man, for you get no nearer to that infinite being by being the sun or the moon than by being a man, or an ant. This is because, in the infinite, there is no difference between those things."[45]

42 Ibid. p.564.

43 Ibid. p.564.

44 Giordano Bruno, *Concerning the Cause, Principle and One*, V. p.91

45 Giordano Bruno, *Concerning the Cause, Principle and One*, V. p.88.

During his trial,[46] Bruno appealed to the principle of the indifference of the finite with respect to the infinite: "*finiti ad infinitum nulla proportion*".[47] Without naming him, he refers to Nicholas of Cusa who had used this proposition to demonstrate the necessity of the Incarnation for the salvation in a world which, by itself and its nature, could have no meaning for an absolute and infinite being. It is only because God Himself wanted to become part of this world, that the world received the quality that gave it divine interest. "*Verbum non propter carnem factum is caro, sed propter seipsum*",[48] this basic formula is the foundation on which Christology transforms the divine self-interest into an interest in the world.[49]

Bruno's argument is the opposite. From his point of view, the infinity of the divine nature and the finitude of human nature in the world exclude a real relation or even a union of two natures of the type understood in traditional Christology. "The impossibility of a particular being in the world having a privileged status leaves only a choice between, on the one hand, the reformation of the Cusan's theory of mediation into a pure principle of transcendence, according to which an involvement in the world could neither be credited nor imputed to the Divinity, and on the other hand, the principle of consistent immanence, according to which the Divinity is already all in all in the same manner forever and by nature."[50] As a result of thinking of absolute power rigorously to the end, Bruno understood the world as the reproduction of divinity. The development of the principle of immanence that flows from this presupposition is neither pantheistic nor polytheistic, because Creation occupies exactly the systematic position that belonged to the 'only-begotten Son' in the theological tradition.[51]

Thus this comparative study of Nicholas of Cusa and Giordano Bruno, of the before and after allows us to better perceive the notion of threshold used by Blumenberg.

Conclusion: The Cusan and the Nolan on Either Sides of the Historical Threshold

"Man does indeed make history, but he does not make epochs."[52] An epoch is the sum total of all interferences between actions and what they make. What is grasped in the patterns of history is more the outcomes than the agents.

46 Specifically during the hearing of 3 June 1592.

47 "There is no proportion between the finite and the infinite.

48 "The Word did not become flesh for the sake of flesh, but for its own sake."

49 Cf. Hans Blumenberg, *The Legitimacy of the Modern Age*, p.575.

50 Ibid. p.575-76.

51 Ibid. p.576.

52 Ibid. p.478.

In this light, Blumenberg argues that neither Nicholas of Cusa nor Giordano Bruno 'made an epoch'. Neither is a founder of an era. However, both are distinguished by their relation to the epochal threshold. This relationship cannot be understood with them or through them but through their interpolation. The method chosen, therefore, was to confront their philosophical systems and to play off one against another. If we put the Cusan and the Nolan side by side, it is obvious that they could not have stood side by side in reality: "The impossibility of substituting one system for the other is due to their respective relations to the epochal threshold."[53]

Their most significant difference lies in their position on issues related to the Copernican revolution: "The pre-Copernican character of Nicholas of Cusa is just as specific to his thought system, insofar as it is 'not yet' modern, as is the post-Copernican character of Giordano Bruno, insofar as it is not a mere assent to an astronomical theory but rather an elevation of it into the guiding principle of cosmological and anthropological metaphysics."[54] The Copernican reform is a systematic point of reference for both systems of thought that at the same time shows that their respective historical places cannot be confused or exchanged.

The Cusan did not anticipate the Copernican turning point as a theoretical event; he did not even foresee it. But he was sensitive enough to consider presuppositions that, while they did not make a change like the Copernican one a historical necessity, could define the meaning (for man's understanding of himself and the world) of its entry into history.

Not wanting to betray the intention of Nicholas of Cusa, we could say that he sought to support the intellectual position, the spiritual substance by and for which he lived, with flexibility so as to deal with what had not been foreseen and could not be foreseen in such an alteration to how the world was viewed.

For the Nolan, the Copernican reform has taken place and has become an unmistakable truth. However, it is not yet really accessible to all and remains trapped in the specialized language of mathematical astronomy with which the common man of that time was certainly uncomfortable; it only masked the need to radically reform the foundation of man's existence and destroying the system in which lay their security.

Both the Cusan and the Nolan have unexpressed motives. "They differ in the degree not to which thoughts were unspoken but to which they could not be spoken, or still more clearly, in their relations to the possible ways of 'putting something into words'."[55] The thing was still possible for the one what would

53 Ibid. p.479.

54 Ibid.

55 Ibid. p.480.

become unachievable for the other: "the compatibility of contradictions as a world principle, represented in the saving datum of the Incarnation, was not a matter of differing degrees of readiness for faith or of differing talents for fate but of what still or was no longer historically possible."[56]

This can be seen in the confrontation between the Nolan and the Cusan. The universe of Giordano Bruno, a necessary and unrestricted realization of the *potentia absoluta* of God the Creator, occupies the space, that was for the Cusan, the intratrinitarian begetting of a divine person, the creation of the world and the linking of both these two in the Incarnation of the Son of God. Their position on the Incarnation enlightens us on the critical difference between the two systems.

For Nicholas of Cusa, the Incarnation of the Word complemented and perfected creation (*complementum et quies*).[57] It is only through this self-involvement of the divine in creation is the full power of God actualized. The duality of generation and creation is integrated into the unity of God's self-expression. But this presupposes that time, by which "an interval is laid between the Creation and the Incarnation in the midst of history, is a purely human measure of successiveness, which is imposed on the inner and essential unity of the divine action."[58] This view is in accordance with the Cusan's theory of time as a category produced by the human spirit.

For Blumenberg, it is only in the temporal form of human discourse that it is permissible and necessary to say that Creation was imperfect and incomplete, and contained a reserve of something that was possible for the Divinity before it received its Christological complement. Nicholas of Cusa, giving this connection a finalist interpretation, used it to demonstrate the singularity of the created world, for the uniqueness of the Son of God presupposed the uniqueness of the world into which he was to enter and whose completion he was to achieve: "*Et ipse quia unus, is unus mundus.*"[59] Moreover, in essence, the constitution of this world was defined by the complement which it was to receive and by which it escaped the contingency. The reserve for perfection determined just what would be capable of this perfection: "*et propter ipsum omnia, quae in mundo sunt, id sunt quod sunt*".[60]

It is precisely this framework that produces the condition that had to be fulfilled by Bruno's cosmological speculations. Inasmuch as for him, creation and generation lose their differentiation and creation is already the totality of what could and had to come forth from the realization of the *potentia absoluta*,

56 Ibid.

57 Nicholas of Cusa, *Dies sanctificatus*.

58 Hans Blumenberg, *The Legitimacy of the Modern Age*, p.565.

59 And itself, because it is unique, is a sole world.

60 "And on account of this, everything that is in the world is what it is."

not only is the Christological complement no longer necessary but it also loses its normative finality for the uniqueness of the world. "The infinite worlds fill the scope that had been left open by discontinuing the restriction teleological intention of the Cusan's speculation, a scope in which the unreserved logic of absolute omnipotence's complete self-exhaustion could now be discharged as the double infinity of the created world."[61]

The universe of the Cusan was the result of the *potentia absoluta* only to the extent that the power imposed on itself ritual of action of a *potentia ordinata*. Only then can one understand that the power posed conditions for man's salvation which made up an agenda separate from that of rational morality.[62] Despite the efforts he made to eliminate the voluntarist element of his metaphysics, the Cusan only managed to shift it further back:

> For the world is not so perfectly created that in creating it God did all that He was able to do, even though the world was created to be as perfect as it could be made to be. Yet, the world was created as perfect as it could be. [...] But that-which-was-made's possibility-of-being-made is not the Omnipotent God's absolute power-to make.[63]

Blumenberg remarks that "this is a desperate attempt to remove the contingency of the world as a scandal to rationality without abandoning God's personhood. The strained character of this attempt indicates the path that leads – instead of to the solution of the problem, which appears impossible - to its elimination".[64]

It is not enough, however, to say that the Nolan philosophized further within the horizon of known questions and only tried to bring new answers. On the contrary, he pressed forward to questioning the questions themselves, that is, as far as to the possibility of their de-legitimization. For example, Bruno notes, rather naively, that the concept of person was invented by Augustine and therefore would find no legitimization in Antiquity, the period from which Bruno takes his models of thought. Consequently, he infers that it should be possible to erase from philosophical theology all questions related to "personhood".

The fact that just before his pyre burst into flames, the Nolan turned away from the crucifix which was shown to him, from the image of the God who became man and was crucified, showed that it was not the defiant gesture of an obstinate heretic but a gesture that was consonant with his vision of a new universe. What had made this vision compelling for the heretic was "the unity

61 Hans Blumenberg, *The Legitimacy of the Modern Age*, p.566.

62 Cf. Ibid. p.566.

63 Nicholas of Cusa, *De Ludo Globi*, I, 19.

64 Hans Blumenberg, *The Legitimacy of the Modern Age*, p.566.

of reality in which everything was indeed self-reproducing self-manifesting God, and man also was a being who becomes God".[65] But this transformation encompassing all realities did not admit the singularity of a God who forces His way into human history, an act of salvation identified as the kenosis of isolation from God. It was therefore necessary to reinterpret this salvific act as an obstacle and a provocative scandal as a counter-symbol. "The great symmetry of man becoming God and God becoming man, which the Cusan had set up against the conflict that was breaking out between the medieval consciousness of God and the new consciousness of self, had been destroyed by the third element of the system, the no longer limited world, which Nicholas himself had introduced, with caution, to balance the transcendent infinity": the world now stripped of its limits, an infinite world![66]

What is now unspeakable in Bruno is the transcendent power of a God revealing Himself in the world. Blumenberg calls this the taking into account of the self-exhaustion of the infinite power of God in the infinite universe. The infinite power of God does not remain a partly unexpressed possibility - always expressible by a free decision of the creator - it has completely and totally asserted itself in the infinite universe. This leads to two consequences: the impossibility of Christology – there cannot be an Incarnation of divine power at a given moment in the history of the world - and a problematic anthropology, i.e. the difficulty intrinsic to the conception of the self-exhaustion of divine power in the infinite universe, to provide a coherent and stable definition of human nature.

In relation to the reason that believes that it can make history, the proceedings we have discussed above under the heading of 'epoch' become acquiescence in contingency. While it is fascinating to see man liberated from the domination of inherited and unexamined truths, at the same time it equally endangers the fragile consciousness of a rationality that can no longer admit that what is elementarily rational could also be an old accepted truth. If the modern age was supposed to have been ushered in by a radical break with its past, then this always implies the admission that it was only from the beginning onward that one could recognise and think what should have been the real issue all along. It appears unavoidable that reason owes man no guarantee of its being always present, and this fact puts every present moment in a difficult situation in relation to what it takes to be certain.

---

65 Ibid. p.593.

66 Ibid.

PART II

THEO-SOPHIA: FAITH MEETING WITH WISDOM

10

Onto-theology, Difference, and the 'Last God'*

Thomas Kalary MSFS

Abstract

Heidegger's diagnosis that occidental metaphysical tradition has right from its inception an onto-theological structure and that the entire history of metaphysics labored hard in approaching the question of being without upholding the essential ontological or theological difference and that the treatment of the question of God within such a framework robbed the divine off its essential relation to the lived human life and relegated it to some dead metaphysical categories opened up possibilities of extremely diverse ways of approaching practically every question in philosophy, which are often unjustly grouped under "post-modern" trends in thinking. This essay is an in-depth analysis of the three Heideggerian foundational notions: onto-theology, ontological and theological difference, and 'the last god.'

Keywords

Onto-theology, ontological difference, theological difference, last god, fundamental ontology, being-historical thinking, sway of being as en-owning.

---

* This essay is a token of my gratitude to Rev. Dr. George Karuvelil, an erudite scholar, an inspiring teacher, a prolific writer, a man on an intimate spiritual journey, and above all a wonderful human being, with whom I have had the privilege of sharing many a wonderful moment.

Introduction

After Heidegger's claim that the entire occidental metaphysical tradition had an onto-theological structure and his indictment of this tradition for having failed to be guided by the essential ontological or theological difference in its engagement with the question of being, terms like "onto-theo-logia" and "ontological difference" has dominated the contemporary philosophical discourse. However, many are still in the dark regarding the actual nuances of these terms or the sense in which Heidegger uses them. This essay is a limited attempt at filling such a vacuum.

In fact, Heidegger was not the first one to coin or use the title "ontotheology." Kant had, for instance, used the title before. However Kant's use of the term "ontotheology" in his *Critique of Pure Reason*, does not form part of any discussion on metaphysics. Steeped as he was in the Wolffian vocabulary, Kant was instead trying to deal with a specific kind of theology under this title. Along the medieval distinction, Kant differentiates within theology a kind of theology based on mere reason from another kind of theology based on revelation.[1] Within the first kind – what the medieval thinkers called natural or rational theology as opposed to revealed theology or theology proper – an attempt is made to capture the primordial being with the help of pure transcendental concepts (like ens originarium, realissimum, ens entium, etc.). However, such a theology has its own limitations as any attempt to grasp the existence of a first being in terms of pure reason can work only with pure transcendental concepts. Beyond postulating the first being as a complete reality in terms of transcendental concepts, mere reason is incapable of determining anything further about this first being that would fall within the experiential realm. It is this transcendentally elucidated discourse about God as the first being that Kant calls ontotheolgoy. In short, ontotheology for Kant is "a theory of God obtained by pure reason with pure transcendental concepts, which imply God's existence as ens realissimum."[2] If, on the other hand, if one moves to the existence of this first being from experience in general or from some aspects of our experience of the cosmos, such a theology is called "cosmotheology." Thus, ontotheology for Kant was one specific kind of rational theology.

1. Heidegger's Understanding of Metaphysics as Ontotheology

We know that the human quest to know initially deals with the things and the factual state of affairs that we experience. We begin by gathering factual

---

1 Immanuel Kant, Critique of Pure Reason, (A631/B659) trans. Werner S. Pluhar (Indianapolis: Hackett Publishing, 1996), 609.

2 Olivier Boulnois , When Does Ontotheology Begin? Aristotle, Thomas Aquinas, and Duns Scotus", in *The Journal of the School of Religious Studies, 44 (2016), 6-7.*

information. But, such factual information alone does not quench the human thirst. It gradually moves away from the factual and inquires into those fundamental aspects and principles that underlie the factual. This is where philosophy in general takes off. The most basic of such a search pertains to the search for that "unifying ground" or "arche" (as it is called in Greek) that "grounds" all the beings of experience or makes them possible at all. It is for this reason that it is said that philosophical reflection as such has an intrinsic metaphysical core. Articulations of such a "ground" have taken different forms during the long history of philosophical thinking. However, irrespective of all such variations, says Heidegger, "what characterizes metaphysical thinking which grounds the ground for beings is the fact that metaphysical thinking departs from what is present in its presence, and thus represents it in terms of its ground as something grounded."[3]

From his intense dialogue with the history of the Western metaphysical tradition from the 20s to the 40s Heidegger came to the conclusion that there are some structural commonalities within this tradition. Firstly, it is an "undeniable fact," says Heidegger, that the occidental-European thinking was always and everywhere guided by the question "what is an entity?" in the sense of what it means for an entity to be. Secondly, this question "what is an entity?" was specifically understood and raised as an inquiry into the "being of entities". When it is asked "what an entity *is*", it is nothing but an inquiry into its *being*. Thus, "whenever it is said of entities, the little word 'is' names the *being* of entities"[4] (GA 10,183). This asking for an account (logos) about an entity qua entity, i.e. with regard to its being, is called the ontological question in so far as it questions an entity "solely with regard to what makes an entity the entity it is: being"[5] (GA 26, 12). Thirdly, It is Heidegger's contention that all the answers regarding the "being of entities" had a "core content" in that they all strive to establish "a truth about the totality of entities as such"[6] (NII 258). Fourthly, the question of being as an inquiry into "the being of entities in their totality" took two subtle directions, namely an inquiry into "the essence" or "whatness" of entities in the sense of an inquiry into what makes an entity that it is on the one hand and an inquiry into "the existence" or "thatness" of entities in the sense of the way in which an entity is what it is on the other.

3 *Ibid.*, p. 7.

4 Martin Heidegger, *Der Satz vom Grund, Gesamtausgabe*, Vol 10. (ed.) Petra Jaeger, (Frankfurt: Vittorio Klostermann, 1997), hereafter referred to as GA 10, followed by page number.

5 Martin Heidegger, *Metaphysische Anfangsgründe der Logik im Ausgang von Leibniz, Gesamtausgabe*, Vol. 26, ed. Klaus Held, (Frankfurt: Vittorio Klostermann, 1978.), hereafter referred to as GA 26, followed by page number.

6 Martin Heidegger, *Nietzsche II, ed. Ingo Seidler,* (Pfullingen: Neske Verlag, 1961), hereafter referred to as N II, followed by page number.

Heidegger calls the former line of inquiry ontology as different from the latter line of enquiry which he calls theology. Based on this distinction he speaks of "the fundamental ontotheological character of metaphysics" (NII 348). We have the clearest formulation of this differentiation in a 1961 manuscript "Kant's Thesis on being": "If we recollect the history of Occidental-European thinking once more, then we will encounter the following: The question of being, as the question concerning the being of entities, is twofold. On the one hand it asks: What is an entity in general as an entity? During the course of the history of philosophy, reflections surrounding this question attain the title ontology. The Question 'What is an entity?' simultaneously asks: Which entity is the highest entity, and in what sense is it? This is the question of God and of the divine. The sphere of this question is called theology. This duality in the question concerning the being of entities can be united under the title ontotheology."[7] (GA 9, 449):

When metaphysics concerns itself with the "most general ground of entities," with that "component element all entities share in common," it functions as ontology. "Ontologists understand the *being* of entities in terms of that entity beneath or beyond which no more basic entity can be "discovered" or "fathomed"; they then generalize from their understanding of this "exemplary entity" to explain the being of all entities. This exemplary entity thus comes to play the ontological role of "giving the ground" (*ergründen*) to all other entities. This basic ontological entity becomes identified as that kind of entity in whose being all other entities share and by which they are thus unified or composed (NII 421). In Heidegger's words, metaphysics as an inquiry into the being of entities is ontology when it "thinks of entities with an eye for the ground that is common to all entities as such"[8] (I&D 70/139). Historically speaking, different metaphysicians articulate this universal ground in terms of large variety of historical molds: *Phusis, Logos, Hen, Idea, Energeia,* Substantiality, Objectivity, Subjectivity, Will, Will to Power, Will to Will, Ousia, and so forth (I&D 66/134). According to Heidegger, it is with '*Ousia*," the proto-substance, that onological 'mold' of the being of entities with which "metaphysics proper begins" (NII, 403)."[9]

The same question "what is an entity?" in terms of its existence or thatness leads to the question "which entity is the highest (or supreme) entity, and in what sense *is* it?" This is the theological dimension of the metaphysical question wherein we could identify two distinct aspects: *which* entity is in the

7 Martin Heidegger, *Wegmarken*, Gesamtausgabe 9, ed. Fr.-W. von Herrmann, (Frankfurt: Vittorio Klostermann, 1976), hereafter referred to as GA 9, followed by page number.

8 Martin Heidegger, *Identiät und Differenz, (Stuttgart: Klett-Cotta, 2002), hereafter referred* to as ID, followed by page number.

9 For a detailed discussion of this element, cf. Iain D. Thomson, *Heidegger on Ontotheology, (Cambridge: Cambridge University Press, 2005),* p. 14ff.

supreme sense and in what sense *is* it? Heidegger calls the first the question of God and the second the question of the divine and believes that treating the latter is a prerquisite in taking up the former. For, "to answer 'the question of God' (of all the entities that are, which of them *is* in the supreme sense?), metaphysics needs to ask 'the question of the divine' (what is the supreme *kind* of being?). The question 'what is an entity?' in its double sense as the "question of God and of the divine" is a *theological* question precisely because "it inquires into and would give an account (*logos*) of the existence of the *theion*, 'the supreme cause and the highest ground of entities' (NII 347)."[10] Metaphysics thinks theologically in so far as it "thinks of the totality of entities as such . . . with regard to the supreme, all-founding entity." (ID, 70-71). It is Heidegger's contention that right from its inception metaphysics thinks theologically as it has always thought of this "highest entity" as the ultimate ground of the being of entities or as an "all-founding entity". Whether as an "unmoved mover" or "self-caused cause" (the very metaphysical concept of God), or as the Aristotelian "first cause", or as the Leibnizian "highest being" which Heidegger translated as "beingest of beings" or as the Kantian "subject of subjectivity as the condition of the possibility of all objectivity" or as Hegel's absolute unconditioned subjectivity" or as the Nietzschean "eternal return of the same" as the highest mode of existence of the totality of entities all the great metaphysicians thought theologically by articulating their own versions of a highest, all-founding entity. In all of them metaphysics received an ontotheological structural framework. Heidegger says: "Since the early days of Occidental thought, being has been interpreted as the ground or foundation in which every entity as an entity is grounded. " (ID 32)

Although there is a grounding taking place both in its ontological as well as in its theological lines of inquiry, there is a difference in the respective manner of their grounding. For ontological grounding, the term used is *ergründen*. It is a matter of the basic entity "giving the ground" to entities. And as such ontology tries to unravel that bedrock beneath all entities beyond which no metaphysical investigation can penetrate and establish them on that ground. For theological grounding, on the other hand, it is a question of *begründen*, a process of establishing the source from which all entities ultimately originate and find their *raison d'être* or justification. "Metaphyscis thinks of the being of entities both in the ground-giving unity of what is most general, that is, of what is uniformly valid everywhere, and also in the founding unity of the all, that is, of the Most High above all others. The being of entities is thus thought of in advance as the grounding ground." (ID, 58) When Heidegger says metaphysics became an ontotheology, the grounding ground grounds in both the ontological and theological senses and the so conceived being of entities in its double

10 Ibid., p. 15.

grounding dimension provided the "changing historical sense of what is." "Metaphysics reinforces its foundational claim about what and how entities are – its 'truth concerning the totality of entities as such' – by coming at the problem from both ends of the conceptual scale simultaneously: Metaphysics effects *both* a bottom-up ontological 'ground-giving or establishing' . . . *and* a top-down, theological 'founding or justification'... (ID 61, 39). All successful, epoch-grounding metaphysical systems *combine* these two different forms of foundationalism, thereby securing our understanding of the being of entities (an so grounding the intelligible order) from *both* the inside out *and* the outside in, microscopically *and* telescopically – or, as Heidegger puts it, ontologically *and* theologically, that is, *ontotheologically*."[11] Thus, according to Heidegger, the metaphysical tradition had always such an onto-theological structure in the form of a bottom-up ontological grounding and a top-down theological grounding. It must, however be noted that not all agree with Heidegger that right from its inception metaphysics had an onto-theological structure.[12]

Heidegger's understanding of metaphysics as ontotheology forms in fact the crucial philosophical background for much of his thought. His objection to this 'onto-theo-logical' approach of the tradition, however, is not an effort at proving that such an approach is totally wrong, but that this metaphysical determination of being as beingness, of man as rational animal, and of god as the highest being is not originary enough in experiencing and articulating the

---

11 Ibid., pp.18-19.

12 Boulnois gives for instance a detailed account of various answers given to the question: When does metaphysics as ontotheology begin? To paraphrase his account, besides the Heideggerian position that metaphysics as ontotheology had already begun with Aristotle and even, in a sense, before him, there are other counter-claims. There are those who say that ontotheology had begun at a precise moment in the history of metaphysics. In this case, it remains to be decided at which moment it begins. One possible answer to this question is given by E.-H. Weber, who makes Henry of Ghent the originator of ontotheology: "The fact remains that his understanding of God-Being [Dieu-Etre] as the first object of our knowledge and, thereby, the basis for all knowledge constitutes the first actual ontotheology of the Latin world." Another possible answer to this question is given by Alain de Libera, who attributes the beginning of ontotheology to Henry of Ghent's immediate successors. According to de Libera, "for a medievalist, this characterization of the essence of Aristotelian metaphysics is actually just one of many Latin interpretations of Avicenna that became established in the university and that, by way of twentieth century Neo-Scholasticism, had decisively pervaded the Heideggerian vision of metaphysics; namely, Scotism. In fact, it is according to Scotus – as an interpreter of Avicenna and not according to Aristotle himself – that metaphysics is presented as a science that has for its object being in common and the most eminent being, God." There is still another opinion, subscribed by Boulnois himself, that maintains that ontotheology is an ambiguous term that has in one sense its beginning with the metaphysical project as such, but in another sense begins at a precise moment in the history of metaphysics. His essay is an attempt at tracing both of those lines of development. Cf. Boulnois, pp. 1-2.

ownmost of being, man and god. On his part, Heidegger initiates a pathway of thinking into the truth of being within a framework provided by both ontological and theological difference.

2. Heidegger's Thinking of Difference

Max Müller credits Heidegger with having "discovered" the "ontological difference." He says that although it is present in every great philosophy, it is somehow pushed aside and identified with something else. "It is actually never taken as itself, always it has its place somewhere else, while it is in effect the place of everything else."[13] Towards elucidating how Heidegger understands ontological difference within the pathway of fundamental ontology, let us begin with a passage from a letter that Heidegger wrote to Max Müller in 1947. In this letter Heidegger speaks of a threefold difference, viz. transcendence-akin[14] difference, a transcendental difference, and a transcendent difference. While subscribing to Müller's elucidations of the ontological difference in his letter to Heidegger, Heidegger adds after a cautionary note: "In the initial working out of the III Division of the first part of *Being and Time*, where a turning to 'Time and Being' unfolds itself, I have called what is intended there (*Gemeinte*) a transcendence-akin difference in relation to transcendental (ontological in a narrow sense) and transcendent (theological) difference."[15] It has been customary up to now to interpret the *transcendence-akin* difference as a difference between extant beings and their beingness, whereas *transcendental difference* has been interpreted as a difference between being and extant beings. But a closer reading of the concerned texts would show that this line of interpretation has already missed the point.[16]

---

13 Martin Heidegger, *Briefe an Max Müller und andere Dokumente*, eds.Holger Zaborowski and Anton Bösl, (Freiburg/München: Verlag Karl Alber, 2003), p.15.

14 I am indebted to Parvis Emad for the rendition of the key German word "tranzendenzhafte" into "transcendence-akin".

15 Heidegger, *Briefe an Max Müller und andere Dokumente*, p.10.

16 Throughout his book *Existenzphilosophie*, Max Müller had already made the topic of ontological and theological difference public, which he had learned from Heidegger through his discussions and correspondence. Although he reproduces in his book all the three titles (cf. Max Müller, *Existenzphilosophie*, 4th edn, Freiburg/München: Karl Alber, 1986, p.86), his understanding and explanation of the first two, as we shall see, is incorrect. He elucidates *transcendental difference* (ontological difference in the narrow sense) as the distinction between a being and its beingness, whereas the transcendence-akin difference (ontological difference in the broad sense) as a distinction of a being along with its beingness from being itself. The problem with his elucidation is not simply a matter of confusion, an accidental mixing up of terms, as Coriando opines (cf. Coriando, letzte Gott, p. 117, footnote 2.), but it is a misunderstanding of the very matter itself. Going by the textual evidences, as will be elucidated in our essay, Heidegger is not at all concerned in the 3rd division of the first of part of *Being and Time* with the difference between

To understand what this transcendence-akin difference and transcendental difference actually stand for, first of all we need to see the context itself. For this we have a relevant clue in Heidegger's *Letter on Humanism*. There he points out that "the subsequent and ongoing unfolding [*Nach- und Mit-Vollzug*] of this other thinking that abandons subjectivity in an adequate manner is surely made more difficult by the fact that in the publication of *Being and Time* the third division of the first part "Time and Being" was held back (cf. *Sein und Zeit*, p. 39). Here [in this third division] the whole [*das Ganze*] turns around. The division in question was held back because thinking failed in the adequate saying of this turning and did not succeed with the help of the language of metaphysics." (GA 9, 327-328)[17] Commenting on this particular text, Heidegger clarifies in his letter to Richardson that the expression used in the *Letter on Humanism* refers to a dynamism "inherent in the very matter designated by the headings: 'Being and Time,' 'Time and Being'." The expression 'the whole' in the above mentioned text refers to "the matter [involved] in 'Being and Time,' 'Time and Being.' A 'turning around' is in play within the matter itself,"[18] a turning around within the third division of *Being and Time*. After having unfolded in the second division ecstatic temporality as the meaning of care – the being of Dasein –, the third division has the assigned task of elucidating the meaning of being as such. This is to be unfolded in two further steps: firstly, the horizonal time that belongs to the existential temporality is to be brought out as the meaning of being as such. Secondly, the manifold modes of being is to be inquired as to how they receive their temporal determination from out of this time-horizon. Up to the explication of horizonal time, i.e., through the first two divisions as well as through the first step of the third division, the perspective moves in the same direction. It is directed towards Dasein and its ecstatic temporality with its horizonal time. After that, "the whole turns around." Understood in this sense, the expression "the whole" here as well as the expression 'what is intended' [*das Gemeinte*] in his letter to Müller refer to the hitherto obtained matter of 'Being and Time' in its belongingness to 'Time

---

beings and their beingness. On the contrary, he is making a differentiation between the pre-thematized, enactmental ontological difference (i.e. trancendence-akin difference or ontological difference in the broad sense) and transcendental-horizonally disclosed and thematized ontological difference (i.e. transcendental difference or ontological difference in the strict sense). This differentiation has been the thrust of Heidegger's thinking right from the War-emergency-lecture-course of 1919 onwards. Thus, although it is Max Müller who made Heidegger's use of "ontological difference" popular, his own understanding of it has been off the mark.

17 Martin Heidegger, "Brief über den 'Hümanismus'," in: *Wegmarken*, Gesamtausgabe Bd. 9, ed. Fr.-W. von Herrmann, (Frankfurt am Main: Vittorio Klostermann, 1976), p.328. Hereafter referred to as GA 9, page number, and included in the running text.

18 William J. Richardson, *Heidegger: Through Phenomenology to Thought,* (The Hague, Martinus Nijhoff, 1974), p.xix.

and Being'. After this, the phenomenological vision re-orients itself in the manner of a turning around from out of the horizonal time towards the modes of being that are determined from out of this horizonal time. This is necessary for showing that all the modes of being such as 'the handy', 'the extant', 'life', 'stock', etc. have the character of presence. Thus, turning as used here is a turning around or a re-orientation of the perspective *within* the fundamental ontological inquiry that takes place within the third step of the transcendental-horizonal approach to the question of being and it is therefore aptly termed a *fundamental ontological turning.* It is in this turning that the transcendental horizonal disclosure of being as such is subjected to a systematic thematization.

In what way does this reference to the fundamental ontological turning become significant for the clarification of transcendence-akin ontological difference as different from transcendental ontological difference? This becomes clear when we turn to another text *The Basic Problems of Phenomenology*, the text that presents Heidegger's renewed attempt at working out the third division of the first part of *Being and Time*. In this text, Heidegger makes an explicit differentiation that is decisive to our elucidations. He says: "The distinction between being and beings is *pre-ontological*, that means, without explicit concept of being, latent there in the existence of Da-sein. As such it can become an *explicitly understood difference*." (GA 24, 454). This text makes it very obvious that the ontological difference can be understood at two levels: (1) the pre-ontological, enactmental level that belongs to the very fundamental ontological constitution of Dasein as existence and (2) the explicitly understood and fundamental ontologically thematized level. We have a further confirmation of this line of interpretation in the treatise *Vom Wesen des Grundes.*[19] While making a distinction between ontic truth as the unconcealedness of beings in their being and ontological truth as the unconcealment of being of beings, Heidegger says that they belong essentially together on account of their relation to the ontological difference, i.e., "*the difference between being and beings.*" He then goes on to add further that if "what distinguishes Dasein consists in the fact that it comports to beings by understanding their being, then *this* being-able-to-differentiate, in which the ontological difference becomes factic, has to have thrust the root of its own possibility in the ground of what is ownmost to Dasein." (GA 9, 134-135).

Thus the distinction between transcendence-akin difference and transcendental difference is this: the former is the pre-theoretical, enactmental difference between being and beings, which can be called the ontological difference in the broad sense. This is a pre-requisite for Dasein's everyday

19 *Vom Wesen des Grundes* was written in 1929 as his contribution to the Husserl Festschrift, which is still anchored in the transcendental horizonal perspective and stands on the basis of the *Grundprobleme der Phänomenologie* (1927) and *Metaphysische Anfangsgründe der Logik* (1928) , the last Marburg lecture-course.

encounter with innerworldly beings in their worldliness (*Weltlichkeit* as its *Bedeutsamkeit*). Only because Dasein has a pre-theoretical understanding of the being of beings, i.e. only because the being of an innerworldly being is always already disclosed to Dasein, it can discover that being in its worldly character. Let us explain this difference between the pre-theoretical disclosure of being and the pre-theoretical discovery of an entity with an example. I encounter or discover a pen *as* an instrument for writing. It worlds for me in its "in-order-to-write" reference. This in-order-to reference is part of a referential totality like pen referring to paper, paper to learning, and learning as a possibility of man. Unless this totality is already pre-theoretically *disclosed* to me, I would not be able to *discover* that entity before me in its instrument character as something in order to write. When this difference is specifically taken in to the phenomenological vision, and phenomenologically, i.e. fundamental-ontologically, thematized in its structure of transcendental-horizonal disclosure without, however, losing its pre-theoretical character, it is called the ontological difference in the strict sense. Thus, the transcendence-akin difference und transcendental difference refers to one and the same difference, the difference between being and beings. When, however, Heidegger speaks of ontological difference in general without making the above-mentioned distinction between unthematized enactmental and phenomenologically thematized difference, difference stands for the transcedental-horizonally disclosed fundamental difference between being and beings, the utmost ground of metaphysics that continues to remain uninquired throughout the history of Occidental metaphysics.

This brings us to the transcendent or theological difference, which is indeed the difference between being and god. But the question that we need to look into is this: what actual role does the thinking of theological difference play in the fundamental ontological unfolding of the truth of being. While speaking of Heidegger's use of transcendent or theological difference in the 20s, it is imperative to keep in mind that it is the theological difference as grasped within the fundamental ontological framework. That is to say that within that framework theological difference is the difference between being - - as disclosed in the transcendental-horizonal manner - - and a god, whose place within the scheme of fundamental ontology we are yet to specify.

It is to be recalled that Heidegger wanted to work out fundamental ontology on its own without appealing to any theo-logical grounds. His conviction that philosophy in itself is essentially "a-theistic" in character prompted him to make the conscious methodological "decision" to inquire into "factic life from out of itself, from out of its own factic possibilities"[20] without any reference to god, in order then to inquire into " Dasein's ontological relation to god." (GA 9, 159)

20 Martin Heidegger, "Phänomenologische Interpretationen zu Aristoteles. (Anzeige der hermeneutischen Situation). In: *Dilthey-Jahrbuch*, VI (1989), 246.

Thus the fundamental ontological pathway of elucidating the transcendental-horizonal disclosure of being took place under the methodological decision of what von Herrmann calls a theological epoché.[21] Thus the "fundamental atheism" of philosophy is essentially a hermeneutic a-theism, a methodological procedure as different from atheism as a theoretical position. Why such a methodological decision was necessary at all is clarified in *Vom Wesen des Grundes* where we are told that "with the ontological interpretation of Dasein as being-in-the-world, no positive or negative decision is made concerning the possible being of god. However, by illuminating transcendence we first of all obtain *an adequate concept* of Dasein, with reference to which we can now *ask*, in what ontological relation Dasein stand towards god" (GA 9, p. 159, footnote 56). Thus, while in the traditional metaphysics, the inquiry into being as beingness culminated in god as the highest being, the fundamental ontology maintains the difference between the transcendental-horizonally disclosed being and god. Consequently, the god-question can be taken up only after the truth of being is sufficiently illuminated in itself.

3. The God-question and Heidegger's Fundamental Ontology

Now the question we need to look into is, whether Heidegger had foreseen any place for the god-question within the fundamental ontological pathway or was the theological epoché his final word on the matter? Had there been no place whatsoever for it in his version of philosophy as fundamental ontology of Dasein? In answering this question, the Heidegger research has by and large let the Heidegger readership hopelessly down. As long as metaphysics understood its leading question as inquiring into beingness of beings and worked out this question in terms of the general principles of being as well as in terms of the highest divine being, the god-question formed an integral part of the leading question of metaphysics. With the outbreak of fundamental

21 Cf. Fr.-W. von Herrmann, "Stationen der Gottesfrage im frühen und späten Denken Heideggers," in: *Die Gottesfrage in der europäischen Philosophie und Literatur des 20. Jahrhunderts*, eds. R. Lanthaler and W. Treitler, (Wien, Köln, Weimar: Böhlan Verlag, 2007), pp. 24f. This is perhaps the best essay to have appeared in print so far that gives a comprehensive orientation to the place the god-question occupies in the entirety of Heidegger's thinking. The same theme is again elaborately treated by the same author in: *Die Metaphysik im Denken Heideggers*, Rome: Urbania University Press, 2004, pp.105 f. Hereafter referred to as von Herrmann, *Die Metaphysik*, followed by page number. This is again a remarkable contribution by the author from two perspectives. It throws for the first time rare light into what is actually happening when Heidegger describes his philosophy as an attempt at overcoming metaphysics. As long as thinking understands the metaphysical tradition as the first beginning of the history of being and being-historical thinking as the other beginning of the same history of being, the history of being forms the onefold within which both of the questions of being fundamentally belong-together. This shows that all talk of Heidegger's thinking as "post-metaphysical" and "post-modern" is senseless talk.

ontology, however, the leading question of metaphysics concerning the beingness of beings gets transformed into the grounding question concerning the more originary phenomenon, the transcendental-horizonal disclosure of being. Along with this transformation, the place the god-question occupies in philosophy also undergoes a substantial transformation.

A clue towards envisioning the place Heidegger had foreseen for the god-question within the fundamental ontological perspective is available in Heidegger's lecture-course given in Marburg in 1928. In this lecture-course, Heidegger clearly indicates that only on the basis of an already elucidated fundamental ontology of Dasein, the god-question can be taken up. Thus we read: "This whole [dynamics] of founding and working out ontology is fundamental ontology; it is 1) the analysis of Dasein, and 2) the analysis of the temporality of being. But the temporal analysis is at the same time a turning, where ontology itself expressly turns back into the metaphysical ontic in which it implicitly always remains. Through this dynamics of radicalizing and universalizing, the aim is to bring ontology to its latent turning over [*Umschlag*]. Here a turning is enacted, and it leads to a turning over, into metontology." (GA 26, 201) The above mentioned 'analysis of Dasein' includes the analysis of Dasein in terms of its temporality that is carried out in the first two divisions of *Being and Time*. The usage 'the analysis of the temporality of being' refers to the thematic that was intended for the third division under the title 'Time and Being'. Now Heidegger says that this analysis of the temporality of being is at the same time a 'turning' in which the fundamental ontology expressly turns back into metaphysical ontic as a turning over into metontology. Metontology stands for the ontological thematization of beings akin to Dasein as well as beings other than Dasein. This in turn presupposes an explication of the full phenomenon of originary time. This means that the turning over in to metontology takes place, after the ecstatic temporality is revealed as the ontological meaning of care -- the being of Dasein --, and the horizonal time as the meaning of being of beings other than Dasein is revealed and after the manifold modes of beings other than Dasein are laid free in their temporal meaning through a fundamental ontological turning. And this turning over into metontology is called the *metontological turning*. This is what Heidegger had in mind, when he stated in the Introduction to *Being and Time* that "the question of being thus aims at an *a priori* condition of the possibility not only of the sciences which investigate beings of such and such a type . . . but it aims also at the condition of the possibility of the ontologies which precede the ontic sciences and found them." (GA 2, 15)[22] While highlighting the priority of the question of being,

22 Martin Heidegger, *Sein und Zeit*, Gesamtausgabe Bd. 2, ed. Fr.-W. von Herrmann, (Frankfurt am Main: Vittorio Klostermann, 1977), hereafter referred to as GA 2, followed by page number.

Heidegger indicates that only under the orientation of the meaning of being as such regional ontologies can be developed, which in turn lay the ground for positive sciences.

Thus, it was Heidegger's stated intention first to work out the fundamental ontology and then in a metontological turning take up all specific questions like man, ethics, god, etc which were to be unfolded into various regional ontologies, which in turn would serve as the condition for the possibility of ontic or positive sciences. It is a fact that Heidegger did not come to an explicit and detailed working out of any of such regional ontologies, and as a result we do not have an ontology of god which would have gone into the question of god from the fundamental ontological perspective. Yet, we find a number of elements that concern such an effort in his lecture "Phenomenology and Theology." Heidegger is of the opinion, as has been his wont right from the early 20s, that from the time of antiquity, through the neo-Platonic, Aristotelian, and medieval times not only was the being question identified with the god-question, but the whole Christian theology on its part was given an essentially Hellenistic formulation. In this lecture, he makes an attempt at a de-Hellenized Christian theology, because he wants to concretely show that moving away from the essentially onto-theological framework of the Greek tradition, a de-Hellenized theology can provide a different and perhaps more meaningful framework for a Christian account of the divine.

Let us single out a few important insights Heidegger provides in this lecture delivered in 1927 in Tübingen.[23] Here he takes 'philosophy' as 'phenomenology' in the sense of 'hermeneutic phenomenology of Dasein' and 'theology' in the narrow sense of 'Christian theology.' As the first insight we should note that the thinking of difference provides the framework for his entire discussion. As he examines the relation between two sciences, 'hermeneutic phenomenology of Dasein' and 'Christian theology,' he stresses their "absolute difference". Philosophy for Heidegger is existential ontology of Dasein, where the inquiry is based purely on being's self-disclosure in the t/here of Dasein. And faith as a specific possibility of existence, insofar as it takes its bearings from revelation stands in "existential opposition" to philosophy. They "are sworn enemies" and in this sense a Christian philosophy is like "wooden steel," a contradiction in terms. Insofar as the framework of their respective inquiries are fundamentally different, they cannot be in principle identified.

While stressing the 'absolute difference' between philosophy and theology, Heidegger points out that what makes theology a positive science, is "Christianness" (*Christlichkeit*) which is initially grasped as 'Christian faith'

23 Cf. Fr.-W. von Herrmann, *Heideggers tübinger und marburger Vortrag von 1927 "Phänomenologie und Theologie"*, unpublished manuscript. Insights from this text is taken in elaborating the points here.

which is articulated as a "way of existence of human Dasein" (GA 9, 52). What is decisive here is that 'faith' is already viewed from the perspective of philosophy as fundamental ontology of Dasein, whose being as existence has a specific ontological structure. Thus 'Christian faith' is not something lying outside the ontological structure of Dasein, but rather it "is itself a manner of existing in t/here."[24] In *Being and Time* Heidegger shows that depending on how Dasein enacts its possibilities of being in each case, whether from the possibilities of itself or from that of the world, it exists in the modes of ownedness (*Eigentlichkeit*), unownedness (*Uneigentlichkeit*) or everyday indifference. While these modes remain what they are, with the enactment of faith as a possibility of existence, there comes an additional mode, which Heidegger calls "re-birth." Faith as a possibility of existence is such that the believing Dasein cannot be in command of this possibility, because in it, Dasein "has become a servant, brought before god and thus *re*-born" (GA 9, 53). Important is Heidegger's usage of pre-believing or un-believing existence of Dasein. The transition to the new mode of faith takes place on the basis of religiously undifferentiated mode of existence. Existence as such is *a*-religious, or, to use Heidegger's terminology, it is pre-Christian existence. This existence in its pre-Christianness is overcome with the transition to Christianness, but even then the mode of existence is itself not overcome, but rather Christianness itself can be understood only as a further modification of existence. Even after the modification of Dasein and existence into Christian existence, man continues to retain his fundamental existential ontological constitution as Dasein. Through careful analysis Heidegger shows that the Christian concept of sin is rooted in the existential phenomenon of guilt. He takes this as an example to illustrate that the religious content of all theological concepts shelters in itself an understanding of being. For this reason, the development of theology as a science with the help of such concepts requires philosophy as existential ontology of Dasein.

By way of summing up, let the following be made clear. First, even in this lecture "Phenomenology and Theology" Heidegger is not concerned with elucidating the details of a thinking of god within the fundamental ontology. He had, while speaking of the metontological turning, indicated the site where such a thinking should be rooted and within what framework such a thinking should unfold. Yet, two things need special mention here. Fundamental ontology has to unfold itself under a theological epoché and only on the basis of what is so unfolded, one can turn to the god-question as one of the regional ontologies, which would provide the ontological basis for a specific theology as a positive science like Christian theology. Second, when Heidegger speaks of God and theology within the fundamental ontological perspective, he is still

24 Ibid., p. 2.

concerned with Christian theology and Christian understanding of God. By shifting his focus from the theoretico-reflexive onto-theo-logical basis of the hitherto Occidental philosophical tradition to a more originary basis, namely the pre-theoretical basis of philosophy that is rooted both in the ontological and theological difference, Heidegger intends to provide a more originary and a de-Hellenized philosophical basis for a fruitful theological reflection. He shows concretely, perhaps without manifesting his own personal stance, how a Christian theology could re-invent itself and in the process re-discover its own unique experiences that got lost in the process of Hellenization. In tracing such a possibility, he provides a number of important insights into what could form the essential basis of a religious ontology, thought out of fundamental ontology of Dasein. But with transition to the being-historical perspective, the thinking of difference in its both forms, namely the ontological difference and theological difference undergoes a transformation. And the location of the god-question also undergoes a radical change. The sway of being as enowning becomes the very site for the self-manifestation of the divine phenomenon. Or to put it differently, the fact that there is fundamental difference between being and god remains decisive for the entire thinking of Heidegger. But this fundamental difference is experienced and articulated quite differently in both perspectives. While the unfolding of the fundamental ontology of Dasein takes place under a strict theological epoché, where the god-question is a matter of one of the regional ontologies, the god-question is very much a co-dimension of the sway of being as enowning.[25]

25 There is an age-old, but totally absurd thesis, propped up and vigorously defended even today by eminent Heidegger scholars, that Heidegger's turning was a 're-turn' to his early position, after having had to concede the failure of the project that *Being and Time* was. According to this line of interpretation, there was already a "turn before the turn." In tune with this line of interpretation Benjamin D. Crowe, [*Heidegger's Phenomenology of Religion: Realism and cultural Criticism*, Bloomington and Indianapolis: Indiana University Press, 2008.] believes that a project of a phenomenology of religion was present in Heidegger's thought throughout. The so called differences between the 'early' and 'later' Heidegger rather "represent shifts of emphasis in a more or less stable, well-established project of critically addressing the religious situation of late modernity through a phenomenological methodology." The evidences "are not sufficient to warrant the claim that his later work is a radical departure" from the earlier one (99). From our elucidations of the thinking of difference and the question of god, it becomes clear that Crowe has not been able to gain an access to Heidegger's thinking of the "divine," especially when he makes statements like: "The 'holy' is Heidegger's term for the objective side of an understanding of being that anchors the intelligibility of religious concepts and practices." (115)

4. Beyond Difference to the Intimacy of the Onefold

Let us begin again with the first dimension of the thinking of difference[26] and ask what happens to the ontological difference with the immanent transformation that occurs in Heidegger's thinking? The first clue towards answering this question is available in a marginal note in *Being and Time* that in a retrospective glance Heidegger jotted down to the third division "Time and Being." It reads: "The transcendental difference. Overcoming of horizon as such. Turning back unto the provenance. Presence from out of provenance."(GA 2, 53) The immanent transformation is a turning back or returning to the provenance, a turning back that "overcomes" both the transcendental-horizonal approach as well as that specific characterization of ontological difference that is rooted in this approach. An appropriate understanding of the usage "overcomes" is important in grasping the direction thinking takes here. The experience of the truth of being as the provenance prompts thinking to realize the inadequacy of the transcendental-horizonal perspective and the transcendental-horizonally understood characterization of ontological difference. When the truth of being is experienced as provenance, it reveals itself no longer as horizon for the disclosure of the being of beings in the sense of *praesens*, but as the counter-resonance of the forth-throw of being and projecting-opening of Dasein.

Section 132 of the *Contributions* clarifies this point further by referring to the counter-resonance of being . On the one hand, Heidegger says, that this trancendental-horizonally conceived distinction between being and being was "necessary" in providing "a preliminary perspective for the question of be-ing" as well as in "safeguarding the question of the truth of be-ing from all confusion." (GA 65, 250/ CP 176) It was precisely because the traditional metaphysics did not preserve the ontological difference in its inquiry into the question of being, that this difference got confused with the beingness of beings as well as with the highest being. Thus it was vital for Heidegger to underline the importance of ontological difference in order to keep the inquiry into being free from all such confusions. But, on the other hand, Heidegger felt that the ownmost of this difference was not adequately grasped by the transcendental-horizonal thinking insofar as ontological difference was conceived as the "condition for the possibility" for the disclosure of being as such. The transcendentaly and horizonally structured distinction had a "tormenting and discording character" as it was still inadequate to reveal the

26 For an excellent account of the thinking of difference in the thinking of being as enowning, cf. Parvis Emad. *On the Way to Heidegger's Contributions to Philosophy*, (Madison, WI: University of Wisconsin Press, 2007), p. 127 f. This is an incomparable work in its effort to think and co-enact the various nuances of the being-historical unfolding of the truth of being in its both ways of dis-enowning as well as enowning. For further elucidations of the thinking of difference, especially in being-historical thinking, cf. von Herrmann, *Die Metaphysik*, p. 107 f.

truth of being in its originary onefold. Therefore, however "necessary" the ontological difference was, it continued to be "disastrous" to the extent this distinction "*does* arise from a questioning of beings as such (of beingness)." (GA 65, 250/ CP 177). Although the traditional metaphysics was leapt over in and through the fundamental ontology as the latter was concerned with going beyond beingness of beings, fundamental ontology still continued to move within the perspective of the structure of transcendence and horizon and to that extent and in that sense it could still be considered metaphysical, in so far as this ontology unfolded the disclosure of being as a transcending of beings. The transcendental-horizonal perspective proposed to arrive at the truth of being by transcending beings, not realizing the fact that this procedure itself was inadequate. When the ontological difference is so conceived, "this distinction *itself* becomes the real barrier" because it actually "misplaces the inquiry into the question of be-ing, insofar as, by pre-supposing this distinction, one attempts to go further than this distinction and to inquire into its one-fold. This onefold can never be anything but the mirroring of the distinction and can never lead to the origin, in view of which this distinction can no longer be seen as originary."(GA 65, 250/ CP 177). What is denied here is not the distinction between being and beings, but the transcendentally and horizonally elucidated structure of this distinction and its appropriateness. Thus, the so conceived distinction becomes a hindrance in reaching the truth of being in its originary onefold: "Therefore the task is not to surpass beings (transcendence) but rather to leap over this distinction and thus over *transcendence* and to inquire inceptually into be-ing and truth." (GA 65, 250-51/ CP 177) What was still inappropriate within the transcendental-horizonal approach, must be leapt over.

Thus it would be a misunderstanding, if one were to think that the 'ontological difference' and with it the 'thinking of difference' as such is 'overcome' and is irrelevant for the thinking of enowning. Heidegger himself says very clearly that "varying attempts were needed to master the 'ontological difference,' to grasp its very origin and that means its genuine *onefold"* (GA 65, 250/ CP 176). The term used here is to "master" and not "abandon." Even the transcendentally and horizonlly conceived ontological difference was an attempt at mastering the 'ontological differencc,' an attempt that proved "inadequate." Thus it is our task to follow the thinking of difference as it unfolds in being-historical perspective. Let it be said in anticipation: while in the transcendental-horizonal perspective, both the ontological difference as well as the theological difference were used as the springboard (as the condition for the possibility) to follow the manner in which being as such discloses itself, being-historical thinking unfolds as the counter-resonance of the truth of being and projecting-opening of Dasein, where the divine phenomenon shows itself as a co-dimension of this counter-resonance. That means, the thinking of difference has its provenance in the intimacy of the onefold of the sway of the truth of being as enowning.

With these preliminary clarifications, we can now follow the being-historical thinking of ontological difference. Being-historical thinking as leap has a two-fold dimension. First of all it leaps over not only the metaphysical tradition of the Occidental thinking, but also the thinking of transcendental-horizonally conceived ontological difference. Secondly, this leap is a leap into the sway of being as enowning which shows itself to thinking in a new light. *Contributions* articulates this as follows: "the thrower of the projecting-open experiences itself as thrown -- i.e., as enowned by be-ing." (GA 65, 239 / CP,169) We recall here that, while elaborating the transcendental-horizonal perspective, Heidegger had explicated thrownness and projecting-open as the two equally-original ontological structural moments of Dasein. In being-historical thinking, the sway of being presents to thinking this ontological structure of Dasein in a new light, providing an insight into the very origin of the existential thrownness. By experiencing the provenance of thrownness from out of the forth-throwing truth of being, the thrower of the projecting-opening, i.e. Dasein, no longer experiences itself merely as the one thrown "into the facticity of disclosedness" and projects-open what is pre-given, but rather as the one "thrown into and being en-owned"[27] by the en-owning forth-throw of the truth of being. With this experience, Dasein experiences itself as the ownhood of the truth of being. However, this experience of being thrown into and en-owned by the truth of being does not in any way level off the projecting-open. If that were to be so, then the actual distinction between being and Dasein would have been totally compromised. The fact is, the enowning-forth throw is just one dimension of the sway of the truth of being as enowning. There is no enowning without the receiving and projecting opening of what is thrown-forth. But, with this experience of being the ownhood of the truth of being, projecting-opening of Dasein does no longer project-open in the manner of a projecting-opening upon a horizon, but rather in the manner of an en-owned projecting-open. It projects open what is en-owningly thrown-forth to it from out of the truth of being.

This turning-relationship of en-owned projecting-opening of Dasein and the en-owning forth-throw of the truth of being is characterized further, in section 133 of the *Contributions,* as a relationship of "*needing* and *belonging*." This dimension of "needing and belonging" builds up further on the co-relationality between thrownness and projecting-open as explicated in the course of the transcendental-horizonal perspective. Specifically, Heidegger says: "Be-ing needs man in order to hold sway; and man belongs to be-ing so that he can accomplish his utmost destiny as Da-sein."(GA 65, 251 /CP,

27 Emad, *op. cit.*, p. 199

177) The turning-relation of being to Dasein, as Emad rightly points out, is "a turning *unto* thinking" because being "needs thinking" to project-open and sustain being's self-unfolding.[28] To this need of being, Dasein responds by acting, which acting as thinking sustains the self-unfolding of being by projecting it open. This demonstrates that the en-owned projecting-opening Dasein *belongs* to the swaying dynamics of the en-owning forth-throw of the truth of being. With its needing, being is turned unto thinking or the projecting-opening Dasein. By acting, i.e. by opening-projecting the unfolding of being, Dasein responds to this need.

With this dynamics of needing-belonging relationship between being and Dasein, Dasein shows itself in a new light. Dasein no longer shows itself in the manner of "*ex-sistere,*" i.e. in the manner of transcending beings for the horizonal disclosure of being, but as an *inabiding* (*Inständigkeit*) in the intimacy of the onefold of the truth of being. The aforementioned dynamics of swaying enacts itself in the wholeness of the turning-relationship. This co-relationality of needing and belonging between being's en-owning forth-throw and Dasein's en-owned projecting-opening is what Heidegger calls "counter-resonance"(GA 65, 251 /CP, 177). This dynamics in its wholeness is what Heidegger calls *enowning*. Being-historical turning stands for the resonance of this counter-resonance, for the alternating co-relationality between the en-owning forth-throw of being and the en-owned projecting-opening of Dasein. This relationship is called "turning in enowning."(GA 65, 57 /CP, 40)

To sum up: in fundamental ontology, it is the thinking of ontological difference that takes us to the disclosure of being as such. Even there, in the disclosure of being, there is a "belonging-together" of being and Dasein as long as t/here ('Da-') of Dasein stands for the disclosure of being. But the transcendental-horizonally conceived structure of ontological difference could not provide an adequate account of the actual dynamics of this "belonging-together." On the other hand, the thinking in being-historical perspective glimpses first into the dynamics of the sway of being as enowning. This sway of being comes to pass as a counter-resonance of the enowning forth-throw of being and enowned projecting-opening of Dasein. Thus the dynamics of the swaying of being shows itself in a genuine onefold of being and Dasein in their needing-belonging relationship. Both the transcendental-horizonally conceived structure of ontological difference as the condition for the possibility of the disclosure of being and the very term "Differenz" seemed to overemphasize the difference so much so that the actual "belonging together" of being and Dasein was not adequately thematized. Being-historical thinking levels off such inadequacies and provides a more originary account of the "belonging-together" of being and Dasein, on the basis of which the ontological

28 *Ibid.*, pp. 190 f.

differentiation can be carried out. On account of this, being-historical thinking uses instead of "Differenz" other terminologies like "Unterscheidung" or "Unter-schied" in order to indicate this transformation in the understanding of ontological difference. While "Differenz" could sound like a permanently prevalent state of affair that would preclude any genuine "belonging-together," the usage "Unterscheidung" has an enactmental tone, implying a dynamics of something being eventually differentiated. And it is to this dynamics that Heidegger's usage of "Unter-schied" refers. He writes the word "Unter-schied" with the separating hyphen in order to indicate that the first part "unter-" stands for the intimacy of the onefold of the swaying of being, while "-schied" names the separateness and distinction between being and beings. It is the dynamism of the 'differentiation' that can appropriately be made only "in the intimacy of the onefold"[29] that is expressed with the term "Unterscheidung." Elucidating the being-historically understood ontological difference, von Herrmann sums it up saying: "Difference and belonging-together of what is differentiated are grasped differently from the swaying of the truth of be-ing as enowning."[30]

After having sufficiently dealt with the nuances of how the thinking of ontological difference, upon which the transcendental-horizonal disclosure of being was investigated, gets transformed into a *thinking of differentiation* rooted in the onefold of the intimacy of the sway of being, we now turn to the question of what becomes of the theological difference within the thinking of enowning. To what extent, if at all, is the theological difference relevant for the treatment of the god-question within the being-historical perspective? To put the same matter from a different perspective, let us recall that the fundamental ontological perspective unfolds in terms of the ontological difference. Within this perspective, the theological difference also played a crucial role in keeping the inquiry into being from not getting mixed up with the question of god. Thus, fundamental ontology unfolds strictly under a theological epoché. Now, the situation in being-historical thinking is quite different. On the one hand, as we have already seen, ontological difference is grasped differently in being-historical thinking. On the other hand, the god-dimension is an integral element of the being-historical thinking, as what is thought under the title "the last god" is one of the six "Joinings" of the jointure of the truth of being as enowning. In what way, then, does the theological difference come into play in the thinking of being as enowning? What is unfortunately overlooked by the hitherto Heidegger research is the fact that an appropriate understanding of this question is crucial to the very understanding of being-historical thinking.

---

29 F.-W. von Herrmann, *Wege ins Ereignis: Zu Heideggers "Beiträge zur Philosophie,"* (Frankfurt am Main: Klostermann Verlag), 1994, p. 79.

30 *Ibid.*

5. The Last God

Let us begin our considerations with the very terms 'the last god'[31] , the title Heidegger gives to the sixth "Joining" of *Contributions*. He sums up the immediate apprehensions the readers would possibly have when confronted with such an odd title by asking, is not the expression 'the last god' a matter of 'debasing god' or even '*the* greatest blasphemy'? Ruling out an obvious tone the title may sound, he hastens to add that it is not an instance of calculative thinking where 'last' means something like 'cessation' or 'end'. The first important insight into the expression 'the last god' is provided in the form of a question: "but what if the last god has to be so named because in the end the decision about gods brings under and among gods and thus makes what is ownmost to the uniqueness of the divine being [*Gottwesen*] most prominent?" (GA 65, 406/CP 286). To be specially noted here, as von Herrmann cautions, is the usage of 'in the end' in this passage: "'in the end' when being shows itself no longer only as beingness of beings, but also as the truth of being in its jointure of enowning, there arises the possibility of thinking in an experiential manner the ownmost of the uniqueness of divine being and with it the last god as the godly god."[32] If we focus our attention on the word 'last' in'the last god,' we cannot miss the implicit yet obvious interplay of the 'first beginning' with the 'other beginning'. For Heidegger the hitherto history of philosophy with its long metaphysical tradition and its leading question of being qua beingness of beings forms the first beginning of the history of being. But this first beginning *as* the first beginning of the history of being already plays forth the possibility of the other beginning of the history of being that begins with the being-historical thinking that thinks the grounding question of philosophy as the truth of being. Alluding to the fact that the god-question occupied a central place in the first beginning, and the fact that the god-question received a specific line of interpretation within this so called onto-theo-logical tradition, with the usage 'the last god' Heidegger wants to convey straight away that the reference is purely to the 'god' of the other beginning. Implied further in the usage is that the 'god' of the thinking of enowning is grasped totally and fundamentally

31 Although Polt's recent work [*The Emergency of Being: On Heidegger's Contributions to Philosophy*, Ithaca and London: Cornell University Press, 2006] is a thoroughly researched book, excellent on many counts, giving a lot of praiseworthy insights into Heidegger's thinking, there are key areas where his elucidations struggle unsuccessfully to come to terms with some of the key aspects of Heidegger's thinking. One such area is his elucidations of Heidegger's "last God". Translating the term "last" as "final," he makes such claims as: "The final god, then, is an 'end' as a goal;" (209) "Heidegger's 'passing' indicates that our relation to the god is an event and advent, not a fixed structure." (210) His elucidations have not been able to get hold of the thinking of difference at all (211 f.) rooted in the onefold of the sway of enowning.

32 von Herrmann, *Die Metaphysick*, p.109.

differently from the 'god' as thought in the first beginning and yet, like in the first beginning, the god-question has a central place within this thinking. That calls our attention to the word 'god' in the usage 'the last god'. How are we to understand this 'god' of the other beginning? It is in this context that the significance of the guiding *dictum* given to sixth "Joining" of *Contributions* immediately after the title "The Last God" becomes obvious: "The totally other over against gods who have been, especially over against the Christian God." (GA 65, 403/CP 283). Even before Heidegger elaborates on the god-question within the thinking of enowning, he absolutely demarcates, as a first hermeneutic step, the last god from all the specific forms of god in the entire history of thinking, especially the biblically revealed Christian God. All of them are for Heidegger some modifications of a god in terms of beingness and highest being. In contrast to such historical forms of god, the last god, the god of the other beginning, is "totally other." We should remember that in the 20s Heidegger had made a distinction between the originary 'Christianness' and its formulation into a "system" in terms of Hellenistic philosophical conceptuality. On the fundamental ontological pathway, he spoke of the need to rediscover this originary Christianness through a process of de-Hellenization. Now, the 'totally other god' of the thinking of enowning should not be identified with even such a de-Hellenized Christian God. For, even such a god is still a form of historical specification. The godly god as the "totally other" stands for the divine phenomenon that is free of any such concretizations.

It is for this reason that being-historical thinking, while referring to the divine phenomenon, uses different, but unusual expressions like 'the last god,' 'godly god,' 'godding of gods,' 'the divine' [*das Gott-hafte*], the plural form 'gods', etc. and takes care to avoid all customary terminologies for it. We have here Heidegger's own clarification: "The talk of 'gods' here does not indicate decided assertion on the extantness of a plurality over against a singular but is rather meant as the allusion to the undedcidability of the being of gods, whether of one single god or of many gods. This undecidability holds within itself what is question-worthy, namely, whether anything at all like being dare be attributed to gods without destroying everything that is divine. The undecidability concerning which god and whether a god can, in utmost distress, once again arise, from which way of being of man and in what way – this is what is named by the name 'gods'." (GA 65, 437/CP 308) Thus, it becomes clear that Heidegger's interest consists in letting the 'godly' to manifest itself in its uniqueness, without already destroying what is divine by beginning the inquiry itself with some already prevalent historical specifications. The "Joining" entitled "The Last God" essentially and exclusively unfolds the originary divine dimension factically from out of the truth of being, becoming thus the utmost god, "the totally other god" of the other beginning, showing itself in its originary dimension that is before every form of individuation and concretization as experienced in and by any particular religious tradition.

Dealing in length with Heidegger's own being-historical explication of the God-question would be the task of another full-length essay. Let it suffice for the moment to say that with this notion of the 'last God" Heidegger opens up one possible way of liberating the question of God from the traditional ontological framework and conceptualities and treating it within an entirely differently conceived horizon. This effort of his has inspired a host of contemporary thinkers to prepare the way for the parousia of the divine in what they envision as the post-metaphysical era. Levinas or Marion would be two good representatives of such a preparatory thinking.

11

Religious Epistemology: A Grammatical Investigation after Wittgenstein

Jose Nandhikkara CMI

Abstract

Religious remarks pervade Ludwig Wittgenstein's published writings, from the early *Notebooks* to the final pages of *Culture and Value*. Wittgenstein's many written thoughts and recorded remarks bear a religious character and he engaged himself extensively with concepts regarding religious belief and practice. The *Nachlass* shows how these themes are intertwined with his thoughts on philosophical matters. In this paper, following Wittgenstein, I "carry out a grammatical investigation" (PI 150)[1] on the use of 'God' in religion. I am arguing that Wittgenstein's way of doing philosophy and his thoughts on aesthetic, ethical, and religious values can be fruitfully applied to throw light on understanding the nature and meaning of religious epistemology.

Keywords

Wittgenstein, grammatical investigation, religion, religious epistemology, religious values.

Introduction

According to Norman Malcolm, "his reflections about himself and mankind, and even about the aims of his intensive philosophical work, were penetrated

1 Wittgenstein, *Philosophical Investigations*, G. E. M. Anscombe (trans.), Oxford: Basil Blackwell, 1953; hereafter PI within the Text.

by thoughts and feelings of a religious character."[2] Wittgenstein's remarks on God and religion are significant. He had a sound grasp of religious beliefs, and his concerns with aesthetic, ethical, and religious values were central to his philosophy.[3] At the beginning of the *Blue Book*, Wittgenstein identified a source of "philosophical bewilderment:" "a substantive makes us look for a thing that corresponds to it" (BB 1).[4] Applied to God, philosophers tend to ask "What sort of entity is God?" and come up with a number of answers, which are often nonsensical. The task of philosophy, according to Wittgenstein, is to raise the questions "How is the word used?" and "What is the grammar of the word?" (WL 35, 3)[5] and to describe the grammar of 'God' and other related words. The God of religion is shown in relation to the world and human beings therein. Wittgenstein's diagnosis that "A main source of our failure to understand is that we do not command a clear view of the use of our words. – Our grammar is lacking in this sort of perspicuity" (PI 122), is true about the use of the word 'God.' I resist the philosophical temptation to force words "on in any single direction against their natural inclination" (PI Preface, vii) so that philosophy can be used to sharpen the blurred edges of our concepts and give a precise religious epistemology. Instead I offer pictures, after Wittgenstein, leaving what's ragged as ragged (CV 51).[6]

A grammatical investigation shows that the use of the word 'God' has a rich filigree pattern and remains a concept without fixed boundaries. We may draw the boundaries to serve particular purposes. However, "A sharper concept would not be the same concept. That is: the sharper concept wouldn't have the value for us that the blurred one does" (LW I, 267).[7] What I learn from Wittgenstein is that one has to take the concept of God as something fundamental and resist the temptation to explain it or to reduce it to something else for which a philosophical or scientific point of view is capable of providing an answer. The concept of God is something fundamental for believers not because of any

2 Malcolm, N. *Ludwig Wittgenstein: A Memoir*, Oxford: Oxford University Press, 1984, 83.

3 Barrett, C. *Wittgenstein on Ethics and Religious Belief*, Oxford: Blackwell, 1993, viii.

4 Wittgenstein, *The Blue and the Brown Books*, Oxford: Basil Blackwell, 1958; Hereafter BB within the Text.

5 Wittgenstein, *Wittgenstein's Lectures: Cambridge 1932-35: From the Notes of Alice Ambrose and Margaret Macdonald*, Alice Ambrose (ed.), New York: Prometheus Books, 2001, Hereafter WL 35 within the Text.

6 Wittgenstein, *Culture and Value*, G. H. von Wright (ed.), Oxford: Basil Blackwell, 1998; hereafter CV within the Text.

7 Wittgenstein, *Last Writings on The Philosophy of Psychology*, Vol. I, (ed.) G. H. Von Wright, and Heikki Nyman, (trans.) C. G. Luckhardt and Maximilian A. E. Aue, London: Basil Blackwell, 1990; hereafter LW I within the Text.

epistemic or phenomenological properties, but by virtue of the place it occupies in their lives.[8]

1. A Scientific World-View

We live in a scientific age. Science dominates many aspects of our lives through technological progress to such an extent that people are tempted to relegate all forms of knowledge other than those of the empirical sciences to the realm of fantasy. In such an intellectual climate, it is tempting to treat religious and moral values as products of imagination and emotion. Even when we think and speak about God and religion, it is difficult to keep it from scientific ways of understanding. It is characteristic of the scientific point of view to offer explanations in the form of theories or hypotheses for everything. A complete theoretical explanation that is objective, verifiable, and universal is seen as the ideal, though often we satisfy ourselves with an inference to the best explanation. It is very difficult to be cured of the disease of wanting to explain (RFM 333),[9] partly because of the enormous success and influence of science and technology in our daily lives. Understanding seems to be identified with scientific explanation in terms of abstraction and theory formation. We become oblivious to other obvious forms of knowledge in aesthetics, ethics, religion, so on, where methods and rules of scientific explanations are not appropriate. We understand more than what we can express, and we express more than what we can theoretically articulate and systematically arrange in a truth-table. According to Wittgenstein, "Philosophers constantly see the method of science before their eyes, and are irresistibly tempted to ask and answer questions in the way science does. This tendency is the real source of metaphysics, and leads the philosopher into compete darkness" (BB 18). Philosophers who were put to sleep by the success of science[10] happily see their roles as under-labourers to the master builders of science.[11]

According to Wittgenstein's point of view in the *Tractatus*, there is an important distinction between the world as the totality of facts, what can be said, on the one hand, and the mystical, what cannot be said but only shown, on the other. Once the totality of true propositions is identified with the whole of natural science (TLP 4.11),[12] the rest is consigned to the realm of silence. He famously

---

8 Phillips, D. Z. *Wittgenstein and Religion*, London: Macmillan Press, 1993, 233.

9 Wittgenstein, *Remarks on the Foundations of Mathematics*, G. H. von Wright, R. Rhees, G. E. M. Anscombe (eds.), Oxford: Basil Blackwell, 1978; hereafter RFM within the Text.

10 "In order to marvel human beings – and perhaps peoples – have to wake up. Science is a way of sending them off to sleep again" (CV 7).

11 John Locke, "The Epistle to the Reader" in *An Essay Concerning Human Understanding*, New York: Penguin Classics, 1998.

12 Wittgenstein, *Tractatus Logico-Philosophicus*, C. K. Ogden (trans.), London: Routledge, 1922; hereafter TLP within the Text.

concluded, "What we cannot speak about we must pass over in silence" (TLP 7). Everything that does not belong to the scientific purview belongs to the realm of the mystical, unsayable. Only nonsense results when people try to say what by nature is unsayable. For those who are under the spell of the scientific point of view there is nothing to be silent about; what we can speak about is all that matters in life. This is not Wittgenstein's point of view: "There are, indeed, things that cannot be put into words. They make themselves manifest. They are what is mystical" (TLP 6.522). The point of the *Tractatus* lies in its pointing beyond world of natural science to the sphere of the mystical. What matters in life lies beyond the world of words. According to Paul Engelman, "Wittgenstein passionately believes that all that really matters in human life is precisely what, in his view, we must be silent about. When he nevertheless takes immense pains to delimit the unimportant, it is not the coastline of that island which he is bent on surveying with such meticulous accuracy, but the boundary of the ocean."[13] The world-talk is about that which is within the boundary of the island. The lives of islanders, however, are not restricted to the conditions of the island; it is related in many ways to the ocean, enhancing the horizons of the meaning of their lives. Though religious language cannot provide the boundaries of the ocean in a manner that scientific views could picture that which is within the boundaries of the island, religious views recognize the reality of the ocean, islanders' dependence on the ocean, and the tendency to transcend the boundaries of the island in their search for truth and meaning of their lives. It is a vision that admits that experience and understanding are not confined to observable empirical data; there is more to life than that can be explained by scientific research and logical language.

Wittgenstein was convinced that scientific views are incapable of answering questions regarding the meaning of life: "We feel that even when all possible scientific questions have been answered, the problems of life remain completely untouched" (TLP 6.52). He wrote: "The use of the word "science" for "everything that can be meaningfully said" constitutes an "overrating of science" (MS 134, 145).[14] He recognized that there are ultimate questions regarding the meaning and the purpose of life, and related them to belief in God:

> The meaning of life, i.e., the meaning of the world, we can call God. And connect with this the comparison of God to a father. To pray is to think about the meaning of life.
>
> To believe in a God means to understand the question about the meaning of life.

13 Engelmann, P. *Letters from Ludwig Wittgenstein: with a Memoir*, L. Furtmuller (Trans.), B.F. McGuinness (ed.), Oxford: Blackwell, 1967, p. 97.

14 Wittgenstein, *Wittgenstein's Nachlass: The Bergen Electronic Edition*, Oxford: Oxford University Press, 2000; hereafter MS within the Text.

> To believe in a God means to see that the facts of the world are not the end of the matter.
> To believe in God means to see that life has a meaning (NB 73-74).[15]

I believe, together with Wittgenstein, that a human being who is in relation to God is strong.[16] I suggest further that contemplating God would help the believer both to know himself better and to become fully human. Wittgenstein wrote:

> To know oneself is terrible because at the same time one recognizes the living call and that one does not sufficiently answer it. There is however no other better means to know oneself than to see the Perfect One. From that the Perfect One must arouse a storm of revolt in people, if they do not want to humiliate themselves completely. I believe, the words: "Blessed, who is not scandalized by me" mean, "Blessed, who holds the sight of the Perfect One" (MS 183, 213214).[17]

Wittgenstein began the *Philosophical Investigations* with a view of language described by Augustine, "a particular picture of the essence of human language:" "Every word has a meaning. This meaning is correlated with the word. It is the object for which the word stands" (PI 1). This is the view Wittgenstein himself held in the *Tractatus*: "A name means an object. The object is its meaning" (3.203). We tend to think that we grasp the meaning of words on the basis of being presented with the object or a sample. According to this view, "once you know what the words stand for, you understand it, you know its whole use" (PI 264). Once we have accepted this picture, confusions arise in our discourses on God, and we need a philosophical treatment for clarification. We begin with a diagnosis, after Wittgenstein.

2. God-Talk: A Grammatical Investigation

From a religious point of view, after Wittgenstein, to speak of God does not necessarily mean that one has to assume the existence of some kind of object that can be pointed at. According to D. Z. Phillips, "When the positivist claims that there is no God because God cannot be located, the believer does not object

15 Wittgenstein, *Notebooks 1914-1916*, Oxford: Basil Blackwell, 1961; hereafter NB within the Text.

16 *Ein Wesen, das mit Gott Verbindung steht, ist Stark* (MS 183.56).

17 *Sich selbst zu erkennen ist furchtbar, weil man zugleich die lebendige/wesentliche Forderung erkennt, und, daß man ihr nicht genügt. Es gibt aber kein besseres Mittel sich selbst kennenzulernen, als den Vollkommenen zu sehen. Daher muß der Vollkommene einen Sturm der Empörung in den Menschen wecken; wenn sie sich nicht ganz, und gar demütigen wollen. Ich glaube, die Worte: "Selig, wer sich nicht an mir ärgert", meinen: Selig, wer den Anblick des Vollkommenen aushält.* The quote is Luther's translation of Mt 11.6: "Blessed is he who takes no offence at me".

on the grounds that the investigation has not been thorough enough, but on the grounds that the investigation fails to understand the grammar of what is being investigated – namely, the reality of God."[18] 'God' does not mean something in the way that names of physical objects refer to those things named. According to G. E. Moore, "The question whether God exists is a question whether to adopt the concept 'God' (the word and its use) into the language, or retain it. For me, the question of the existence of God is the question whether I can find a use for the word 'God' in my talk."[19] Moore could not find any meaningful use for 'God' and, accordingly, held that there is no reason to retain it or to talk about it. It is quite useful to eliminate it; because, according to Alfred J. Ayer, "... the mere existence of the noun is enough to foster the illusion that there is a real, or at any rate a possible entity corresponding to it. It is only when we inquire what God's attributes are that we discover that 'God' in this usage, is not a genuine name."[20] According to this view, there cannot be something that is real that is not in the world, which could be independently verified. God is not in the world as an object that could be identified and verified; therefore it is better to eliminate 'God' to avoid the illusion that there is some corresponding real (or possible) entity.

Some Wittgensteinians like Rush Rhees and D. Z. Phillips tried to clarify the grammar of 'God': "'God exists' is not a statement of fact. You might say also that it is not in the indicative mood. "There is a God", though it appears to be in the indicative mood, is an expression of faith."[21] According to this view, to think that existence can be applied to God is to confuse the grammar of God-talk with the grammar of physical objects. Rhees clarifies: "We use "it exists" chiefly in connection with physical objects and anyway we use it where we can ask whether it exists or not. This goes with the sense of finding out whether it exists. Now the "it", whatever it is, is something we could identify in such an investigation . . . by, for example, finding out."[22] If we raise the question "whether God exists?" we must be able to find out, one way or the other. Since we cannot verify whether God exists, it is claimed that we cannot know what it would mean for God to exist independent of knowing what the word 'God' means.[23] So

18 Phillips, D. Z. *Wittgenstein and Religion*, London: Macmillan Press, 1993, 2.

19 Moore, G. *Believing in God*, Edinburgh: T&T Clark, 1988, 39-40.

20 Ayer, A. J. *Language, Truth and Logic*, London: Penguin Books, 1990, 122.

21 Rhees, R., D. Z. Phillips, assisted by M. von der Ruhr, *Rush Rhees on Religion and Philosophy*, Cambridge: Cambridge University Press, 1997, 49.

22 Rhees, R. *Without Answers*, London: Routledge, 1969, 131.

23 "If one lays emphasis . . . on the fact that 'God' is a substantive, and especially if one goes on . . . to say that it is a proper name, then the natural thing will be to assume that meaning the same by 'God' is something like meaning the same by "the sun" or meaning the same by "Churchill." You might even want to use some such phrase as "stands for" the same. But nothing of that sort will do here. Questions about "meaning the same" in connexion

when believers affirm that "God exists", according to this view, they can only claim that 'God' has meaning in their God-talk. They cannot claim that anything in particular exists because the "technique of comparison" between the word 'God' and God is not like that between a name and an object or that between a picture and the object pictured; picture of a tropical plant and the actual plant, for example (LC 63).[24] Therefore, according to this view, existence or reality in relation to God is guaranteed only by the meaning of religious language and religious practices.[25]

This is not, however, how believers see their quest for and experience of God. Nor is it how they use the word 'God' in their religious discourse. Users of religious language are committed to the existence of God. Though denying God's existence will make God-talk meaningless, confessing his existence is not merely to say the use of 'God' is meaningful in religious forms of life. The mystery of God cannot be reduced to the semantics of 'God'. It is true that religious language is mischaracterized when treated as if it aims to represent a state of affairs. It does not, however, follow that it cannot be understood as corresponding to something real. The meaning of a statement is to be found in its use. Although religious language is expressive, this does not mean that the objects it speaks of are not real. They are not real in the way the physical objects are real. They are real, from a religious point of view, not from an empirical point of view. The word 'real' cannot be reserved to speak only about physical objects. We use 'real' in a variety of ways to qualify life, love, pain, time, number, mind, will, and so on. They are all real in their own ways as they have their roles in the characteristic forms of life. There is no one use as the real.

with the names of physical objects are connected with the kind of criteria to which we may appeal in saying that this is the same object ... Supposing someone said "the word 'God' stands for a different object now." What could that mean? I know what it means to say that "the Queen" stands for a different person now, and I know what it means to say that St. Mary's Church is not the St. Mary's Church that was here in So-and-So's day. I know the sort of thing that might be said if I were to question either of these statements. But nothing of that sort could be said in connexion with any question about the meaning of 'God'. It is not by having someone point and say "That's God." Now this is not a trivial or inessential matter. It hangs together in very important ways with what I call the grammar of the word 'God'. And it is one reason why I do not think it is helpful just to say that the word is a substantive" (Rhees *Rush Rhees on Religion and Philosophy*, 45-6). Rhees is referring to the grammatical fact the word 'God' does not refer in the way names refer to physical objects. At the end of the paper he makes it clear that it is wrong to conclude from his discussion that 'God' means nothing. His point was to draw our attention to the grammatical fact that we cannot apply the same kind of criteria in using "standing for" and "meaning the same" in connexion with the names of physical objects and 'God'.

24 Wittgenstein, *Lectures and Conversations on Aesthetics, Psychology and Religious Belief*, C. Barrett (ed.), Oxford: Basil Blackwell, 1966; hereafter LC within the Text.

25 McCutcheon, F. *Religion within the Limits of Language Alone: Wittgenstein on Philosophy and Religion*, Aldershot: Ashgate, 2001, 138.

Because we are over-familiar with the use of real with empirical objects and also because of the enormous success of empirical sciences, we are tempted to reserve 'real' for empirical objects. Bewitched by such a view, philosophers of scientific temper tend to ask: "How can something be real and not in the world?" As Wittgenstein remarked, "Not empiricism and yet realism in philosophy, that is the hardest thing" (RFM 325). To show a way of achieving such a point of view after Wittgenstein is the objective of this paper.

God is beyond description because he is not an object. 'Real' finds its home not in metaphysical discourses but in the description of lived human experiences. The referring functions of 'I', 'pain,' and so on are characteristically different from words referring to physical objects. Believers also use 'God' as a name and refer to God in religious language knowing that it is not like referring to physical objects or anything else other than God. Considering how issues concerning 'referring' could be settled in these religious contexts could clarify the similarities and differences. We have different criteria for referring to physical objects, persons, sensations, etc. The methods for settling these questions clarify the grammar of 'referring' in the respective contexts.

> Wittgenstein observed,
> Augustine says in the *Confessions* "*quid est ergo tempus? si nemo ex me quaerat scio; si quaerenti explicare velim, nescio*". -- This could not be said about a question of natural science ("What is the specific gravity of hydrogen?" for instance). Something that we know when no one asks us, but no longer know when we are supposed to give an account of it, is something that we need to remind ourselves of. (And it is obviously something of which for some reason it is difficult to remind oneself.) (PI 89).

Wittgenstein also points to the difference in "the way music speaks": "Do not forget that a poem even though it is composed in the language-game of information is not used in the language-game of giving information" (Z 160).[26] Religious language describing God, though given in the language of describing objects, is categorically different. It is also different from our language for sensations, abstract concepts, music, etc. (The differences are shown in the ways believers use religious language.) It is not without reason that religious traditions often preferred the *via negativa* in speaking about God. Aquinas qualified his *quinque viae* to show the existence of God: "Now we cannot know what God is, but only what he is not; we must therefore consider the ways in which God does not exist, rather than the ways in which he does."[27] This is done by ruling

26 Wittgenstein, *Zettel*, G. E M. Anscombe and G. H. von Wright, (eds.), Oxford: Basil Blackwell, 1967; hereafter Z within the text.

27 Aquinas, *Summa Theologiae* 1a.2.3 < http://www.newadvent.org/summa/1002.htm> (22 February 2019).

out from God everything inappropriate, such as compositeness and change. This is not to say that there is no God to speak about, but rather to draw attention to the fact that our God-talk is different from our talk about physical objects. The realm of the mystical is of enormous importance to Wittgenstein. It is the ocean surrounding our small island, as Engelmann characterised it.[28] Believers speak about God, and Wittgenstein himself spoke and wrote about God. It is interesting to note that Aquinas who wrote copiously about God reverted to silence once he had a mystical vision, claiming that whatever he had written was mere straw. Wittgenstein, on the other hand, moved from the realm of silence to the realm of words, perhaps following the admonition of Augustine: "*Et vae tacentibus de te quoniam loquaces muti sunt.*"[29] Perhaps his later attitude regarding God-talk is expressed in the following remark: "don't for heaven's sake, be afraid of talking nonsense! Only don't fail to pay attention to your nonsense" (CV 64). Both silence and words can be responses to God-experience.

3. A Religious Point of View

'God' is not a meaningless word; its meaning is given by various uses of the word. When believers use the word 'God', they refer to God, though referring to God is different from referring to material objects. 'God' cannot be constructed on the model of 'name and object'. We use words in various ways to refer to material properties, human subjects, subjective experiences, and other abstract concepts. Philosophy cannot judge on the truth of the statements that refer to God; it can only clarify their meaning so that those who use the term 'God' have a critical understanding of it. A critical understanding of the use of the word would involve looking into the actual uses of the word, their internal coherence, their functions in the stream of life, and how they are related to the

---

28 Engelmann, P. *Letters from Ludwig Wittgenstein: with a Memoir*, L. Furtmuller (Trans.), B.F. McGuinness (ed.), Oxford: Blackwell, 1967, 97.

29 Augusine, *Confessions* 1.4: "And woe to those who are silent about you, since the talkative are dumb". G. E. Moore, at the beginning of his lectures, had told the students that he had nothing to say on the "philosophy of religion", though he was required to lecture on the topic. M. O'Drury thought a Professor of Philosophy had no right to keep silent concerning such an important subject and told so to Wittgenstein, Wittgenstein responded with this quote from *Confessions*. Not satisfied with the translation that Drury had, Wittgenstein translated it: "And woe to those who say nothing concerning thee just because the chatterboxes talk a lot of nonsense." He added "I won't refuse to talk about God or religion" (Rhees, R. (ed.). *Ludwig Wittgenstein: Personal Recollections*, Oxford: Basil Blackwell, 1984, 104). The passage appears also at the end of Wittgenstein's remarks to Moritz Schlick as recorded by Friedrich Waismann on the subject of Heidegger's paradoxical statements on Being and Anxiety: "*Augustine sagt: "Was, Du Mistvieh! Du willst keinen Unsinn reden. Rede nur einen Unsinn, es macht nichts*!"" (Augustine says: "What, you swine! You don't want to talk nonsense. Go ahead talking nonsense, it doesn't matter".) (Wittgenstein, *Schriften* 4, Frankfurt: Suhrkamp, 1937, 69, quoted in Spiegelberg 1979, 322).

rest of life. Such a critical investigation might strengthen or weaken the faith of a person. Philosophy cannot, however, just get rid of God-Talk, thinking that it will solve all the problems that are connected with it. Such short-circuiting or rewriting of the problem so that one can solve it is not worthy of a philosopher. We could eliminate the use of 'God' as a name for an object and could argue that 'God' does not refer to any object. Believers do not use the word 'God' to refer to a material object; they refer to God, often using words, pictures, idols, or experience of natural events. If there were no meaningful use for the word, the word would become obsolete. Words are used in a variety of ways for a variety of purposes.

Classical theism understands God to be the Being different from all other beings; the Being beyond all representations. Wittgenstein's discussion on the neighbourless level of 'I' could be applied to the God-talk in classical theism. God "has no neighbours". He is the One and there is no other god beside, above or below him. It is not just "that it happens to be alone but that its grammatical position is that of having no neighbour" (refer PO 229).[30] God is a class by itself (refer to LW 35, 21). It is not only that one cannot represent Him, but that nothing would count as representing Him. We cannot pick, identify, and label God. Description, definition, and representation are suitable in the world of objects and not for God: "And now we might say: There can be a description of what it would be like if there were gods on Olympus – but not: "what it would be like if there were God". And this determines the concept 'God' more precisely" (CV 94). This is to clarify that we cannot use language to refer to God as we use to refer to objects and persons. What is difficult, however, is to articulate the uniqueness of referring to God. If we follow Wittgenstein, we can only point to similarities and differences. "What happens with the words 'God' and 'soul' is what happens with the word 'number'. Even though we give up explaining these words ostensively, by pointing, we don't give up explaining them in substantival terms. The reason people say that a number is a scratch on the blackboard is the desire to point to something. No sort of process of pointing is connected with explaining 'number'..." (WL 35, 32). Yet, we do not give up using 'number'; we refer to numbers without pointing. Even when we point, it is different from pointing to an object; we point to the numerals. We may remind ourselves that pointing was also different in the use of 'I,' 'pain,' 'joy,' etc. A different kind of referring is involved in using 'God, which we learn when we learn the word 'God' and come to believe in God. The referring to the nameless and formless Spirit using words, pictures, icons, and idols functions, because of what lies around such uses, namely believers' life in which these uses have meaning.

30 Wittgenstein, *Philosophical Occasions*, Klagge, J. and A. Nordmann (eds.), Indianapolis: Hackett Publishing Company, 1993; hereafter PO within the Text.

In the *Zettel*, to the observation by the interlocutor that "Joy" surely designates an inward thing," Wittgenstein replied: "No. 'Joy' designates nothing. Neither any inward nor any outward thing" (Z 487). This is not the same as to argue, however, that joy and other feelings do not exist; nor that they are identified with forms of behaviour. Wittgenstein admitted that they are real and they are important aspects of human life. Like other words, they have their roles in the stream of life. We can say the same about God and other words that refer to the Divine. They are used to express, describe, and explain religious experience and religious life. They cannot be used on the model of 'object and name'. God is not an inner or outer object: "It is not a something, but not a nothing either!" (PI 304). This is also not to claim that the word 'God' is used like the sensation words, 'pain', 'joy', etc., but to draw attention to the fact that the referring functions of words differ. Referring to objects and their qualities, subject and subjective experiences, God and religious experiences differ. The relation between God and 'God' is different from other uses of words, including words that refer to subject and subjective experiences. Believers do not use it because they recognize a particular object with certain characteristics that is in heaven. Expressions such as "That's God!" "Check whether this is God!" and "I know what/who is God; but I am not sure whether this is God!" are excluded from meaningful religious language. There are no criteria, identification, or misidentification. Yet the word 'God' is used as corresponding to the reality of God.

Following Wittgenstein, instead of searching for an ostensive definition of 'God', we should better raise the question: "How is the word 'God' used?"(refer to PI 370). We should explore the contexts of applications involved and look at the various language-games in which the word occurs, how it is being used, etc. "What sort of entity is a God?" – like "What sort of entity is a number?" – can only be answered insisting that God, like a number, is not a 'sort of entity'; neither empirical nor fictional. It is also not a matter of opinion that God exists (refer to PI p. 178). God is neither a discovery nor a product of human intelligence and ingenuity, individually or collectively. A proper account of God-talk has to take into account its differences and similarities with ways of speaking about physical things, persons, sensations, numbers, etc. Though they all refer, there are categorical differences and one kind of use (name-object) should not be taken as the norm for other uses. A believer is not typically puzzled about how the word 'God' refers to God. His search for God is categorically different from the philosophers' search for the reference of 'God'. Philosophers should stop stripping the leaves in vain attempts "to find the real artichoke" (PI 164, BB 125), the essence of God, leaving behind God of religion expressed in religious mythologies, pictures, parables, etc.

Conclusion

To conclude, the human tendency and need to talk about God is a fact of our natural history. Wittgenstein himself shared this common tendency and respected it immensely.[31] What we need is a synoptic view of language that would show the connexions and clarify the special status of our God-talk. Learning from Wittgenstein, what we really need to do is "to call to mind the differences between the language-games" (PI 290) and note the differences and similarities of the various uses of 'God'. We need to clarify its grammar rather than eliminate it or deny its referential function. Indeed, "One cannot guess how a word functions. One has to look at its use and learn from that. But the difficulty is to remove the prejudice, which stands in the way of doing this. It is not a stupid prejudice" (PI 340).

Wittgenstein was sensitive not to place God just at the beginning of creation. It is equally miraculous that something exists now, and not just that something had a definite beginning:

> It is remarkable that one says, God has created the world, and not: God creates, continually, the world. For why it should be a greater miracle that it has to be begun, than that it is to be continued. One is misled by the example of the workman. That one makes a shoe is a work but once made (out of available), it remains so for some time. Does one not think however God as a creator, the maintenance of the universe has to be a just as great a miracle as its creation, – yes, are both not one? Why should I postulate a unique act of the creation and not a lasting act of sustaining – that once begun has, that had a temporal beginning or, what runs out on the same, a constant creating?[32]

In religious terms, both the beginning and the continued existence depend on God totally. We may also compare the relation between God and the world to

31 "My whole tendency and I believe the tendency of all men who have ever tried to write or talk Ethics or Religion was to run against the boundaries of language. This running against the walls of our cage is perfectly, absolutely hopeless. Ethics so far as it springs from the desire to say something about the ultimate meaning of life, the absolute good, the absolute valuable, can be no science. But it is a document of a tendency in the human mind which I personally cannot help respecting deeply and I would not for my life ridicule it" (LE 11).

32 *"Es ist merkwürdig, daß man sagt, Gott habe die Welt erschaffen, und nicht: Gott erschaffe, fortwährend, die Welt. Denn warum soll es ein größeres Wunder sein, daß sie zu sein begonnen hat, als daß sie fortfuhr zu sein. Man wird von dem Gleichnis des Handwerkers verleitet. Daß Einer einen Schuh macht, ist eine Leistung aber einmal (aus Vorhandenem) gemacht, bleibt er von selbst einige Zeit bestehen. Denkt man sich aber Gott als Schöpfer, muß die Erhaltung des Universums nicht ein ebensogrosses Wunder sein als seine Schöpfung, – ja, sind die beiden nicht eins? Warum soll ich einen einmaligen Akt der Schöpfung postulieren und nicht einen dauernden Akt des Erhaltens – der einmal angefangen hat, der einen zeitlichen Anfang hatte oder, was aufs Gleiche hinausläuft, ein fortdauerndes Erschaffen?"* (MS 183, 206 207: 24/27.2.37).

that of a dancer and the dance.[33] In a dance, the dancer is in the dance, though the dance is not the dancer. When the dancer stops dancing, there is no more dance. There is no dance without a dancer. The dancer is not just an element in the dance; he is the inner and outer limit of dance. Dance and dancer are internally related, and any talk about dance or dancer needs to take into account this empirical and logical relation. Similar relations can be seen between music and the musician. Applied to the relation between the world and God, at the empirical level there is the world of things – the dance; from a theistic point of view, "the totality of facts" becomes "God's world". Theistic God-talk, however, keeps the world and God distinct, but related. They are identified in pantheism. Monism reduces all reality to God, and materialism reduces all reality to the world. The difficulty is to see the connections right and to express the relation between God and the world without reducing one to the other or separating one from the other. The examples of eye and the field of vision, subject and experience, and dance and dancer point to the difficulties involved in speaking about God in relation to the world. The proposed book, *The World as I Found It* (TLP 5.631) would not mention the I; nor could it mention God. For a theist, God is not in the world as other objects are in the world; rather, the world is created and sustained by God.

Wittgenstein helped us to liberate ourselves from the bewitching object-name picture in his conceptual elucidation on words that refer to self and sensations, and it is my contention that those grammatical investigations could help us to understand and use meaningfully the words that refer to God and religious experiences. On both occasions the referring function is different from referring to physical objects. In his description of sensation words, Wittgenstein clarified that they are not defined either by ostensive definition or by introspection. "If we construe the grammar of the expression of sensation on the model of 'object and name' the object drops out of consideration as irrelevant" (PI 293). This does not, however, deny the existence of the sensation; it means that a sensation is not an object like other material objects with which we are familiar and use 'object and name' model to refer to them. This is applicable to our God-experience and God-talk: if we construe the grammar of the expression of God-experience on the model of 'object and name' the object drops out of consideration as irrelevant. This does not mean that God is absent or the existence of God is irrelevant; the language-game of religious experience and religious expression is played with different rules.

Philosophy is not called upon to pass judgements on the truths about God; they are given in revelation and are accepted in faith. These truths are not susceptible to empirical verification either. Nonetheless we cannot be genuinely

33 In the Hindu tradition, Lord Siva is also presented as dancer, Nata Raja. Creation is depicted as his dance. A similar picture is that of Lord Krishna with a flute. The world is seen as the *lila* (play or performance) of the Lord in these theistic views.

indifferent to the question of whether what we believe is true or not. If we discover that those truths are false, we reject them. There are in our lives, however, many more truths than are acquired by way of personal verification. Though we seek the truth, we live also by beliefs. Religious beliefs are, by nature, not available for empirical verification. That does not mean that they are not real. As in other matters of philosophy, though hard to achieve, realism but not empiricism (RFM 325) is the noble goal in a philosophical discourse on God, after Wittgenstein. The role of philosophy is to critically examine the meaning of these beliefs, clarify the concepts, and come to a certain understanding of the contents of faith. Therefore, resisting the temptations to seek further explanations and justifications, I rest content with conceptual elucidations of the religious use of words that refer to "the living God." This is a philosophical praxis that I learn from Wittgenstein. Though faith seeks understanding, in religion a believer typically believes in order to understand the truths about God. The God of religion is a mystery worshipped by believers and not a problem to be solved either by science or philosophy.

12

Theology for a Scientific Age: A. R. Peacocke's Vision of God, Human and World

Isaac Parackal OIC

Abstract

A.R Peacocke views evolution as continuing creation and on this view he has based his whole philosophy without making any conflict between science and religion. He is of the view that creation is not static that has been completed but a continuing process which generates new forms of being each and every moment. That means God is still acting in the creation and guiding it through his spirit to the fulfilment. God is a "living" God who is directing whole creation to its fulfilment and is vigilant over the world processes. Peacocke holds the panentheistic view that everything is "in God." Therefore, creation is the self-offering of God and God suffers with creation. God limited his omnipotence and omniscience so that human beings can co-operate with him with his or her free will to co-create the world. So, God is presented as a "Living and Loving God" who creates and sustains the world with his providence.

Keywords

Continuous creation, continuing Creator, living and loving God, whole-part model, self-limiting omnipotence and omniscience.

Introduction

Our age that has witnessed marvellous discoveries in the field of science and technology. New discoveries have enhanced the scientific understanding of the universe and corrected the age old misconceptions about it. The tremendous success in the field of science has given a new face to humanity and profoundly transformed the human life. Today we know more about the origin not only of our human race but also of the universe. In the light of the new scientific discoveries Arthur Peacocke makes a synthesis between science and theology. Without losing much the traditional theological concepts he conjoins theology with science. He holds that in the wake of the evolutionary theory the place of God has been stressed more than ever before. In this paper we will discuss Peacocke's vision of creation and of God as the Creator. The continuing presence of the transcendent God is made visible in the continuing creation of the universe. God is conceived as the Source and Ground of evolution and therefore, God is the continuing Creator. For Peacocke, creation is 'in' God.

1. Evolution as Continuing Creation

We begin our study with the Peacocke's vision of creation and evolution. For Peacocke, creation takes place through evolution and evolution is conceived as continuing creation. In this sense, God is *semper Creator* and the world is *creatio continua.*[1] Creation, for him is not a 'past once and for all' act but which continues every now and then, through the creative natural processes in which the interplay of chance and law plays an important role. So, God is not seen as someone who intervenes and interfere in regular intervals to fill the 'gaps' but the one who creates at every moment of the world's existence in and through the perpetually endowed creativity of the very stuff of the world. This is an enhanced idea of creation which emphasizes the immanent and dynamic nature of God's relation to the world.[2]

Peacocke views evolution as continuing creation and in this view he has based his whole philosophy without making any conflict between science and religion. He is of the view that creation is not static that is completed but a continuing process which generates new forms of being.[3] That means God is still acting in the creation and guiding it through his spirit to the fulfilment. Peacocke continues: "For that perspective is of a cosmos in which creativity is ever-present, in which new forms of matter emerge and in which,

---

1 Cf. A.R Peacocke, "Biological Evolution – A Positive Theological Appraisal", *Evolutionary and Molecular Biology: Scientific Perspective on God's action*, eds. R. J. Russel, W. R. Stoeger and F. J. Ayala, Berkley, California, Vatican Observatory, 1998, 359.

2 A.R. Peacocke, "Biology and A Theology of Evolution" *Zygon*, 34 (1999), 707.

3 A.R. Peacocke, *Science and the Christian Experiment* (London:Oxford University Press, 1971), 123.

with many thrusts in many fruitless directions, nevertheless in the end there emerged man, mind, human society, human values, in brief the human spirit."[4] This development for Peacocke is genuinely creative.[5] The matter has the permanent potentiality to whose actualization depends on the circumstances. This potentiality for Peacocke is not injected into the cosmos from outside. In all this world process, God is ever present and continues to hold it on by his will with these potentialities.[6] Peacocke rejects the mechanical understanding of the universe and he views God as not the 'God- of- the- gaps' but a God ever-present in the cosmos and continues to create all the time through the matter and the laws governing its transformations.[7]

2. Understanding of God as Continuing Creator

Peacocke conceives God as the continuous Creator. God is ever present in the process of evolution and he is continuously creating and guiding it.

The world is seen to be in the process of evolution, in which new forms of its basic stuff emerge continuously, creatively but according to the regularities of relationship which we call the 'laws of nature' of the stuff of the world.[8] Peacocke rejects the static conception of creation and he holds that the world is still being made and, on the surface of the earth human being has emerged from biological life and his/her history is still developing. "Any static conception of the way in which God sustains and holds the cosmos in being is therefore precluded, for the cosmos is in a dynamic state..."[9] He observes that the scientific outlook of a cosmos in development introduces a dynamic element into our understanding of God's relation to the cosmos which was, even if obscured, always implicit in the Hebrew conception of a 'living God', who is dynamic in action.[10]

The universe in its being continuously manifests wonder because of its intelligibility and rationality. The scientific understanding based on pure scientific method is not able to give a complete answer to the existence of the world. Einstein has written, "The eternal mystery of the world is its comprehensibility...The fact that it is comprehensible is a miracle."[11] The comprehensibility does not answer the 'why' of the world. These 'why' questions in the search for meaning lead one from scientific to a religious

---

4 *Ibid*, 127.

5 *Ibid*, 129.

6 *Ibid*, 130.

7 *Ibid*, 130.

8 A.R. Peacocke, *Science and the Christian Experiment*, 156.

9 A.R. Peacocke, *Creation and the World of Science* (Oxford: Clarendon Press, 1979), 80.

10 *Ibid*, 80.

11 A. Einstein, *Out of my later years* (Westport: Greenwood Press, 1970, 61.

search, because according to Peacocke, God is the best explanation to the search of intelligibility and meaning in the universe.[12] He explains that this ultimate Reality, 'God' who is the end of all searches is the Ground of everything. For Peacocke, the Divine being is the Ground and Source of everything that exists and he speaks of God as being and becoming. In his attempt to understand God from the scientific perspectives, Peacocke describes God as *becoming* through the process of the world. But at the same time, it is to be noted that for Peacocke, the distinction is not absolute because every becoming is based on being. He presents it as the two poles of the question of God: what God is and how God interacts with the world?[13] The 'being nature' of God could answer the 'why' of the created world and the 'becoming nature' of God could answer the 'why' of the evolving world as described by science. According to Peacocke 'becoming' is neither an attribution of change in God nor God actualises some potency through becoming. But, it is the revealing or unveiling of God to the creatures. It is the creative emergence of God through which the presence of God becomes more visible and God becomes more immanent to the creatures.

3. God's Creative Activity

Much discussion was made to answer the question about creation and evolution. The principal answers are given on the basis of science and religious scriptures. Peacocke offers his answer by presenting of Scriptures and science in the light of the new scientific discoveries. Peacocke observes that the scientific picture of the world, especially the living world, inexorably impresses upon us a dynamic picture of the world of entities, structures and processes involved in continuous and incessant change. This has encouraged us to reintroduce into our understanding of God's creative relation to the world a dynamic element.[14] He shows that the Scripture also presents the picture of an active God in the history. In the Hebrew conception, God was conceived as a 'living God' who is dynamic in action. But this idea "has been obscured by the tendency to think of 'creation' as an event in the past."[15]God has again to be conceived as continuously creating, continuously giving existence to, what is anew.[16] Creation, for Peacocke "is not confined to a restricted period of time but is going on all the time (and indeed modern physics would support seeing

12 A. R. Peacocke, *Theology for a Scientific Age: Being and Becoming-Natural and Divine* Minneapolis: Fortress Press, 1993), 91.

13 A.R. Peacocke, *Theology for a Scientific Age,* 99-100.

14 A.R. Peacocke, *Paths from Science towards God*, 137.

15 A.R. Peacocke, *Paths from Science towards God*: *The End of All Our Exploring* (London: One World, 2001), 137.

16 *Ibid*, 137.

time itself as an aspect of the created order)."[17] So, if we identify the creativity of the world with that of its Creator, then it must be emphasized that God's relation to the world is perennially that of Creator.[18] For Peacocke, all these show the need to affirm more strongly than at any other time in Christian(and Jewish and Islamic) history that in a very strong sense God is the immanent Creator creating through the processes of the natural order. "The processes are not themselves God, but the action of God as Creator."[19] God's creation is continuing every moment and God is not acting in the gaps or in some certain intervals. This means there is no need to look for any extra supposed gaps in which, or mechanisms whereby, God might be supposed to be acting as Creator in the world.[20] God is very much in the world as he expresses his own inner being in the act of creation. Peacocke argues that if the world is God's creation and if it expresses God's own inner being, then we can say that God is never absent from his world and he is as much in his world as, say, Beethoven is in his Seventh Symphony during a performance of it.[21] Beethoven–as-composer was to be found only in the music itself. Beethoven-as-composer is/was other than the music(he transcends it) but his communication with us is entirely subsumed in and represented by the music itself –he is immanent in it and we need not look elsewhere to meet him in that creative role.[22]

3.1. Chance as God's Radar of Creation

Peacocke is making use of different metaphors to explain the creative action of God through the interplay of chance and law. Among these metaphors the important one is that of radar. The main function of radar is to control and to protect planes and to direct air routes. In the same way, chance functions as radar of God to direct the evolution and protect and control its processes.[23] According to Peacocke chance explores through the process of evolution. In evolution there is an interplay between random chance at the micro-level and the necessity that arises from the stuff of the world having its particular 'given' properties and law like behaviour.[24] Peacocke holds the idea that God makes things make themselves. Here chance is seen as part of God's toolkit. God has fashioned a system which has the potential for self-creation. God uses chance

17 A.R. Peacocke, *God and the New Biology* (Gloucester: Peter Smith, 1994), 95.

18 *Ibid*, 95.

19 A.R. Peacocke, *Paths from Science towards God*, 137.

20 *Ibid*, 137.

21 A.R. Peacocke, *God and the New Biology*, 95-96.

22 A.R. Peacocke, *Paths from Science towards God*, 137-138.

23 A.R. Peacocke, "God's Action in the Real World", *Zygon*, 26(1991), 467.

24 A.R. Peacocke, *God and the New Biology*, 97. Also, see J. D. Bartholomew, *God of Chance*, (London: SCM Press, 1984), 148.

to ensure the variety, resilience and freedom necessary to achieve his purposes in the world as a whole. In this evolutionary process each stage is a launching pad for the next. Proposing the idea of chance, Peacocke gives the picture of a God who is always vigilant and active in the world and not just a 'watch maker' who has given all the laws and left it determined without any openness and freedom. God's choice of chance gives creativity and flexibility to nature without reducing it into a pre-determined machine. Both chance and law, Peacocke argues, are necessary for a creative and ordered universe. If chance alone is ruled, no forms, patterns or organizations would persist long enough for them to have identity or real existence and the universe would never be a cosmos and susceptible to rational inquiry. It is a combination of the two which makes possible an ordered universe capable of developing within itself new modes of existence. It is *the interplay of chance and law that is creative.*[25]

3.2. Creation as the Self-offering of God

Creation, for Peacocke is the self-offering of God. He believes that "the very stuff of the universe is in this act manifest as the means whereby the self-offering, self -emptying, self -limiting of the Creator in the very act of creation is made explicit as also involving the perennial suffering of God."[26] Peacocke describes God as 'love' because, in creation, God deliberately limits himself, by allowing a cosmos to remain in being which is other than himself, which is given its own autonomy and so limits his freedom, and in which Man can consciously repudiate his Creatorhood.[27] Putting forward the idea of self–offering of God in creation Peacocke shows that creation is costly process and it is the self-manifestation and self-emptying of God. To explain this we have no other option but only to use anthropomorphic language. In the creative processes God strives to bring into existence new forms of matter and ultimately human beings. Peacocke acknowledges the self-emptying love of God in all the evolutionary process.

The notion of self-offering love of God which is expressed in self-limitation for Peacocke, is very important and it is the root of everything in the world. "This self-limitation on behalf of the good and well–being, indeed the existence of another being can properly be designated as being consistent with, and so exemplifying the ultimate character of *God as 'Love'*."[28] In human life, it seems that love is supremely manifest in self-limiting, costly action on

---

25 A.R. Peacocke, "God as the Creator of the World of Science", *Interpreting the Universe as Creation* ed. Vincent Brümmer (Kampen: Kok Pharos Publishing House, 1991), 103-104.

26 A.R. Peacocke, *Paths from Science towards God*, 149.

27 A.R. Peacocke, *Science and the Christian Experiment*, 137.

28 A.R. Peacocke, *Theology for a Scientific Age*, 123.

behalf for the good and existence of another.[29] The self offering love of God finds its full expression in the suffering love of God with the creation.

3.3. God Suffers with Creation

According to Peacocke God's love is manifested in the creative process and God suffers with the creation.[30] Peacocke envisages love, as we have seen, as the foundation of God's suffering for his creation. He suggests that "love may justifiably be attributed(with all the reservations such analogies necessitate) as a primary characteristic of the Creator in relation to his creation, for amongst human beings love is basically characterized self limitation and self denial on behalf of the ultimate good of the another."[31] From the 'panentheistic' understanding follows Peacocke's idea of God's suffering.[32] "Now, when the natural world, with all its suffering, is panentheistically conceived of as 'in God', it follows that the evils of pain, suffering and death in the world are internal to God's own self. So, God must have the experience of the natural."[33]

The suffering of creation, for Peacocke, affects God also, because the world is 'in' God. Since God is creating the world from within and, the world being 'in' God, "God experiences its suffering directly as God's own and not from the outside."[34] He argues that God is immanently present in and to natural processes, on particular those that generate conscious and self-conscious life. Therefore we cannot but conclude that God suffers 'in', 'with' and 'under' the creative processes of the world with their costly, open ended unfolding.[35] Peacocke uses the feminine image to depict the suffering of God with his creation. Moreover, the panentheistic feminine image of the world, as being given existence by God in the very 'womb of God', is a particularly apt one for evoking an insight into the suffering of God in the very process of creation.[36]

4. God's Relation with the World

The world is in continuous dynamic creation. If the world is evolving with its inherent potentialities what is the role of a Creator God in this evolving world? How does the world relate to God in its continuing creative process?

---

29 *Ibid* 123.

30 A.R. Peacocke, *Creation and the World of Science*, 213.

31 *Ibid*, 213.

32 Panentheism means that the world is 'in' God. We shall deal with this concept in the coming section.

33 A.R. Peacocke, *Paths from Science towards God*, 142.

34 *Ibid*, 142.

35 *Ibid,* 126.

36 A.R. Peacocke, *Paths from Science towards God*, 142.

Is God immanent and transcendent at the same time? What is God's relation with time?

4.1. Panentheistic Understanding of Creation

Peacocke holds the panentheistic idea regarding the relation between God and the world. What is then, panenetheism? Peacocke defines: "Panentheism is the belief that the Being of God includes and penetrates all-that-is, so that every part of it exists in God and (as against pantheism)[37] that God's Being is more than it and is not exhausted by it."[38] There is no place 'out side' of God and everything exists in God. This points us in the direction of postulating that the ontological gap(s) between the world and God is /are located simply everywhere-or, more precisely, because the world is 'in God' , God can influence the world in its totality, as a System of systems.[39] Peacocke uses another example to clarify the notion of panentheism. He distinguishes panentheistic model from the western classical concept. According to Peacocke in the western classical concept, there is too much stress on the externality of the creative process-God is regarded as creating rather in a way the male fertilises the female from outside. However, the mammalian females nurture new life within themselves and Peacocke argues that this idea provides a much–needed corrective to the purely masculine image of divine creation.[40]

For Peacocke, the panentheistic model is capable of explaining the relation between God and the world. He also believes that "the panentheistic model allows one to combine a strengthened emphasis on the immanence of God in the world with God's ultimate transcendence over it."[41]

4.2. Immanence and Transcendence of God

From the panentheistic understanding of Peacocke follows the immanence and transcendence of God. In the light of panentheism Peacocke explains both the immanence and the transcendence of God. For him, God as continuing Creator and Sustainer is immanent in his creation. At the same time, he is transcendent to the creation. Peacocke stresses both aspects simultaneously. Some times, he uses the terms 'immanence in transcendence' and 'transcendence in immanence' to refer to God.[42] Peacocke's idea of immanence of God is inferred from the understanding of God as continuing Creator. He writes: "From the continuity and creativity of the processes of the natural world we inferred

37 Pantheism is a belief that everything is God.

38 A.R. Peacocke, *Paths from Science towards God*, 57.

39 *Ibid*, 58.

40 A.R. Peacocke, *Paths from Science towards God*, 139.

41 *Ibid*, 141.

42 A.R. Peacocke, *God and the New Biology*, 132.

that God's creative relation to the world must be conceived of as continuous, sustaining creative action within these natural processes."[43] This makes him say that the Creator is immanent in his creation. This is why, we can look for God's 'meanings' within the world of which we are part.[44]

By immanence of God Peacocke proposes the idea that God is creating in the whole process of the world continuously through and through. For him, the natural, causal, creative nexus of events themselves are God's creative action. "It is this that the attribution of immanence to God in his world must be taken to convey. God is not some kind of diffuse "spiritual" gas permeating everything (like the discarded ether of the nineteenth century), but all-that-is in its actual processes is God manifest in his mode as continuous creator."[45] By transcendence, Peacocke means that God is more than the world although he is immanent in his creation. Peacocke seems so convinced to assert that God transcends both humanity and nature, "for God is either in everything created from the beginning to the end, at all times and in all places or he is not there at all."[46] Whatever is 'in' the world is 'in' God and there is not something more in the world that is not 'in' God. He believes that "there is no part of the world where God is not active and present in the events and processes themselves, and because there is infinitely more to God's being than the world, we could say that the world is in God, there is nothing in the world not in God."[47]

4.3. Whole - Part Model

Peacocke uses the term *whole-part constraint* in order to show the causal connection between God and the world. *Whole-part constraint*, for Peacocke is a constraint exercised by the whole of the system on its parts.[48] This does not mean that *whole-part constraint* model derogates from the continued recognition of the effects of its components on the state of the system as a whole. This notion of *whole–part constraint* has become more and more significant in evolutionary development with the evolution of brain as the whole state and behaviour of the individual organism itself play an important role. "The state of the system-as-a-whole is influencing (i.e. acting like a cause

---

43 *Ibid*, 130.

44 *Ibid*, 130.

45 A.R. Peacocke, *Intimations of Reality*, 63.

46 A.R. Peacocke, "Chance and Law in Irreversible Thermodynamics, Theoretical Biology, and Theology" 139-140.

47 A.R. Peacocke, *Intimations of Reality*, (Notre Dame: Notre Dame University press, 1984), 64.

48 A.R. Peacocke, "God's Interaction with the World: The Implication of Deterministic "Chaos" and of Interconnected and Interdependent Complexity", *Chaos and Complexity: Scientific Perspectives on God's Action*, foot note no.23, 272.

on) what the parts, the constituents, actually do."[49] God is acting from a higher level over nature and exerts *top-down causality* on the world. He says that "the term *whole- part influence* will be used to represent the net effect of all those ways in which a system-as-a-whole, operating from its higher level, is a causal factor in what happens to its constituent parts, the lower level."[50] Peacocke applies this to the interaction between God and the world: "If God interacts with the world-system as a totality, then God, by affecting its overall state, could be envisaged as being able to exercise influence upon events in the myriad sublevels of existence of which it is made without abrogating the laws and regularities that specifically apply to them."[51]

For Peacocke the *whole-part constraint* is not a transfer of energy but a transfer of information or communication: "There is a flow of information from higher to lower levels in single, hierarchically stratified complex. The higher level is seen as constraining and shaping the patterns of events occurring among the constituent units of the lower ones."[52] He uses the example of mind-brain interaction with the body. The total state of human brain-as-a-whole is a constraint upon, and so causally effective, on the individual neurons of the body.[53] In this way, God is shaping and influencing the whole state of all-that-is over all space and all times. Peacocke affirms that "the best model for God's interaction with the world is that of God as 'informing,' influencing through an input of information and so shaping and influencing, the whole state of all-that-is over all space and times."[54]In this model God is seen as exerting a top-down causative constraint on the higher level so that particular patterns of events at lower levels within that whole can be different, if God so wills, from what they would otherwise have been if God has not willed.[55]

4.4. God and Time

One of the fundamental issues related to the discussion about creation and evolution is the problem of time. Among the principal questions frequently dealt in are the following: what is time, who created time and how did time begin, how can we relate temporality and eternity and etc? According to Peacocke time is created by God. "God is also the creator of physical time

---

49 A.R. Peacocke, *Paths from Science towards God*, 52.

50 *Ibid*, 52.

51 *Ibid*, 109.

52 *Ibid*, 53.

53 A.R. Peacocke, *From DNA to DEAN: Reflections and Explorations of a Priest-Scientist,* Norwich, the Canterbury Press, 1996, 206.

54 A.R. Peacocke, "Religion of a Scientist: Explorations into Reality", *Zygon*, 26(1994), 653.

55 A.R. Peacocke, *From DNA to DEAN: Reflections and Explorations of Priest-Scientist,* 207.

which is closely integrated with space, and so with energy and so with matter, in the understanding that 20th century physics has given us."[56] For Peacocke, God is eternal in the sense that he can transcend time but at the same time, God is temporal because God experiences a succession in relation to events and persons. God transcends physical time as its Creator but is himself immanent in created time, being present to every moment of it as he creates it.[57] "There is no created time to which God is not present as he gives its existence, just as he is present to all space."[58]God has to be 'inside' time in order to relate to the evolving processes of the world. If God is totally 'outside' time, it is not possible for him to interact with the world. In other words, Peacoke affirms that God has to be in some sense 'temporal' in order to relate with the 'temporal' world.

The idea of a temporal God is derived from the following ideas: Peacocke considers God as 'personal'. Peacocke shows that this is the Judeo-Christian experience of God. This shows that the transcendent God has been in some sense immanent and present 'in time'. According to Peacocke, "to be a person with consciousness is to be aware of the succession of states of mind"[59] The human experience of psychological time as a succession of our conscious states is intimately related to physical time. "Our own sense of psychological time, the sense of succession of our conscious states, with which our own sense of personhood is so bound, is closely related to the created physical time."[60] Peacocke applies this parallelism to God. By creation, Peacocke means that it is "the activity whereby God gives existence to each instant of physical time, the 'now' of the hand of the clock, and each instant has no existence prior to its being so created with all the entities, structures, and processes that fill it."[61] Then, the future does not exist not even for God as God creates each instant of physical time, fecund with possibilities and the outcomes are not yet actualised.[62] But still God can have purposes to implement in the forthcoming future. God is the Creator of space and time and God can transcend space and time, for they owe their being to him. Further, space and time can exist 'within' God in such a way that he is not precluded from being present at all points in space and time [63] According to Peacocke the idea of God as having no

56 A.R. Peacocke. "Science and God the Creator", *Zygon*, 28 (1993), 481.

57 According to Peacocke, God gives existence to each instant of physical time. Each moment is being created by God.

58 A.R. Peacocke, *Theology for a Scientific Age,* 132.

59 A.R. Peacocke, *Theology for a Scientific Age,* 128.

60 A.R. Peacocke. "Science and God the Creator", 481.

61 *Ibid*, 481.

62 *Ibid*, 481.

63 A.R. Peacocke, *Creation and the World of Science*, foot note no.53, 80.

knowledge about the future does not mean that God cannot have the knowledge about the probabilities of the outcomes of the processes in the world. In the same manner, he argues with regard to the problem of free will. Peacocke puts it in this way, "if human free will is to be genuine and not illusory, even if more constrained than we think as we experience it, then God cannot so 'transcend' the time in which we act that he can know precisely and definitively what our future free actions will be."[64] Regarding free will Peacocke says that God can have complete knowledge of the probabilities of the outcomes of the operations of our free will as a parent might(have some knowledge) in relation to a child's decisions, or a wife in relation to the husband's.[65] God limits his omniscience to safeguard human freedom. This model of a "loving God" gives more meaningfulness to human life.

Conclusion

In this article, we have analysed Peacocke's understanding about God, humans and the world in the light of the new discoveries and evolutionary theories. God's continuing action holds the cosmos in existence. Peacocke tries to project a "living and loving God" who is always vigilant to his creatures through his unfailing immanence in the world. God is always acting in and with the world processes with his loving care. In this understanding God, human being and the world are not seen closed entities but they are interconnected and interrelated. God has limited his omnipotence so that human beings would have free will to collaborate with him in re-making the world. Here, we see a loving God who suffers with creation and guide it towards its destiny.

Bibliography

Books

Peacocke, A. R.: *Science and the Christian Experiment* (London: Oxford University Press, 1971).

______: *Creation and the World of Science* (Oxford: Clarendon Press, 1979).

______: *An Introduction to the Physical Chemistry of Biological Organization* (Oxford: Clarendon Press, 1983).

______: *Intimations of Reality,* (Notre Dame: Notre Dame University Press, 1984).

______: *Theology for a Scientific Age: Being and Becoming – Natural and Divine* (Oxford: Blackwell, 1990), IInd enlarged edition, (Minneapolis: Fortress Press 1993).

______: *God and the New Biology* (Gloucester: Peter Smith, 1994).

64 A.R. Peacocke, *Theology for a Scientific Age,* 129.

65 A.R. Peacocke, *Theology for a Scientific Age,* 129.

______: *God and Science: A Quest for Christian Credibility*, London, SCM Press, 1996.

______: *From DNA to DEAN: Reflections and Explorations of a Priest-Scientist* (Norwich: The Canterbury Press, 1996).

______: *Paths from Science Towards God: The End of All Our Exploring*, London, One World, 2001.

______: *The Music of Creation* (Minneapolis: Fortress Press, 2006).

Articles

Peacocke, A. R.: "God's Action in the Real World", *Zygon*, 26 (1991), 455-477.

______: "Religion of a Scientist, Explorations into Reality", *Zygon*, 29 (1994), 639-659.

______: "Science and God the Creator", *Zygon*, 28 (1993), 469-484.

______: "Biology and Theology of Evolution", *Zygon*, 34 (1999), 694-712.

______: "Biological Evolution – A Positive Theological Appraisal" in *Evolutionary and Molecular Biology: Scientific Perspectives on God's Action*, eds. R. J. Russell, W. R. Stoeger and F. J. Ayala, Vatican, Vatican Observatory; Berkley, California, The Center for Theology and Natural Sciences, 1998, 357-376.

Other References

Bartholomew D.: *God of Chance*, (London: SCM Press, 1984)

Einstein, A.: *Out of my Later Years* (Westport: Greenwood Press, 1970).

Farrer, A.: *Faith and Speculation* (London: A & C Black, 1997).

Gibbins, P.: *Particles and Paradoxes: The Limits of Quantum Logic* (Cambridge: Cambridge University Press, 1987).

Polkinghorne, J.: *Science and Creation* (London: SPCK, 1988).

______: *Science and Providence*: *God's Interaction with the World* (London: SPCK, 1989).

______: *Scientists as Theologians: A Comparison of the Writings of Ian Barbour, A. Peacocke, and J. Polkinghorne (* London: SPCK, 1996).

13

The Mystery of God and the Dialectics of Evil

Savio Martires

Abstract

Humanity has through the ages struggled with the problem of evil, but more so today, the thesis that posits the non-existence of God in the face of immense evil and insurmountable suffering seems to be fortified. This article endeavours to make sense of this perennial problem by examining the manner in which St. Augustine and St. Ireneaus attempt a justification of God in the face of evil in their theodicies and then moves on to the modern philosophical distinction between the Logical and Evidential problem of evil. In attempting to offer motivation to responding to the reality of suffering and evil, it delves on human relationality and freedom before presenting the virtues of Faith, Hope and Charity as Christian motivation to being active agents in the battle against evil and in the alleviation of suffering.

Keywords

St. Augustine, St. Ireneaus, justification, evil, human relationality, freedom.

Introduction

A journey down human history would reveal the experience of evil as one being built into our very human fabric, such that, at pivotal moments in time, the thought of questioning God's existence wouldn't be unconvincing.

How ought we to respond to say, Hume who, in paraphrasing Epicurus in his *Dialogues Concerning Natural Religion* for the sake of philosophical discourse, states, "Is he [God] willing to prevent evil, but not able? Then is he [*sic*] impotent. Is he able, but not willing? Then is he [*sic*] malevolent. Is he both able and willing? Whence then is evil?"[1] Potent, isn't it?

In fact, the excruciating suffering of innocents in wars, the horrors of the concentration camps, the extreme poverty and the suffering of the marginalized, rapes, murders, ISIS killings in the name of God, the dehumanization of people in detention camps, etc. seem to fortify a thesis against the belief in a benevolent, omnipotent God. A belief in such a God and the fact of evil seem irreconcilable and stand juxtaposed.

1. The Theodicies of St. Augustine and St. Irenaeus

Augustine had a literal understanding of the *fall* as stated in Genesis and, consequently, the only way for him to maintain belief in the God of classical theism was to shift the blame for the existence of evil entirely onto human beings.

Manichaeism posited good and evil as two independent principles. However, Augustine rejects this ultimate duality, affirming the victory of good. He posits evil as non-substantial, defining evil as *privatio boni* – a 'privation of good'. In this context, being a theist, we see how he comes to hold God alone as the ultimate reality, defining evil as a mere privation.[2]

This definition fortifies his claim that God created a perfect world, but, through the misuse of free will, humankind realized the inherent potency for evil, resulting in a rift between God and humanity. In having ceased to be what we were meant to be, we are solely responsible for evil and suffering in the world.[3]

Now, critics could argue, if the world was perfect as Augustine claimed, whence did evil emerge? Did it create itself *ex nihilo*? Either the world wasn't created perfect, or it was, and then, God allowed evil. Further, if humans were perfectly created, how do they come to choose evil? Evolution challenges the notion of a perfect world and Hick says Augustine's view suggests predestination.

Irenaeus, on the other hand, held a dynamic view of creation, suggesting that God created human beings in an imperfect world so that they would be driven to grow morally and spiritually. In the quest for becoming fully human and fully alive, moral evil becomes a natural consequence of human finitude.

1 Cited by John S. Feinberg, *The Many Faces of Evil: Theological Systems and the Problem of Evil* (Wheaton: Crossway Books, 2004), 18.

2 Masao Abe, "The Problem of Evil in Christianity and Buddhism," in *Buddhist-Christian Dialogue: Mutual Renewal and Transformation*, eds. Paul O. Ingram and Frederick J. Streng, 148-149.

3 Cyril Desbruslais, *Guidelines for the Study of the Philosophy of Religion* (Pune: Jnana-Deepa Vidyapeeth, 2000), 51-52.

He wasn't implying that humans are not culpable for their actions, but rather that the measure of one's responsibility is proportionate to how knowledgeable and free one is at the time of committing actions, which in turn need to be situated in their proper context. Even physical evils are not to be viewed as the wrath of God, but as a necessary consequence of having an evolving world.[4]

1.1. Influences of Irenaean Thinking

John Hick proposes that in creating a finite person, God must give some epistemic distance, i.e. a certain relative autonomy over and against Himself. God must not be forced upon us, consequently, He is veiled by creation. To man, the world must be, to an extent, *etsi deus non daretur.* God becomes knowable only through a personal free response. Thus, epistemic distance is certainly not a spatial distance to be traversed, but a cognitive freedom which ensures a certain degree of human autonomy from God. This is necessary, or else humans wouldn't be able to love, or learn to love, or grow to the fullness of maturity.[5] We may call epistemic distance, the distance between immaturity and maturity. A question to contemplate at this juncture is, 'if suffering is essential for moral development, what is really served by the suffering of children and of animals?'

Hick's thought is echoed by Polkinghorne, who states that God puts a limitation on Himself in creating; it is a kenotic act, so that creatures may be free. Therefore, it follows that all that occurs will not conform to divine will. Polkinghorne also claims that science can explain physical evils e.g. malignancy will occur when organisms evolve freely. Thus, omnipotence is not an unlimited power, but an unlimited ability to act in accordance with the laws of nature.[6]

2. The Logical Problem of Evil

J. L. Mackie's formulation is the paradigm of the 'logical problem of evil'. The 3 premises are: 1. God is omnipotent; 2. God is wholly good, and 3. Evil exists. He says there is a contradiction between the propositions, such that if any two were true at a given time, the third must be false.[7]

To demonstrate incompatibility, he introduces premises: Firstly, good is opposed to evil, from which it follows that a benevolent omnipotent being

4 Ibid., 53-54.

5 John Hick, *Evil and the God of Love* (New York: Palgrave Macmillan, 2010), 281.

6 John Polkinghorne, "Religion and Science," in *Philosophy of Religion: Classic and Contemporary Issues,* eds. Paul Copan and Chad Meister (Oxford: Blackwell Publishing, 2008), 26-27.

7 J. L. Mackie, "Evil and Omnipotence," in *God and Evil: Contemporary Perspectives in Philosophy Series*, ed. Nelson Pike (Englewood Cliffs: Prentice-Hall, 1964), 47.

would eliminate evil completely. Secondly, there is no limit to what an omnipotent being can do.[8]

Mackie says that denying any one of the attributes of God or the reality of evil is an adequate solution, but, being incompatible with Classical theism, it is rejected by theists. Even if one denies that evil is ultimately real, why then would there be an 'apparent' evil? Denying evil would seem to solve the problem at the cost of common sense. Mackie's personal response, however, is to deny that God is omnipotent and wholly good.[9]

To debunk Mackie's argument we need to look at some premises:

1. There is no limit to what an omnipotent being can do. Theists would say God can't do the logically impossible and this doesn't limit God's omnipotence, e.g. making square circles.[10]
2. A good being always eliminates evil as far as it can. In talking about God, we should modify the premise as follows: An omni-being always eliminates evil as far as it can, without eliminating a greater good that outweighs the evil.[11]

To arrive at Mackie's conclusion, we need another premise: There is no morally justified reason for God to permit evil he could prevent.[12] To which, Peter Kreeft would say that we haven't considered God's wisdom, which is different. Perhaps, He sees a greater good, we do not.[13]

2.1. Alvin Plantinga's Free Will Defence

Alvin Plantinga introduces the premise: God is omnipotent, and it wasn't within His power to create a world with moral good, but no moral evil.[14] This attacks the premise: 'there is no morally justified reason for God to permit evil he could prevent'. Thus, God would have good reason for creating a world with evil.[15]

---

8 Daniel Howard-Snyder, ed., *The Evidential Argument from Evil* (Bloomington: Indiana University Press, 1996), xii-xiii.

9 Mackie, "Evil and Omnipotence," in *God and Evil: Contemporary Perspectives in Philosophy Series*, 47-48.

10 Luke Muehlhauser, "*Arguing about Evil: Mackie's Argument*," September 12, 2009, http://commonsenseatheism.com/?p=3115 (accessed January 03, 2014).

11 Ibid.

12 Ibid.

13 Peter Kreeft, *The Modern Scholar: Faith and Reason: The Philosophy of Religion* (Prince Frederick: Recorded Books, 2005), 18.

14 Alvin Plantinga, *God, Freedom and Evil* (Grand Rapids: Wm. B. Eerdmans Publishing Co., 1977), 45.

15 Ibid., 31.

Now, if it is logically possible that God creates us such that we freely choose the right thing always, then can the free will defence be sustained? Plantinga, here, makes a distinction between creating and actualizing, saying God could not have actualized any possible world he pleases.[16] Our counterfactuals of freedom are such that, in a situation, assuming we are free, every possible person suffers from 'transworld depravity', becoming capable of at least one act of moral evil, e.g. a person is free to take a bribe or not. Either one could take place, which means God cannot actualize all possible worlds.[17]

Plantinga attempts to show consistency between premises: 1. God is omnipotent, benevolent, omniscient and 2. Evil exists. He does so by introducing an implicit proposition 3. God actualizes a world containing moral good and every human suffers from 'transworld depravity'. This new premise 3 is consistent with premise 1 and entails premise 2. Thus, Plantinga solves the problem.[18]

Critics say this solution offers explanation only for some evil, but we see much more moral evil. To which, he says, it is at least logically possible that the counterfactuals of freedom are such that our world has a better balance of moral good and evil than any other possible world God could have actualized.[19]

3. The Evidential Problem

The evidential argument claims that the existence of evil provides prima facie reasons for the improbability that God exists. William Rowe states:

1. There are instances of intense suffering which an omnipotent, omniscient being could have prevented without losing some greater good or permitting evil equally bad or worse.
2. An omniscient, wholly good being would prevent any intense suffering it could, unless it could not without losing some greater good or permitting some evil equally bad or worse.
3. There does not exist an omnipotent, omniscient, wholly good being.[20]

Premise 2, he says is acceptable to both theists and atheists, and to support premise 1, he gives the example of a fawn, trapped in a forest fire, that

16 Alvin Plantinga, "The Free Will Defense," in *God and the Problem of Evil*, ed. William L. Rowe (Malden: Blackwell Publishing, 2001), 95-100.

17 Ibid., 100-114.

18 Ibid., 114-115.

19 Ibid., 116.

20 William L. Rowe, "The Problem of Evil and Some Varieties of Atheism," in *The Evidential Argument from Evil,* ed. Daniel Howard-Snyder (Bloomington: Indiana University Press, 1996), 2.

dies only after enduring terrible and prolonged pain. Thus, we have rational grounds to believe that premise 1 is true.[21]

Through the *G. E. Moore Shift*, the theist can come up with a counter-argument that rationally justifies his belief, i.e. if you have an argument p, q and therefore, r, instead of directly arguing against p, you create another argument not-r, q, therefore, not-p. Both are valid, but both can't be accepted.[22]

To the rationality of the theist's belief, Rowe says an atheist can take the following positions: unfriendly atheism; indifferent atheism; or his position, which is friendly atheism, i.e. where the atheist holds some theists as justified in their belief. In support of friendly atheism, he says truth is not a necessary condition for being rationally justified in holding a belief. Thus, if the atheist holds the theist as rationally justified in his belief, it doesn't mean the atheist thinks the belief of the theist is true.[23]

Rowe illustrates how we can be justified in our counter-beliefs. Say you are lost at sea due to a plane crash. People are unable to find you and conclude that you are dead. They are rationally justified in their belief. While you, who are alive, are justified in the opposite.[24]

So the theist has a counter-argument, but what is the evidence for God's existence? Rowe says the theist may use traditional arguments to justify God on the basis of phenomena. But the problem is both the theist and the atheist use the same justification i.e. diverse phenomena and end with opposite conclusions. This he calls the paradox of friendly atheism. Though the argument for theism is logically valid, it doesn't make it true. Rowe, therefore, says it is more reasonable to believe the atheistic one.[25]

3.1. Wykstra's CORNEA Argument

In the CORNEA argument, Stephen Wykstra infers that, because Rowe doesn't see a good served by the fawn's suffering, he can claim that 'it appears there is no such good'. But he can do so only if he is sure that, given his cognitive faculties, if there were such a good, he would likely see it.[26]

He gives an analogy of a college dean who hears a candidate speak in Greek, which he doesn't understand. Could he say the sentence spoken has no

21 Ibid., 4.

22 Ibid., 6-7.

23 Ibid., 8.

24 Ibid.

25 Ibid., 9.

26 Stephen J. Wykstra, "Rowe's Noseeum Arguments from Evil," in *The Evidential Argument from Evil,* ed. Daniel Howard-Snyder (Bloomington: Indiana University Press, 1996), 129.

meaning? Obviously not! Similarly, Rowe has no epistemic access to God's intent. Thus, Rowe's premise 1 doesn't stand.[27]

4. Human Finitude

The ignorance of not knowing God's intentions is built into the limits of our finitude. Basil Mitchell's parable of the partisans demonstrates human finitude. The parable goes thus: a member of an underground resistance meets a stranger who assures him that he is with the resistance and is its leader, but warns that his actions may seem contrary at times, i.e. he would seem to be in league with the enemy. As time unfolds, the evidence is ambiguous, but the stranger had a charismatic effect on the partisan, such that, even in the face of counter-evidence, he continues to believe that the stranger is with the resistance. When questioned as to the motives of the stranger, the partisan says that he doesn't know why, but that the stranger must have his reasons.[28] Thus, we can say of pain and suffering, that they aren't decisive against God's love, because we don't know what is happening within the suffering person and what happens after death.

Contemporary philosopher Martin Heidegger says that 'thrownness' is our inevitable facticity. The ultimate givenness, death, places a limit on our choice of possibilities.[29] So if we understand our finitude, it is not hard to accept that we can't understand God's intentions.

5. Human Relationality

The ability to transcend is part of our very essence as human beings and here, it is opportune to reflect on one of the transcendentals of Scholastic philosophy, i.e. Transcendental Unity, which posits that there is an inherent interconnectedness that is true to our experience. For a theist, finding perfection of unity in God and in us an imperfection echoes St. Augustine's sentiments, "Thou hast made us for thyself, O Lord, and our heart is restless until it finds its rest in thee." Transcendental unity gives us an identity of who we are, due to the unity in substance of a being and it would follow that it also gives rise to equality. To know one's own identity would call us to respect the identity of the other. Kant's categorical maxim of never treating others 'merely as a means', but as 'ends in themselves', expounds this very idea of equality. If we were to use the

---

27 Stephen J. Wykstra, "The Humean Obstacle to Evidential Arguments from Suffering: On Avoiding the Evils of 'Appearance'," in *Oxford Readings in Philosophy: The Problem of Evil*, eds. Marilyn McCord Adams and Robert Merrihew Adams (New York: Oxford University Press, 1990), 151, 156.

28 David Stewart, *Exploring the Philosophy of Religion* (Englewood Cliffs: Prentice-Hall, 1980), 132-133.

29 Johnson Puthenpurackal, *Survey of Contemporary Western Philosophy: Part I* (Pune: Jnana-Deepa Vidyapeeth, 2013), 24, 31.

'butterfly effect' analogy, this would mean that all that we do in this life today has ramifications elsewhere, that even the slightest action of malice has some effect to the detriment of the society and the public.

Heidegger tells us that *Dasein* is ontologically related to the world. In relation to persons, *Dasein* is for the sake of others. *Dasein,* therefore, as being-in-the-world, is a relational paradigm, where *Dasein* has no being apart from the world and there is no world apart from *Dasein's* Being. Thus, human beings can't afford to be deistic spectators. We are called to alleviate pain and suffering. Our relationality demands a response which hinges on the extent of our freedom.

6. Freedom: The Criterion for Authentic Praxis

Gabriel Marcel calls freedom a grace through which one can create oneself and commit to God and others. Our free activity is marked by finite freedom. Therefore, freedom hinges on the recognition that we are finite.[30]

In the quest for authentic existence, let us look at Kierkegaard's 3 stages of existence and compare with Fulton Sheen's 3 levels of existence. Kierkegaard's stage of the 'lone individual' is where one has an attitude of non-commitment; thus, a person would hate being constrained by choice and relating to God or people becomes impossible.[31] At Sheen's level of the ego, an egotist would make his ego the central interest of his life.[32] An egocentric life ensures narcissistic tendencies and a thriving of moral evils. People would be treated as mere means and never as ends in themselves. Both Kierkegaard's and Sheen's first level shows that a person fixated at this stage could never reach out to anyone.

Kierkegaard's second stage is the 'ethical stage', where one has some constancy and consistency. There is a choice for a moral standard. A person is influenced by society and one's individual fantasies become subservient to society and law. Yet, by being ethical, one still misses the category of the exceptional.[33] Sheen's 'I' level is the stage where the ego is subordinated to the 'I', but one is still on a purely human level; thus, there are boundaries the 'I' cannot transcend on its own.[34] But, positively, both agree that despite limitations, there is openness to the other.

Kierkegaard's 3rd stage is the 'religious stage', where one is before God. From commitment to the impersonal law, one takes a leap to a personal

30 Ibid., 36.

31 Ibid., 33.

32 Fulton J. Sheen, *Lift up your Hearts: A Guide to Spiritual Peace* (Bangalore: Asian Trading Corporation, 1998), 6-7.

33 Puthenpurackal, *Survey of Contemporary Western Philosophy: Part I,* 33-34.

34 Sheen, *Lift up your Hearts: A Guide to Spiritual Peace*, 176-177.

Absolute. Therefore, a wrongdoing is not just against the law, but against God. In taking this leap of faith into the dark, one attains genuine selfhood.[35] In Sheen's third level of the Divine, Christ is central and the 'I' is on the periphery. The ego has been sublimated. There is the surrender of one's freedom to God and, in such a surrender, one becomes truly free. At this stage, there is an understanding of suffering.[36] Kierkegaard would say the weaker the human, the stronger God is in him.

Sheen, obviously operating on the level of faith, seems to go further in saying that Christ is central to the person at this level. Thus, though unasked suffering exists, at the level of the divine existence, one can make meaning through seeking union. While Kierkegaard says that moving from one level to another depends on individual choice, Sheen would say, there is also divine help.

This covers a freedom and authentic existence from a theist's point of view, but atheistic thinkers like Sartre would say that man is condemned to be free, and thus the onus of responsibility is on oneself. Responsibility is the price of freedom and to abandon it is bad faith.37 Camus too says that, though evil is greater than good, we must still extend a helping hand to others to combat the plague of absurdity.38 So atheism, too, can be seen as a faith-like driving force that impels actions. From a theistic or atheistic perspective, what is clear is that freedom is the bedrock and criterion for an impetus to praxis. Which provides greater motivation? I propose theism over atheism.

7. Faith, Hope and Charity: Christian Motivation to Praxis

Peter Kreeft, in *Three Philosophies of Life,* examines the theological virtues of faith, hope and charity. He says that Ecclesiastes, an existential book focused on human existence, teaches the necessity of faith. For without the eye of faith, using mere reason, experience and observation to see and think is inadequate to save one from the "vanity of vanities." He says,

> Ecclesiastes has intellectual faith; he believes in God. But that is not enough. "The demons also believe, and tremble" (James 2:19). Ecclesiastes proves that need for real faith, true faith, lived faith, saving faith, by showing the consequences of its absence, even in the presence of intellectual faith.39

Kreeft says Job offers the insight that in the midst of all destruction, pain, suffering and misery, hope is what helps him to endure, to persist in the good fight that eventually leads to victory.40 This is amply evident in the theist at

35 Puthenpurackal, *Survey of Contemporary Western Philosophy: Part I,* 34.

36 Sheen, *Lift up your Hearts: A Guide to Spiritual Peace*, 11-12.

37 Puthenpurackal, *Survey of Contemporary Western Philosophy: Part I*, 39.

38 Ibid., 42.

39 Peter Kreeft, *Three Philosophies of Life* (San Francisco: Ignatius Press, 1989), 11.

40 Ibid.

Sheen's level of the divine, whose real faith offers hope, by which he/she could possibly find meaning in suffering.

Lastly, Kreeft claims that it is in the Song of Songs that we learn the most important lesson, i.e. Love. This is what lends ultimate meaning to life. Love is what allows us to reach out in authentic charity.41 A person at Sheen's level of the divine, where Christ, the God of love is the cynosure, would certainly be in a position to understand suffering and reach out to others.

Christian theistic responses attempt to reconcile the experience of evil and of a good and omnipotent God. God is never in question as the theist has antecedent reason for his belief. His is not a mere intellectual faith, but one based on the experience of, and, at a deeper level, on a union with the God who is love, which encourages reaching out to fellow suffering human beings, e.g. people like Mother Theresa. For a naturalist, however, God is not transcendent, but a hypothesis to be proved. Consequently, we conclude that, bereft of faith, one becomes a sceptic and though atheism can provide impetus to praxis, a theist's faith seems like a far greater motivation to work to alleviate pain and suffering around.

Conclusion

The problem of Evil viewed logically doesn't contradict the existence of God. Plantinga's Free Will defence aptly demonstrated this. While the theodicies attempt a justification of God, given the fact of evil, Plantinga's approach is to show consistency between an all-perfect God and evil, i.e. a consistency where Mackie did not find one. Wykstra's response to the Evidential Problem was to acknowledge that we don't have an epistemic access to God's intentions. This makes sense, given our finitude.

But just because atheistic arguments do not disprove God, we cannot stop there. Our relationality, intertwined with the extent of our freedom, necessitates a personal response. Praxis hinges on freedom. Only in being free can one be said to have authentic existence.

Aldous Huxley quite adequately says, "Experience is not what happens to a man; it is what a man does with what happens to him."42 On this note we may conclude, with the suggestion that the experience of real faith, in true freedom, is what leads to authentic existence. It is, in Frankl's language, that 'WHY' which lends meaning and purpose to life, enabling us to cope with any 'HOW'. Thus, we may contend that it is true freedom and hope, which real faith offers, that alone enables humanity to respond to the problem of evil.

---

41 Ibid.

42 Aldous Huxley, *Text and Pretexts: An Anthology with Commentaries* (London: Chatto & Windus, 1932), 5.

14

Encounter of Christian Faith with Deleuze and Vattimo

Arun Philip SJ

Abstract

As the humble offering to my professor, who taught me a method of Christian philosophizing, following the example of St. Thomas Aquinas, an exemplar, who philosophized using the philosophies of his time, I have attempted to have an encounter between Christian philosophy and two ideas of Gilles Deleuze and Gianni Vattimo. The contemporary world context reveals the important role religion has to play. The multifaceted religious faith needs to interact with various dimensions of reason. These are much more than certain proofs for the existence of God. I have introduced the concepts of 'difference preceding identity' from Deleuze and is applied to the Christian faith to see it as difference. Probably to overcome the common criticism against postmodernism that 'anything can go', the judging criteria for the faith is brought in by the concept of charity of which Vattimo speaks. I am not attempting to Christianise Deleuzian philosophy or vice versa, but facilitating an encounter between three streams of thought which may be fruitful for the Christian faith.

Keywords

Faith, reason, Deleuze,Vattimo, post-modernism, post-structuralism, 'difference', machinic thinking, weak thought.

Introduction

George Karuvelil SJ, is a philosopher, teacher and friend to me, who has taught me a few insightful courses accompanied by the philosophical rigour of an analytical philosopher. One of main inspirations for this article is his course on Faith and Reason, where he considers Thomas Aquinas as an exemplar, a man who theologized with the help of the dominant philosophical trends of his time. George's course was an attempt to follow the example of this exemplar to have an interaction of his Christian faith with the cultural and philosophical movements of our time. Moving along these lines of thought, I have attempted in this paper to see how some of the ideas of an atheistic, post-structuralist philosopher called Gilles Deleuze and a contemporary philosopher Gianni Vattimo can be helpful in our dialogue between faith and reason.

There is a powerful dialogue in the movie, 'Fiddler on the Roof', which says "traditions, traditions. Without our traditions, our lives would be as shaky as... as... as a fiddler on the roof!" Few dares to become a fiddler on the roof, risking their lives. Though philosophy is a critical and reflective branch of study, deviant thinking is not always appreciated. Spinoza and Nietzsche along with many others belong to that group of few, who dared to think differently from the mainline philosophical thinking. I think Gilles Deleuze also belongs to that group who had the audacity to think beyond identity, to sing the praises of chaos and differences. Attempts are made here to engage with this thinker, who was a firm believer of immanence, no transcendence, difference and creation.

1. Context for the Article

A discussion on faith and reason has always been a part of the philosophy curriculum, especially philosophy of religion. In that sense, this article is part of that normal tradition. But the context, which I describe in the first section reveals the need for faith to have encounter with different sets of reasons.

1.1. A Set of Books[1]

There are a set of recent books written by sociologists and thinkers[2] describing the phenomenon of an increase in atheists in many traditionally religious countries. These countries also occupy top positions in the social indices like World Happiness report, human rights index 2018, human freedom index 2018 etc. In the book entitled *A Society without God,* Phil Zuckermanan, an American sociologist, speaks of his experience of living in Denmark and

1 Personal Experiences in the country where I am staying now attest to some of these conclusions of the books. I see many atheistic individuals who are extremely service minded, who works tirelessly for the cause of refugees and migrants.

2 I am not describing of the people like Richard Dawkins who are apologetics of atheism.

Sweden, two Scandinavian countries with high ratings on these indices with very less economic inequality (India and US[3], two religious countries have high and growing rates of economic inequality), low crime rates (jails are empty) and very good care for the old and dying and good social security schemes. This record of Scandinavian countries is nothing new. Most of the citizens call themselves Christians by culture and not by beliefs.

> It is a great socio-religious irony—for lack of a better term—that when we consider the fundamental values and moral imperatives contained within the world's great religions, such as caring for the sick, the infirm, the elderly, the poor, the orphaned, the vulnerable; practicing mercy, charity, and goodwill toward one's fellow human beings; and fostering generosity, humility, honesty, and communal concern over individual egotism—these traditionally religious values are most successfully established, institutionalized, and put into practice at the societal level in the most irreligious nations in the world today.[4]

In the book *Religion without God,* Ray Billington tries to go beyond the binaries of theism and atheism; he tries to look at the possibility of a religion without God. A question that is asked by him is, "Why the theistic religions have the monopoly over the transcendence and the fundamental nature of being?"[5] He is trying to look into the eastern religions, especially Buddhism, Taoism and the non-dualistic aspects of Hinduism.

1.2. Revival of Religions in the World

A prophetic prediction that has been proven wrong is that religious faith will decline as we progress in the age of reason. A survey published in a Guardian article says 84% of the world population identifies themselves with the major or minor religions of the world.[6] When there are growing populations of non-religious (agnostics, atheists or people who don't want to identify with any religion) are increasing in the European countries, the number of religious people are increasing in countries like China.[7]

1.3. Religion, Fundamentalism and Politics

While fundamentalist tendencies are not limited to any religion, the growing influence of fundamentalist groups in the political scenarios of the major

3 https://economictimes.indiatimes.com/news/economy/indicators/inequality-increased-in-china-india-and-us-imf/articleshow/61039705.cms (Accessed on 8 November,2019).

4 Phil Zuckerman, *Society without God* (New York: New York University Press, 2008), 30.

5 Ray Billington, *Religion without God* (London: Routledge; 2002), ix.

6 https://www.theguardian.com/news/2018/aug/27/religion-why-is-faith-growing-and-what-happens-next (Accessed on 8 November,2019).

7 https://www1.cbn.com/cbnnews/world/2017/april/china-gripped-by-spiritual-revival-as-hundreds-of-millions-turn-to-religion-and-faith (Accessed on 8 November,2019).

democracies is an issue of concern. The support of Hindutva politics in India, the support of Trump politics by the white evangelical Americans are good examples of such a trend. The growing polarization in the lines of religion is the byproduct of all these.

1.4. Pope Francis and Catholicism

Although he couldn't settle all the problems in the Catholic Church, especially sexual abuse, financial irregularities connected with Vatican Bank and the role of women in the Church, Pope Francis is still considered as a moral authority in the world. But beyond this, he is trying to reshape the church in the mold of Vatican II, to become a church of the people of God. There is a regular invitation in the Synod of Bishops to speak freely and courageously, to hear diverse opinions.[8] He constantly invites the church to be the church of the poor, a church which is ecologically conscious and the church which looks outward.[9] One strong message from the conclusion of the Synod in Amazon is, "We, all of us, are in need of salvation, to consider ourselves righteous is to leave God, the only righteous one, out in the cold."[10]

1.5. Certain Remarks:

From these descriptions of the context, I would like to summarize some essential characteristics of the post-modern world especially connected to theme religion.

1. Religion plays a major role
2. Fundamentalist tendencies are prevalent in many religions
3. We live in an inter-religious context
4. There is a prophetic call from certain number of atheists to religious people, to live the life much more authentically according to their religion.

1.6. A Word on Reason

As faith is multi-faceted,[11] it is foolishness to think that we can discover it with a uni-dimensional reason or logic (or the so-called Aristotelian logic). But this will include fuzzy logic, modal logic and all other systems of logic; and it may go beyond the ideas of scientific and mechanistic reason based on Newtonian

8 http://www.synod.va/content/synod2018/en/news/address-by-pope-francis-at-the-opening-of-the-synod-of-bishops-.html (Accessed on 8 November,2019).

9 https://www.vaticannews.va/en/pope/news/2019-10/pope-francis-amazon-synod-closing-speech.html (Accessed on 8 November,2019).

10 https://www.ncronline.org/news/vatican/closing-synod-francis-warns-against-righteous-who-leave-god-out-cold (Accessed on 8 November,2019).

11 This dimension will be discussed in detail in the next sections.

mechanics, but it includes scientific reason based on relativity and quantum physics and the reason seen in social sciences, philosophy, art and culture. In this article, I have tried to juxtapose faith with post-modern/post-structuralist reasons present in the ideas of Deleuze and Vattimo.

2. Introduction to Deleuzian Thinking and the Concept of Difference

Gilles Deleuze (1925-1995) is a French philosopher belonging to the generation of Levinas, Derrida, Lyotard and Foucault. The labels like post-structuralist, post-modernist and pure metaphysician (he uses this term)[12] are attributed to him. Michel Foucault, a prominent French Philosopher, proclaimed that the century might be called Deleuzian, which was considered a joke by Deleuze himself, "meant to make people who like us laugh, and make everyone else livid."[13] On my part, I am interested in focusing on the title, 'the philosopher of difference,' especially after his ground-breaking work called *Difference and Repetition*. Most of his later works (popular and famous) like *Anti-Oedipus* and *A Thousand Plateaus* are built upon this foundation of difference.[14] If Heidegger's central thought in his entire philosophy was the question of being, then the central thought of Deleuze is the subjugation of 'difference' to 'representation'.

In our day to day circumstances, we speak of a difference between or difference from something, and that something has an identity. When a claim is made that red is different from blue, it speaks of the difference between the two colours after having an understanding of their identity. The clarity of the concept of difference will depend on the clarity of the concepts of identity. In otherwords, identity is privileged over difference. Deleuze understands and accepts this separation of concepts and privileging, but he states such a concept of difference is historical baggage that we are carrying. The words like diversity could be used instead of difference (difference from or difference between), but Deleuze speaks of the difference which is prior to identity. Identity is created from the difference. Difference[15] is defined by itself. The Deleuzian phrase is, "difference is behind everything, and behind difference there is nothing."[16] "Difference is not diversity. Diversity is given, but difference is that by which the given is given, that by which the given is given as diverse. Difference is

12 Henry Somers-Hall, *Deleuze's Difference and Repetition: An Edinburg Philosophical Guide* (Edinburg: Edinburg University Press Ltd, 2013), 1.

13 Gilles Deleuze, *Negotiations 1972-1990*, trans. Martin Joughin (New York: Columbia University Press, 1995), 4.

14 Foundation and Difference are opposing terms, but the paradox of the structure is the essence of his philosophy.

15 From now on, I use the term difference in this Deleuzian sense unless otherwise specified.

16 Gilles Deleuze, Difference and Repetition, trans. Paul Patton (London: Athlone Press,1994), 57

not phenomenon but the noumenon closest to the phenomenon." [17] The notions of identity or the order unfolds out of the difference or the world in motion.

I saw a beautiful summary of Deleuzian thinking in a YouTube video, "His work is a call to see the entire world in terms of difference. Because if the world is fundamentally immanent, in motion and rhizomatic, then to embrace all that, complexity and the inter-connectedness is to affirm existence. To affirm existence is to affirm difference."[18] In other words, the affirmation of existence is much more than affirmation of a single or multiple identities.

2.1. Deleuzian Political Ontology: A Concrete Application of Difference

The traditional liberal political theory (Locke, Hobbes) starts with the individual. The question that was asked is, "Why is the government required? or Is the government justifiable?" Traditional political theorists argued about the original condition of the human being and based themselves on different parameters (e.g.: preservation of natural rights of life, liberty and property in Locke), and each one claimed a government (type of government is different for each one) based on social contract is the best possible way for peace and development. The questions have not changed even for the contemporary political thinkers like John Rawls and Robert Nozick.[19] The strong point of these political theorists is the central figure called the human individual, with his or her personal interests and preference. Using Deleuzian terms, Todd May says, this is a translation of the dogmatic image of thought (which Deleuze criticizes very explicitly in the third chapter of *Difference and Repetition*). A journey is made from individual to government via representation.[20] Politics in this framework is a matter of stability and anarchy is completely opposed. Many questions are asked in this framework. Deleuze may ask, can we think, live and govern differently?[21] Could there be a starting point which is not prejudiced towards any of the particular units like individual, society, state, ethnic groups, subaltern groups, different genders and so on. Deleuze attempts for a fluid ontology which is not privileging one group in any form.

---

17 Deleuze, Difference and Repetition, 222.

18 https://www.youtube.com/watch?v=jHZXQCEjtjY (17:40-18:05) (Accessed on 8 November, 2019)

19 Todd May, Gilles Deleuze: An introduction (New York: Cambridge University Press, 2005), 118.

20 May, Gilles Deleuze: An introduction, 120.

21 May, Gilles Deleuze: An introduction, 121.

2.1.1. Concept of Machine

One of the starting points offered by Deleuze is the concept of machine.[22] The Machines does establish connections and couplings with other machines. The fluidity of the concept ensures that it can be situated at the level of various particular units described above like individual, state or different groups. Claire Colebrook's differentiation between organisms, mechanism and machine is very apt here to clarify the terms.

> In *Anti-Oedipus* and *A Thousand Plateaus* Deleuze and Guattari use a terminology of machines, assemblages, connections and productions. In Anti-Oedipus they insist that the machine is not a metaphor and that life is literally a machine. This is crucial to Deleuze's ethics. An organism is a bounded whole with an identity and end. A mechanism is a closed machine with a specific function. A machine, however, is nothing more than its connections; it is not made by anything, is not for anything and has no closed identity.[23]

Thus, the central figure in a Deleuzian political ontology won't be individuals, but to consider individuals as machines entering into various connections with the environment.[24] Colebrook gives the example of bicycle as machine. Rather than considering it as having a fixed identity, we could consider it as made of several connections. There is no fixed purpose for the combination of connections as the use depends on the future connections made by the bicycle. It could be a work of art in museum; it becomes a vehicle for transport in the hands of a rider. There are several other possibilities as it makes connections with other things. The difference which was the main theme of the *Difference and Repetition* continues to define the concept of machines.

2.1.2. Critique and A response

One of the first critical thoughts that emerge is, is machinic thinking a supporter of neo-liberal policies, with less and less governmental controls, helping the rich to be richer and poor to be poorer. When Marx says economics is the superstructure over which character of machinic connections are determined, and if this is valid, then the above criticism holds a lot of weight. But Deleuze considers machinic connections as being more primordial and economic modes of production are defined by the machinic connections.[25]

---

22 We shouldn't easily carry the baggage of scientific revolution along and equate machine with the process of mechanization.

23 Claire Colebrook, *Gilles* Deleuze (New York: Routledge, 2007) 56.

24 May, Gilles Deleuze: An introduction, 122.

25 May, *Gilles Deleuze: An introduction*, 126.

We could use the concepts of micro and macro politics (molecular and molar thinking respectively) to further answer this possible criticism. When macro-politics (Capitalism and Marxism) are interested in the grand scheme of things, micro-politics is an issue of quantum flow and machines.[26] A quantum flow could be a virtual field that actualizes itself; there is no question of fixed identities. Suppleness, and not large/small distinction, is the feature of micro-politics. Deleuze is not saying macro-politics doesn't exist, but they co-exist with micro-politics, but micro-politics is primary just like difference is primary to identity. Machinic thinking also allows us to see the connections and modifications of connections which are not normally seen in the macro-politics. Todd May gave the example of the Palestinian issue being ignored as they are neither representatives of major streams of thinking like capitalism or socialism. They are molecular stream of thought which are ignored. The issues of ethnic, religious minorities are often ignored as they are minor streams of thought which are not of much relevance to the major streams of thought. The recent awarding of the Nobel Prize for economics (2019) to Abhijit Banerjee, Esther Duflo and Michael Kremer "for their experimental approach to alleviating global poverty" is further encouragement to micro-economics along with macro-economics.

2.1.3. Subject and Subjected Groups

The concepts of subject groups and subjected groups finally help us to answer the critical question– the similarity of machinic thinking with neo liberal economic policies increasing the inequality. Subjected groups function with the understanding of suppressing desires, whereas the subject group considers desire as the molecular phenomena which are productive.[27] Subjected groups make a clear cut distinction between us and them (sedantry distribution); subject groups rely on collectivities, not knowing yet the full potentialities of the subject groups.[28] Yes, the way out is not alone, but by forming subject groups which employ machinic thinking leading to the discovery of streams of micro-politics along with the macro-politics. There is definitely not a fixed way, but this is a possible trajectory and being in touch with the virtual will reveal more trajectories. Politics is an experiment and not a deduction.[29]

In his book, *A Thousand Plataeus* Deleuze advocates the rhizome-based thinker instead of a tree thinking. When we look at most of the plants, they have a hierarchical structure leading from root to the trunk. You destroy the

26 May, *Gilles Deleuze: An introduction*, 127.

27 May, *Gilles Deleuze: An introduction*, 148.

28 May, *Gilles Deleuze: An introduction*, 148-149.

29 May, *Gilles Deleuze: An introduction*, 152.

roots and the tree is destroyed. But there are some plants like crab grass where the roots grow on all sides. We can't say which is the central root because it is connected to innumerable roots. Thus, if we destroy one cluster of the crab grass, nothing much is going to happen to the whole plant. It will still continue to expand and grow. The structure of Ginger or ant colonies are other examples of rhizome. Pure rhizome is infinitely connectable with no beginning and no end. It could be considered like a map (and not algorithm), where you can begin from anywhere.

Some of the examples that could be seen from the contemporary life situations are Arab Spring (which didn't have a committee monitoring the situation, where the message of liberation got spread through social medias), many peoples' campaigns based on Social Media, Liberation theology, inter-disciplinary approaches (there may be a person for coordinating, but none is supreme; all are connected with others), alternative medicines like Ayurveda (which attempts to heal the body by understanding the connections rather than pinpointing a particular cause in a particular part to settle the issue).

This political ontology is an application of Deleuzian thinking in concrete situation, where themes like machinic thinking, micro-politics, subjected groups and rhizomes are more significant than mechanisms, macro-politics, and subject groups; difference holds prominence over identity.

3. Why Deleuze in this Discussion on Faith and Reason?

Colebrook clearly mentions of the human intimacy with the concept of transcendence, either by divining the platonic forms or by subjugating the materiality to rationality as in the Cartesian subject. Deleuze considers Cartesian dualism as being extremely dangerous and the world becoming 'manipulable' matter. The Deleuzian affirmation of life is a release from all these subjections to the systems[30].

In his article titled *God in the Margins: Deleuze and Immanent theology*, Peter Paul Elicor shows one way of interaction between the atheistic philosopher Deleuze and Christian theology. He sees in Deleuzian thinking, an invitation for living a real life. The Deleuzian affirmation of life, which he borrows from Nietzsche and expands is similar to the Christian affirmation of life. [31]

30 *Claire Colebrook, Deleuze and the Meaning of Life (NY: Continuum International Publishing Group, 2010),* 26.

31 One of the powerful sayings of Jesus is "I have come to give life and life in its abundance" John 10:10. Though Deleuzian affirmation of life and Christian fullness of life have a lot of differences, something that links them together is the affirmation of life, here and now. Like the author, this has been one point of invitation for me to look into the Deleuzian thinking.

He distinguishes between the mainstream and marginal theology[32] and sees a possibility of encounter between Deleuze and the marginal theology[33].

3.1. Christian Faith in Deleuzian Terms[34]

Religious faith is mostly associated with an experience of transcendence of a particular person, which is original to that person and it becomes the foundation stone for the faith of other followers. Jesus, Buddha and Ramana Maharshi could be some of the great examples of the original pioneers. But it is equally true that some of the religious believers or followers have a personal religious experience, which complements the experience of their leaders.

Even among the Christians, the faith of one person is different from the faith of another, though there can be many commonalities. Thus, there is a sense of uniqueness for our faith. Thus, creating or assuming a structured identity to that faith is quite a problematic theme. That's exactly because faith is connected to a reality called God who is beyond our comprehension (definitions of identity). Assuming a structured identity to the human person is also a problematic theme.

When reason has to interact with Christian faith, it can interact with the faith of identity and faith of difference. Even when I say it is a faith in Jesus Christ, the question is whether I am treating Jesus as an identity (which is quite well defined) or Jesus as a difference (which precedes our images of God in the form of identity).God as mystery and God as difference[35] can be homeomorphic equivalents in the Panikkarean sense.[36] I think mystical experiences can further support this claim.

Mysticism and mystical experiences are normally considered to be a special type of religious experiences, though we have examples for mystical experiences not originating from an explicit religious belief.[37]A question that always inspired many of the seekers of different tradition is... How mystics

32 In the mainstream theology, we speak of the closest approximation humanity can speak and grasp of the fundamental nature of a transcendent God using metaphysical tenets. But marginal theology resists any form of identification with hierarchical systems, but rely on intuitive or mystical faith. Though Christian theology is necessarily in the form of mainstream theology, marginal dimensions are not completely excluded.

33 Peter Paul Elicor, "God in the Margins: Deleuze and Immanent Theology," *Diwa: Studies in Philosophy and Theology* 42, no .2 (2017) 98.

34 This article is not an attempt to Christianize Deleuze or Deluezianise Christian faith, but just to point out some possible avenues of encounter.

35 It is worthwhile to see the Deleuzian interpretation of Nietzschean Death of God, eternal return and will to power in the article; Marie Chabbert, On Becoming-Secular: Gilles Deleuze and the Death of God. *Working Papers in the Humanities* vol. 13 (2018), 50–59.

36 Raimon Panikkar, *The Intra-religious Dialogue* (New Jersey: Paulist Press, 1998; 18-19).

37 George Karuvelil, Mysticism, Language and Truth. *Journal of Dharma* 35 no.3 (July-September 2010) 263-264.

agree and theologians disagree? I think Deleuzian difference preceding identity' can give an answer. Theologians are more interested in the identity of the transcendent manifested or revealed, whereas mystics have got a sense of the 'unfathomableness' of the reality (difference), which is infinitely more powerful than the innumerable manifestations (identity).

When Christian Faith is connected to the relationship between two realities, who can be considered difference, it is better to consider that relationship also as difference, of which one expression is the identity of my faith today. One of the many critical questions can be similar to the common critique against post-modernism – Can anything go as Christian faith? Probably I take the help of Vattimo to answer it.

4. Gianni Vattimo[38]& Weak Thought

Gianni Vattimo is one of the most influential living philosophers, who was influenced by the idea of the Death of God by Nietzsche and the end of metaphysics by Heidegger. Vattimo is introduced here for two reasons. The first reason is that Vattimo's explanations could be seen as a concrete example for the case I am putting forward, to see faith as difference. Secondly, he gives a criterion called Charity for the Christian faith, thus it tries to dispel the allegation that anything goes. Vattimo clarifies weak thought as "the idea of a thinking that is more aware of its own limits, that abandons its claims to global and metaphysical nature, but above all a theory of weakening as the constitutive character of Being in the epoch of the end of metaphysics."[39] Hermeneutics is the expression of weak thought. Weak thought is also an attempt to find the traces from the history of thought, which are more compatible with the postmodern thinking. 'Weak' in the weak thought is its strength and weakness, as it is not possible to define it in a precise manner, but it is a description of the post-metaphysical trend originated with Heidegger and continued with post-Heideggerians, hermeneuticians and postmodern philosophers.[40.]

---

38 The reasons for choosing Italian Philosopher Gianni Vattimo are 1. Influential in the contemporary post-modern scenario, especially in the field of religion and politics. 2. Contemporary Philosopher whose ideas are interesting for me.

39 Jeffrey W Robbins, "Introduction: After the death of God," in *After the Death of God*, ed. Jeffrey W Robbins (New York: Columbia University Press), 19.

40 Andrzej Zawadzki, "Literature and Weak Thought," in *Cross-Roads: Polish Studies in Culture, Literary Theory, and History,* ed. Ryszard Nycz and Teresa Walas (Frankfurt: PL Academic Research, 2013), 2:13

4.1. Weak Thought to Kenosis

For Richard Rorty, weak thought in Christianity expresses itself as a journey from 'Christianity as power' to 'Christianity as love.'41 Vattimo uses the central idea of Christian history of salvation (kenosis) to drive the message of weak thought to Christianity. He invites the church to strip off all those things that prevent its encounter with other religions and cultures, and to understand the meaning of kenotic incarnation in the present scenario. It needs throwing away of superstitions like faith as the objective knowledge of God. For him, salvation is throwing away the tendency to identify God with natural order and metaphysical objective being, and this is kenosis.42 God shouldn't be viewed as absolute and truth, but an ability to see God in terms of charity, 'God is love'.

Vattimo says that secularization43 is the postmodern version of Christianity if it needs to survive. The death of God of Nietzsche, for him, is the death of Jesus on the cross where absolutist foundations of metaphysics are put into a coffin giving rise to nihilism.44 He justifies his claims by saying that Jesus' command to love the enemies is against natural order; thus, Jesus didn't come for the protection of the natural (or law based),45 but for demolishing it in the name of charity. Secularization is the process where the process of kenosis that happened with Jesus is continued in religion. It is the interpretation of the biblical message beyond the sacred, ecclesiastical and sacramental realm.46 As weakening of being is symbolically same as kenosis of God, secularization is the realization of Being's religious vocation.47

4.2. Post-Modern Christianity and Charity

As Christian theology of 20th century was still under the influence of the shadow of Christendom after the decline of Christian power, theologians like

---

41 Richard Rorty, Gianni Vattimo, and Santiago Zabala, 'What Is Religion's Future After Metaphysics" in *The Future of Religion* ed. Santiago Zabala (New York: Columbia University Press, 2005), 56.

42 Gianni Vattimo, *A Farewell to Truth*, trans. William McCuaig (New York: Columbia University Press, 2011), 55.

43 I think Vattimo is closer to the French secularism than Indian secularism as the basic context of his article is European. Some of the implications of the proposal are equally applicable to many other Asian, African and American contexts, especially when the Church is powerful.

44 Vattimo, *A Farewell to Truth*, 58.

45 Echoes of similarities with Deleuze and his opposition to law.

46 Gianni Vattimo, *After Christianity*, trans. Luca D'Isanto (New York: Columbia University Press, 2002), 45.

47 Vattimo, *After Christianity*, 24.

Bonhoeffer speak of religionless Christianity.48 Kierkegaard also stood for anti-institutional and individualized church.49 Quoting Gustavo Bontadini, Vattimo says that the church speaks of freedom when the church feels itself weak and speaks of truth when it feels itself as strong.50 A church which subscribes completely to Biblical anthropology and having strong opposition to the universalization of science and human rights issues won't sustain longer.51 He modifies the Heideggerian experience 'Only a God can save us' to 'Only a relativistic God can save us.' Though he feels Heidegger wouldn't be upset to see that translation because of the evils of fundamentalism, Vattimo further suggests a less provocative title called 'Only a kenotic God can save us.'52

Dostoevsky writes: "If I had to choose between Jesus Christ and truth, I would choose Jesus Christ."53 The future of Christianity, and of the Church, is to become an ever more refined religion of pure charity. The promised salvation in the New Testament is fuller than being objective and literal. For him, real religiosity is in secularization, and there is no uniform code or authority to guide you.54 The religion which is returned in the postmodern world is a secularized religion, and it is as a result of secularization. Thus, in the postmodern world, a religion has meaning only with secularizing characteristics. Vattimo says, "I believe that ecumenism is inconceivable except as a lightening of the burden of dogma and the wider preaching of charity. This is the discourse of hermeneutics, Gadamer's discourse, the discourse of much of the most reasonably acceptable contemporary philosophy."55 When identities are not lost completely in this process, any identity based on absolutist structures becomes untenable. Only Charity remains there.

Conclusion

Friedrich Nietzsche says, "One must still have chaos in oneself to be able to give birth to a dancing star. I say to you: you still have chaos in yourselves.56 Bertrand Russell would say, "The trouble with the world is that the stupid

48 Robbins, "Introduction: After the death of God," 22.

49 Robbins, "*Introduction: After the death of God*," 8.

50 Vattimo, *A Farewell to Truth*, 53.

51 Vattimo, *A Farewell to Truth*, 53.

52 Vattimo, *A Farewell to Truth*, 47.

53 Vattimo, *A Farewell to Truth*, 77.

54 Gianni Vattimo, "A Prayer for Silence," in *After the Death of God*, ed. Jeffrey W Robbins (New York: Columbia University Press, 2001), 95.

55 Vattimo, *A Farewell to Truth*, 79.

56 Friedrich Nietzsche, *Thus Spoke Zarathustra: A Book for All and None*, ed. Adrian Del Caro and Robert B Pippin, trans. Adrian Del Caro (New York: Cambridge University Press, 2006), 55.

are cocksure and the intelligent are full of doubt.” The context of the world, especially in the religious dimension, showed many troubling signs. Are we diligent enough to see this as an opportunity to renew the religion (probably as Vatican II did for Catholic Church) or we will continue to be sure of the solutions and fortify the walls (as the Church attempted to do against modernism till Vatican II)? I have introduced two basic ideas from Deleuze (difference) and Vattimo (weak thought/charity) to have an encounter with the faith. Probably they are attempts of the post-modern/post structuralist reason to encounter with Christian faith. How the evolution will emerge can't be predicted. But these interactions are invitations to the Christian faith to re-discover the life-affirming nature of the faith, the mystery aspect of the faith and Charity (faith that does work), which is the cornerstone of Christian faith.

PART III

RELIGIO-SOPHIA: RELIGION MEETING WITH WISDOM

15

All Quadrant – All Level (AQAL): Wilberian Way to Understand Religious Diversity Today

Maxim Pinto

Abstract

Kenneth Earl Wilber, popularly known as Ken Wilber, is well known for his integral vision of reality. The AQAL (All Quadrant, All Level) is his most original contribution to the integral approach. The four quadrants are the four holarchies that deal with the inside and the outside of a holon, its both individual and collective forms. Through this 'meta-theory,' Wilber attempts to honour and include as much research as possible from the largest number of disciplines in a coherent and creative fashion. By this he argues that it is possible for every person, every paradigm, every worldview, and every methodology, including those of modern science and postmodern philosophy, as well as traditional religions to have their own valuable yet partial truths to contribute to the understanding of the reality. In other words, an event, a person or a tradition cannot be understood in isolation; on the contrary, it must be perceived within the network of things to which it is explicitly and implicitly connected. One of the major concerns of the world today is religious fundamentalism. The AQAL is one of the key factors to understand growing religious intolerance. This method invites everyone to deepen one's own religious experience by learning to integrate that of others. The dynamic nature of reality demonstrates that our religious experience is not static but ever evolving and as human beings, we do not possess the whole truth. This encourages us to weave together different partial truths. This rational outlook can help us to appreciate others for their difference rather than to appreciate others because they vibe with us.

Keywords

Ken Wilber, all quadrant, all level, holon, meta-theory.

Introduction

A few years ago, there was an advertisement for the Steel Authority of India Limited (SAIL), which ended with this captivating caption: "There is little bit of steel in everybody's life." Marvelling at the phenomenal rise of religious consciousness in our world today, we may say, and rightly, that there is a little bit of religion in everybody's life. Or better still, in the Asian context, we may recast erstwhile Pepsi's motto: We eat religion, drink religion and we sleep religion. Religion has a sweeping influence on every sphere of life – social, cultural, economic, political, technological, etc. Truly, religion has a "totalising tendency,"[1] or a 'totalitarian character.'[2] While we acknowledge the positive influences of religion in every sphere, we are also aware of the harm disseminated by it. In the process of each religious tradition lawfully asserting its rightful place and pressing for making its presence felt, the result has often been 'injurious to the health' of the society. The recent history of the world, and of our own nation reminds us of the dark influences of religion. We are reminded of the apt saying, "Men will wrangle for religion; write for it; fight for it; anything but –live for it."[3]

Besides this, there is another but related danger that decidedly churns the foundations of the world today, what is usually christened as 'clash of civilizations' or 'war of religions.' In the struggle to establish hegemony and spread imperialistic ambitions, many religions have locked horns, which has resulted in killing of the innocent and mass destruction. At the same time, we must gratefully acknowledge that there are people who have articulated and still articulate positive responses in the face of emerging religious consciousness of different religious traditions and their legitimate claim for dignity, respect and validity. Moreover, there is a genuine concern to come to terms with religious diversity, as it has become the order of the day. There are three major responses to religious diversity. They are exclusivism, inclusivism and pluralism.[4]

1 George Karuvelil, *Philosophy of Experience* (Pune: Jnana-Deepa Vidyapeeth, 2002), 12.

2 Gavin D' Costa, *Theology and Religious Pluralism –The Challenge to Other Religions* (Oxford: Basil Blackwell Ltd., 1986), 55.

3 In Cyril Desbruslais, *Guidelines for the Study of the Philosophy of Religion* (Pune: Jnana-Deepa Vidyapeeth, 2000), 6.

4 But there are not just three options to understand religious pluralism. For example, Schubert Ogden accepts the typology of exclusivism, inclusivism and pluralism, but, in a criticism of all of them, he proposes a fourth option –"not that there *are* many true religions, but only

Exclusivism[5] is the view that 'true religious claims are found only among the doctrines and teachings of the home religion"[6] and this home religion offers the only valid path to salvation and alien religions are marked by "humankind's fundamental sinfulness and are therefore erroneous."[7] Inclusivism is the view that one's own religion contains the final truth and other religions merely contain approaches to, or approximations of it; one's own religion offers the most effective path to salvation, but those outside of it can be somehow saved or liberated.[8] In other words, it is possible that one's own religion and other religions may teach truth; in its open variety, it affirms the possibility that other religions may teach truths not already explicitly taught by one's own religion, while in its closed variety, it denies this possibility. Pluralism can be defined as: "[A] single ultimate religious reality is being differently experienced and understood in all the major religious traditions; they all, as far as we can tell, offer equally effective paths to salvation or libration."[9]

Ken Wilber[10] is famously known for his integral vision of reality. It is in this context, Wilber skillfully develops All Quadrant-All Level (AQAL), his

---

that there *can* be," Andreas Grünschloß speaks about fourth option that is, 'inferiorism/exotism' which means, "viewing other religions as superior to one's own." Paul Knitter calls this model 'acceptance model' and Richard Plantinga adds 'universalism' as the fourth option. For details see, Perry Schmidt-Leukel, "Exclusivism, Inclusivism, Pluralism –The Tripolar Typology: Clarified and Reaffirmed," in Paul Knitter, ed., *The Myth of Religious Superiority –A Multifaith Exploration* (New York: Orbis Books, 2005), 14-15.

5 Exclusivism can be further classified into doctrinal exclusivism and soteriological exclusivism. Doctrinal exclusivism is the view that "the doctrines of one religion are completely true; the other doctrines of all others are false whenever there is conflict". Soteriological exclusivism is the view "that only one religion offers an effective path to salvation or liberation. Though the two kinds of exclusivism are logically independent, they are usually held together" Craig Edward gen. ed., *Routledge Encyclopedia of Philosophy* 6 (New York: Routledge, 1998), 260.

6 Cf. Paul J. Griffiths, *Problems of Religious Diversity* (USA: Blackwell Publishers, 2000), xiv. Griffiths makes a distinction between home religion and alien religions. Home religion is that which one belongs to and alien religions are those to which one does not belong. Cf. *Ibid.*

7 Gavin D' Costa, *Theology and Religious Pluralism –The Challenge to Other Religions, 52.*

8 Cf. Craig Edward gen. ed., *Routledge Encyclopedia of Philosophy* 6, 260.

9 Cf. Craig Edward gen. ed., *Routledge Encyclopedia of Philosophy*, 260

10 Kenneth Earl Wilber, famously known as Ken Wilber, was born on 31st January, 1949 in Oklahoma City, US. He lived in many places during his school years, due to his father being in the army. He completed high school in Lincoln, Nebraska. In 1967, he enrolled himself as a pre-medical student at Duke University and was almost immediately disillusioned with what science had to offer. Thus he lost all interest in pursuing a career in science and started to read in psychology and philosophy both east and west. He went back to Nebraska to study biochemistry. But after a few years, be dropped out of the university to devoted all his time to studying his curriculum and writings books. So far he has written more than

most original contribution to understand different faith traditions. In the paper, we shall only focus on AQAL, which renders us integral vision of reality, as an alternative to understand religious diversity today.

1. AQAL –All Quadrant-All Level

The acronym AQAL stands for "All Quadrants, All Levels" and it is also known as 'AQAL Approach,' or 'AQAL Meta-theory' or the 'AQAL Model.'[11] Though it stands for 'All Quadrants, All Levels,' it also represents the larger embrace of "all-quadrants, all levels, all-lines, all-states, all–types and all-worldviews."[12] These four quadrants are the four holarchies[13] that actually deal with the inside and the outside of a holon,[14] in both its individual and collective forms. Inside and outside, singular and plural –they are present in every holon. All four of these holarchies are dealing with real aspects of real holons. These four quadrants, according to Wilber, are the very bedrock of realities –four corners of the Kosmos.[15] Further, Wilber asserts that this meta-theory "attempts to honor and include as much research as possible from the largest number of disciplines in a coherent fashion (which is one definition of an integral or

two dozen books and translations in more than twenty countries. Wilber is now the most translated academic author in the US. For the fundamental and pioneering nature of his insights, he has been called "the Einstein of Consciousness." His vision extends across many eras and encompasses most stands of thought –from Pre-Socratic, to Neo-Platonic, from Plato to Plotinus, and covering such trends as Existentialism, Phenomenology, Pluralistic Pragmatism, Nihilism, Post-Structuralism, Critical Theory, Logical Positivism, etc. Specialized scholars continually gain insight from Wilber's 'Vision-Logic.' He clearly elucidates the thought of such diverse thinkers as Bergson, Whitehead, Teilhard de Chardin, Ernest Becker, Freud, Aurobindo and Nagarjuna. Since a long time, Wilber is a practicing Buddhist, and many of the key ideas in his approach are Buddhist-inspired. From 1987, Wilber lived in Boulder, Colorado, where he worked on his Kosmos trilogy and oversaw the work of Integral Institute. He now lives in Denver, Colorado. For details see, "Ken Wilber's Biography," (accessed 21 September, 2019); available from http://www.worldofkenwilber.com; Internet; "Who is Ken Wilber?" (accessed 21 September, 2019); available from http://integralnaked.org/contributer.aspx?Contributor?=1; Internet.

11 Brad Reynolds, *Where Wilber At? –Ken Wilber's Integral Vision in the New Millennium*, 4.

12 *Ibid.*, 4.

13 The term 'holon' or 'holarchy' (instead of hierarchy) is coined by Arthur Koestler. It is derived from the Greek *holos meaning whole, with the suffix on which, an in proton or neutron, suggests a particle of part. Hence, holon refers to that which, being a whole that is simultaneously a part of some other whole, infinitively. For details see, Ken Wilber Integral Psychology (Boston: Shambala, 2000); Arthur Koestler, Ghost in the Machine (London: Picador Pan Books, 1975), 48; Ken Wilber, Up from Eden –a Transpersonal View of Human Evolution, xii-xiii.*

14 See footnote no. 13.

15 Ken Wilber, *A Brief History of Everything (Boston: Shambhala, 2007), 109.*

more comprehensive view of the Kosmos)."[16] In other words, it is possible for every person, every paradigm, every worldview, and every methodology, including those of modern science and postmodern philosophy, as well as traditional religions to have their own valuable yet partial truths to contribute to the understanding of the reality. Before we explain the four quadrants, we shall briefly explain the terms such as, (a) 'All Levels,' (b) 'All Quadrants,' (c) 'The Big Three,' (d) 'All Lines.' and (e) 'All States.'[17] (a) All Levels: They refer to the basic waves found in the spectrum of consciousness[18] or the AQAL matrix, based on qualitatively distinct classes of recurrent structures within developmental lines thus measuring high or more complex and low or less complex. 'All Levels' is synonym with 'wave stage' (that is sequential unfolding) and structures (that is enduring patterns) which are found in 'The Great Chain of Being.'[19] In general, it represents the pre-modern worldview. (b) All Quadrants: They refer to the multiple perspectives of holons (the whole/parts of the universe). They are categorized as having both interiors (subjective 'I' and inter-subjective 'We/You'), and exteriors (objective 'It' and inter-objective 'Its' realms), reaching from sub-atomic particles to the inner realities of consciousness and spirit. They also involve the 'eight zones' or the inside/outside of each quadrant's perspective. (c) The Big Three: The four quadrants have been simplified to reflect modernity's 'value spheres' or qualitative differentiation of subjective self/aesthetics (languages in the first person), inter-objective culture/morals (languages in the second person), and objective science/nature (languages in the third person). In general, it represents the modern worldview. (d) All Lines: They refer to the developmental structures that comprise the evolving components of the self-system. They are defined as being relatively independent streams or capacities that proceed through

---

16 Ken Wilber, *A Brief History of Everything, 2.*

17 For details see, *Ken Wilber, The Eye of Spirit –An Integral Vision for a World Gone Slightly Mad*, 254-271.

18 The basic waves in the spectrum of consciousness are archaic, magic, mythic, rational, psychic, subtle and causal. Cf. Ken Wilber, *The Essential Ken Wilber –An Introductory Reader, 61.*

19 The Great Chain of Being is presented as having three levels: matter, mind, and spirit. Other versions present it with five levels –matter, body, mind, soul, and spirit. Others still give very exhaustive breakdown of it. For example, *Vedānta, an eastern tradition groups them into three –body, mind and spirit or gross; Christianity and Islam indicate five levels – matter, body, mind, soul, and spirit; the Great Chain according to Kundalini, another eastern yogic discipline, shows seven levels –matter, sex, gut reactions, love and belongingness, discursive intellect, higher mental-psychic powers and transcendence. There are other traditions which show very sophisticated breakdown of the levels often running into 12, 30 and even 108 subdivisions. Cf. Ken Wilber, Integral Psychology – Consciousness, Spirit, Psychology, Therapy, 6; Ken Wilber, Up from Eden –a Transpersonal View of Human Evolution, 38-39, 150-152.*

the unfolding levels of development. It includes ethics, emotional/affective, interpersonal, needs, self-identity, aesthetics, values, psychosexual and spiritual levels. (e) All States: Wilber makes a clear distinction between deep patterns or basic level of consciousness, which tend to be enduring and the usually temporary states of consciousness, which include waking (gross body) dreaming (subtle body) and deep dreamless sleep (causal body). He also adds various altered or non-ordinary states, including peak experiences of higher levels. 'All States' also involves the sequential unfolding of states-stages usually from the result of intensive training (from gross to subtle to causal to non-dual). Thus, the single goal of the AQAL metatheory is the integration –'what modernity put asunder, post-modernity must heal.'[20]

In *A Brief History of Everything*,[21] Wilber explains how he arrived at the concept of 'the four quadrants.' Earlier, he had looked at various 'new paradigms' theorists –from holists to eco-feminists to ecologists to system thinkers and found that they offer various types of holarchies or hierarchies. Even the anti-hierarchy eco-philosophers offer their own hierarchy, saying, atoms are parts of molecules, which are part of cells, which are parts of individual organism, which are parts of families, which are part of cultures, which are the parts of the total bio-sphere.[22] Many other researchers offer their own hierarchies, such as hierarchies in moral development, in ego development, in cognitive development, etc. Most of the maps of the world, argues Wilber, that have been offered are in fact holarchical for the simple reason that holarchies are impossible to avoid. Collecting such holarchical maps from around the world, he realized that these maps were all referring to the same territory. He thought they were all different versions of an essentially similar holarchy. There were too many similarities and overlapping in all of them. By comparing and contrasting them all, Wilber thought, that he might be able to find the single and foundational holarchy that they were trying to represent in their own ways. But that would not work, confesses Wilber, as many holarchies had undeniable similarities but differed in certain profound ways. And the exact nature of the difference was not obvious. And most confusing of all, "in some of these holarchical maps, the holons got bigger as development progressed, and in others, they became smaller (I didn't yet understand that evolution produces greater depth, less span)."[23] He thought for some time that nothing would come

20 Brad Reynolds, *Where Wilber At? –Ken Wilber's Integral Vision in the New Millennium, 6; See also, Ken Wilber, "Introduction to the Fourth Volume of the Collected Works," (Accessed 20 September 2019), available from http://www.kenwilber.shambhala.com. Internet.*

21 Ken Wilber, *A Brief History of Everything, 104-109; See also, Brad Reynolds, Where Wilber At? –Ken Wilber's Integral Vision in the New Millennium, 175-177.*

22 Cf. Ken Wilber, *A Brief History of Everything, 106.*

23 Ken Wilber, *A Brief History of Everything, 107.*

out of this strenuous research. But gradually it dawned on Wilber as he looked at various holarchies that they were actually four very different holarchies, four very different types of holistic sequences. It had not been spotted before and this insight was a revelation for Wilber. And then, he put various holarchies into four groups and instantly they fell into place at that point. Thus, it became clear to him that each holarchy in each group was indeed dealing with the same territory, but overall they had four different territories. Simultaneously, they are not just radically different holistic sequences; they need to touch each other somehow. Hence, he concluded that the four type of holarchies deal with the inside and outside of a holon, in both its individual and collective forms and that's how Wilber arrived at the concept of four quadrants. We shall explain the four quadrants in some length below.

1.1. The Upper-Right Quadrant[24]

The Upper-Right (UR) quadrant is the objective or exterior form or structure of an individual holon. It runs from 'the centre to subatomic particles to atoms to molecules to cells to neural organisms to triune-brained organisms.'[25] In the case of the human holon, this quadrant is the one emphasized by behaviourism, positivism or any sort of sensory empiricism. Sensory empiricism (which also includes behaviourism and positivism for Wilber) is concerned primarily with what can be seen –and this is what the Upper Right quadrant is concerned about –the behavior of holons. It has nothing to do with introspection which involves the interiors of individuals. The language of this quadrant is *it*-language. This quadrant, thinks Wilber, is of such importance today because of the increasing dominance of cognitive science, evolutionary psychology, neuroscience, biological psychiarchy, etc. And the reasons for this are, (a) this quadrant is investigated by the scientific method, or empiric-analytic inquiry which is fairly objective in its operation and interpretation; (b) There is an enormous amount of work already being done in this quadrant; (c) the data gathered in this quadrant, once verified, tend to be stable and trustworthy, requiring only modest amount of interpretation.[26]

24 The Upper Right quadrant which is individual, objective and behavior, Wilber adds the following fields: (a) *physical* –pritikin, ornish, eades, atkins, vitamins, hormones; (b) *structural* –weightlifting, aerobics, hiking, etc.; (c) *pharmacological* –vaious medication/ drugs, where appropriate; (d) *brain/mind machines* –to help induce theta and delta states of consciousness. Ken Wilber, *One Taste –Daily Reflections on Integral Spirituality*, 121-122; Ken Wilber, *Integral Psychology –Consciousness, Spirit, Psychology, Therapy*, 113; Ken Wilber, *The Essential Ken Wilber –An Introductory Reader, 105.*

25 Cf. Ken Wilber, *Sex, Ecology, Spirituality –The Spirit of Evolution, 127.*

26 Cf. Ken Wilber, *The Eye of Spirit –An Integral Vision for a World Gone Slightly Mad, 397, no. 25.*

This quadrant wears the assumption that true knowing consists of making an accurate map of a pre-given objective territory. This assumption is not totally false but it is a very small part of the holon. The one who views reality with an impartial and scientific mine, lights up the third-person (*it*) dimension of the holon. While that is said, one must realize that the *it* dimension does not stand alone nor it is cut off from the rest of the holon. The disaster occurs when one thinks that the investigation into the Upper Right is the only right investigation that gives true and valid knowledge. In other words, 'only those and those objects alone that one sees out there are real.'[27] This amounts to quadrant absolutism.

1.2. The Upper-Left Quadrant[28]

The Upper-Left (UL) quadrant represents the interior of the individual, the subjective aspect of consciousness or the individual awareness. It runs from the centre to pre-hension, sensation, impulse, image, symbol, concept and so on and includes the entire spectrum of consciousness as it appears to any individual, from the bodily sensations to mental ideas to soul and spirit. The integral psychograph is a graph of this quadrant. The language of this quadrant is *I*-language. It is the first-person account of the inner stream of consciousness. This also, says Wilber, "is the home of aesthetics, or the beauty that is in the "I" of the beholder."[29] In other words, one can look at a reality from the inside, in which case one can observe various feelings, hopes, fears, sensations, and perceptions that one might have in any given moment.

One must remember that what is interior or subjective is also partly the product of social, cultural systems. This indicates the relation between different quadrants or, at least for now, between two quadrants. However, the subjective and many of its forms is not entirely an illusory game, just as with

---

27 Ken Wilber, "Excerpt A –An Internal Age at the Leading Edge; Part V. Integral Methodological Pluralism," (Accessed 23 June 2009); available from *http://wilber.shambhala.com/html/books/kosmos/excerptA/Part.5.cfm.* Internet.

28 In the Upper Left quadrant which is individual, subjective and intentional, Wilber includes the following: (a) *Emotional–breath – t'ai chi, yoga, bioenergies, circulation of* praṇa or feeling-energy, qi gong; (b) *mental –psychotherapy, cognitive therapy, shadow work; vision –adopting a conscious philosophy of life, visualization, affirmations; (c) spiritual –physic –shamanic, nature mysticism, beginning tantric; subtle –deity, yoga, yidam, contemplative prayer, advanced tantric; causal –vipasana, self-inquiry, bare attention, witnessing; non-dual –dzogchen, mahamudra, kabbalah, zen, Eckhart, etc.* Ken Wilber, *One Taste –Daily Reflections on Integral Spirituality*, 122; Ken Wilber, *Integral Psychology –Consciousness, Spirit, Psychology, Therapy*, 113-114; Ken Wilber, *The Essential Ken Wilber –An Introductory Reader, 106.*

29 Ken Wilber, *Integral Psychology –Consciousness, Spirit, Psychology, Therapy, 63.*

empiricism, it can disclose many important occasions not disclosed or enacted by any other level or stream.[30]

But when one takes up the interior or subjective part of a holon, one lights up its first-person dimensions. What one finds depends on many variables, including the level of consciousness and the stream of consciousness that one feels. Conflicts can occur in the quadrant when one of the many levels or streams of awareness is absolutized as the one and only true level or stream and all others are but surface currents. This amounts to what Wilber calls, "level or stream absolutism."[31] Nevertheless, the subjective or interior with its many forms such as bodily, spiritual, mental is very important resource in any integral interpretation of reality.

1.3. The Lower-Right Quadrant[32]

The Lower-Right quadrant represents all the exterior forms of social systems, forms that also can be seen, forms that are empirical and behavioral in nature. In other words, it involves the exterior forms of holons, and, in this case, it is a 'social holon.'[33] It runs from "the Big Bang to superclusters to galaxies to stars to planets to (on Earth) the Gaia system to ecosystem to societies with division of labor to groups/families."[34] In the case of humans, this quadrant runs from kinship tribes to villages to nation-states to the global world-system. Moreover, this quadrant refers to any of the concrete, material, embedded social forms of communities (the exterior forms of social systems), including modes of tools and technology, forces of production, architectural styles and concrete institutions. In other words, the Lower-Right quadrant represents all the exterior forms social systems, forms that can be seen, forms that are empirical and behaviour as it involves the exterior forms of holons.

30 Ken Wilber, "Excerpt A –An Internal Age at the Leading Edge; Part V. Integral Methodological Pluralism," Internet.

31 For example, the Piagetian stream absolutism i.e., the belief that Piaget's cognitive line is the one deep line against which all other developmental lines are surface currents. Of course, much of what Piaget discovered about the cognitive line may be valid and accurate, but it must be seen as one of the many relatively independent developmental lines. Cf. Ken Wilber, "Excerpt A –An Internal Age at the Leading Edge; Part V. Integral Methodological Pluralism," Internet.

32 In the Lower-Right quadrant which is social, inter-objective, Wilber includes the following: (a) *systems* –exercising responsibilities to Gaia, nature, bio-sphere, and geopolitical infrastructures at all levels; (b) *institutional* –exercising educational, political, and civic duties to family, town, state, nation and world. Cf. Ken Wilber, *One Taste –Daily Reflections on Integral Spirituality*, 122; Ken Wilber, *Integral Psychology –Consciousness, Spirit, Psychology, Therapy*, 114; Ken Wilber, *The Essential Ken Wilber –An Introductory Reader, 106.*

33 Cf. Ken Wilber, *Sex, Ecology, Spirituality –The Spirit of Evolution, 128.*

34 *Ibid.*, 128.

The evolution of an individual holon, for example, cannot be understood apart from the ecological system in which it is embedded. In certain cases, a holon does not exist on its own; but what actually exists is an organism-environment system, and ecological web, itself embedded in even larger webs, and it is an understanding of these systems and webs that constitutes significant knowledge. Hence, it is not the "behavior of objects" but the "behavior of systems" that becomes the focus of this quadrant. This system-theory perspective[35] is primarily a third-person inquiry, but now executed with an eye on the plural and the collective, not in the singular and atomistic.

But in system theory one finds no first-person accounts of desire, feelings, levels, streams, and so on and neither does one find authentic or non-reductionistic second-person accounts of mutual understanding, hermeneutics, collectively shared horizons; nor any account of the interior levels of consciousness and so on. At times these concerns have been addressed, most often they are reduced to their exteriors appearing in dynamic systems of interwoven '*its*.'

In spite of the above short-coming the dimensions of the system theory forms are real; they are a relatively objective fact about systems in the world. They disclose the Lower-Right quadrant or the objective dimension of communal holons.[36] All the inter-objective approaches recognize the fact that all holons have a Lower-Right quadrant, a holistic web of mutually interpenetrating patterns across space and time that can be described in a third-person perspective, and which, although far from the whole story, are a crucial aspect of a more integral view.

1.4. Lower-Left Quadrant[37]

The Lower-Left quadrant involves all those patterns in consciousness that are shared by those who are in a particular culture or sub-culture. If one wants to understand others, then one needs, to say the least, to share certain linguistic

35 The system-theory perspective resulted from *developmental structuralism to genealogical anthropology to evolutionary systems theory to the ecological sciences and Web-of-Life* theories to the wide variety of dynamic systems theory. Cf. Ken Wilber, "A Summary of the Psychological Model of Ken Wilber –(Or, Outline of An Integral Psychology)," (Accessed September 2019); available from http//www.kenwilber.shambhala.com. Internet

36 *Ibid.*

37 In the Lower-Left quadrant which is cultural, inter-subjective, Wilber includes the following: (a) *relationships* –with family, friends, sentient beings in general, making relationships part of one's growth, de-centering the self; (b) *community service* volunteer work, homeless shelters, hospice, etc.; (c) *morals* –engaging the inter-subjective world of the Good, practicing compassion in relation to all sentient beings. Cf. Ken Wilber, *One Taste –Daily Reflections on Integral Spirituality*, 122; Ken Wilber, *Integral Psychology –Consciousness, Spirit, Psychology, Therapy*, 114; Ken Wilber, *The Essential Ken Wilber –An Introductory Reader, 107.*

semantics, numerous perceptions, world-views, shared values, perception, meanings, semantic habitants, cultural practices, ethics and so on. This is what Wilber calls culture or the inter-subjective patterns of consciousness.[38] In other words, the Lower-Left quadrant is the study of shared interior meaning that constitutes the world-view or common world space of collective or communal holons.

One can say that individual organism exists only as inseparable aspects of webs of ecological interaction and these inter-objective webs actually have interiors that cannot be reduced to, or explained by, the web themselves. The social systems possess interiors of inter-subjective dimension (I and We) that escape detection by the ecological and system sciences. The Lower-Left quadrant or the inter-subjective pattern is truly irreducible. It is not some sort of haphazard product of the interaction of pre-meditated separate objects that somehow come together, interact, and then form an inter-subjective horizon. Rather, inter-subjectivity is present, from the start, as an intrinsic aspect of the tetra-arising of this and every moment.[39] Hermeneutics, the art and science of interpretation, attempts to reconstruct and emphatically enter the shared cultural world-space of human beings and usher an understanding of the values contained therein.[40] When one engages himself/herself in hermeneutics or inter-subjective activity, one lights up the second-person (and first-person plural) dimensions of a holon. These dimensions are real; they are present; and they constitute an essential part of an integral search.

For an easy understanding of the AQAL, we shall summarize it in the following way. One can look at a reality from the inside (the interior of the individual/Upper Left quadrant) in which case, one can see his/her various feelings, hopes, fears, sensations, and perception that one might have in

---

38 Ken Wilber, *A Theory of Everything –An Integral Vision for Business, Politics, Science and Spirituality, 50.*

39 Even evolutionary sciences support this claim. They say there are no first instances in evolution. When the first instance of a new species arises, for example, the first mammal, it never arises by itself; what first shows up is an entire population of mammals. This means that the inside and outside of the singular and plural arrive on the scene simultaneously; the four quadrants together arise and mutually tetra-evolve. Cf. Ken Wilber, "Excerpt A –An Internal Age at the Leading Edge; Part V. Integral Methodological Pluralism," Internet.

40 Cf. Ken Wilber, *Sex, Ecology, Spirituality –The Spirit of Evolution, 133. According to Wilber, hermeneutics is not solely the patrimony of self-reflexive humans. For hermeneutics, contends Wilber, in its pre-reflexive mode exists "all the way down." Holons, even at the sub-atomic level, are engaged in interpreting their environments. Signal systems and exchanges of particles/energies/forces exist at even the most fundamental of levels. Unfortunately, because the novelty of the most fundamental holons' approaches, it mistakenly appears that interpretive freedom is completly absent at the ground levels.* Cf. Ken Wilber, "A Summary of the Psychological Model of Ken Wilber –(Or, Outline of An Integral Psychology)," Internet.

any given moment. This is the first-person phenomenal view, described in 'I' language. But consciousness can also be looked at in an objective –in a scientific fashion, in which case one might conclude that my consciousness is the product of objective brain mechanisms and neuro-physiological systems. This is the third-person or objective view (Lower-Right quadrant). But my consciousness/self or reality does not exist in a vacuum; it exists in a community of other selves. So in addition to a singular view of consciousness or reality, one can look at how consciousness or reality exists in the plural –as a part of a group, a community, a collective. And just as we can look at the inside and the outside of an individual, we can also look at the inside and the outside of the collective. For example, we can try to analyze any group of people from the inside, in a sympathetic resonance of mutual understanding or, we can understand them from the outside, in a detached and objective manner. These both views are useful and one must honour them both. On the inside of the collective, one can see all the various shared worldviews (archaic, magic, mythic, rational, etc.) ethics, and inter-subjective structures held in common by those in the collective (whether that be family, corporation, organization, tribe, town, nation and globe). The insides of the collective are described in 'we' language (Lower-Left quadrant) and include all of those inter-subjective items that one might experience if one is truly a member of the collective. From the outside (Lower-Right quadrant), one can see all the objective structures and social institutions of the collective, such as the physical buildings, the infrastructures, the techno-economic base (foraging, horticultural, agrarian, industrial, informational), the quantitative aspects of society (the objective data), modes of communication and so on. These are all 'its' –patterns of inter-objective social systems. Thus there are four perspectives –the inside and the outside of the singular and the plural: *I*, *it*, *we* and *its*. Since the objective dimensions (the outside of the individual and the outside of the collective) are both described in third-person *it*-language, they can be reduced from the four quadrants to just three: *I*, *we* and *it*.[41] The main point is that each of the levels, lines, and states of consciousness has these four quadrants. This model explicitly integrates first-, second- and third-person accounts of consciousness at each of the states, levels and lines. This gives a more comprehensive and integral view of consciousness or reality.

Wilber points out a number of correlations between the scheme of the four quadrants. For example, the entire Right half, the exterior self, can be described in 'it' language and can be studied empirically. The entire Right half is something one can see 'out there,' something one can register with the senses or their extensions. The components of the Right half, -both Upper-

41 Cf. Ken Wilber, "All Quadrants, All Levels," (Accessed on September 28, 2019), available from *http://integralpoitics.info/articles_all_quadrants_all_levels.php*. Internet.

Right and Lower-Right quadrants are, in themselves, neutral surfaces, neutral exteriors, neutral forms, all of which can be described in 'it' language. One need not have to engage oneself in the interiors of any of those holons; neither in the introspection or interpretation or meaning or values. One has to just describe the exterior form in its behavior. One observes the surface form and describes it. The surface form is existence; it is legitimate and is necessary. But that is not the whole story. Wilber often calls the study of both the Upper-Right and Lower-Right quadrants as the Right-Hand path –the path of that which can be seen with the eye of flesh or its exteriors.[42] In short, it is the path of 'it' language. This Right-Hand path has two major warring camps: the atomists, who study the surfaces of the individuals, and the wholists, who say that whole systems, and not individuals, are the primary object of study. Both these are equally exterior approaches confined to surfaces only and they are thoroughly empirical.

The entire Left half of the diagram, on the other hand, cannot be seen with the eye of flesh. Hence, it cannot be described in 'it' language. Rather, the Upper-Left is described in 'I' language, and the Lower-Left is described in 'we' language. And Wilber christens them as the Left-Hand path.[43] The Right half can be seen, the Left half must be interpreted. Because the surfaces can be seen and therefore, anyone can have a look at them but the depth cannot be directly perceived –it has to be interpreted. The Right-Hand path asks, "what does it do?" or "how does it work?" while the Left-Hand path asks, "what does it mean?"[44]

Wilber points out that the social theory is divided into two often sharply disagreeing camps: hermeneutics –the art and science of interpretation, and structural-functionalism or systems theory –that looks at the external social structures and social systems that governed the behavior of the action system. But to reconstruct meaning (the Left-Hand path) one must engage in interpretation; one must try to enter the shared depths, shared values, etc; one must try to understand and describe the culture from within as meaning

---

42 Cf. Ken Wilber, *Sex, Ecology, Spirituality –The Spirit of Evolution, 132.*

43 *Ibid.*, 132.

44 Wilber gives the following example to understand the correlations better. "A deer sees me approach. It *sees* my exterior form, my shape, and registers all the appropriate physical stimuli coming from my form to the deer. But what do they *mean*? Am I the friendly with the food, or the hunter with the rifle? The deer must *interpret* its stimuli in the *context* of its own *worldspace* and how I might *affect* it. And this is not just a matter of seeing: the deer sees just fine. But it might be *mistaken* it its *interpretation*; I might actually have the rifle, not the food. All the physical stimuli are hitting the deer fully (that's not the problem); the problem is, what do they actually *mean*? The surfaces are given, but what is lurking in the depths? What are the intentions lying behind the surfaces? What is transmitted empirically but not merely given empirically?" Ken Wilber, *Sex, Ecology, Spirituality –The Spirit of Evolution, 132-133.*

cannot just be seen from outside. When the Right-Hand path asks, "what does it do?" it seeks to offer explanation based on naturalistic, empirical, observable variables. When the Left-Hand path asks, "what does it mean?" it attempts to arrive at understanding that would be mutual. To conclude, we can say that there are important truths in both the Left- and Right-Hand approaches and both are required for a balanced or "all-quadrant" view. Every reality or holon has at least four aspects or dimensions and therefore, it must be studied in its intentional, behavioral, cultural and social settings. No holon exists simply in one of the four quadrant; each holon has four quadrants.[45]

2. Critical Appraisal of AQAL

Today, more than ever, the rise of religious fundamentalism is threatening to destabilize human civilization. Religious fundamentalism can be described as, "that global impulse to retrieve, nourish and institutionalize with a strongly reductionistic flavour the spiritual aspects of the past that modern and postmodern life seem to have obscured particularly in the face of the scientific revolution and the rise of modernity."[46] In Wilberian terms, any terror activity appears to be the behavioural manifestations (Upper-Right) of religious fundamentalistic ideology which, to a certain extent shaped by one's personality (Upper-Left), culture (Lower-Left) and society (Lower-Right). In other words, any behavioural manifestation, or any manifestation for that matter, is interrelated to the other three quadrants. But often, the combat techniques attempt to arrest only the behavioural dimensions by generally resorting to the "eye for an eye" ideology without even at times paying heed to the other quadrants.[47] A quadrant absolute or reductionist approach can be dangerous as a long term solution. It might create more problems than to solve them. In short, Wilber's AQAL meta-theory does help one to analyze the problem of religious fundamentalism in a comprehensive way.

There are limitations of this theory as well. Wilber's AQAL meta-theory is a holistic attempt to integrate the 'Great Chain of Being' with the three modern value spheres. In Wilber's own words: "[T]o integrate the Great Chain with the Differentiation of modernity."[48] This means that each of the levels

---

45 Cf. Ken Wilber, *Sex, Ecology, Spirituality –The Spirit of Evolution, 135.*

46 M. C. Abraham, "Religious Fundamentalism –A Psycho-Social Perspective." *Jnanadeepa: Journal of Religious Studies* 4, no.1 (2001), 239.

47 For example, on December 14, 2003, the media broke out the news of Saddam Hussein's capture by US led coalition forces. While then President of USA George Bush was elated at the fall of Saddam but he was prompt in cautioning the coalition forces and the people of Iraq of a possible flare up of violence. And one can see bomb blasts and other subtle violence in Iraq, threatening its stability. Cf. "Saddamned," *The Indian Express*, December 15, 2003, 1.

48 Ken Wilber, *The Marriage of Sense and Soul –Integrating Science and Religion*, 14.

in the traditional Great Chain needs to be carefully differentiated in the light of modernity.[49] It would follow naturally, then, that a consistent and faithful implementation of this idea should preserve and integrate all levels of knowing and being in the 'Great Chain' within all the four quadrants. For example, integration of the Upper-Left and Upper-Right (the 'I' and 'It') would mean, the two quadrants must look like the knowing and being columns of the 'Great Chain,' with each quadrant having a hierarchy of transcendent, subtle, and gross levels of the 'Great Chain.' Surprisingly, this is not what Wilber's Upper two quadrants look like. Although the 'Great Chain' with all its levels of knowing is included in the 'I' domain, the 'It' domain is not the traditional hierarchy of being at all. Wilber's hierarchy of being is limited to the level of matter alone. Thus, the transcendent and subtle levels of objective being are not included in Wilber's individual exterior ('It') domain. Similarly, an analogous omission is made in Wilber's hierarchy for the Lower-Right quadrant. All the levels in this quadrant are also just material levels of collective complexity (from primitive collections of atoms in the form of galaxies, to collections of atoms and molecules in the form of planets, up through collections of organisms into ecosystems, and collections of human organisms into societies). In other words, in both exterior quadrants (Upper-Right and Lower-Left) the hierarchy includes only the gross level of matter, and omits the subtle and transcendent levels of objective being.[50] The fact that Wilber's AQAL meta-theory excludes the deeper subtle or transcendental levels of ontological reality is a serious defect: two quadrants of his AQAL omit the most significant levels of the 'Great Chain' and therefore, one can argue that his AQAL model is not a faithful integration of the 'Great Chain' with the four modern value spheres. There are limitations as well. First, because these deeper realities are excluded, Wilber's model is stripped of nature or Kosmos in its intrinsic depth and meaning. As Wilber would say, "Although consciousness and value and meaning are intrinsic to the depth of the Kosmos, they cannot be found in the cosmos. That is, they inhere in the Left Hand dimensions of the Kosmos, not in the Right

49 Cf. *Ibid.*, 14.

50 One can also point out in contrast to Wilber's scheme, that all the wisdom traditions recognize all the ontological levels of being that correspond to all the levels of knowing. "As Plotinus writes in his *Enneads*, "Knowing demands the organ fitted to the object." For example, the subtle realities of angels, archetypes, celestial hierarchies, archetypal deities, and so on, are all the objects of subtle mental knowing, just as the gross realities of the physical plane are objects of gross perceptual knowing. Thus, the levels of being in the true great chain of being include not just the gross, physical levels of matter and their increasingly complex degrees of organization, but also the subtle and transcendental levels of being." Thomas J. McFarlane, "A Critical Look at Ken Wilber's Four Quadrant Model," Accessed on September 28 2019, available from *http://www.integralscience.org/wilber.html*.

Hand surfaces."[51] But this assertion is based on the assumption that the mind and soul cannot take exteriors as their objects, that exteriors can only be known through bodily sensations alone. Of course, if one artificially restricts one's knowledge of being to perception alone, one will see the perceptual surfaces of objects. This can blind one seeing any depth in the Kosmos and one can reduce the meaning of 'exterior' to the physical alone, as Wilber has done in this case. Second, Wilber's assumption is also inconsistent with experience as well. For example, with subtle conceptual thought, one can see beyond the perceptual surfaces of exterior objects and know their deeper subtle nature (as mathematics allows insight into subtle physical laws of the exterior world). Third, since Wilber's AQAL model bypasses ontological depth from the exterior world, it provides no way to understand how modern physics could converge with the mystical views of the world. These above limitations are quite disturbing because Wilber presents the AQAL model as 'A Theory of Everything' and an integral model for the whole Kosmos. In fact, the AQAL meta-theory is not integral since it excludes very significant dimensions of reality. And the result is that a partial vision is presented as being a complete vision of the whole.[52] Moreover, Andrew P. Smith makes another valid observation.[53] Noting that the four aspects of a holon have undergone a round of breeding, Smith opines that in the new generation of holons, every one of the original-found dimension has an inside and an outside. Smith contends that one might have thought that the terms interior and exterior would adequately convey these notions. But according to Wilber, the interiors have both insides and outsides, as do exteriors. This looks to be confusing. Further still, one can notice that Wilber's AQAL meta-theory conflates two different meanings of the individual versus social dynamic.[54] One meaning used by Wilber is the distinction between an individual and a social holon. The other meaning is the individual (or agency) versus social (or communion) aspect of any holon, individual or social. This means that sixteen quadrants are needed to convey the complete world of holons. Also, Wilber has recognized the existence of multiple developmental streams (for example, cognitive, emotional, interpersonal, moral etc.) within a single holon. Since these streams do not necessarily develop simultaneously in any individual, they are all the more complications to any description

51 Ken Wilber, *A Brief History of Everything*, 265.

52 Wilber has refined his AQAL meta-theory in the wake of serious criticism against it. For details see, Thomas J. McFarlane, "A Critical Look at Ken Wilber's Four Quadrant Model," Internet.

53 In Andrew P. Smith, "Wilber's Eight-Fold Way: How Many sides Does a Holon Have?" (Accessed September 28 2019); available from *http://www.geocities.com/andybalik/8f.html.* Internet.

54 Cf. Andrew P. Smith, "Wilber's Eight-Fold Way: How Many sides Does a Holon Have?" Internet.

of holon.[55] This can also hurt the comprehensive understanding of the four quadrants.

Conclusion

In his AQAL meta-theory, Wilber attempts of articulate an integral vision of reality and how this meta-theory is actually applicable in the real world of religious, social and economic conditions. It offers 'constructive postmodernism' or a 'post-postmodern' approach based on universal integralism that reflects unity in diversity. Wilber says, "Integral means, if it means anything, the integration of all that is given to humankind."[56] The AQAL meta-theory is also a classic example of Wilber's on inter-subjective dimensions. He perceives human person as a human holon, who manifests the process of Spirit-in-action. One of the important contributions of Wilber toward integralism is his AQAL meta-theory –which is actually applicable in the real world of social, economic and religious conditions. It is deeply involved with integral transformative practices or engaging in actual methodologies that transform consciousness and increase valid knowledge acquisition. In spite of many criticisms against his theory, we must note that Wilber has been always attentive to the critical comments of critics and colleagues. He modifies his thinking in the light of the criticism he has invited. Lastly, it is worth noting Wilber's attitude –that his system or philosophy is a 'open-ended and not a closed system;'[57] a map and not a territory. In other words, every human being must take upon himself/ herself to promote integral vision –not by a mere theory but by integral living. Keeping in mind the present problems of religious disharmony, we are called upon to subscribe to this integral vision of reality, which will help us to be conscious of inter-religiousness in everyone's religious belief.

---

55 Cf. Andrew P. Smith, "Wilber's Eight-Fold Way: How Many sides Does a Holon Have?" Internet.

56 Ken Wilber, *Integral Psychology –Consciousness, Spirit, Psychology, Therapy*, 56.

57 Cf. Brad Reynolds, *Where's Wilber At? -Ken Wilber's Integral Vision in the New Millennium*, 7; Cf. Ken Wilber, *One Taste –Daily Reflections on Integral Spirituality*, viii.

16

Religious Experience: Is It Rational to Believe in Religious Experiences?

Doni Raja SJ

Abstract

Religious experience is a fluid term and hard to find one definition for it, since many people have multiple understanding of religious experience. Here the author tries to form a sweeping definition of religious experience to help the readers make sense of the paper. Religious experiences are perceptions of God contrasted with conceptualizing and judging. It involves more of perceiving than taking or interpreting or inferring. Religious experiences are direct awareness of God. God presents himself to the subjects of these experiences. These subjects in the experiences directly perceive God. The basic principles of rationality used by Swinburne is used to prove the rationality of Religious experiences. Principle of credulity is for the subjects involved in the religious experience. The subject is justified in believing what he seems to perceive in the absence of special considerations. Principle of testimony tells that in the absence of special consideration we ought to believe what people report of their experiences. Then using a cumulative case, we show how it is rational to believe in the religious experiences in the absence of special considerations. Finally, we try to respond to some of the critiques against the veridicality of the religious experience and the beliefs formed from them. The critiques are shown that they have been unjustly applied to religious experiences. Those who critique have applied double standard or epistemic imperialism. There are no convincing and persuasive reasons to show that religious experiences should not be trusted. Therefore, it is rational to believe them.

Keywords

Religious experience, tradition, principles of rationality, principle of credulity, principle of testimony, non-sensory perceptual experiences.

Introduction[1]

Life in the modern world has challenged some of the transcendental dimensions only because they seem to lie beyond the reach of our sense-dependent experiences. One such truth is God. Is there God? This question has evoked a lot of debates. Those who answer affirmatively call themselves believers and those who respond negatively are called non-believers. A non-believer's question to a believer is that if there is a God, how he/she can know Him/Her. If a believer has no reasons for his belief, his belief is blind. Every believer has some reasons for his/her faith. Science seems to have made many believers suspicious of their faith. What kind of answers will help these believers to regain or return to their faith? The many arguments for God's existence, in the past, are purely metaphysical and impersonal. This paper attempts to respond to the genuine search of people. If there is God, he should have revealed himself at least to some people somewhere in history. And many religious traditions do speak about the experiences people had of God. These experiences are the possible means through which we can know God. Many religions are founded on religious experiences.

Religious experiences are direct awareness of God. God presents himself to the subjects of these experiences. These subjects in the experiences directly perceive God. The basic principles of rationality show that in the absence of special considerations, one ought to believe what one seems to perceive and what others report about their experience. Often the recipients of religious experience are very communitarian and do not have any selfish motives in proclaiming their experience. They are trustworthy and so it is rational to believe in what trustworthy people say, unless and until there is evidence to prove otherwise. There are no convincing and persuasive reasons to show that religious experiences should not be trusted. Therefore, it is rational to believe them.

1. Framing (Defining) the Religious Experience

There are different religious traditions and every tradition understands the religious experience in a way that is unique to itself. Here, it is important to

1 The author remains grateful to Dr. George Karuvelil for encouraging and initiating him to philosophical thinking. The author is ever thankful for the rigor of research he learned while working his B. Ph thesis with Dr. George Karuvelil.

specify what type of religious experiences the author is concerned with. An experience always involves the subject (one who experiences) and its relation with an object (a thing, experienced). It is a conscious activity. What makes an experience religious is when the object involved is religious; to be more precise, the object of religious experience is God. Richard Swinburne defines religious experience,

> ...what makes an experience religious is the way it seems to the subject. This definition seems fair to the use of the expression 'religious experience' in our context – for the characteristics of such experiences have always been supposed to be that in some way they wore their religious origin on their face. What is it for the subject to be right, in fact to experience God, i.e. to be aware of God, and so in the very general sense to perceive god.[2]

The religiousness of experience is in the way it appears to the subject. The subject experiences a direct awareness of God. God is the object of the experience. When we say direct awareness of God, it implies that there are many other possibilities of becoming aware of God. Here we consider the experiences where God reveals or to use the words of William P Alston, experiences that involve "a presentation, givenness, or appearance of something to the subject, identified by the subject as God."[3] The experiences of this sort can be contrasted with "thinking about God, calling up mental images, entertaining propositions, reasoning, or remembering something about God, just as seeing a tree contrasts with these other cognitive relations to it."[4] God presents himself to the subject. A caveat is that one cannot deny the possibilities of other religious experiences that are prevalent in other religious traditions. We are interested in the epistemic knowing of the object of the perception.

Alston concentrates on non-sensory perceptual experiences.[5] The reason Alston Gives, for preferring them to sensory experiences is that those non-sensory experiences have greater chance of presenting God who is disembodied, spiritual, indescribable, metaphysical, external being as He is.[6] Alston's interest is in mystical experiences. But here we will involve the kind of perceptions that Swinburne discusses. This more extensive understanding would be inclusive of many people's experiences. Much of the ambiguity we

2 Richard Swinburne, *The Existence of God* (Oxford: Clarendon Paperbacks, 1991), 247.

3 William P. Alston, *Perceiving God: The Epistemology of Religious Experience* (London: Cornell University press, 1995), 5.

4 William P. Alston, "Religious Experience as Perception of God," in *The Ten Essential Texts in The Philosophy of Religion: Classics and Contemporary Issues*, ed. Steven M. Cahn (New York Oxford: Oxford University Press, 2005), 444.

5 Ibid, 442.

6 Ibid, 442.

have of them will be solved as we proceed. Now comes the major question; Do we need to believe these experiences? Our effort in this paper is to show that we do have justifiable reasons to trust these experiences.

2. Principles of Rationality

What we present here are the principle of credulity and the principle of testimony, the two basic principles of rationality, according to Swinburne.

2.1. Principle of Credulity

All of us will agree that what seems to be the case is the case in the absence of counter evidence. The experience of you seeming (epistemically) to reading this paper is good and enough evidence for supposing that you are reading it. We can define the principle of credulity as, in the absence of special circumstances or counter-evidence, one ought to believe what one seems (epistemically) to perceive. To put it more clearly, we can say, "In the absence of special circumstances, it is wise to believe that what we appear to perceive is actually present."[7] Now we apply this principle to the religious experience of the subjects.

> How things seem to be is good grounds for a belief about how things are. From this it would follow that, in the absence of special considerations, all religious experiences ought to be taken by their subjects as genuine, and hence as substantial grounds for belief in the existence of their apparent object – God, or Mary, or Ultimate reality, or Poseidon.[8]

The principle has been stated in the affirmative, i.e., "how things seem positively to be is the evidence of how they are, but how things seem not to be is not such evidence."[9] For instance, that its seeming to us that there is no tiger in the classroom cannot be taken as an evidence for supposing that there is not, unless there are reasonable grounds (i) that we have looked everywhere in the classroom, (ii) that we have healthy eyes with good functioning ability and (iii) that we have the cognitive ability to recognize the tiger when we see one as we have seen in the past. If a non-believer says that there seems to be no God in the universe, his 'not seeming' to perceive God cannot be evidence for supposing that there is no God. For two (i & iii) of the prerequisite grounds would refute his perception. Therefore, his statement that there is no God would not stand justified. One may perceive the absence of God in his or her life, but it is not proper to say that there is no God at all. The principle of credulity seems to help only those who have had religious experiences. Their

7 Beverley Clack and Brian R. Clack, *The Philosophy of Religion: A Critical Introduction* (Cambridge: Polity press, 2008), 44.

8 Richard Swinburne, *The Existence of God,* 254.

9 Ibid, 254.

total is very minimum comparing to those who don't have such experiences. How can they believe in religious experiences? Do we have any principles for them?

2.2. Principle of Testimony

The second principle of rationality helps us gain knowledge. For much of our knowledge about the world, science or even about ourselves, we rely on testimony. We can define the second epistemological principle as

> ... (in the absence of special considerations) the experiences of others are (probably) as they report them. This latter principle I will call the Principle of Testimony. I used this principle in claiming (on the basis of what they tell us) that very many people have religious experiences. The special considerations which lead us to doubt a subject's reports of his experiences are evidence that generally or in matters of a particular kind he misremembers or exaggerates or lies. But in the absence of such positive evidence we have good grounds to believe what others tell us about their experiences.[10]

You have a severe problem on your knees. You meet a doctor, and he tells You that your meniscus tissues were torn, and You need to be operated immediately, and it might cost 50,000 rupees. Despite not having money, you would still be ready to borrow some and get the operation done. Suppose, before You came to him for treatment You have heard of the doctor, being money-oriented and he builds another clinic in the city, and he needs money for it and so the number of operations he is doing these days has increased. Because of this positive evidence, you would probably take a second opinion from another doctor who is not building any other clinic and, therefore, not money minded and more reliable and confirm your condition and then would proceed with the treatment.

In the absence of special considerations, other things being equal, we believe what others testify that they experienced. We see that religious experiences transform those who have them. The veracity of their verbal testimony is stronger with their life testimony. Their whole life manifests the deep experience. Their life stands as a witness to the religious experience they have had. William James writes, "by their fruits ye shall know them not by their roots."[11]

Let me give you one of the not-so-often quoted examples, St. Ignatius' life - before and after his conversion. Ignatius himself dictates to Da Camara about his early life, "Up to the age of twenty-six he was a man given to the

10 Richard Swinburne, *The Existence of God,* 272.

11 William James, *The Varieties of Religious Experiences* (London and New York: Routledge, 2002), 26.

follies of the world; and what he enjoyed most was exercise with arms having a great and a foolish desire to win fame."[12] As we further read the testament and testimony we come to know how God has filled Ignatius with grace after grace. He had many religious experiences. His experiences led him through a great transformation. William James writes about Ignatius, "Saint Ignatius was a mystic, but his mysticism made him assuredly one of the most powerfully practical human engines that ever lived."[13] So many millions of people have come to experience God through the spiritual exercises of St. Ignatius which is itself the fruit of his own religious (mystical) experiences.

3. Cumulative Case

Swinburne uses the argument from religious experience as cumulative argument and not in isolation. The evidential force or veridicality of cumulative argument is much stronger in the absence of challenges than a simple perceptual claim.

> Critics look at one-dimensional arguments for the existence of God, find each of them flawed or inadequate, and then reject them all. What they fail to see is that these arguments can interact in such a way that their combined weight overcomes individual inadequacies. .... such an argument would be a "synergism," in which the combined effect of the components exceeds the sum of their individual effects.[14]

In the absence of special consideration (in the presence of positive evidence) and with long history of testimonies that affirm that God did appear to so many people, it is more probable and rational that a person's perceptual claim from his experience is true than not.

3.1 Absence of Special Consideration

Among all the other arguments from religious experience, Swinburne's argument is preferred because he premeditates what he calls special consideration which may have a possible stance against any perceptual claim of religious experience and responds to them convincingly. The principle of credulity tells us that what a person seems to perceive is probably so. Why then we need to discuss the special consideration. Here is an answer given by Davis for discussing the possible considerations and objections.

---

12 Luis Concalves Da Camara, *Testament and Testimony: The Memoirs of Ignatius of Loyola,* trans. Parmananda R. Divarkar, 17.

13 William James, "The Significance of Mysticism", in *Religious Belief and Philosophical Thought: Readings in the Philosophy of Religion,* ed. William P. Alston (New York: Harcourt, Brace & World, Inc., 1963), 144.

14 Caroline Franks Davis, *The Evidential Force of Religious Experience* (Oxford: Clarendon Press, 1999),109.

> If we wish others to accept an important experiential claim, we must, like a scientist proposing a new theory, *anticipate* possible challenges. The principle of credulity does not entitle us to regard our claims as 'proven' just because no challenges have yet been issued. Where it is demanded by the nature of the claim, a thorough investigation must be carried out into possible sources of challenges. It would be a complete misuse of the principle of credulity to say, "The onus is on the sceptic to produce challenges and therefore I can completely trust all unchallenged religious experiences." That would be blind faith, not an argument from religious experience.[15]

The person who claims to have religious experience may have had an experience. But the major dilemmas are two. The first is that the object of the experience is not God. The second is that there is no such event occurred. The claimant concocted it to gain popularity or monetary favours. Here, we discuss the special considerations discussed in detail by Swinburne. The considerations are

> "that perceptual claims are generally false when made under the influence of LSD (Lysergic acid diethylamide), which is good inductive grounds for believing that a particular new perceptual claim made by S or made under the influence of LSD is false. Secondly, one may show that the perceptual claim was to have perceived an object of a certain kind in circumstances where similar perceptual claims have proved false.[16]

It is not impossible to verify if the claimant had had any LSD at the time of religious experience. We can confirm that there is no possibility for the person to be influenced by drugs. Therefore, we can confirm that the person must have been fully aware of what happened to him. The other variant of consideration whether the claimant has necessary empirical experience required to identify the experience of God is not also valid "as it is not at all evident a priori what kinds of experience people need in order to make probable true perceptual claims; and clearly people vary enormously in this respect."[17]

The second dilemma of concoction could be shown to be true or false by checking on the probable favours and motives the claimant may surreptitiously have. This also we can see from the history of religions that many of those who have claimed to have experience of God have lost more than what they gained. Some of them went to the extent of giving their lives for the good of their brethren and the progress of humanity. Our history is full of such people. Beginning from the disciples of Jesus to St. Oscar Romero, we have seen what

---

15 Caroline Franks Davis, *The Evidential Force of Religious Experience,* 102.

16 Richard Swinburne, *The Existence of God*, 260 - 261.

17 Richard Swinburne, *The Existence of God*, 261.

the religious experiences demanded from them; not just the renunciation of comforts, but the very lives.

4. The Critiques Against the Argument from Religious Experience

4.1. Principle of Credulity not Proper for Religious Experiences

There have been arguments for restricting the application of the principle of credulity only to the ordinary (mundane) realities and not to the religious experience. The reason is that there is no inductive justification to prove religious experiences. So the principle of rationality would need an inductive justification, and religious experiences lack the inductive justification.

> ....an induction from past experiences to future experiences is only reliable if we correctly recall our past experiences. And what grounds have we got for supposing that we do? Clearly not inductive grounds-an inductive justification of the reliability of memory-claims would obviously be circular. Here clearly, we must rely on the principle that things are the way they seem, as a basic principle not further justifiable; that we seem to have had such and such experience is in itself good grounds for believing that we had.[18]

Therefore, there is no need for an inductive justification every time we experience an object.

4.2. Inter-subjective Confirmation

The unavailability and impossibility of intersubjective confirmation, which is so abundant in sense perception make one suspect the integrity of Religious experience. It also makes others who hear from the recipient of Religious experience think that this is a very subjective report. In his critique of William Alston's Perceiving God, Keith Augustine writes,

> SP (Sense Perceptual Practice) based beliefs can be checked against each other due to the allowance for intersubjective confirmation within SP; but the lack of intersubjective confirmation in CMP (Christian Mystical Perceptual practice) prevents M-beliefs from being checked against each other. This gives us strong grounds for doubting that CMP qualifies as a rationally engaged in doxastic practice, for prima facie justification of CMP cannot occur if CMP cannot be overridden. If CMP is to be rationally engaged in, it must be capable of being overridden on other grounds, grounds that come from outside of the insufficient overrider system of CMP itself.[19]

---

18 Ibid, 256.

19 Keith Augustine, "Can Mystical Experience Be a Perception of God?" infidels.org/library/modern/keith-augustine/alston.html (accessed on November 20, 2013),12.

Keith has argued that justification of CMP (Religious perception) is not possible if CMP has no overrider system other than itself. Sense perceptual based beliefs do have such overrider system. One such is the intersubjective testability. Religious perception is not sense perception. Even in SP we rely on SP to override a particular belief. Now let us consider other belief-forming practices. Is memory reliable? How do we measure its reliability? We use memory to arrive at a conclusion because, in the past, our memory has not deceived us in similar conditions. There is a kind of epistemic circularity in many of the belief-forming practices we engage in our day to day life.

We can't deny that senses are the doors through which we receive beliefs about the physical world and environment. But can we say that *only* through them it is possible? There may be a different world if we see from the perspective of other beings. God presents himself not through sense but beyond senses. In Alston's words,

> Why should we suppose that the possibilities of experiential givenness, for human beings or otherwise, are exhausted by the powers of *our* five senses? surely it is possible, to start with the most obvious point, that other creatures should possess a sensitivity to other physical stimuli that play a role in their functioning analogous to that played by our five senses in our lives.[20]

We are not spiritualizing or mystifying things by saying these things. We are trying to be as rational as possible. How do we know a person has experienced God and his beliefs about God are true? We do know by learning his longing for God before experience and by seeing his transformed life of sanctification that has put him in the world with the rest of the human beings to spread the joy and love that she/he experienced.

Therefore, the argument is that it is not proper to apply SP's standard of testing its reliability to testing the reliability of religious experience When SP itself does not have any ground other than itself to test its reliability. If a person insists on doing so, he is trying to exhibit what Alston calls 'epistemic chauvinism.'[21] Religious perceptual beliefs are tested on some other reliable grounds. Therefore, the beliefs formed from one's religious experience are rational.

4.3. Response to the Challenges of Naturalism and Neuroscience

Alston writes that "science is fitted for the exploration of the natural world that is accessible to sense perception. How could its procedures throw any light

20 William P. Alston, "Religious Experience As Perception of God," in *The Ten Essential Texts in The Philosophy of Religion; Classics and Contemporary Issues,* ed. Steven M. Cahn, 442.

21 William P. Alston, "Perceiving God," *The Journal of Philosophy* (1986), 662.

on whether or not there are orders of reality not cognitively accessible in the same way?"[22] The rise of naturalism and neuroscience seems to question the authenticity of the external intervention that many recipients of the experience claim to have perceived in or during their religious experiences. Cognitive and neuroscientific research has begun to see religious experiences and practices as part of brain activity. On studying the chemical reactions and intersecting of neurons that go on under the scull, while having religious experiences or participating in religious rituals, cognitive scientists think that they could put a full stop to the long search for the divine, saying that there is nothing as divine, but only the temporal lobe activity. The three fundamental principles of Naturalism are Materialism[23] (everything that exists is material, and everything that happens is the result of interactions between material things), causation[24] (all events are caused by other physical events: this causation is governed by universal physical laws), and reductionism[25] (all of the worlds are reducible to the laws of physics). They try to prove that the religious experiences have no supernatural divine interventions as the believers claim and these are "associated with a complex circuit of neural structures."[26] In his critique against Alston's Perceiving God, Keith Augustine, though differs from him in many ideas, accepts that naturalism operates based on "the metaphysical thesis that the only causes influencing the physical world are natural causes."[27] This paper while itself standing for vindication "cannot disqualify alternative metaphysical views for rational acceptance."[28]

"A wealth of clinical and experimental evidence demonstrates a close connection between various aspects of religious experience and physiological processes in the brain."[29] What the experiences that the neuroscientists claim to have studied are not religious experiences but laboratory experiments where individuals have been stimulated to get religious feeling in a simulated religious environment. There may be some brain activity during the religious experiences that can be traced through brain imaging. Is it justifiable to conclude that the recipients have such experiences because of the specified

---

22 William P. Alston, *Perceiving God: The Epistemology of Religious Experience,* 247.

23 Vance G. Morgan, "The Metaphysics of Naturalism," *American Catholic Philosophical Quarterly,* Vol. LXXV, no. 3 (2001), 413.

24 Ibid, 414.

25 Ibid, 415.

26 Patrick McNamara, *The Neuroscience of Religious Experience* (New York: Cambridge University Press, 2009), xi.

27 Keith Augustine, "Can Mystical Experience Be a Perception of God?" 14.

28 Ibid,14.

29 Paul F. Cunningham, "Are Religious Experiences Really Localized in The Brain? The Promise, Challenges and The Prospects of Neurothelogy," *The Journal of Mind and Behavior,* V. 32, no. 3 (Summer 2011), 225.

physiological processes in the brain? The presence of chemical reactions and neural connections is no argument against religious experiences. It seems that different Studies related to brain functions are construed to show that it is by the brain all religious experiences are derived. This would be wrong. The correct statement or assumption would be that it is the brain by which all experiences, whether religious or otherwise, are mediated.

> "If religious cognition, emotion, and behavior are mediated by the same neural systems as ordinary experience, then it would appear that what is distinctive to religious experience is not to be found in the brain but somewhere else."[30]

Therefore, we can reasonably think that there cannot be any separate anatomy in the brain with the specific sensory activity by stimulating religious experiences. If still the cognitive scientists think that they can reduce the religious experiences to material explanations alone, ignoring the divine intervention, we, along with William James call this attitude as "the vice of intellectualism."[31]

Conclusion

This paper tried to explore the terrain of epistemology and religious epistemology to show that it is rational to believe in religious experiences. If a person fails to accept the rationality of the religious experience, he operates on his incredulity. The non-sensory or a-phenomenal character of the object of the religious experience makes it not possible for the claimant to produce empirical evidence, as available and possible in the sense perception. This type of justification in the words of George Karuvelil is called 'intra-personal propositional justification.'[32] In this type of justification, the experiencer has "evidence to which he alone has a privileged access."[33] But this limitation has been overcome by presenting the positive evidence and showing the occurrence of the experience in the absence of special considerations. The problem arises when we keep the religious perception on par with sense perception and thereby judging the belief in religious experience irrational. The rationality in humans would help the skeptics, the evidentialists, the naturalists and their ilk to see the rationality and truthfulness in the religious experiences and thereby leading humanity to become fully human through the experience of the divine as it had happened in the lives of, Muhammad, Buddha, Shankara, Ignatius, Arrupe, and

30 Ibid, 227.

31 William James, *The Varieties of Religious Experiences*, 106.

32 George Karu, "Epistemic Justification and The Possibility of Empirical Evidence," *Journal of Indian Council of Philosophical Research,* Vol.12, no. 1 (September-December 1994): 33.

33 Ibid, 33.

so many others. One of the significant and difficult challenges to the argument from religious experience is the problem of religious diversity. The author is not dealing this in this paper 'because of' the limitation of his knowledge in the field of religious epistemology. Many religious epistemologists have tried to respond to this problem, though. Prof. George Karuvelil, in whose honour this book is published, is one such original thinker who has made efforts to reasonably establish the rationality of religious experiences amidst diverse religious traditions. The author remains grateful to Dr. George Karuvelil for his guidance in writing this paper during his philosophy studies. This paper is the modified and edited work of the author's thesis during his philosophy studies.

Bibliography

Alston, William P. *Perceiving God: The Epistemology of Religious Experience.* Itheca and London: Cornell University press, 1995.

Alston, William P. "Religious Experience as Perception of God." In *The Ten Essential Texts in The Philosophy of Religion: Classics and Contemporary Issues*, edited by Steven M. Cahn. New York Oxford: Oxford University Press, 2005. 394 – 449.

Alston, William P. "Religious Experience and Religious Belief." *Noûs, Vol. 16, No. 1 (Mar 1982):* 3 – 12.

Alston, William P. "Perceiving God." *The Journal of Philosophy*. 1986. 655 – 666.

Augustine, Keith. "Can Mystical Experience Be a Perception of God?" infidels.org/library/modern/keith-augustine/alston.html (accessed on November 20, 2013).

Clack, Beverley., and Brian R. Clack. *The Philosophy of Religion; a Critical Introduction.* Cambridge: Polity press, 2008. 13 – 53.

Concalves, Luis Da Camara. *Testament and Testimony: The Memoirs of Ignatius Of Loyola.* translated by Parmananda R. Divarkar. India: Gujarat Sahitya Prakash, 1994.

Cunningham, Paul F. "Are Religious Experiences Really Localized in the Brain? The Promise, Challenges and The Prospects of Neurothelogy." *The Journal of Mind and Behavior,* V. 32, no. 3 (Summer 2011): 223 – 250.

Franks, Caroline Davis. *The Evidential Force Of Religious Experience.* Oxford: Clarendon Press, 1999.

James, William. *The Varieties of Religious Experiences.* London and New York: Routledge, 2002.

James, William. "The Significance of Mysticism." In *Religious Belief and Philosophical Thought: Readings in the Philosophy of Religion,* edited by William P. Alston. New York: Harcourt, Brace & World, Inc., 1963. 126 – 163.

Karu, George. "Epistemic Justification and The Possibility of Empirical Evidence." *Journal of Indian Council of Philosophical Research,* Vol.12, no. 1 (September-December 1994): 29 - 48

McNamara, Patrick. *The Neuroscience of Religious Experience.* New York: Cambridge University Press, 2009.

Morgan, Vance G. "The Metaphysics of Naturalism." *American Catholic Philosophical Quarterly,* Vol. LXXV, no. 3 (2001): 409 – 431.

Swinburne, Richard. *The Existence of God.* Oxford: Clarendon Paperbacks, 1991. 244 – 276.

17

'Family Resemblance' For Conceptual Clarifications: Tasks of Fundamental Theology and Theology of Religions

Sathya Balan SJ

Abstract

This paper has two parts; the first deals with *Family Resemblance*, one of Wittgenstein's central notions. With this notion, he was able to clarify one of the sources of conceptual confusions, resulting from the human craving for generality. The second part explores Fr Karuvelil's article, "*Who am I speaking? Communication, Culture, and Fundamental Theology*" by applying this notion to spell out the distinct roles of fundamental theology and theology of religions. Taking a communication perspective, Fr Karuvelil explicates the similarities and differences of these two disciplines of theology in the context of our pluralistic society. Lack of clarity between them would lead us to a generalisation of their significant roles as is the case with pluralists like John Hick. They consider particularities of different religions as historical accretions to be overcome. Such an intellectual approach to religions attempts to bring them on par with each other on a level playing field. This is problematic as it downplays the unique features of each religion.

Keywords

Communication Perspective, Craving for generality, Family Resemblance, Fundamental Theology, Theology of Religions

Introduction

At the outset, I would like to say that it was truly a blessing for me to be a student of Fr. George Karuvelil, one of the finest professors I have come across in my four years of student life at JDV, which includes both B.Ph and M.Ph. Right from the start, I liked the subjects he taught as well as his teaching method; two terms sum up his teaching: 'clarify and show the way'- first clarify the concepts then show a way out of the philosophical problems! In this regard, his two important courses, *Religious Pluralism* and *Faith & Reason*, revealed his intense and continuous research. His approach, as always, was to clarify the concepts of the problems of epistemology and to show the way out of the entanglement. His main concern was that students should understand the concepts and be able to assimilate them. Philosophy is not merely an academic exercise, but 'a way of life' – this is one of the valuable lessons I have learnt from him and witnessed in his life and teaching.

A constant companion of his courses was the great twentieth century philosopher, Ludwig Wittgenstein. Fr Karuvelil effectively applied some key Wittgensteinian philosophical notions such as the distinction between grammatical and empirical sentences, hinge proposition, language games, autonomy of language games, etc. to clarify important nuances of the course. The memory of the courses offered by Fr Karuvelil is ever fresh in my mind and his attempt to show the way out of certain philosophical issues was a true learning experience. Wittgenstein said that the aim of Philosophy is to show a fly the way out of the fly bottle. Fr Karuvelil stands out as a model to emulate in this regard.

In this paper, I present the concept of Family Resemblance, one of the central notions of Wittgenstein. He employed this notion to clarify issues manifested in language, caused by certain human tendencies and attempted to show the way out of these philosophical issues. The second part of this work, as an application of family resemblance, discusses a nuanced study of the differences between the fundamental theology and theology of religions explicated by Fr Karuvelil himself in his article, "*Who am I speaking? Communication, Culture, and Fundamental Theology*"[1] At first glance, all looks similar (human craving for generality as Wittgenstein would call it); it appears that there is not much difference between the two kinds of theology. However the nuanced study by Fr. Karuvelil reveals both the similarities and the clear differences between the two and their relevance in contemporary society.

1 George Karuvelil, "To Whom Am I Speaking? Communication, Culture, and Fundamental Theology," *Theological Studies* 76, no. 4 (2015), 675-697.

1. Family Resemblance: A Central Theme of Wittgenstein

The term 'Family Resemblance' was in use prior to Wittgenstein. Nietzsche used it in his 1886 work, *Beyond Good and Evil*,[2] to explicate the similarity among the diverse ways of philosophising, "*The strange family resemblance of all Indian, Greek, and German philosophizing speaks for itself clearly enough.*"[3] But Wittgenstein applied the term in his analytic philosophy to highlight some philosophical issues, using it effectively to point out confusions and conflicts caused by human tendencies for essentialism and generality while attempting to resolve some of the philosophical problems. A study of Family Resemblance gives clarity to the thought of earlier and later Wittgenstein analytic philosophy. It could well be argued that the notion, Family Resemblance, is a meeting point of the many dimensions around the seminal ideas of one of the greatest Western philosophers of the 20th century.

1.1. Family Resemblance: A Shift from Earlier to Later Wittgenstein

In *Tractatus*, Wittgenstein maintained a picture theory of meaning which states that the function of language is to picture reality. In this way, he draws a limit to language as having one defining feature. What cannot be put in pictorial representation is simply nonsense as he writes, "*The limit can, therefore, only be drawn in language and what lies on the other side of the limit will be simply nonsense.*"[4] In *Philosophical Investigations*, Wittgenstein asks us to '*look and see*' the use of words and observe the over-lapping and criss-crossing. That is to say, language no longer has only one function to represent reality but there are many language games. Words acquire meaning by their use. The later Wittgenstein is clearly a shift from his earlier position regarding language. If the aim of *Tractatus* is to look closer, then *Philosophical investigations* can be considered as looking closer by having a wider look around. Thus, *Tractatus* is all about a homogeneous description of language whereas the later Wittgenstein is about its heterogeneous description. Each description is a language game. There exists a great multiplicity of language games such as asking, commanding, requesting, pleading, joking, debating, shouting, yelling, praying, etc.

The importance of language games is that the meaning of one language game should not be confused with another. We run into confusions when we overlook the fact that the function of words varies from one language game

---

2 Hans-Johann Glock, *A Wittgenstein Dictionary* (Oxford: Blackwell Publishers, 1996), 120.

3 Friedrich Nietzsche, *Beyond good and evil: prelude to a philosophy of the future*, trans. Norman (Cambridge: University Press 2002), 20.

4 Ludwig Wittgenstein, *Tractatus Logico-Philosophicus*, trans. C.K. Ogden & F.P. Ramsey (London: Routledge & Kegan Paul, 1922), 23.

to another. For example, take the word 'good;'[5] what is common among the following expressions: a good joke, a good tennis player, a good man, feeling good, good will, good breeding, good looking, and good for nothing? Here the word 'good' is common in all the expressions, but is used in different situations. Is there anything common in these expressions? Wittgenstein gives his insightful analysis: "Instead of producing something common to all that we call language, I am saying that these phenomena have no one thing in common which makes us use the same word for all,— but that they are related to one another in many different ways" (PI 65).

Though the word 'good' is used in all the phrases, there is nothing common among them, only a network of similarities and differences. Wittgenstein himself took the example of games (PI 166) to explain this phenomenon. There are a variety of games and there is no common essence among them. Some are solitary while some are competitive; some individual, others team activities, some depend on skills whereas others on chance. Some games are played for amusement while others played for gain. Some are played with balls, some with cards, sticks, etc.; some games are played at the local level while some played at the Olympics. Still we call all of them games, but what is common to all of them? Wittgenstein states:

> "Don't say: "There must be something common, or they would not be called 'games' "—but look and see whether there is anything common to all. For if you look at them you will not see something that is common to all, but similarities, relationships, and a whole series of them at that. To repeat: don't think, but look! ...And the result of this examination is: we see a complicated network of similarities overlapping and criss-crossing." *(PI 66)*

To describe this aspect of the nature of language Wittgenstein uses the expression 'Family Resemblance': "I can think of no better expression to characterize these similarities than "family resemblances"; for the various resemblances between members of a family: build, features, colour of eyes, gait, temperament, etc. etc. overlap and criss-cross in the same way." *(PI 67)* Because the concept of family members brings out effectively the similarities and differences they share. Family members have different traits and yet to consider them all similar as one family clarifies what a word or term could mean in language. In that sense, the term 'family resemblance' is more appropriate and it does justice to the 'similar and yet different' nature of the terms in the language we use.

5 John Heaton and Judy Groves, *Introducing Wittgenstein* (Cambridge: Icon Books Ltd, 1999), 129.

1.2. Family Resemblance: A Reaction to Essentialism and Human Craving for Generality

For Wittgenstein, all philosophical problems are first of all problems of language. He was convinced that on studying the logic of language, we would be able to solve many philosophical problems. In this context, his concept of family resemblance is an attack on essentialism, coming right from Plato's idealism that all things have an essence (an idea or a form) and the task of philosophizing is to seek and formulate the essence of things. Wittgenstein points out that this tendency to look for the essence has led us astray, causing many confusions and conflicts.

The concept of family resemblance is not limited to language alone. It also addresses the problems caused by the human tendency to seek the essence of things; it is not merely a linguistic analysis but a deep philosophical issue arising from essentialism: "There is no reason to look, as we have done traditionally—and dogmatically—for one, essential core in which the meaning of a word is located and which is, therefore, common to all uses of that word. We should, instead, travel with the word's uses through "a complicated network of similarities overlapping and criss-crossing."[6] In this way, Wittgenstein brings to light the problem of strict boundaries and exactness of a word or term in the use of language. Such boundaries, right from Plato's essentialism to even his own form of proposition in *Tractatus*, create confusions and conflicts. His notion of family resemblance is aimed at overcoming such confusions caused by the strict boundaries and exactness favoured by the human tendency for essentialism.

Another main source of problems, according to Wittgenstein, is the human tendency to crave for generality which is a method of science that tries to narrow down natural laws to the smallest possible number, in the form of equation and definition. Applying such form of generalization or unification, a method of science, to philosophy creates confusions and conflict. "Philosophers constantly see the method of science before their eyes, and are irresistibly tempted to ask and answer questions in the way science does. This tendency is the real source of metaphysics, and leads the philosopher into complete darkness. I want to say here that it can never be our job to reduce anything to anything or to explain anything. Philosophy is 'purely descriptive'."[7]

One of Wittgenstein's major contentions is that *philosophy is purely descriptive.* The concept of Family resemblance seeks to describe the use of a particular word or term in language in a given context, as opposed to the

6 "Ludwig Wittgenstein," Stanford Encyclopaedia of Philosophy, substantive revision May 2, 2018, https://plato.stanford.edu/entries/wittgenstein/.

7 Ludwig Wittgenstein, *The Blue and Brown Books: Preliminary Studies for the 'Philosophical Investigation*' (New York: Happer Colophon Books, 1965), 18.

scientific method of generalisation in all situations. It needs to be clarified that human actions are so varied and nuanced that mere generalisation is misleading; instead describing the event would avoid errors and confusions. Reality cannot be exhausted as it has infinite layers of meaning; it looks similar and different and we, humans, also understand in a way that is similar and different. Conceptual confusions manifest themselves when we tend to generalize things at the cost of ignoring the 'similar yet different' dimension of reality. In this regard, the notion of family resemblance intends to resolve a serious philosophical issue resulting from the human tendency for generality.

2. Different Tasks of Fundamental Theology and Theology of Religions

This part is aimed at using the notion of *family resemblance* to distinguish the roles of fundamental theology and theology of religions. These two disciplines of theology are similar yet their tasks differ in the context of our pluralistic society. Lack of clarity between them would lead to a generalization of their significant roles. Such rash generalization becomes a serious concern, Wittgenstein warns us, as it dilutes the distinct roles played by the two disciplines in effectively reaching out to the contemporary world. To illustrate, John Hick's conception of theology of religions is one such example of such generalization. He searched for a level playing field where no religion is considered superior or inferior. But such a hunt for an objective paradigm made pluralists like Hick consider particularities of different religions as historical accretions to be overcome. This kind of intellectual approach to religions is scientistic' as it claims science as the only norm for everything else. The same approach of generalizing religions to bring them on par with each other or with their rival worldviews, to bring them onto a level playing field would result in downplaying the unique features of each religion.

There is also a danger of generalizing the distinct tasks of fundamental theology and theology of religions. Here, the notion of family resemblance could serve as a wake-up call to seek clarity in order to avoid conceptual errors. And in our pluralistic context, it becomes crucial to spell out the distinct roles of fundamental theology and theology of religions, avoiding any generalization of their unique characteristics. Vatican II genuinely wanted to read the signs of the times and communicate the message of the gospel in an intelligible way to the contemporary world. Its sincere efforts to re-evangelize the world resulted in creating Councils for Culture, for Interreligious dialogue and for Promoting New Evangelization. In fact, the role of fundamental theology is to reach out to the contemporary world with an approach of faith seeking acceptability. But the Council's efforts have not borne much fruit, because the nature of fundamental theology as a discipline is itself in dire need of clarity in the context of a pluralistic society.

Set in this context, Fr Karuvelil's article, '*To whom Am I speaking? : Communication, Culture and Fundamental theology*' is an eye-opener. He spells out clearly the task of fundamental theology, not from the perspective of looking for a clear definition and meaning of the term, but from the perspective of its active and dynamic role in the context our pluralistic society. Moreover, he explicates, the sharp differences between fundamental theology and theology of religions. His close observation of the different roles of these two disciplines of theology draw admiration as it could serve well to resolve some of the conceptual confusions arising from our tendency to generalize the meaning and the purpose of these two theological terms. Fr Karuvelil argues that the distinction between the two terms emerge from a good communication perspective and the diverse addressees of our pluralistic society.

This part explores the (he)art of a good human communication theory, as presented by Fr Karuvelil in his article, and presents the diverse addressees in today's context. It further clarifies, considering Thomas Aquinas as exemplar, the distinct roles of fundamental theology and theology of religions based on the communication theory.

2.1. A Healthy Communication Perspective and the Different Addressees of Contemporary Society

We now live in a world of great diversity; there are many forces at work in society today such as religion, science, politics, etc. In the present scenario, a significant task of fundamental theology is to make the gospel intelligible to the contemporary world. Since it is a matter of communicating the gospel in the context of our times, fundamental theology should have a healthy communication perspective. As the addressees could come from diverse cultural backgrounds, the communication perspective should account for this diversity. If it neglects or undermines the importance of the cultural background of any system, it would be inadequate in dealing with the diverse and pluralistic nature of society today. A good and effective communication theory bears in mind the inevitable role of culture of the diverse addressees. The problem with modern epistemology was that it looked for an Archimedean point (from outside of all received traditions and belief systems) to seek objectivity and truth. But such an a-historical epistemology has caused many problems, because it neglects and underestimates the existential dimension or the rootedness of the people of any particular culture.

A successful communication theory, unlike the bullet theory of communication[8], genuinely accounts for the existential dimension or the lived horizon of both the communicator and the recipient. Culture plays a vital role

8 Bullet theory of communication is problematic as its focus is only on the communicator to shoot the message, ignoring the role of the recipient.

in encoding and decoding the message by the communicator and recipient respectively; the communicator, the recipient and the message then form a triadic relationship. It is necessarily a doubly-mediated dynamic process of making an entry into the horizon of each other. In the process, to overcome the distance between the source and the destination, there exists a tension in aligning the source and the destination of the message. But the driving force (a sense of ought to communicate) and the engaging force (being profoundly open to the other) as two wings, keep the dynamic process alive. In this dynamic, doubly-mediated process of human communication, the slow and steady enlargement of the shared horizon (arising from the fusion of the horizons of both the communicator and the recipient) is the eventual outcome of a successful communication. However it is easier said than done as it involves a constant tension to ensure the process of the communication in progress. The qualities required to manage this unavoidable tension are empathy with the other and respect for the otherness of the other which would keep the process of human communication alive.

When applied to religious communication, it is imperative first of all to know the addressees in a pluralistic society; it has to be very clear as to whom the message is directed since we live with people from diverse backgrounds. Here, we can look up to Saint Thomas Aquinas who excelled in reaching out to the three general categories of addressees of his time (the Gentiles, the Jews and heretics and the co-believers). His model successfully took natural theology as propaedeutic to faith in the 13th century, when it fitted well in the Christian world. But our time is very different from the 13th century as many divergent worldviews coexist with increasing secularisation of social and political structures. Hence, considering Thomas Aquinas as our exemplar, we need to divide today's contemporary society into three broad categories of addressees: religious kin (from the same tradition), religious aliens or religious outsiders (from different religious traditions), and the non-religious.

This complex and diverse scenario demands a healthy communication approach to suit the needs of the addressees. It is in this context of diverse addressees that the distinction between the fundamental theology and theology of religions emerges and it becomes necessary to differentiate their roles.

2.2. Distinct Roles of Fundamental Theology and Theology of Religions based on the Communication Perspective

It may be fitting to say that religious communication creates a spectrum, stretching from addressing fellow religious kin (maximally shared horizon) to members of other religious traditions and then to non-religious recipients (the least shared horizon). In the first kind of religious communication, which addresses religious kin, since communication is done within a maximally shared faith horizon, available conceptual resources of the religious tradition are used. The aim of this communication is to understand already existing beliefs and to solidify those beliefs. But when addressing religious outsiders and the non-religious, the shared territory and available resources are not the same - they are relatively minimal when addressing the non-religious, and comparatively more when addressing religious outsiders. Besides, the aim and purpose of such communication is also different – that is, it is not so much about faith seeking understanding as when done with religious kin, but is more about faith seeking acceptability.

This acceptability becomes the guiding theme and it plays an important role in the emergence of the task of fundamental theology. If theology is addressed to religious kin with the view of faith seeking understanding, then fundamental theology is addressed to religious outsiders and non-religious to seek acceptability of faith. This is clearly in continuity with the classical apologetic tradition of defending faith, not with the traditional confrontational and polemic attitude, but with an attitude of dialogue and friendly appeal to reason. It has to be emphasised that fundamental theology, following the method of Thomas Aquinas, takes the insider approach. Hence it is a theological discipline. It attempts to seek acceptability of the Christian faith in a pluralistic society without relying on the authority of the Church or Christian revelation. As 20th century successor to the older traditions of natural theology and apologetics, it adopts a comprehensive approach in the context of increasing secularisation of the pluralistic society to avoid any of the polemic characteristics of traditional apologetics.

In today's context, another problem emerges - many Christians have the same serious questions and doubts about the Christian faith like their other religious counterparts. The task of fundamental theology then cannot be reduced to reaching out only to outsiders, but must be comprehensive enough to encompass the concerns of co-believers as well. Besides, in terms of communication theory, another difficulty arises in addressing religious kin since both the communicator and the addresses are in the same boat, having doubts and questions about their faith, but with no message to communicate and with no interest and motivation to do so. In this complex situation, there is a possibility of giving up religious communication (as there is no message that ought to be communicated) or a denial that co believers are in the same boat. This delicate situation causes a dilemma.

Overcoming this dilemma would clarify the role of fundamental theology today. Firstly, we realise that we live in a pluralistic context and the addressees are rarely a single person or a homogenous group. Unavoidably, others are present in the background when communication takes place between two persons/ groups; that is the reality today. And in this context, Pearce proposes the *daisy model of communication* which takes into account simultaneously the main addressee/s and the secondary addressee/s potentially present in the background. It is best illustrated with the example of a judge pronouncing the verdict in a courtroom. The primary addressee could be explicitly the accused, but the judgement is implicitly to the others such as other judges, journalists, fellow citizens, potential criminals and so on. Keeping the daisy model of communication in mind, the roles of theology and fundamental theology could be defined. The primary addressees of theology of religions would be fellow believers; religious outsiders and nonbelievers would be the secondary addressees. Roles are reversed as far as fundamental theology is concerned. Moreover, this daisy model of communication, having the primary addressees in the foreground and potential secondary addressees in the background, demands that the message is tailored to reach out to the concerned primary addressee, but not at the cost of diluting the core message of the communication (as the co-believers are potential secondary addressees).

Along the same line of thought, the distinct roles of fundamental theology and theology of religions are made clear through the work of interreligious dialogue. It is a need of the hour in today's diverse religious society. Though we need both fundamental theology and theology of religion for the important task of interreligious dialogue, their contribution to dialogue is distinguished based on the communication theory. Theology of religions' primary addressees would be religious kin in order to resolve the rival truth claims made by religious outsiders and others. As it is directed at religious kin, i.e. to the maximally shared horizon, it makes use of the available resources to resolve the tension and solidify the faith of religious kin, precisely in the role of faith seeking understanding. Whereas, fundamental theology is addressed to the secular world (to the group not sharing the same resources of traditions and to the group with the minimally shared horizon), making its contribution to interreligious dialogue different. Its vital task is to provide a framework for communication to explore the substantive commonality shared between religions. This search for shared ground is essential for successful communication. With its exploration of the shared ground and the genuine desire to increase the shared ground, the role of fundamental theology becomes prominent in the diverse context of our contemporary world.

To sum up, a mere generalisation of the addressees of our diverse cultural backgrounds would be problematic as such an approach would fall back to modern philosophy which downplayed culture and history. Philosophers like John Hick, looking for a level playing field to prove objectivist epistemology, try to filter out the unique features of different religions. They fall back on modern philosophy, seeking a neutral, ahistorical matrix for objectivistic epistemology. It is in this problematic situation that the communication theory offers a boundary that underscores the distinct roles of the fundamental theology and theology of religions. Without clarity of the diverse addressees of our society, these roles get blurred.

Conclusion

The greatness of Wittgenstein lies in his ability to bring Philosophy as a constant engagement, making it a way of life. In other words, Philosophy is an activity and not mere theory. And with his concept of family resemblance, he reminds us to 'look at and see' carefully the use of language and how it is intimately connected to human activity. He urges us to become aware of our tendency to generalize terms and concepts, and be freed from the ensuing conceptual confusions caused by such an attitude. One such confusion has come about in distinguishing the roles of fundamental theology and theology of religions. In the pluralistic context of our time, both these terms need to be clearly defined and their tasks are to be distinguished. Both are similar yet different in their purpose in the contemporary world. Their roles get blurred if we tend to generalize them. Fr Karuvelil, with the help of the communication theory, provides a framework to understand the similar yet different tasks of both these theological terms. His article is a revelation, not only about the distinction between the two theological terms, but also about his commitment to conceptual clarifications.

Bibliography

Glock, Hans-Johann. *A Wittgenstein Dictionary*, Oxford: Blackwell Publishers, 1996.

Heaton, John, and Judy Groves., *Introducing Wittgenstein*. Cambridge: Icon Books Ltd, 1999.

Karuvelil, George. "To Whom Am I Speaking? Communication, Culture, and Fundamental Theology." *Theological Studies* 76, no. 4 (2015): 675-697.

Nietzsche, Friedrich. *Beyond good and evil: prelude to a philosophy of the future*. Translated by Norman. Cambridge: University Press, 2002.

Stanford Encyclopedia of Philosophy. "Ludwig Wittgenstein." Substantive revision May 2, 2018. https://plato.stanford.edu/entries/wittgenstein/.

Wittgenstein, Ludwig. *Tractatus Logico-Philosophicus*. Translated by C.K. Ogden & F.P. Ramsey. London: Routledge & Kegan Paul, 1922.

Wittgenstein, Ludwig. *The Blue and Brown Books: Preliminary Studies for the 'Philosophical Investigation*. New York: Happer Colophon Books, 1965.

18

Reflecting Our Religion

Subhash Anand

Abstract

In the West, many are moving away from traditional religions; elsewhere, they have been co-opted by the consumer market and political forces. This development seems to confirm the earlier rejection of religion by some modern and contemporary thinkers. Only reflection may redeem religion. The Japanese Origami Craft is a good model for theological reflection. The artist takes a piece of paper and folds it in different ways to give it a particular shape. With one and the same sheet, he can come up with different products: arrow, boat, bird, etc. A creative theologian takes the foundational experience very seriously; he reflects over it again and again so as to interpret it meaningfully and articulate it intelligibly for our times. Our household mirror helps us to understand existential reflection. A good mirror reflects almost all the light that falls on it. Ancient people illumined a dark interior by using this technique. A true follower of religion allows the foundational experience to enlighten him; his life may make religion more respectable in the eyes of others. Enlightened religion would mean a shift from belief to faith, from rituals to values, from law to discernment, from prayers to contemplation, from religiosity to humanity.

Keywords

Contemplation, discernment, humanity, law, prayers, reflection, rituals, values.

Introduction

A national survey on priestly ministry in the mid-eighties makes a disturbing but not unexpected conclusion:

> by and large, the people who accept and respect the priests today are the uneducated, not the educated... We cannot dismiss the educated laity's disaffection with the clergy simply as an expression of the disenchantment of the educated with religion in general. The survey data does not support the popular perception that the educated are generally less 'religious' than the uneducated.[1]

That was before the Tsunami of Child Abuse came to light. Since then many have left their churches.[2] Besides Christians, many more have lost faith in traditional and organized religions. Even Hindu thinkers have been critical of organized religions. Vivekananda once remarked: "If you want to be religious, enter not the gate of any organised religions. They do a hundred times more evil than good, because they stop the growth of each one's individual development."[3] Organized religions have become competitive corporates: "We see today a rivalry, a war going on among different religions as to the number of adherents each can boast of…we are denying our God and being untrue to ourselves."[4] The disillusionment with organized religions is much more pervasive than some are prepared to admit.

Today the Abrahamic religions are facing a special crisis. Postmodernism questions the reality of foundational events and the normative character of overarching narratives.

> In the present cultural scenario of pluralism, liminality and mobility, common people out of socio-cultural compulsions construct a faith which does not make them belong to any religion per se...People are quite

---

1 Paul Parathazham, "Catholic Priests in India: Reflections on a Survey", *Vidyajyoti Journal of Theological Reflection*, 52 (1988), 388.

2 See the following sites, all accessed on 24-09-2019:

http://religion.blogs.cnn.com/2012/03/30/7-reasons-catholics-leave-church-in-trenton-1-is-sex-abuse-crisis/.

https://www.christianpost.com/by/stoyan-zaimov#Churchtoo: Women Share Stories of Rape, Sexual Abuse, Leaving Church.

https://www.usatoday.com/story/news/nation/2019/04/22/sex-abuse-catholic-church-why-more-americans-leaving/3507437002/.

https://catholics4change.com/2012/03/12/catholics-leaving-church-over-abuse-issue/.

3 Swami Vivekananda, *The Complete Works of Swami Vivekananda*, 9 vols., Mayavati Memorial Edition, Kolkata: Advaita Ashrama, 2002-04, vol. 1, 474.

4 M. K. Gandhi, *In Search of Supreme*, 3 vols., ed.: V. B. Kher, Ahmedabad: Navajivan Publishing House, 1962, vol. 3, 342. See also T. P. Urumpackal, *Organized Religion according to Dr. S. Radhakrishnan*, Rome: Gregorian University, 1972.

> imaginative and intelligent in this regard and take profound freedom to interpret their faith in context. People increasingly say that they believe in 'spirituality' rather than 'religion'.[5]

This phenomenon generates a lot of insecurity especially among traditional 'priests' of all religions. Not only their religion but—and for many of them this may be a greater concern—but also their livelihood is facing a powerful threat. They may pretend that nothing is happening and try to keep their flock in the dark.

Yet religion will continue to be part of human life. "The immense mysteries and uncertainties of the world and man's own inquiring and evaluating self-consciousness make inevitable a reaching out for some sort of ultimate values and realities—which is but another name for the religious quest."6 Certain phenomena that were mysterious to our ancestors are no longer so for moderns. The biggest mystery humans experience is when they come in the presence of other humans. Then reason alone does not suffice. The other is understood in self-disclosure, provide I have faith in the other: the other as truthful. Then I accept not only the disclosure, but the mystery that is self-disclosing. I accept the other as other: the mystery remains a mystery even after the self-disclosure. I come in the presence of the unknown, the unpredictable, the uncontrollable. I become vulnerable. Deep in my heart I hope the other will accept and respect my otherness. My encounter with the other is an engagement with a mystery humans, demanding faith, hope and love. Hence, whatever be the failures of religions, I cannot side-line religion.

Years ago, I decided to opt for ministry within the Church; I committed myself to promote the religious within humans. Even though my understanding of ministry has changed almost radically, my commitment remains, though at times I was found lacking. There are four reasons why I feel responsible for the future of religion. First, religion has been successfully co-opted and domesticated by commercial corporates. "The temples, *gurudwaras* and other religious institutions attract not only devotees but also allied businesses of all kinds such as jewellers, garland makers and so on, seeking opportunities to make money. In short, religion has become a growth industry."[7] Religion has become part of the advertisement industry. "The gods in over 16 religious

5 Anthony Kalliath, "Believing-Faith to Awakening-Faith: Asian Hermeneutics of Faith and Meaning of Conversion", *Third Millennium*, 18/1 (January - March, 2015), 40.

6 Winston L. King, "Religion", in Mircea Eliade (ed.-in-chief), *The Encyclopedia of Religion*, 16 vols, New York: Smon & Schuster Macmillan, 1993, vol. 12, 292a.

7 Pushpa Sundar, "*Rich Gods and Poor People in the Era of Commercialised Religion*", thewire.in/religion/religion-commercialisation; accessed on 01-08-2019. Pushpa Sundar, founder of Sampradaan—Indian Centre for Philanthropy, has authored Business and Community: The Story of Corporate Social Responsibility in India, and Patrons and Philistines: Arts and the State in British India.

shrines in India have income which runs into crores. They live or travel out in silver and gold bedecked sanctums and chariots, clothed and ornamented in the finest of fine clothes and jewellery, fed sumptuously and sung to sleep."[8] Consumer glamour has trapped many—thank God, not all—cultic leaders. They make sure that even if their religious mission may not succeed, their commission should not be lacking. Their life-style reflects that of their gods. Their message is clear: all those who are devoted to those gods will eventually become prosperous! They will "receive a hundredfold now in this time" (Mk 10.30).

My second reason for being concerned about religion is its relation to politics. Political leaders, past and present, know that if the majority of the people follow their religion, then they have a better chance of acquiring political power and holding on to it. This explains why the growing polarization that is taking place in our country, aggressively explicit during election times.[9] Religious differences provoke people to indulge in violence and mob-lynching; many observers believe that people in power are tacitly supporting this sort of behaviour.[10] In a broader sense, politics is the art of managing power. Many religions have acquired a corporate character. They have a lot of money at their disposal. Hence people are eager to get positions of power so that they control, and thereby get their share of, those funds. Positions of power within corporate structures brings social status, and that has many benefits attached to it.

Third, I have a personal reason to be involved in the effort at the revisioning of religion, especially in India and within the Church. What is disturbing me very deeply is that many of the people who have spent years in studying philosophy and theology—at least that is their claim, are also responsible for the degradation of religion. I say, it is disturbing me very deeply, because for thirty-five years I was one of their 'teachers' and 'formators'.[11] As students, they demanded a lot of freedom; now many of them are knowingly or unknowingly using religion to enslave others. Then they claimed to be grown-ups, knowing what was good for them. Now they treat laypeople, who are so often much more educated than they are and who have much more experience

8 *Idem.*

9 See the following websites, all accessed on 28-07-2019:

H. Kumar (ed.), "Polarization of Indian Politics", www.lawctopus.com/academike/polarization-indian-politics.

S. Motiram and N. Sarma, "Polarization, Inequality and Growth: The Indian Experience" Mumbai: Indira Gandhi Institute of Development Research, June 2011, www.igidr.ac.in/pdf/publication/WP-2011-011.pdf.

10 See Subhash Anand, "Mob Lynching: Some Pastoral Reflections", *Third Millennium*, 21\3 (2018, July – September), 35-80.

11 On purpose I have used 'teachers' and 'formators', because I can neither teach nor form anybody for religious ministry.

of real life than they do, as school kids, who need to be given detailed rules for their life. They dish out to them an ideology which they have not critically examined. "They are blind guides. And if the blind lead the blind, both will fall into a pit" (Mt 15:14).

Fourth, if religion is to survive it has to be credible. When I started studying philosophy, one professor explained to us the importance of reflection. He quoted a Greek thinker: "The unexamined life is not worth living."[12] More recently, Christopher Hitchens maintained that "the burden of proof regarding the truthfulness of a claim lies with the one who makes the claim; if this burden is not met, then the claim is unfounded, and its opponents need not argue further in order to dismiss it."[13] He is believed to have taken the idea from a "Latin proverb *quod grātīs asseritur, grātīs negātur* ('What is asserted gratuitously may be denied gratuitously'), which was commonly used in the 19th century."[14] If religion has to survive, it needs to be adequately grounded. If we make a claim without good reasons, then people have good reasons to reject our claim. But can any religion provide good reasons for its claims? Here Blaise Pascal may help us: "The heart has its reasons, of which reason knows nothing" ("*Le cœur a ses raisons que la raison ne connaît point.*").[15] I shall try to spell out what could be the reasons which reason may not easily understand, but which the heart could find acceptable.

1. From Ideology to Theology

Ideology is the discourse put out by an organization in power to ensure its survival, position, power and income. As such, it is a defence mechanism and resists critical scrutiny. Ideology is guided by authority, not by reason. It is discussed behind closed doors. Persons who question are marginalized and eventually excommunicated. Those who formulate an ideology, also put out a moral discourse. Obedience, humility, loyalty and uniformity are primary virtues. Theology, on the other hand, is the quest for meaningful religion, religion that will effectively nurture authentic human existence. Hence, it encourages questions, and at times even admits that it does not have an answer. It is the work of persons who have a real commitment to people, whoever and wherever they are. It is shaped by honesty and humility. It promotes open dialogue. It cherishes discernment, sincerity, creative criticism and diversity.

Theology, on the other hand, calls for reflection. We could think of theology in terms of the Japanese Origami Craft. "The goal is to transform a flat

12 https://en.wikipedia.org/wiki/The_unexamined_life_is_not_worth_living; accessed on 04-10-2019.

13 https://en.wikipedia.org/wiki/Hitchens%27s_razor; accessed on 04-10-2019.

14 *Idem.*

15 https://en.wikiquote.org/wiki/Talk:Blaise_Pascal; accessed on 04-10-2019.

square sheet of paper into a finished sculpture through folding and sculpting techniques."[16] In the paper factory big sheets of paper are manufactured. Then they are cut into small sizes: A3, A4, etc. As the Upanishads declared, the reality is one, with many shapes (*rūpa*) and corresponding names (*nāma*). The Origami artist will take one sheet and bend it many times till he comes to the form he has in mind: a boat, an arrow, etc. Once again, we have many shapes (*rūpa*) and corresponding names (*nāma*). Then he can carefully undo what he has done, press the paper gently and proceed to make another shape with another name. It should not surprise us that "modern origami practitioners generally discourage the use of cuts, glue, or markings on the paper."[17] Good artists believe the piece of paper before them has great potential. They also believe in the power of their imagination.

Today some teachers carry pliable wires to their class. The kids learn the letters of the alphabet by doing. Every kid is given one piece of wire and told to make D, M, N, etc. This involves bending and straightening the same piece of wire in different ways. Among those kids two ignore the teacher's words. Both make a spiral. The teacher is annoyed and demands an explanation. One says that he wants to be like the spiral, moving from superficial marginalities to the all-important centre. The other too, wants to be like the spiral, moving away from his little ego and embracing the whole reality. Both interpretations are beautiful; both challenge us; they complement each other. The teacher who is annoyed, represents the establishment. She is keen that the students learn what has been prescribed by the syllabus. The two 'deviant' kids are critical thinkers. They make the establishment uncomfortable.

Many think that reflection demands logic: you have the correct premises and you get the right conclusion. But that may not be always helpful. Hence, theological reflection calls for discernment. Who am I? Where am I? Am I where I should have been? How did I get here? Where do I need to go from here? How do I reach there? Reflection is the art of bending again: re-flecting. Religious leaders and theologians are 'discoursing' about the Mystery that grounds our capacity to think. A claim to absolutely correct knowledge about this Mystery, is an attempt to paste a piece of our imagination on It. We are desecrating the Mystery and resorting to an idol, "the work of human hands" (Ps 115.4). All religions and theologies are our constructions. As such they ridden with all the liabilities that are part of human existence. But they can be beautiful, meaningful and prophetical, challenging us to go beyond. This anticipates the question that is bound to crop up: if all religions and theologies are provisional interpretations, can we depend on them? The answer to this question lies with us: if our religion and its theology helps us effectively and

16 https://en.wikipedia.org/wiki/Origami; accessed on 24-09-2019.

17 https://en.wikipedia.org/wiki/Origami; accessed on 24-09-2019.

affectively to be more human and humane, then there is some legitimacy in the claims made.

I now pass on to articulate more what I am trying to suggest: we need to existentially reflect the religious claims we make. But before doing that we need to understand that "the essence of religion is the relation of man beyond himself to the unknown reality that faith calls God. It is man's capacity to go beyond all tangible, measurable reality and to enter into the primordial relation... This relationship itself, I would say is, properly speaking, the content of religion."[18] Religion is the depth dimension of human existence. Humans being essentially social, religion gets a social format. Here, as in many other areas of our life, we need to distinguish between the central and the marginal, between the essentials and the accessories.

2. From Belief to Faith

Today we are facing a critical moment. When the tortoise feels threatened it withdraws into itself. Modern claims make many traditional believers uncomfortable and insecure. They resort to fundamentalism: "a tendency among certain groups—mainly, although not exclusively, in religion—that is characterized by a markedly strict literalism as it is applied to certain specific scriptures, dogmas, or ideologies, and a strong sense of the importance of maintaining ingroup and outgroup distinctions."[19] This attitude could lead to obscurantism: an uncritical rejection of the findings of contemporary scholarship. No religion is immune to fundamentalism.

A fundamentalist religious management, however, does not encourage questions, not only about doctrinal matters, but also about its way of functioning.[20] Many religious leaders do not like to discuss religion! They rather talk about the weather. What is even more sad is that a fundamentalist management will block research that could threats its survival. The importance fundamentalists give to credal tenets gives the impression that salvation depends on right knowledge. What is even more disturbing is that people who speak of God as love and compassion can be very violent towards those who reject some credal tenets. Heretics do not deserve to live! The situation becomes tragically comic when different groups make conflicting claims about God. The certitude with which they make their claims borders on blasphemy: they claim that they can know the divine mystery as it really is.

18 Joseph Ratzinger, *Salt of the Earth: The Church at the End of the Millennium* (an interview with Peter Seeward), San Francisco: Ignatius, 2007, 22.

19 en.wikipedia.org/wiki/Fundamentalism; accessed on 31-08-2019.

20 See Donald Cozzens, *Sacred Silence: Denial and the Crisis in the Church*, Collegeville (Minn): Liturgical Press, 2002.

To avoid falling into the trap of fundamentalism, we need to clarify the nature of faith as different from belief. Reason enables us to come to some knowledge of things. When it comes to persons, only through faith, hope and love, can we come to some understanding. Addressing God, Anselm of Canterbury said: "I do not seek to understand in order to believe, but I believe so that I may understand."[21] Faith brings understanding. Thus, reason and faith complete each other in the human journey unto understanding. "Reason always stands in need of being purified by faith: this also holds true for political reason, which must not consider itself omnipotent. For its part, religion always needs to be purified by reason in order to show its authentically human face. Any breach in this dialogue comes only at an enormous price to human development."[22]

Reason will help me to see that what I believe is not dehumanizing me. Reason will empower me to be critical of my own beliefs; and to honestly examine the claims made by the followers of other religious traditions. But reason as such cannot provide me absolute certitude of the other. It is here that we are cautioned by contemporary epistemological and hermeneutical studies. They alert us to the fact that religious 'truths' can be generated and 'texts' constructed. They invite us to follow a historico-critical method in examining our 'truths', and be guided by a 'hermeneutic of suspicion' when reading our texts.[23] If we all make absolute claims, can we dialogue and collaborate with each other? Yes, if we can move away from the claim of epistemological objectivity and move towards existential truth; if we clarify what we mean by faith.

We need to keep in mind the distinction Benedict XVI notes between the act of faith and the content of faith or belief: "At this point I would like to sketch a path intended to help us understand more profoundly not only the content of the faith, but also the act by which we choose to entrust ourselves fully to God, in complete freedom."[24] Our failure to distinguish between faith and belief has led to some horrific tragedies in the past. We have burnt some people to death because we thought they denied one or the other aspect of the Christian faith, or held on to some wrong beliefs. The fact that those people

---

21 "*Neque enim quaero intelligere ut credam, sed credo ut intelligam*" (*Proslogion*, 1).

22 Benedict XVI, *Caritas in Veritate*, no. 56.

23 "The 'hermeneutics of suspicion' is a phrase coined by Paul Ricoeur to capture a common spirit that pervades the writings of Marx, Freud, and Nietzsche…they share a commitment to unmasking 'the lies and illusions of consciousness;' they are the architects of a distinctively modern style of interpretation that circumvents obvious or self-evident meanings in order to draw out less visible and less flattering truths" (Rita Felski, "Critique and the Hermeneutics of Suspicion", journal.media-culture.org.au/index.php/mcjournal/article/view/431; accessed on 31-08-2019.

24 Benedict XVI, *PORTA FIDEI*, NO. 10.

accepted death rather than deny what they were convinced was true showed, that they were people of deep faith. They knew that God would not abandon them. They are real martyrs.[25] Perhaps their faith was greater than that of their persecutors. The Church has been divided into many fragments because Christian leaders failed to differentiate adequately between faith and belief and the different levels on which beliefs are related to faith. We can illustrate the claim that people may appear to hold on to wrong ideas about God, and yet be people of deep faith by citing the example of Abraham, "who best exemplifies the notion of faith in the religion of ancient Israel. Perhaps that is the key role from a purely theological point of view that Abraham plays."[26]

Paul quotes what the Old Testament (Gen 15:6) says about Abraham: "Abraham believed God, and it was reckoned to him as righteousness" (Rom 4:3). Paul is contrasting the way of the works of Law with the way of faith. Explaining God's plan for Abraham, Paul says: "The purpose was to make him the father of all who believe without being circumcised and who thus have righteousness reckoned to them" (Rom 4:11). Abraham is our father in faith, even though his ideas about God were far from adequate. Today we know with certainty "that Israel believed in the existence of only one God and worshipped that one God from the latter part of the sixth century BCE..The popular religion of the Israelites was polytheistic up to the Exile."[27] Thus we can safely say that Abraham was a polytheist. His was a monolatrist covenant with God, a covenant initiated by God.

When Abraham accepted the call of God, he believed that there where many gods but Yahweh had chosen him as his own and he had accepted Yahweh as his only God. That was about 1800 years BC. Then about 1200 B.C., we have the Exodus. As the Jews move out of Egypt, they felt that Yahweh had done

25 John Huss (1372-1415), "was summoned to the Council of Constance (1414) where, despite an imperial guarantee of safe conduct, he was arrested and burned as a heretic" ("Hus, John", in Richard P. Mcbrien, *The Happercollins Encyclopedia of Catholicism*, New York: HarperCollins Pbs., 1989, p. 425a.p. 646a). "By his death Huss became a national hero. The university of Prague [of which he was the Rector] declared him a martyr and fixed his feast on the day of his execution" ("Huss, John", in L. cross and E. A. Livingsone, eds., *The Oxford Dictionary of the Christian Church*, 3rd rev. ed., Oxford: Oxford University Press, 2005, 811b). St. Joan of Arc (1412-1431) was burnt to death as a heretic. She was tried by a large court made up of theologians, civil and church lawyers—all men; but later on canonized by Benedict XV in 1920. The canonization was a very meagre reparation for a heinous crime. In his *Divina Disponente Clementia*, the Pope described her trial as "*iniquus processus*" (www.vatican.va/holy_father/benedict_xv/bulls/documents/hf_ben-xv_bulls_19200516_divina-disponente_lt.html, accessed on 18-07-2010).

26 Joseph P. Healey, "Faith: Old Testament", in David Noel Freedman et al. (eds.), *The Anchor Bible Dictionary*, 6 vols., New York: Doubleday, 1992, *ABD*, vol. 2, 745b.

27 Leslie J. Hoppe, "Monotheism", in Carroll Stuhlmueller (ed.), The Collegeville Pastoral Dictionary of Biblical Theology. Bangalore: Theological Publications India, 2005, 641b.

mighty deeds for them. Their god had helped them to outwit the Egyptians. Yahweh is not just one god among others: he is more powerful than all the other gods (Ex 18:1). He is the God of gods (Deut 10:17). Then 600 years later when the Jews are carried away to Babylon, their faith deepens: Yahweh is not simply the God of gods but that he is the only God, the one God of all times and of all nations (Is 44:8; 45:22). Here we have real monotheism, but this is not yet the Christian faith in a triune God.[28] Thus, for over a thousand years the descendants of Abraham continued with their faulty beliefs, and yet many of them were people of deep faith.

How then is Abraham a model of faith for us Christians? The *Letter to the Hebrews* gives us the answer. Abraham, we are told, began his journey not knowing where he was to go (11:8). He knew that the Lord was the good shepherd, who takes care of him wherever he leads him (Ps 23:1–4). Abraham did not know where he was going, but he knew that Yahweh was walking by his side, all the time holding his hand. Faith is an existential attitude of surrender.[29] It means that we put ourselves in God's hands, trusting Him, allowing Him to shape our life. It is He who will keep us on the path of faith, because He is faithful. God repeatedly tells Abraham that his descendants would be as numerous as the stars in the heaven, and that He would give him and his offspring the land where he was then as an alien (15:2-3; 17:4-8; 18:10). Yet when God asked him to sacrifice his only legitimate son, He does not hesitate. He knows that God is much greater than all that He gives us. He knows that He can fulfil His promises in ways that totally surpass our imagination (Eph 3:20-21).

We all need some signs and symbols, accept some creed and code, take part in some cult and celebration. For a person of deep faith, however, only God is really necessary. All our signs and symbols, creeds and codes, cults and celebrations, rules and rubrics, and even doctrines and dogmas are secondary and, therefore, dispensable. When we absolutize them, we abandon the true God and become idol-worshippers. A person of deep faith is not dogmatic about his dogmas, nor does he canonize his canons. For a person who has really understood what faith is all about, meaningfulness—person relation within human life—is more important than objective truth—the reality exactly as it is. In any case, the claim to know the Real as it is leads to idolatry. We de-absolutize and domesticate God and end up with an idol convenient to us. Like Abraham, the true believer understands that faith is the invitation to be a pilgrim, to set out on a journey not knowing where he is going, constantly

28 Many Jews would think that the Christian confession of the Trinity and Incarnation is a betrayal of monotheism.

29 The Roman centurion did not share the beliefs of the Jews, but Jesus found in him a faith that he did not find even in the children of Israel (Mt 8:10).

moving unto the receding Horizon, yet the Horizon is with him carrying him. For such a person covenantal fidelity is more important than dogmatic correctness and institutional security.

3. From Rituals to Values

Humans are characterized by creative self-articulation and self-communication. This is indicative of a depth dimension within them, an urge for self-transcendence. We could interpret religion as "the organization of life around the depth dimension of experience—varied in form, completeness, and clarity in accordance with the environing culture."[30] Slowly, however, due to different reasons, the depth dimension of human existence is almost forgotten, and human behaviour becomes stylized and routinized. It becomes more a sign of belonging to a group here and now, than a spontaneous expression of the human longing for the mystery that grounds our here and now, and takes us beyond its banality.

As embodied beings, we need to express our inner feelings through visible realities. Ernst Cassirer considered humans as *animal symbolicum*' ("symbol-making" or "symbolizing animal"). He "claimed that man's outstanding characteristic is not in his metaphysical or physical nature, but rather in his work. Humanity cannot be known directly, but has to be known through the analysis of the symbolic universe that man has created historically."[31] If we include 'sign' within 'symbol', then all human languages are symbolic. Signs and symbols permeate all spheres of human life. Hence, religions too have their signs, symbols and symbolic actions. A ritual brings together symbols and symbolic gestures in a continuous 'narrative'.

Slowly correct ritual behaviour becomes more important than upright living. Rituals acquire a power of their own. A person may rape and even murder his victim. He then goes through a ritual—bath in a holy river, disclosure to a priest, etc.—and he feels forgiven! He may even bribe the deity by making a big donation, using the money he has acquired through exploitation. The deity blots out his crime! Religion can make life here and now comfortable, totally obliterating the challenge of transcendence. The major religious traditions have always witnessed reform movements, but the impact of these movements either did not last or remained alive in the hearts of a few.

Rituals have an originating context, within which they have some significance. With the passage of time, that significance is lost, because the situation is changed. Yet people continue performing those rituals, lest some harm may befall them. This explains why some observers have "criticized certain religious behaviours as irrational or as reflecting an incorrect

---

30 King, "Religion", 286a.

31 https://en.wikipedia.org/wiki/Animal_symbolicum

understanding of both nature and divinity."[32] This unenlightened mentality was and is still common among many people. Pope Francis notes: "We are suffering from religious illiteracy to the point that, in some shrines around the world, things get confused: people go there to pray. There are shops that sell objects of devotion...But there are others that sell objects of superstition because people seek salvation in superstition."[33] Rituals are effective if people consciously internalize the meaning that is being suggested and respond appropriately.

The French thinker, Voltaire, is reported to have said: "If God has made us in his image, we have returned him the favour."[34] When religion becomes superstitious, then even our understanding of God becomes distorted. Jesus is reported to have made some special promises to Margaret Mary Alacoque: "I promise you that my all powerful love will grant to all those who will receive Communion on the First Fridays, for nine consecutive months, the grace of final repentance...my Heart will be their secure refuge in that last hour."[35] I find it impossible to believe that for the Risen Lord nine first Fridays have any special importance. To be truly religious we need not hold on to some special place or time (Gal 4.10).

The priests of all religions keeping on introducing new rituals. The more the rituals, the greater is their income. Even when it retains its significance, the ritual itself becomes more important and the reality that ought to be evoked recedes into the background and at times is almost forgotten. Slowly the rituals are seen as operating automatically, as if they were magic acts. They have their effect even if you do not understand or accept them. The less religiously informed people are, the greater is their concern for rituals. Thus, for the priestly caste,[36] religion becomes a lucrative business; but it is opium for the masses. For those who exploit the poor and make money through immoral and illegal activities, religion becomes some psychedelic drug that deadens their conscience. They think that by their gifts they can bribe the deity!

Rituals are easy; they do not call for competence or integrity. Rituals are populist gestures: they do not make demands. If rituals really promoted love of God and love of neighbour, then the members of the priestly class would be normally the most spiritual persons in their community. The opposite is so often the case. This explains why the priestly class of all religions are not held

32 Mary R. O'Neil, "Superstition" in Eliade, *The Encyclopedia of Religion*, vol. 14, 163b.

33 w2.vatican.va/content/francesco/en/speeches/2016/july/documents/papa-francesco_20160727_polonia-vescovi.html; accessed on 01-08-2017.

34 www.goodreads.com/quotes/640344-if-god-has-made-us-in-his-image-we-have; accessed on 31-08-2019.

35 en.wikipedia.org/wiki/First_Friday_Devotion; accessed on 31-08-2019.

36 I have, on purpose, used the word 'caste', as it denotes a hierarchy. In many ancient societies the 'high' cultist was the highest authority in his tribe or clan.

is much esteem by the educated. Rituals even encourage immoral behaviour. They can wash away my crime. I can rape a woman and then murder her. Then I can 'validly' celebrate the Eucharist.

Rituals get surrounded with worldly pomp and consumer glamour. People who donate funds to promote them think they are very religious people. They are made much of by the followers of their religion. The priestly classes oblige people to sponsor and participate in rituals. Rituals may give people emotional fulfilment. Correct rituals do not necessarily promote right behaviour. Then religion loses its meaning. The prophets of Israel came down heavily on decadent religion: God hates the solemn liturgy of Israel, which has become an abomination to him; his soul just cannot endure it. He invites his people to return to justice and concern for widows and orphans (Is 1, 12-17; Amos 5, 21-24).

4. From Law to Discernment

Closely connected with ritual, is the notion of sacred and profane, pure and impure. Many laws are enacted to ensure the purity of persons, places, times and things. If they violate these rules and regulations, they have to pay a penalty. That too is a source of income for the priestly caste. They generate a discourse: their rituals are of divine origin; only people who have been especially chosen by God are competent to officiate at rituals. Thus, they ensure their livelihood, find importance within the society, and perpetuate their clan. This was possible because many of the religions emerged when the vast majority was not critically awakened.

On the other hand, all humans have the capacity to distance themselves from the given. This difference explains why existential thinkers reserve 'existence' only for humans. The other creatures are totally defined by their nature. Humans, on the other hand, 'stand out' (ex-ist). As for other creatures, "their nature or essence is already given to them. The human being exists actively, by standing out or emerging through the decisions and acts that make this person the unique being that he or she is."[37] In other words, humans can become humans only by exercising their freedom. They become humane when they do this in a responsible manner. If there is one area where human freedom becomes central, then it is the realm of religion. Through religions humans approach the Mystery that grounds their existence. Then the Depth of God calls to the depth within (Ps 42.7). Then no human laws can be of any avail. In our journey unto God we journey unto our unique personality, the unique call of a Mystery that is Love. The journey unto God is possible only by taking the narrow path; at times so narrow that no two pilgrims can walk side by side!

Most of the first Christians were of Jewish origin. From their childhood onwards they were instructed to observe the Law, which during the many

---

37 John Macquarrie, "Existentialism", in Eliade, *The Encyclopedia of Religion, vol. 5, 223a.*

centuries before Jesus, had been concretely expressed in many rules and regulations. It was understandable that they wanted the other disciples to observe the same laws. Paul is totally against this. Sure, we need guidance along our journey, but then that guidance can come only from people who are *real* presbyters—people who have grown in maturity by learning from life, who have journeyed and continue journeying. They have learnt to listen to the depth within them. They can help us to do the same. This is one way of understanding what Paul meant when he invited his readers not to go by the Law, but to listen to the Spirit. Authentic religious guides enable others to learn the art of discernment. They can do it because they themselves have learnt it by experience. Religious cult ministers insist on rules, rubrics and regulations. For this they assert their authority, as they have no experience to fall back upon. They do not encourage discernment for fear of losing their clientele.

5. From Prayers to Contemplation

Organized religions have a long list of many kinds of prayers; many devotees recite those prayers. Yet, somehow, we do not seem to be improving. Kabir Das has lamented: "Ages have gone by reciting the rosary, but the crookedness of my mind has not gone." Hence, he advises us: "Abandon the beads of the rosary and focus on the beads of the mind." This explains why "silence is looked upon as a very important thing among our people. Samadhi means silence. Muni (sage) and mauna (sagehood, silence) are both derived from the same root."[38] Repeating prayers whether in common or all alone does not allow us to go deeper into ourselves. We need another path to find our unique person.

Silence helps us to get closer to ourselves, to others and the Other. Silence helps us to understand ourselves better, for only then we can understand in some way, others and the Other. Without this understanding discernment is difficult. Real discernment demands inner freedom. For this we need to become aware of the subconscious blocks that force us to play games and put on masks. We have to own them and slowly work towards greater freedom. This is what the Asian sages mean when they speak about self-knowledge that leads to freedom. In a certain sense, the contemplation of God and self-knowledge demand an inward journey, a journey with oneself, within oneself, because God is not out there. He is the ground of our being, the Breath that keeps us alive, the Path that walks with us, and the Awareness that makes us aware. To find him and ourselves we need to enter the cave of our heart.[39] Contemplative prayer slowly helps us to be free from ourselves, free for others.

38 M. K. Gandhi, *Prayer, ed.: Chandrakant Kaji*, Ahmedabad: Navajivan Publishing House, 1977 (www.mkgandhi.org/ebks/prayer.pdf; Accessed on 01-01-2019), 110..

39 The Upanishads frequently tells us that God dwells in the cave within us. See *Taittirīya-upaniṣad*, 2. 1. 1; *Kaṭha-upaniṣad*, 1. 14; *Śvetāśvatara-upaniṣad*, 2. 10; *Maitri-upaniṣad*, 2. 6; *Muṇḍaka-upaniṣad*, 2. 1. 10.

6. From Religiosity to Humanity

Sometimes, the way we derive a word may help us to understand it better. "The Latin term *religiō*...is of ultimately obscure etymology."[40] But "popular etymology among the later ancients (Servius, Lactantius, Augustine) and the interpretation of many modern writers connects it with *religare* 'to bind fast'...'place an obligation on,' or 'bond between humans and gods.'"[41] Some of our Indian languages use '*dharma*' to indicate religion. The word *dharma* "is one of those Sanskrit words that defy all attempts at an exact rendering in English or any other tongue."[42] The word is derived from the root *dhṛ*—to hold, to sustain, etc.,[43] and *dharma* is that which holds our life with all its aspects in harmony. Thus, thus it seems to me that there is some affinity between religion and *dharma*. The concern to inter-relate people and sustain them is a fundamental human concern.

In our mother's womb we are just humans. I may be circumcised for religious reasons, but my son will be born like any other boy child. My wife may have undergone religious genital mutilation, but her daughter will be born like any other girl child. My wife and I go about with a dress that indicates our religious affiliation—mostly due to socio-religious pressure. Fortunately, my children will be born naked. The boundary-markers will come much later. My parents were very devout and traditional Christians, but I was born without any religion. We need to return to our womb: to our fundamental humanity.

The ancient peoples of all lands did not make a watertight distinction between religion and life, and therefore, between individual and society. Life in all its aspects was to be governed by *dharma*, not any religion as understood today; but by *sanātana dharma*, the eternal religiosity that comes from being human: our humanity. The real *sanātana dharma* promotes *mānava dharma*. Through *mānava dharma* we become *manu*, people who can think and discern (*man*), persons who are gifted with *manīṣa* (wisdom).[44] Wisdom will enable us to choose what promotes better the good of all (*śreyas*) and to reject what may give some pleasure to some (*preyas*).[45] Only our humane way of life will legitimize our religion. Only when life reflects religion does it have some credibility.

---

40 https://en.wikipedia.org/wiki/Religio; accessed on 04-10-2019.

41 https://www.etymonline.com/word/Religion; accessed on 04-10-2019.

42 Pandurang Vaman Kane, *History of Dharmaśāstra, 5 vols., Poona: Bhandarkar Oriental Research Institute, rev. ed., 196875, vol. 1, 1.*

43 Vaman S. Apte, *The Practical Sanskrit-English Dictionary, Delhi: Motilal Banarsidass, rev. ed., 1912, rep. 1998, p. 522.*

44 *Ibid., 739b.*

45 See *Kaṭha-upaniṣad*, 2.1-2.

Conclusion

Religions all over the world have some form of organization—creed, cult and code. This gives the followers an identity, holding them together. The creed, cult and code of different religions do not have the same binding degree. Some religions are more liberal, while others are very strict. All creeds, cults and codes are human creations. They are an attempt to understand the Mystery that grounds us; to communicate that understanding through symbols and symbolic actions; to spell out the behaviour pattern which would be an appropriate response to that understanding. The fact that by our very human character we are pilgrims means that all religions with their theologies are provisional. They are not based on objective facts, but on interpretations, which are bound to be provisional. Any person who claims to have objective knowledge of God is talking about an idol. If this is the case, then theology demands the courage to re-flect, to bend again and come to a new shape and a new name; thereby to reflect it more meaningfully. This demands discernment, to know which is the appropriate shape and name needed for our situation.

Allow me to conclude with a text that gives us a very profound and unsettling vision. The prophet sees a man with a measuring line in his hand, wanting to measure Jerusalem to find out its width and its length. Then an angel tells that person: "Jerusalem shall be inhabited as villages without walls, because of the multitude of people and livestock in it. And I will be to her a wall of fire all around, declares the LORD, and I will be the glory in her midst" (Zech 2.4-5). The city of God cannot be measured: it has no boundaries. God is that City! Authentic religion brings us existentially closer to the Mystery that enwombs us. Slowly we become aware that we are surrounded by an impregnable wall, the Love that calls all of us—not only humans but all creatures, a Love that does not permit any walls to stand in between, definitely not the walls of our dogmas, rituals and laws.

PART IV

INDO-SOPHIA: INDOLOGY MEETING WITH WISDOM

19

'*Tat-tvam-asi*' in the *Chandogya Upanisad* and its Interpretation by *Dvaita Vedanta*

Henry D'Almeida SJ

Abstract

The study especially focuses on Madhva's interpretation of the *mahavakya tat-tvam-asi* in the Chandogya Upanishad in order to highlight his contribution to shruti Hermeneutics. Madhva achieves his great goal of *Vishnu-sarvottamattva* (sovereignty of Visnu) by employing a hermeneutical device known, as *Paramamukhyavrtti* (the supreme being as the semantic referent of the scriptures). As an illustration of Madhva's interpretation we focus on *'tattvamasi'* in the Chandogya Upanishad. Justification for Madhva's reading it as *'atattvamasi'* is also explained. The various devices employed to understand the meaning of *'tattvamasi'* are taken up and it culminates with the understanding of *'tattvamasi'* as '*Bimba-pratibimba-bhava*' (relation of prototype and the image) between Brahman and jiva.

Keywords

Chandogya Upanisad, Brhadaranyaka Upanisad, Tat-tvam-asi, atattvamasi, atmatattvamasi Gitatatparya.

Introduction

The *Chandogya*[1] *Upanisad*[2] belongs to the singers[3] of the *Samaveda.* It is a section of the *Chandogya Brahmana*[4] which has ten chapters[5]. Chapters three to ten in this Brahmana form the *Chandogya Upanisad.*

Together with the *Brhadaranyaka Upanisad, Chandogya Upanisad* represents the oldest and the most classical upanishadic tradition. Its oldest parts may date back to 9C BCE.[6] Each chapter of *Chandogya Upanisad* is an independent whole and shows the unity of contents. It contains some of the important theological and philosophical utterances of ancient Hindus.[7] This is especially seen in the sixth chapter where our specific concern lies. Hence there is first the treatment of the context. This is done to locate 'tat-*tvam-asi'*. After this, the justification for Madhva's reading it as '*atat-tvam-asi*' is discussed. The rest of the chapter deals with the interpretation according to *dvaitavedanta* and the critique of Sankara and Ramanuja. We conclude with the meaning of '*tat-tvam-asi*' as '*bimba-pratibimba-bhava*' existing between *Brahman* and *Jiva.*

1. The Sixth Chapter of the Chandogya Upanisad

1.1. Context

Uddalaka sent his son *Svetaketu* to study the Vedas and get religious instruction as per the family tradition. Having studied for twelve years the son comes home conceited, haughty and egotistical.[8] He was proud of his newly acquired knowledge and thought he knew everything. The father in order to humble his son's pride asked whether *Svetaketu* knew that central principle by knowing which everything would be known.[9] Svetaketu was ignorant of it and appealed to his father to teach it. He knew that he had not yet penetrated to the heart of the matter. The correcting instruction follows in the form of a dialogue. The father becomes the teacher; the son becomes the student. *Uddalaka* gives

---

1 *'chandoga' is the singer of the Saman (chando Sama gayati iti Chandoga). The upanishad belongs to the followers of the Sama Veda. See S. Radhakrishnan, The Principal Upanishads, 335.*

2 The word '*upanisad' means the knowledge of Brahman, source of liberation and means to know Brahman. It is known as vedanta and serves as the important source for Vedanta philosophy.*

3 They are called '*udgata'*

4 Hence the name *Brahmanopanisad.*

5 Paul Deussen, Sixty Upanishads of the Veda.63

6 Belvalkar and Ranade, The creative period, p.102

7 Like *tat-tvam-asi (Ch.U. 6.8.7) and sadeva somya idam agra asit (Ch.U. 6.2.1)*

8 *'mahamana' translated as greatly conceited' in S. Radhakrishnan, op.cit. 446*

9 *yenasrutam srutam bhavati amatam matamavijnatam vijnatam iti, (Ch.U. 6.1.3)*

instruction on Being and the place of human person in the universe in relation to the great Being. The famous proposition: By knowing one that is the central entity, everything is known is illustrated by various illustrations. *Uddalaka* tells *Svetaketu*: *Sa atma tat tvam asi.*

1.2. Madhvacharya's Reading of *'atat-tvam-asi'* in *Chandogya Upanisad*

Madhvacharya's interpretation of '*tat-tvam-asi*' is based on two different ways of splitting the key sentences into either *sa-atma tat- tvam-asi*' or sa atma-'*atat-tvam-asi*'. Madhva has adopted the reading '*atat-tvam-asi*'in his commentary on the *Chandogya Upanisad.*[10]. In he has taken '*atat-tvam-asi*'[11]11. Thus he has shown that preferring a particular form does not change the thrust of his theological enterprise.

The *Upanisad* itself does not contain any independently worded sentence '*tattvamasi*' where '*tat*' stands for Brahman and '*tvam*' for the individual soul. The part wherein '*tattvamasi*' occurs reads as '*atmatattvamasi*' with '*atma*' and '*tattvamasi*' joined together.[12]

Actually there is no grammatical bar agaist Madhvachrya's word division. The Padacchedha '*atat-tvam-asi*' is based on *savarnadirgha sandhi* between the final long vowel in the preceding word '*atma*' followed by the initial short vowel of the following word '*atat*'. Hence the rendering according to Madhva would be: *Sa atma atat tvam asi*[13]

Further by the analysis of the nine illustrations[14] occurring in the sixth chapter of *Chandogya Upaniaad* Madhva justifies his reading. Besides the reading '*atat-tvam-asi*' directly and categorically conveys the truth of '*Jivesvara-bheda*'. Vyasatirtha justifies this in his famous work, Nyayamrta.[15]

---

10 In *Visnutattva-vinirnaya also Madhva adopts the reading atat-tvam-asi*

11 HDVL,178

12 D.N. Shanbhag, "In defense of difference", 361 – 362.

13 MM, 177.

14 The nine illustrations are: A bird tied to a sting, flower-juices and the honey, rivers and the sea, tree and the sap, banyan seed, salt in water, sick man on the deathbed, blind folded person, thief and touching hot iron to prove innocence.

15 *adhinatvasya eva uktatvat atat ityeva chedah yuktah.*

2. Interpretation of '*tat-tvam-asi*'[16]

2.1. Introduction

Having seen '*tat-tvam-asi'* in the *Chandogya upanisad* with its justification, now we shall take a look at various attempts of Madhva and his followers[17]17 to bring out the import of '*tat-tvam-asi'*. Madhva and his followers resort to various interpretive methods. As it is stated already in the first part whether one adopts '*atat-tvam-asi'*[18] or 'tat-tvam-asi'[19] it does not bring any change to Madhva's grand theological and philosophical enterprise. Madhva himself followed '*atat-tvam-asi*' in his commentary on the *Chandogya Upanisad* and '*tat-tvam-asi'* in *Gita-tatparya-nirnaya*. We shall see the interpretation of *'tat-tvam-asi'* under various headings. It is quite interesting to see how Dvaita interpretation is informed by Panini's Grammar, *Purvamimamsa* exegetical rules and rhetoricians' technique of *laksana*. They also employ the popular maxims like *'sakhacandranyaya.'*[20]

2.2. Interpretation of 'tat-tvam-asi' in the Light of its Context in the Chandogya Upanisad[21]

The context shows that the purpose of Uddalaka's *upadesa* was to rid Svetaketu of pride[22] and awaken a sense of the presence of a power greater than everything, subsisting in all and controlling without being controlled. Uuddalaka has this forthright statement:

Sanmulah somya imah sarvah prajah sadayatanah satpratisthah[23]

The above statement couched in Bahuvrihi compounds[24] like 'Sanmula' clearly points to the supreme power as the support and sustaining force of the universe. Thus the whole purpose of the *upadesa* is to overcome the egoism

---

16 For this section I am heavily depending on BNK Sharma's views found in his '*Mahatatparya of Mahavakyas and other Advaita srutis.*

17 Especially Vyasatirtha (c.1539) in his Nyayamrta and Jayatirtha (c.1388) in his commentary on Madhva's *Visnu-tattva-vinirnaya.*

18 Madhva adopts '*atat-tvam-asi' in Chandogya upanisad-bhasya and Visnutattvavinirnaya.*

19 '*tat-tvam-asi' is the reading in Gita-tatparya-nirnaya.*

20 This is the maxim of the branch and the moon. As the moon, though considerably distant from the *branch is spoken of as 'moon on the branch' because of proximity. See Apte, The practical Sanskrit-English Dictionary, 575.*

21 BNK Sharma, op.cit, 174

22 See 'Essentials of *Dasaprakaranas,*'34 *sarvan vedanadhitya mahamanah anucamani stabda eyaya iti atmanah anyam anucanatvadigunapradam puramavijna,stabdasya paradhinatvajnapanena stabdatam nirasya tannisthah hi atropadisyate.*

23 Ch.U. 6.8.4

24 In *Bahuvrihi compound two or more nouns in apposition to each other are made to qualify another substantive which is outside the compound; see Apte, op.cit., 697*

of *Svetaketu* who was afflicted with an attitude of spiritual conceit born of ignorance of the supreme power.[25]

2.3. Interpretation Based on *Laksana*[26]

Madhva and his followers use the concept of '*laksana*' to bring out the import of '*tat*' and '*tvam*'. Let us first get some idea of this '*laksana*'.[27]

2.3.1. Characteristics of Laksana

In addition to their primary semantic power *abhidha* words have also secondary semantic power known as *laksana*. When in a given context the primary meaning of a word is unintellible the word is credited with the secondary meaning related to the primary meaning. The famous example is: The village is on the Ganges (*Gangayam ghosah*) Since the primary meaning (Village on the water) in the given context is impossible, the sentence '*Gangayam ghosah*' is understood as '*Gangatate ghosah*'(The village is on the bank of the river).

2.3.2. Classification of *Laksana*

Laksana is divided into three kinds:

i. **Exclusive (*Jahallaksana*)** – In this type the primary meaning is completely abandoned and the new secondary meaning is posited, e.g. The village is on the Ganges.[28]
ii. **Inclusive (*ajahallaksana*)** – This type includes the primary meaning in addition to the secondary meaning. E.g. Protect the ghee from the crows.[29]
   The meaning of the sentence would be to protect the ghee not only from crows but also from other animals.
iii. **Quasi-Inclusive (*jahadajahallaksana*)** – In this type a part of the primary meaning is abandoned and part of it is retained. e.g. 'This is that *Devadatta*.'[30]

To arrive at the identity of *Devadatta* qualified by 'this' referring to the present time and 'that' referring to the past time are rejected and '*Devadatta*' bereft of spatio-temporal qualifications is retained. *Advaita Vedanta* makes use of this kind of *laksana*[31] to bring out the significance of '*tat-tvam-asi*'.

---

25 *sa Harih sarvasvami tvam tu na kadapi tat param Brahmasi iti See Ch.U.Bh. Khandartha*

26 Mahatatparya, 178 - 193

27 John Grimes, Problems and Perspectives in Religious Discourse, 118 – 119.

28 The implied meaning is: The village is on the bank of the Ganges(*gangatate ghosah*).

29 The Sanskrit version is:*kakebhyo dadhi rasyatam*

30 *So'yam Devadattah*

31 It is also called '*Bhagatyagalaksana*' (literally: part abandoning implication)

2.3.3. *Laksana* on '*tat*'[32]

i. Association Expressed as Identity

Dvaita followers make use of an example under the *Panini*'s rule (4.2.63)[33] given by *Patañjali,* the great Grammarian the author of *Mahabhasya.* The example '*vasantadhyayanam*' (spring study) does not refer to the object of study called '*vasanta*' but the association of 'spring-time' with study.[34] The word 'tat' in '*tat-tvam-asi*' means close association of *Jiva* with *Brahman.* This association of *Brahman* is understood as Brahman's control.[35]

ii. Basic Relation or Identity[36] (*tadasritattvena taditi vyapadesah*)

According to Panini's Sutra: *samarthah padavidhih* (2.1.1) the term '*samartha*' in the sutra stands for syntactic competency of words in a compound. Hence here '*samartha*' means *samarthasrita-padavidhi.*[37] Such part and whole relation (angangi-bhava) is intended by Uddalaka when he says:*sanmulah imah sarvah prajah sadayatanah satpratisthah.*[38] Hence 'tat' means a fundamental relation of *Brahman* with *Jiva.*

iii. Source of Another Expressed as Identity[39] (*tato jatatvat tad vyapadesah*)

The Vedic Statement: The *Brahmana* was his face[40] refers to the *Purusa* from whose face the *Brahmana* is produced. Similarly *Jivas* owe their genesis to the Lord.[41]Hence '*tat*' expresses the meaning of creation understood as *paradhinavisesapti* in *Dvaita.*[42]

---

32 MM. pp. 180 - 183

33 The Sutra of Panini (4.2.63) reads: *vasantadibhyastak.*

34 *vasanta-sahacaritamadhyayanam vasantadhyayanam.*

35 *tat sahacaryat taditi vyapadesah.Prasiddham ca jivasya brahmasahacaritvam dvasuparna ityadau.*

36 MM, p.180

37 Compounding based on semantic competency

38 Ch.U.6.8.4

39 MM, p.181

40 Rv 10.90.2

41 Since Madhva believe in eternal souls, the word genesis is taken in the sense of 'embodiment'.

42 *Paradhinavisesapti* means the acquiring of a new trait that depends on the will of the 'other' (God). This is a distinct contribution of Madhva.

iv. Dependence on Another Expressed as Identity[43]43 (*tadadhinatvat taditi vyapadesah*)

We have the reference to the husked rice as grain in the Vedic passage: *dhanyamasi dhinuhi devan*[44] *Mimamsakas* explain it as a *laksana* based on dependence. Hence the sentence would mean: *dhanyadhinotpattike tandule dhanyasabdaprayogah.*[45]

This is exployed in understanding the meaning of '*tat*' as *sanmula*[46]

v. Resemblance Expressed as Identity[47]

In the Panini-Sutra: *bahugunavatudati sankhya*(1.1.23), according to *Patañjali*, the purpose is not to designate *bahu*, *gana*, *vatu*, *dati* as numerals (*Sankhya*). The word '*Sankhya*' here means '*sankhyavat*' expressing similitude. Even in the world there is a tendency to equate when similarities are found. Accordingly for *purvamimamsa* the sentence *adityo yupah*[48] (The sacrificial post is the Sun) is understood in its resemblance.[49] Since *Jiva* resembles *Brahman* to a certain extent in *jñana*, *anandaù* it is expressed as identity.

vi. '*Tat*' Standing for all its Oblique Cases.[50]

According to Panini sutra '*supam suluk*' (7.1.39) the case ending of a noun can be deleted without affecting its oblique case sense. Hence according to the word '*tat*' has all its case senses. So this enables one to contrue the term '*tat*' as.[51]

a) *Tena tvamasi* ------ you are by Brahman
b) *Tasmai tvamasi* ------ you are for his service
c) *Tasmat tvamasi* ------ you are from Brahman
d) *Tasya tvamasi* ------- you are Brahman's servant
e) Tasmin tvamasi ------ you are in Brahman,

---

43 MM, p.181

44 *Taittiriya Brahmana 1.1.6.1*

45 PMS, 9.1.38

46 existential root

47 MM, p. 182

48 *Taittiriya Brahmana 2.1.52*

49 *adityo yupa itivat sadrsyartha tu sa srutih.Na svarupaikata tasya yuktasyapi virupatah. Svatantrapurnatannapyateparatantryo virupyate(Anuvyakhyana)*

50 MM, p.179

51 *yacca supam sulugityadi sutrat trtiyavibhaktyadih luk prathamaikavacanadeso tatastena tvam tisthasiti va tatastvam jata iti va tasya tvamiti va tasmin tvamiti va'rthah.*

2.3.4. *Laksana* on *tvam*

i. Sense of Vicinity[52]

By '*Sakhacandranyaya*' 'the moon is said to be between the branches of a tree. Here the word '*sakha*'signifies 'sakhasadesya'(in the vicinity of the branches) In a similar manner '*tvam*' means Brahman nearest to the *Jiva* as '*antaryami*' (*tvatsadesyam brahma*)[53]

ii. As One's Sustaining Force:

In the statement: *Brahmana* is all the gods,[54] the word '*Brahmana*' is understood as the mainstay of all *varna*s to his functions. Similarly *Brahman* is the sustaining force of the *Jiva*. *Brahman* is called *tvam* as he is the abode of the *Jivas*[55]

iii. Being the Source of All

The sentence '*yajamanah prastarah*'[56] (The sacrifice is called the *darbha* grass). Jaimini in his *Mimamsasutra* (1.4.23) understands it as the source.[57] In a similar manner Brahman being the source of all is identified with the *Jiva.*[58]

2.3.5. Spirit of '*tat-tvam-asi*' from the Meaning of the Antecedent '*aitadatmyam*'[59]

In the declaration of *Uddalaka*, '*tat-tvam-asi*' is preceded by '*aitadatmyam*'. According to the *Dvaita* interpreters it stands in apposition to its consequent 'tat' relating to *Brahman*. Further '*aitadatmyam*' is the secondary nominal derivative of *aitadatma* with a suitable suffix. The derivative suffix conveys the sense of belonging to the *atman*, i.e. *Brahman*. This is beautifully explained by Jayatirtha[60]60, the famous commentator of Madhva. The sense

52 MM, p. 184

53 *sakhasadese candre sakhasabdavat jivantaryamitaya jiva sadese brahmani tvamiti vyapadesah*

54 *brahmano vai sarvah devatah vasanti.*

55 *yasya brahmano vai sarva devatah ityadivat jivasrayatvat brahmani tvamiti vyapadesah.*

56 Tatittiriya Samhita 1.7.4, see Sayana's Remarks:*yajamanavad yagasadhanatvat prastare yajamanotvopacarah*.PMS 1.4.23 stress its metaphorical use.

57 *tat siddhi*(PMS 1.423)

58 *yatha narthah sruterabhaveta. Brahmatvamapi jivasya pratyaksyavisesatah*(Anuvyakhya na v.36), p.4 in SMG

59 MM, 189 -191

60 *etena aitadatmyam etat svamikametadiyamiti siddhyati* - (*VTN tika*), MM, P.189

of '*aitadatmyam*' as "belonging to' suits the context and the import of the nine illustrations used in the sixth chapter of the *Chandogya Uanisad.*[61]

2.3.6 Illustrations Revealing the Meaning of 'tat-tvam-asi'[62]

According to Madhva, the nine illustrations found in the sixth chapter of *Chandogya Upanisad* clearly bring out the aspect of difference between *Jiva* and *Brahman.*[63] Let us see the explanations and interpretations of these illustrations occurring in the *Upanisad*s.

i. A Bird tied to a String at One End and to a Peg at the Other

The bird flies here and there and at last finding no place to rest comes back to the peg and rests. In a similar manner the sentient *Jiva* having wandered endlessly in his dream rests near the source and engrossed in deep sleep. The bird and the rope in the illustration are compared to *Jiva* and Brahman respectively. As there is difference between the bird and rope, similarly there is difference between *Jiva* and *Brahman*.

ii. Nectar of Different Flowers Collected by Bees and the Honey

Bees suck the nectar of different flowers and prepare honey by mixing juices. Though all nectars mix to produce honey yet each nectar maintains its individuality even if they do not knows it. Similarly *Jiva*s are with God inseparably maintaining their individuality.

iii. Rivers Joining the Sea

Though rivers join the sea they do not lose their individuality even though they do not know it. River particles and sea particles remain separate without losing their properties. Similarly *Jivas* joining *Brahman* retain the difference.[64]

iv. Tree and its Life Giving Sap

When the living tree is cut in different places the sap goes out and the tree withers. The withering of the tree is due to the leaving of *Vrksa-Jiva.* This *vrksa-jiva* itself in turn is sustained by the *antaryami Brahman*. The tree is

61 Like everything else in the entire universe *Jivatman too has the one supreme Being for his inner rules and indwelling principle (aitadatmyam). The neuter 'tat' (pronoun) how has for its antecedent the compound 'aitadatmyam'(neuter) which provides a smooth anvaya (syntactical connection) Thus the overall Samanvaya of the whole gamut of upanisad in the majesty of Brahman is achieved. See BNK Sharma, Dvaita Philosophy, p.35.*

62 A.V. Nagasampige, "*Visnutattvavinirnaya" tattvavada, pp. 26 – 30.*

63 *na hi sakunisutrayoh nanavrksarasanam nadisamudrayoh jivavrksayoh animadhanayoh lavanodakayoh gandharapurusayoh ajnah prananiyamakayoh stenapaharyayoh aikyam(VTN)*

64 '*tah samudrat samudramevapiyanti.Sa samudrah eva bhavati ityatrapi bheda evocyate. Anytha tah samudra eva bhavatiti vyapadesah syat(cVTN)*

compared to *Jiva* and the emerging principle is compared to *Brahman*. The aspect of difference is clearly seen here.

v. Cutting Open the Banyan Seed

Svetaketu is asked by *Uddalaka* to cut open the seed of the banyan fruit progressively till he sees 'nothing'. Then the father enlightens him saying that it is by the invisible power[65] hidden inside the tiny seed makes the mighty *Nyagrodha* come into being. Here seed is the sentient *Jiva* and the invisible power is *Brahman*. Again the illustration points to difference.

vi. Salt Dissolved in Water

Salt is present in the solution yet it is not visible to the naked eye. It can be felt only by taste. As salt is in salt solution *Brahman* is immanent in the whole universe including the *Jiva*s. The relation between Brahman and *Jiva* is same as the salt and the water.

vii. Blind-Folded Person[66]

A wayfarer who is blindfolded is led by a kindly traveller to his right destination. The struggling wayfarer is the *Jiva*; the kindly traveller is the *guru*. The individual who is enabled to see God by Guru's guidance is different from the goal he has to reach. Thus the thesis of difference is clearly illustrated.

viii. The Thief and the Touching of Red Hot Iron

The thief who has stolen in order to prove his innocence has to touch the red hot iron. If he is innocent he is not burnt. A *Jiva* who is not *Brahman* becomes a thief if he thinks he is one with God. Advocating and meditating on non-difference is punishable. The failure to accept difference is a robbery.[67]

ix. The Sick Person and the Ability to Recognize Relatives

As long as the power of God animates the sick person his senses would be alert and he is able to recognize his relatives who are beside his death-bed. This illustration speaks of the overall control of God on *Jiva*.

Thus *Madhvcarya* has brought out import of '*Tattvamasi*' as 'difference' between *Brahman* and *Jiva* by interpreting the nine illustrations.

65 The word used is, '*animnah' (the atomic essence)*

66 The illustration is named '*gandaharebhyo abhinaddhaksah purusah'*

67 The words, *apaharsit, steyamakarsit clearly indicate difference HDVL, 176 – 177.*

2.4. Interpretation of '*Tat-tvam-asi*' by Sankara and Ramanuja and Madhva's Critique

2.4.1. '*Tat-tvam-asi*' according to Sankara[68]

According to Sankara the words '*tat*' (that) referring Brahman and '*tvam*' (thou referring to the *Jiva*, should not be understood in the literal meanings (*vacyartha*). In a *vacyartha* the word 'thou' means "consciousness connected with the internal *organ* (*antahkarana*) and illuminated as object (*alambana*) of the word "I". The word 'that' means that which has maya as its limitation (*Isvara*) which is the cause of the universe, omniscient etc." Since the meanings are incompatible one has to resort to the implied or the secondary meaning (*laksyartha*). Sankara uses a special kind of *laksana* called *jahat-ajahat-laksana* or *bhaga-tyaga-laksana*. The explanation of this type of *laksana* we have already seen. In the process of applying this kind of *laksana* one "leaves out the part consisting of the internal organ and the reflection of consciousness from the direct meaning of the word 'thou' and also leaves out that part consisting of '*maya*' and the reflection of consciousness from the direct meaning of the word 'that'. Thus the only possible meaning of '*tat-tvam-asi*' (thou-art-that) according to Sankara would be: the one indivisible entity with its existence-knowledge-bliss having no connection either with *maya* or the internal organ or with the reflection of consciousness in either form."Hence the focus of Sankara is on identity between '*tat*' and '*tvam*' in its implied meaning.

2.4.2. Ramanuja on '*tat-tvam-asi*'[69]

For Ramanuja, "both the terms 'that' and 'thou' are in mutual predication and signify *Brahman* alone under two aspects. The term 'that' refers to *Brahman*, who is the cause of the universe, the abode of all auspicious qualities, the flowers and the changeless one; where as the term 'thou' signifies that same *Brahman* who , because he hs is the inner controller of finite selves, has these services, along with their bodies, as His modes"

Thus Ramanuja in his interpretation of '*tat-tvam –asi*' strikes a middle course between *dvaita* and *advaita* with his doctrine of *visistadvaita.*[70] Further according to Ramanuja '*tattvamasi*' is not the main proposition but an extension of the earlier pronouncement *aitadatmyamidam sarvam.*[71]

---

68 M.A. Devasia, some Hermeneutical Reflections on Religious speech Acts, pp, 66 – 67.

69 J.B. Carman, The Theology of Ramanuja, p.124

70 *cit-acit-visista-brahmanah advaitam.*

71 BNK Sharma, Dvaita Philosophy, p.50

2.4.3. Critique of Sankara by Madhva[72]

Sankara reduces the meaning of '*tat-tvam-asi*' to a bare consciousness without any characteristic. The procedure adopted by him in interpretation empties the constituent parts by their denotative content leaving only a hazy notion of pure consciousness. A bare 'identity' without reference to any correlates makes no sense.

Further resort to *laksana* is optional for Madhva. By taking the reading '*atat-tvam-asi*- he has dispensed with *laksana*. Even if one were to insist on '*tat-tvam-asi*' *dvaita* interpretation manages with a single *laksana* on any one of the terms at a time. This we have seen already. By applying *laksana* on both '*tat*' and '*tvam*' simultaneously advaita incurs the fault of '*Kalpana-gaurava.*'[73] In the light of the context and illustrations of '*tat-tvam-asi*' in *Chandogya Upanisad*, Madhva further explains the untenability of Sankara's interpretation.

2.4.4. Critique of Ramanuja by Madhva[74]

According to Ramanuja Brahman exists in manifold forms as sentient souls and insentient matter. Thus there are both distinction and identity. Madhva criticizes the Ramanuja system for advocating mutually opposed relations among the three fundamental entities (i.e. God, sentient soul and insentient matter). Further there is a logical difficulty and impossiblility of making the Independent real actually transform[75] itself into souls and matter without loss of authentic being and nature. Since Ramanuja advocates real transformation of Brahman into the word and souls, an illusory transformation of Brahman into the world and souls an illusory transformation[76] has no place.

2.5. Madhva's Analogy of '*Bimba-Pratibimba*' Highlighting the Meaning of '*atat-tvam-asi*'

The meaning of '*atat-tvam-asi*' is succinctly summed up by Madhva in his analogy of '*bimba-pratibimba*' (prototype – reflection). This is derived by Madhva from *Rgveda* 7.47.18.

> '*Rupam rupam pratirupo babhuva*
> *Tadasya rupam praticaksanaya*'

---

72 MM, pp. 163 - 175

73 Greatness of effort in expression. Dvaita can manage the interpretation of any term in '*tattvamasi' with a single laksana at a time.*

74 MM,p xviii

75 It is called *Brahmaparinamavada*

76 This is known as *vivartavada*

(With reference to each form of *Jiva* He (the Lord) becomes the original form. His form is for this one (.e. the *Jiva*) to perceive.)[77] By this analogy Brahman is the '*bimba*' and '*Jiva*' is the '*pratibimba*'. As '*pratibimba*' (reflection) owes its existence to '*bimba*' (prototype) so *Jiva* is dependent on Brahman. "Madhva emphasizes *Jiva*'s dependence on *Brahman* for its existence, consciousness and activities for all the time".[78] *Brhaman* is the sole independent source of all reality.

Madhva is careful to distinguish his understanding of '*bimba-pratibimba*' analogy from *Advaita*. *Pratibimba* is not a false reflection. According to Sankara the *Jiva* is a false appearance or projection of *Brahman* on the screen of *avidya* (ignorance). Hence the relation can be transcended which is not the case in Madhva. The relation of '*bimba-pratibimbabhava*' between God and soul is a sacred and inviolable relation true for all time. This relation goes to the very core of *Jiva* constituting essence and could never be annulled or transcended.[79] '*Pratibimbatva*' is not a false relation which the *Jivas* are to be ashamed of and should try to shake off as in Sankara. In fact, *Moksa* (liberation) is the complete realization of metaphysical dependence on and similarity to the Supreme.[80]

Madhva wants to drive home through the analogy of '*bimba-pratibimba*' three truths concerning the nature of relation between God and soul.[81]

1. The finite spiritual being is similar to *Visnu.*
2. It is completely distinct from *Visnu.*
3. It is radically dependent on *Visnu.*

Conclusion

Madhva's interpretation of '*atat-tvam-asi*' emphatically brings out the significance of difference. The methods of interpretation (context, *laksana*, illustrations, *Padacchedha*, *aitadatmyam,* critique of Sankara and Ramanuja and the analogy of '*bimba-pratibimba*') highlight the aspect of difference. '*Atat-tvam-asi*' is a metaphysical statement of relation. It is a metaphysical relation of radical dependence of *Jiva* on *Brahman.* Though in certain respects there is similarity,[82] the difference and distinction is clearly stated by Madhva through his interpretation of '*tat-tvam-asi*'.

---

77 PM, 306

78 PM, 307

79 ibid

80 ibid

81 I. Puthiadam, Visnu, the Ever Free, p.230

82 PM, p.318

Abbreviations

ABMM: Akhila-bharata-madhva-mahamandala
C.: Commentary
Ch.U.: Chandogya Upanisad
DVSRF: Dvaita Vedanta Studies and Research Foundation
HDVL : History of the Dvaita School of Vedanta and its Literature by BNK Sharma
MM: Mahatatparya of Mahavakyas and other Advaita Srutis by BNK Sharma
Pa.: Panini's Astadhyayi
PM: Philosophy of Sri Madhvacharya by BNK Sharma
PMS: Purvamimamsa Sutras of Jaimini
PSM: Purnaprajna-Samsodhana-Mandira
RV: Rgveda
SMG: Sarvamulagranthas of Sri Madhvacharya ed. By Bannanje Govindacharya.
VTN: Visnu-tattva-vinirnaya

Bibliography

Primary Sources

Chandogyopanisad with the Khandartha of Raghavendratirtha. Ed. with Introduction by Malagi.Bangalore: PSM, 1988.

Sarvamulagranthah of Sri Madhva Charya. Ed. Bannanje Govindacharya. Udupi: ABNM, 1969-1974.

Visnu-tattva-vinirnaya of Anandatirtha.English tr.with notes. K.T. Pandurangi. Bangalore: DVSRF, 1991.

B. Secondary Sources

Archak, K. B.Tattvamasi in Brahmasutra-Sankara- bhasya. Dharwad: Shruti Geeta Prakashana,1996.

Belvalkar and Ranade.The Creative Period.Poona, 1927.

Carman, J. B. The Theology of Ramanuja: An Essay in Inter-religious Understanding. London:Yale University Press, 1974.

Deussen, Paul. Sixty Upanisads of the Veda. Delhi: Motilal Banarsidass, 1980.

Devasia, M. A. Some Hermeneutical Reflections on Religious Speech-acts. An M.Phil dissertation submitted to the University of Delhi. Department of Philosophy, 2001.

Grimes, John. Problems and Perspectives in Religious Discourse: Advaita Vedanta Implications. New York: State university Press, 1994.

Nagasampige, A. V. "Visnutattvavinirnaya". Tattvavada, vol.2/4 (Sept.-Oct.), 2002, 26-30.

Pandurangi, K. T. Essentials of Dasaprakaranas. Bangalore: PSM, 1994.

Puthiadam, Ignatius. Visnu, the Ever Free. Madurai: Arul Anandar College, 1986.

Radhakrishnan,S. The Principal Upanisads. New Delhi: Harper Collins, 1994.

Shanbhag, D. N. Sri Madhvacharya and His Cardinal Doctrines. Dharwad: Bharat Book Depot and Prakashan,1990.

Sharma, BNK. Philosophy of Sri Madhvacharya. Delhi: Motilal Banarsidass, 1986.

_______, Mahatatparya of Mahavakyas and other Advaita Srutis. Bangalore: ABMM, 1999.

20

Contemporary Interpretations of Shankara's Advaita and the Affirmation of the World

Joseph Kaipayil MCBS

Abstract

Shankara's Advaita Vedanta has been very influential in India, both as a well-articulated philosophical system and a weighty theological position. However, Advaita's supposedly dismissive attitude toward the world always remained its Achilles' heel. Thinkers whose sympathies lie firmly with Advaita are at pains to give a philosophically satisfactory explanation of the ontological status of the world. This article briefly discusses the efforts and resultant views of four such contemporary thinkers – K.C. Bhattacharyya, S. Radhakrishnan, P.T. Raju, and Richard De Smet.

Keywords

Advaita, Shankara, maya, Advaita and the world, K.C. Bhattacharyya, S. Radhakrishnan, P. T. Raju, Richard De Smet

1. The Problematic of the World in Advaita Vedanta

During the entire 20th century, Advaita Vedanta was the single most influcntial philosophy in India. This was due in part to its endorsement by western Indologists like Max Mueller and Paul Deussen in the late 19th and early 20th century. However, Advaita's supposedly, or allegedly, dismissive attitude toward the world always remained its Achilles' heel, especially in the contemporary period when the empirical world has been given significant philosophical and scientific importance. It is no easy task for any Advaitin to give an adequate world-affirming interpretation of Advaita, given that the system dismisses all distinctions as ontologically impossible and that the system was repeatedly dubbed *maya-vada* (theory of illusion) and crypto-Buddhism by its adversaries.[1]

The Advaita doctrine as epitomized in Shankara's *Brahmasutra-bhashya* presents a robust form of monistic idealism.[2] On the authority of the Upanishads, the *Brahma-sutra*, and the *Mandukya-karika*, Shankara accepted Brahman as the absolute truth about reality. If Brahman is the sole reality, the reality of the world has to be toned down. Shankara explained the world in terms of illusion (*maya*) and superimposition (*adhyasa*).

The world for Advaita is an illusory appearance of Brahman and the world's ontological status as real is only an erroneous superimposition on Brahman. In the classic rope-snake example, the illusory snake is superimposed on the rope. Until the discrimination between the rope and the snake takes place, the snake is regarded as real, on account of the reality of the rope. Similarly, when discriminatory knowledge (*vidya*) arises, you realize that all differences are unreal and reality is ultimately non-dual (*advaita*). This non-dual reality of your higher experience is Brahman, and the world of your empirical experience, which is Brahman's appearance, is only apparently real. Advaita explains away all empirical experience and knowledge as ultimately your erroneous superimposition on Brahman. A well-known epigram attributed to Shankara captures the gist of Advaita: "Brahman is real, the world is unreal, and the individual self is identical to Brahman."[3]

We discuss briefly the views of four academic philosophers of Advaitic leanings, who tried to give some reinterpretations to Advaita, so it can better and more positively account for the world of our empirical and human experiences. K.C. Bhattacharyya (1875-1949), S. Radhakrishnan (1888-1975), P.T. Raju (1904-92), and Richard De Smet (1916-97) are chosen for their long-

---

1 See S. M. Srinivasa Chari, *Fundamentals of Visistadvaita Vedanta: A Study Based on Vedanta Desika's Tattva-mukta-kalapa* (Delhi: Motilal Banarsidass, 1988), 5; Hajime Nakamura, *A History of Early Vedanta Philosophy*, vol. 1 (Delhi: Motilal Banarsidass, 1989), 121, 459; Sengaku Mayeda, "Sankara and Buddhism," in *New Perspectives on Advaita Vedanta: Essays in Commemoration of Professor Richard De Smet*, ed. Bradley J. Malkovsky (Leiden: Brill, 2000), 18-19.

2 By scholarly consensus, the *Brahmasutra-bhashya* is considered the most authentic work of Shankara. The Shankarite authorship of the *Upadeshasahasri*, the *Brihadaranyaka-bhashya*, and the *Taittiriya-bhashya* is also generally accepted. See Karl H. Potter, ed., *Advaita Vedanta up to Samkara and His Pupils*, vol. 3 of *The Encyclopedia of Indian Philosophies* (Delhi: Motilal Banarsidass, 1981), 115-16.

3 In verse 20 of the *Brahma-jnanavali-mala*, a non-Shankarite work of later period, we read, "Brahma satyam, jaganmithya, jivo Brahmaiva naparah."

standing stability in the Advaitic tradition and their divergent readings of that very same tradition.

1.1. K.C. Bhattacharyya

Bhattacharyya tried to understand Vedanta in light of Kant and Hegel, and Kant and Hegel in light of Vedanta.[4] From Kant he learnt the importance of the rational, ethical and aesthetic aspects of human subjectivity, and from Hegel, the dialectic of the Absolute. But at the same time he rejected the Kantian agnosticism about the transcendent (noumenon) and the Hegelian absolutization of the Absolute.

Bhattacharyya disagreed with the Kantian thesis that the Transcendent (the Self) as a thing-in-itself is not knowable to theoretical reason but is accepted only as an object of moral faith (practical reason). He classified epistemological objects into speakables, thinkables, and knowables. All speakables are knowables, but not all knowables are thinkables. The Self is speakable, though inadequately, but not thinkable using empirical categories. Even as the Self is not thinkable empirically (intellectively), it can be known transcendentally (intuitively).[5]

Different levels of human consciousness are involved in understanding different speakables. At the level of empirical consciousness, the objects of our knowing are empirical facts. Such abstract concepts as universals, life, and mind are the objects of pure objective consciousness. The ego-sense, the awareness of my empirical (psychological) self, constitutes subjective consciousness. The highest level or form of consciousness is transcendental consciousness. Here the object of our knowing is the inner Self (the Absolute), known intuitively.[6] At the empirical level, which is the level of science, speaking is literal and the aim is to get information about the world. At the other three levels, which are the levels of philosophy, the speaking is symbolic and the aim is to find the meaning of our experience.

Related to the levels of consciousness are the three levels of self-realization (realization of our subjectivity). In bodily subjectivity, we identify our self with the body; in psychic subjectivity, the self is identified with the mind; and in pure subjectivity, the self is realized as freedom (freedom from all objectivity), the Absolute.

The Absolute as pure subjectivity is devoid of all objectivity. In this regard, Bhattacharyya believed that the concept of *maya* is indispensable

4 For Bhattacharyya's writings, see Krishnachandra Bhattacharyya, *Studies in Philosophy*, ed. Gopinath Bhattacharyya (Delhi: Motilal Banarsidass, 2008).

5 For an Advaita Vedantin, knowledge (*vidya*) is the paramount way toward the summum bonum, namely the *Brahma-sakshatkara* (Self-realization).

6 From the advaitic (non-dualistic) point of view, this intuitive knowing of the Self is nothing but the Self (the Absolute) knowing itself.

to the Shankarite monism and its understanding of the world. The reality of cosmic *maya*, the world, and our experience of it is akin to the illusory snake in the rope-snake example. The illusory snake is experienced in three stages, according to Bhattacharyya. In the first stage the snake is believed to be real. In the second stage this belief is corrected and we come to know the snake is unreal. In the third stage we know the snake is unreal at all times, both now and at the time we perceived it as real. Like the snake in the third stage, *maya* is neither existent nor non-existent but absolute nought. Both its appearance and its retraction are unreal.

Bhattacharyya's most remarkable idea is his notion of the Absolute as alternation. Instead of the Hegelian absolutization of the Absolute, he chose the dialectics of alternation both at transcendental and empirical levels of reality. The triple functions of consciousness in relation to its contents are: knowing, feeling, and willing. Each of them has its own formulation of the Absolute, namely truth, value, and freedom respectively. When cognition is given importance, the Absolute is viewed as truth; when emotion (devotion) is given importance, it is viewed as value; and when volition is given importance, it is viewed as freedom. These conceptions of the Absolute cannot be unified into one, because each is Absolute in turn.[7] For Bhattacharyya, this *alternation* is not just our symbolic speaking about the one Absolute in three distinct ways, but the very constitution (dynamics) of the Absolute.[8]

1.2. S. Radhakrishnan

Radhakrishnan tried to make Vedanta, especially the Shankara Vedanta, more appealing and meaningful to the modern mind.[9] Besides Advaita, his principal source of philosophizing, Radhakrishnan made use of ideas from Western idealism, modern science, Christianity, and Buddhism.

Radhakrishnan was a devoted defender of religion and spirituality against the challenges of modern science. In his philosophy, it is hard to distinguish between philosophical thinking and religious thinking. As against the usual understanding of intellectual reflection (discursive reasoning) as the method of philosophy, he proposed intuition as the method. While science describes the empirical world, philosophy interprets and explains the ultimate nature,

7 This gives reason and legitimacy to philosophical and religious pluralism.

8 If the alternation (alternation of truth, value, and freedom) itself is constitutive of the Absolute is an open question, however. Cf. Gopinath Bhattacharyya, "Editor's Introduction," in Bhattacharyya, *Studies in Philosophy*, xliii. The similarity appears not so much to the Hegelian dialectic as to the Kantian notion of triple-reason (pure reason, practical reason, and aesthetic reason).

9 For Radhakrishnan's philosophical views, see mainly his *An Idealist View of Life* (1932, 1937) and the introduction to his *The Brahma Sutra: The Philosophy of Spiritual Life* (1960).

meaning, and purpose of the universe by intuitive knowledge. The intuitive apprehension (understanding) provides us with immediate, personal experience of reality. This intuitive apprehension is the very activity of the spirit within us.

The idealist view of life and reality, which Radhakrishnan calls religion of the spirit, perceives the universe as ultimately spiritual. Brahman (Atman/ the Spirit) being the ultimate truth and the universe its self-manifestation, the spirit is our deepest self. Radhakrishnan wanted all historical religions to transform themselves into the religion of the spirit, a spiritual vision that transforms the world and ensures human unity, universal moral order, and world peace.

Radhakrishnan tried to work out a positive account of the world by interfacing three concepts – Brahman (the Absolute), Ishvara (God), and the world. Brahman considered in its self-identity as pure consciousness is beyond all distinctions, qualifications, and descriptions. This one, absolute being, however, manifests itself as the world. The world is just one possibility of Brahman's self-manifestation; other possibilities we may not know. Brahman in its relation to the world is Ishvara (God). Ishvara is Brahman's creative aspect, conceived as creator, redeemer, and judge. Immanent in the world, Ishvara guides and transforms it. Ishvara lasts as long as the world-process lasts.

Although the transformation of the world is God's action, it is essentially linked with human transformation. Despite limitations, human evolution and progress is teleological and moves toward a greater good.[10] Human calling is to co-operate with the divine plan for the world's transformation. Typical of an Advaitin, Radhakrishnan held that our deepest self (atman) is identical to the transcendental Self (Atman) and is above transmigration. What is subject to transmigration is *jiva*, the empirical self. The world-process lasts until all *jivas* are liberated.[11] When all *jivas* are liberated, the world will be transformed into *Brahma-loka* (the kingdom of God). The world and all *jivas* become one with God and God will be all in all. And finally the *Brahma-loka*, along with Ishvara, will lapse into Brahman. Thus Brahman remains the beginning and the end of the world. If and when another world-process begins is left to the freedom of Brahman.

1.3. P.T. Raju

Raju's entire philosophizing revolved around the concept of I-am.[12] The uppercase I-AM stands for the supreme Self (Brahman) and the lowercase

---

10 According to Radhakrishnan, regress rebirth is a remote possibility. For human beings there may not be a going back to sub-human levels.

11 Meanwhile, the liberated *jivas* take birth as *bodhisattvas* (*jivan-muktas*) for the benefit of humanity.

12 For Raju's philosophical views, see mainly his *Spirit, Being, and Self* (1982) and sections on "General Estimate and Constructive Comment" in his *Structural Depths of Indian*

I-am for the individual self (atman). The latter is the gateway by which we access the former. The philosophy of I-am, according to Raju, accounts for the Vedantic doctrine of the transcendence and immanence of the spirit.

My existence is fundamentally an I-am experience, as my existence (am-ness) and consciousness (self-awareness) are united in it. I-am experience is self-evident, as it does not require any external proof. In my I-am experience, I am directly aware of my am-ness. It is on this fundamental I-am experience that all other experiences are founded. The philosophy of I-am thus forms the foundation for a philosophy of life.

I-am is involved in all my cognitive activities. All my mental activities presuppose the existence of a dynamic I. I cannot meaningfully make even a simple statement like "This is a pen," if I am not aware that I am aware of a pen. In this regard, Raju draws a distinction between I-am (ontological self) and I-think (empirical or phenomenological self). The former continues and the latter changes. The latter is an aggregate of psychological experiences and the former is the synthesizer of this aggregate. The empirical self undergoes changes, but the ontological self endures through these changes. My ontological self is involved in all my activities, and yet transcends them all. Without a dynamic self to synthesize our experiences, we cannot experience the world. It is the ontological self in us that organizes our empirical experiences into time, space, and causality.[13]

If my existence is fundamentally an I-am experience, the Supreme Being must also be an I-AM experience. The argument is from unity of being. Being (is-ness) is the same for all entities. The difference is only in how this one being is manifested. A horse and a human are ontologically (in is-ness aspect) same, but phenomenologically different. The source from which all is-ness derives is the supreme I-AM. The world has no is-ness of its own, apart from that of Brahman. On the question of how the world of objectivity comes out of Brahman, which is pure subjectivity, Raju would say the world does not come out of Brahman directly, but from its power (*shakti*). The world comes out of Brahman's *shakti* and is absorbed back to Brahman through the same *shakti*. In other words, the world is the transformation of Brahman's power, rather than of Brahman itself.[14] Brahman and its power are nonetheless inseparable, like fire and its power to burn.

The world, for Raju, is very much real and it cannot be dismissed as illusion (*maya/mithya*). The world is said to be illusory or unreal only at the

---

Thought (1985).

13 Raju is not denying the objective reality of time, space, and causality. Rather, the point is to underscore the importance of ontological self, I-am.

14 In "Transcendence and Historicity in the Self as Atman" (*Idealistic Studies* 20 [1990]: 203-29), Raju speaks of three forms this transformation: God (*Ishvara*), subtle cosmic from (*Hiranyagarbha*), and gross cosmic form (*Virat*).

higher level, where it is contrasted to Brahman, who is the ontological source of all existents. The word *maya*, in fact, should be taken in its etymological meaning. According to Raju, the word *maya* is derived from the verbal root *ma*, meaning "to measure." The world is called *maya*, because it is "measured" in time and space, in contrast to Brahman that cannot be measured.

And coming to the question whether the individual I-am (atman) is identical to the supreme I-AM (Brahman), Raju seems to neither affirm nor deny it. He would rather say they are ontologically the same, because the being of my I-am is derived from the supreme I-AM. So it may be said that my I-am is inherently infinite and essentially one with I-AM. Moreover, for me my I-am is the gateway to the supreme I-AM. I can know and experience I-AM only as my I-am.

1.4. Richard De Smet

The Belgian-born Indian philosopher Richard De Smet tried to give a Christian, or rather Thomistic, reading to Shankara's non-dualism by interpreting Brahman as the non-dual substantive (existence-giving) cause, standing in a non-reciprocal relation to the universe.[15]

The Brahman of Advaita, the non-qualified Brahman, has usually been taken to be impersonal, in contrast with the personal God (the qualified Brahman) of other Vedantic schools. But De Smet would argue that personality (personhood) is applicable to the non-qualified (*nirguna*) Brahman of Advaita as well.[16] The concept of "person" signifies the ultimate subject of attribution of intellectual activities like knowledge and consciousness. If pure consciousness is the defining characteristic of Brahman, the non-dual Brahman can also be referred to as person, indeed a super-person.

Regarding the Advaitic view of the world, De Smet would hold that Shankara's philosophy is not illusionistic and acosmic. The notion of *maya* implies not so much the negation of the world as the affirmation of Brahman who is the substantive cause of the world. On the level of ordinary speaking, both the world and its substantive cause (Brahman) are beings.[17] But Brahman transcends its effects so immensely, that compared with Brahman the universe is considered unreal (*maya*). The being of the world is only a participation

---

15 For De Smet's writings, see Richard De Smet, *Brahman and Person*, ed. Ivo Coelho (Delhi: Motilal Banarsidass, 2010); Richard De Smet, *Understanding Sankara*, ed. Ivo Coelho (Delhi: Motilal Banarsidass, 2013).

16 According to De Smet, Brahman is called *nirguna* not because it is impersonal or without qualities, but because its qualities are identical to itself. Brahman's *nirgunatva* is here considered as analogous to the Thomistic notion of divine simplicity.

17 "On the level of ordinary language, creaturely effects and their Cause are beings (*sat*), are imbued with existence (*satta*)" (De Smet, *Understanding Sankara*, 377).

in the being of Brahman, and as a participated being, the world is ultimately non-being.[18]

De Smet further interprets the meaning of Shankara's "advaita" (non-dualism) as "tadatmya" (identity) of non-reciprocal nature. As non-reciprocal relation, *tadatmya* is having *Tat* (That, i.e. Brahman) as one's own *atman*, inner being. What it means is that Brahman is the substantive cause of one's being.[19] *Tadatmya* is not unique to the individual self (atman) alone, but it imbues all effects of Brahman. Brahman, being the substantive (existence-giving) cause of the universe, is the innermost self of every entity. All things have their self, their being, in Brahman, but Brahman has not its self in them. Thus the non-duality implied by *tadatmya*, at both individual and cosmic levels, does not eliminate distinctions, but only underscores the pervading causal presence of Brahman, immanent in all things and at the same time transcendent.

2. Observations and Comments

The philosophers we discussed above have provided diverse views as to how we can better understand Advaita's take on the ontological status of the world in relation to Brahman. Here the question of who remained more faithful to the Advaitic tradition is immaterial. As creative thinkers, they took the freedom of philosophizing, and hence their different interpretations. Even as remaining committed to classical Advaita in their own way, they critiqued that very same tradition to make it more relevant and meaningful in contemporary times.

Out of the four, Bhattacharyya is stronger and more focussed in the analysis of human subjectivity at its various levels. But he appears lacking in his analysis of the world. This does not mean that Bhattacharyya is dismissive of the word as total *maya*. His philosophy is not without some inherent potential to give a positive account of the world. The first two levels human consciousness, namely empirical consciousness and pure objective consciousness, do not make sense without reference to the real world. Nor can we explain bodily subjectivity and psychic subjectivity without taking into consideration the world of our empirical experience. And his idea of the triple-absolute, the Absolute as truth, freedom, and value alternatively, is apparently

18 Here the Thomistic idea of participation, i.e. creatures participate in God's being, is at the back of De Smet's mind.

19 Unlike a reciprocal relation, the two terms (here Brahman and atman) are not interchangeable in a non-reciprocal relation. In order to substantiate his view, De Smet appeals to the analogy of the face and its reflection (in the mirror) discussed in *Upadeshasahasri*, chapter 2.18. Just as a face is reflected in a mirror, the Self is reflected in the ego (the empirical self) and make it appear like the Self. De Smet takes this to imply that the individual self is a reflection (image) of the supreme Self and thus in *tadatmya* relation with it. It seems that De Smet has taken here a view different than what the chapter in question originally meant. The original import of part 2, chapter 18 of the *Upadeshasahasri* was to show "that" and "thou" in "that art thou" express the same reality (see US 2.18.170-71).

the prototype of the three subjective functions – knowing, willing, and feeling – we perform in relation to the world of our everyday experience.

Unlike Bhattacharyya, Radhakrishnan attempted at constructing a grand metaphysical narrative after the manner of Western idealists like Kant and Hegel.[20] He tried to bring into his system all aspects of reality we experience – religious, empirical and scientific, and ethical. The world for Radhakrishnan is very much real and it cannot be underrated as illusion. The world, however, is called *maya* because of its temporal (passing) character. The world is being, for it exists for a time; the world is non-being, for it does not exist for all times. Brahman is the only being that exists for all times, and it is the substratum of all other forms of existence. So we may say the world as *maya* is neither real nor unreal. Radhakrishnan's real explainer of the world is not *maya* but his Ishvara concept though. He presented Ishvara as the connecting link between Brahman (pure subjectivity) and the world (objectivity), thus keeping his idealist view of reality compatible with a realist view of the world. Ishvara is the creative aspect of Brahman. Endowed with the creative power of *maya*, Ishvara will endure as long as the world-process continues. Ishvara is Brahman immanent in the world and becoming its organizer and guide. Ishvara is not Brahman just looked at in relation to the world, as commonly understood, but rather the very first phase of Brahman's unfolding.

Raju shared many of his philosophical views with Radhakrishnan, as both were interested in defending a grand idealist view of life. In the later part of his philosophical career, however, Raju narrowed down his reflections to a single unifying concept, namely I-am. He used the concept of I-am as the hermeneutic key to interpret and understand reality at different levels. In I-am, consciousness and existence meet and merge into a single entity. This becomes the basis of the Advaitic view of reality. Brahman, atman, and the world are different levels of I-am existence and experience. At the subjective individual level, reality is experienced as my enduring self, my I-am. In my self-transcendence, the supreme Self is experienced as I-AM. The world of objectivity (I-think) may be out there, but I cannot experience or comprehend it without linking it to my I-am, so much so that I can say my I-am is conferring existence on the world. Here Raju is not denying the objective existence of the world but only trying to explain the ontological and epistemological link that exists between subjectivity (the self) and objectivity (the world). It is ultimately the supreme I-AM that confers existence on the world, which is the modification of its creative energy (*shakti/maya*).

---

20 But owing to syncretic style and idea overload in his writings, it can sometimes be hard to identify his definitive position on a specific problem. As for his views on the ontological character of the world, however, we have relied primarily on the final chapter of his *An Idealist View of Life* and his introduction to *The Brahma Sutra: The Philosophy of Spiritual Life*.

While Bhattacharyya, Radhakrishnan, and Raju philosophized from within one main tradition, De Smet did his thinking from within two, namely Advaita and Thomism. On the one hand it put some constraint on his interpretation of Advaita, but on the other it provided him with an opportunity to explore a new line of reflection. He argued that the Brahman of Shankara can also be viewed as a person, granted that consciousness is the hallmark of personality. For De Smet the ultimate truth about "advaita" is that Brahman is the substantive cause, inherent in all beings. As the source of all being, Brahman is the only reality. As to the ontological status of the individual self and the world, theirs is only a participated existence. What is denied by Advaita is not their reality but their independent reality. They are ontologically dependent on Brahman, who De Smet sees as eminently personal in nature and the object of intellectual contemplation and love. On the whole, De Smet's interpretation of Advaita may have been greatly influenced by Thomism, but his philosophy as creative cross-cultural philosophizing is a case in point.

21

Hindutva of our Minds

Victor Ferrao

Abstract

Hindutva is a measure of all things Indian. Paradoxically, it imitates the West in form and asserts what may be called cultural matrix of the upper caste into it. Hidutva result of hybridization that has emerged as a result of our encounter with the colonization. It is a recovery of a lost self under colonization. It is also a completion of colonization of our mind. In this study, we study this colonization of our minds with respects to three forms borrowed from the West. The three forms under our study are the Nation, Text and Religion. As a colonization of our minds, it has become a hauntology that haunts all Indians. Every Indian is rendered not Indian enough. Hindus are not Indian enough unless they become sankari Hindus the same is true of minorities in our country. The study hopes that it will provoke an wakeful awareness and set in a process of de-colonization of our mind.

Keywords

Hindutva, colonization, hauntology, de-colonization of mind, nationalism etc.

Introduction

The famous words of George Orwell which say,' who controls the past controls the future and who controls the present control the past',[1] seem to

1 See S. P. UdayaKumar, '*Presenting*' *Past*: *Anxious History*, *Ancient Future in a Hindutva India* (London: Praeger 2015), 2.

be the way Indian society has been evolving for a long time. The Hindutva[2] forces have been working to control the past, presents and the future of Indians. They have tried to control all pluralistic conversation of Indians and have tried to homogenise Indian society. This has led to the mono-culturing of as well as semiticization of Hinduism. Some scholars refer to it as syndicate Hinduism. Viewing Indian openness and tolerance of diversity as weakness, protagonists of Hindutva strive to inject masculine Hindu supremists ideology into our society. They have constructed an anxious history and envisioned an ancient future for India and proudly call it the Hindu Rashtra. Much has been manifested about their fascination as well as structural resemblance with the Fascists and Nazi groups of Europe. Their coupling of communalism and nationalism is viewed as parallel to Hitler's combination of Aryan Racism and German Nationalism. Like the Fascists in Italy, they have infiltrated police and administration and use religion as a convenient myth. The Machiavellian policy of end justifying of the means is followed as a Krishnaneeti. They have craftily usurped the politico-moral authority as divine royalty and speak for the entire Hindu community and nation with no much opposition. This is why their Sarsangchayalak and pracharyaks are very powerful figures in our society. They believe in the power of fear that induces anxiety in our society both in the minority as well as the majority communities.

Hindutva successfully makes use of the social, cultural and religious symbols embedded in our society. It is important to explore how Hindutva by spinning a web around Ram develops a theology that animates the politics of BJP. It grew alongside of Islam, particularly its political organisation, the Muslim league. It seems that Islamic communalism provided background and continues to inspire a constant back drop to the growth and consolidation of Hindutva communalism. There are many India(s). These many India(s) have many historie(s). Unfortunately, Hintudva paints a simple monochromic history over the plural past(s) of our people. It has an ambiguous relation with the West. In imitates its form and enfleshes it into the Indian cultural matrix of the upper castes. In the context of this study, we wish to understand the Hindutva of our Minds. It has reflects on the matter and form(s) of Hindutva. There are several forms from the West that have been enfleshed to make Hindutva what it is. We shall consider Nation, Text and Religion that have been cross pollinated under colonisation and led to the formation of Hindutva in this study. The notions of Nation and Nationalism inspires Hindutva nationalism and reinforces the longing for a Hindu Nation, Textualisation of what was mainly an oral tradition has given us the text of *Bhagvad Gita* as the holy book and has led to the singularization of Ramayana. The construction of religion

2 See Joytirmaya Sharma, *Hindutva: Exploring the Idea of Hindu Nationalism* (Noida: Harper-Collins, 2015).

unto the model of the Semitic form gave birth to Hinduism and as a result we have Hinduness that we call Hindutva.

1. The West(s) of our Minds

The philosophical horizons of enlightenment, the academic discipline we know as history and the political organisation that we call nation-state came under colonization into south Asia, mainly through the work of orientalists. In several ways, we in India have mimicked the West. There are many west(s) in the minds of Indians. Under the influence of Enlightenment, the Western civilization was viewed as the product of human rational action under the light of scientific reason. This absolutization of rationality of nature and human mind was appropriated by local positivists with the academic discourse in India. They denied other Indians the right to represent themselves and took it on themselves to do so. Like other parts of the colonial world, in India, nation and the kind of its national history that was crafted emerged in tandem with the struggle for independence. This copying or mimesis of the West is complex and is a disruptive anti-colonial strategy. In this context, we examine only three areas of *Imitatio* West, namely Primacy of Nationalism, Primacy of Textual Tradition, and the Primacy of Religion as they are intimately linked with conceptualization and the political formation of Hindutva. Mimesis is born out of desire to become a recognizable other as a subject of difference that is almost the same but not quite. Becoming a subject of difference, Indians constructed parity with the colonizer and reinforced and legitimated their struggle to displace the colonizer.

2. Construction of the Primacy of Nation

The idea of nation emerged as a powerful historical idea in the West. There is a constitutive liminal dimension to the idea of a nation. Among other things, this liminal side includes its mobilising power and teleology of progress. This gives us an impression that a nation emerges out of an immemorial past and is marching towards a limitless future. Nations emerged as a representation of cultural life as well as a disciplining practice. As a disciplining practice, it has performative power. The nation calls its citizens into being. This was chiefly achieved through homogenization of culture. Such a social organization is viewed as progress although cultural diversity has to often give way to what maybe called a monoculture. The paradox is that such a mono-culturing is never possible as the local cultural forms may manifest resemblances but not identities. It is in this gaps that are either blurred or opened up that cultural as well as political authority is negotiated. Although Enerst Renan places the origin of a nation into the mythical moorings of the Germanic tribes,[3] we are

3 http://ucparis.fr/files/9313/6549/9943/What_is_a_Nation.pdf accessed on 30/08/2019.

more familiar with the idea that modern nations as we know them today are products of the treaty of Westphalia.[4] Late colonialism was the springtime for the colonies to embrace idealism of a nation and become the other of the colonizer by taking his position of power. Indian nationalism also followed this trajectory as it built it's on the colonial difference.

3. Constructing the Primacy of Text

West is a tradition of the Book. This means it is chiefly a textual tradition. Bible was central to the West. This may be a reason why visibility emerged as an important cultural technology of power in the West. The colonial project was entirely based on this visibilization of difference between the colonizer and the colonized. One can trace that textual practices are central to the construction of colonial difference. The colonizers used textual practices to gather, classify and codify knowledge systems that they found in the colonies.[5] They employed the modalities of writing like the writing of histories, grammars of the vernacular languages, recording of birth, deaths and marriages, surveying of land and people, introducing of print technology, etc. This manifests that textual practices were central to the building of the colonial empire. Textual practices have emerged as powerful technologies of power and have become part of the bureaucracy of a modern nation state. We can see that textual primacy is appropriated in post-colonial societies in several ways. In India, they are also employed to the field of religion by the local elites. Where orality was sacred, written text has steadily come to occupy its space. The Indian tradition of the upper caste always regarded that which is heard, smrti as the highest revelation. But in the encounter with the colonizers, local elites began to accept the written text as having the authority of revelation. The tradition which regarded Vedas as authorless took up a written text, the revered Bhagvad Gita as the holy book for the Hindus in the 19th century. This is how the form of the Holy Book of the West informed the choice as well as kind of text to match the Bible and Koran. We have also witnessed conflicts over plural Ramayanas and arrived at an absolutization and singularization of one text.

4. Constructing of Primacy of Religion

If anything is so widespread and appears universal to humanity, it is religion. There is a rich diversity of beliefs, rituals and practices among religions. Scholars like Jonathan Zittel Smith teach that religion is an academic

4 https://courses.lumenlearning.com/boundless-worldhistory/chapter/nation-states-and-sovereignty/accessed on 30/08/2019.

5 Bernand S. Cohn, *Colonialism and Its Forms of Knowledge: The British In India* (New Delhi: Oxford University Press, 2002),3-5.

invention and has no independent study apart from the academy.[6] He teaches that the phenomenon of religion is a second order reflection and a construct of comparison. Religion as a notion developed in the context of Abrahmic religions. There were other sacred formations besides these religions of one God, one prophet and one book. They were shamanic in nature but they were also assimilated as religions. Religion, thus, is not a universal given. Several anthropologists think that religion is not a human universal. The idea that religion is a human universal has more to do with western culture than human culture.[7] One might trace a steady semiticization of Hinduism in our country. Several scholars think that Hinduism of today became organised in the image and likeness of the Semitic religions in the 19th century under British colonizers. Before that, it appears that caste was the most important identity marker of our people than religions. It said that with the archival power of the British, caste became rigid and fixated in India.[8] Hinduism that was a geographical ascription steadily becomes a term that describes their faith acceptable to the rest of India in the 20th century. Hinduism does not have one central all presiding deity and one prophet yet it is steadily appropriated into the categories of Semitic religions.

5. Nations of our Minds

Benedict Anderson taught that a nation is an imagined community. This meant that nations are not products of race, religion and language. Nations everywhere are imagined into existence. This has happened not by mere mimesis. It is not identity but difference with its colonial other that led to the construction of nationalisms in Asia and Africa where nationalism arose as a political battle with the imperial other who was the colonizer.

6. Nation and Nationalism

Several thinkers like J. J. Roseau teach that Nations are a product of natural destinies of Humans. Nations are no accidents in history.[9] Marxist and liberal-rationalist take up a constructivist position when they say that nations arose out of the intersection of politics, technology and social transformations that provided impetus to universal human urge for liberty and progress.[10] Benedict

---

6 https://aeon.co/ideas/is-religion-a-universal-in-human-culture-or-an-academic-invention accessed on 30/08/2019.

7 See S. N. Balagangadhara, '*The Heathens in their Blindness...' Asia, the West and the Dynamic of Religion* (New York: Brill, 1994), 1.

8 Nicholas Dirks, *The Castes of the Mind: Colonization and the Making of Modern India* (Princeton: Princeton University Press, 2001).

9 See S. P. UdayaKumar, '*Presenting' Past*, 18.

10 *Ibid.*

Anderson views nations as imagined societies.[11] He asserts that nationality, nation-ness and nationalism are cultural artifacts developed to gain and maintain power. Just like the Monarch legitimated its rule through divine election, nations seek to naturalise their power domain over the people through invented traditions. Eric Hobsbawn teaches that communities invent traditions to legitimate their identities as nations.[12] Anthony Smith rejects theories of imagination and invention and asserts that role of the elite/ intelligentsia is far more circumscribed.[13] Thus, nations are constructed from above through a strong binding narrative. These narratives interpellate the people to become subject by embracing a collective identity. Bruce Lincoln teaches that nation is constructed on the basis of sentiments, internal affinity and external estrangement.[14]

7. Indian Nationalism(s)

There are several Indian nationalism(s). They are not merely born out of a response of Europeanization. They did not just arise vis-à-vis inner struggles due to historical and political situation in the region. They rather arose in the contestation of the British Raj in Indian and borrowed models or forms from Europe but dressed them in Indian clothing. M N Roy thus, for instance, compares the Indian National Congress to orthodox nationalism of the revivalist as he finds its social radicalism inadequate. He thinks that the nationalist tried to dress the backwardness of India in the glorious garb of its ancient spiritual civilization.[15] The Congress largely attempted a nationalism that would assist in building the nation that is largely inclusive though one could trace moderates and extremists that leaned to what is thought to be orthodox nationalism amidst its followers.[16] Bal Gangadhar Tilak took the position of an extremist and promoted orthodox nationalism and thought that it was an integral nationalism.[17] His followers like Pal and Ghose thought of independence as spiritual uplift rather than political progress.[18] Nehru and Gandhi brought more economic and social content to nationalism. They tied to transform India into an industrialised, secular and liberal democracy.[19] Alongside of several nationalism(s) that evolved in the congress the Muslim nationalism developed

11 Ibid.

12 Ibid.

13 Ibid, 18-19

14 Ibid, 20.

15 Ibid, 22.

16 Ibid.

17 Ibid.

18 Ibid, 23.

19 Ibid, 24-25.

by leaders like Syed Amed Khan, Muhammad Ali Jinnah and Muhammad Ali.[20] They started as nationalists but ended as communal. Being afraid of Hindu domination, Jinnah is said to have developed his two-nation theory.

8. Hindutva Nationalism

The concept of Hindutva was articulated by Vinayak Damodar Sarvarkar.[21] He thought that everyone who had ancestral roots in India is a Hindu and That they all constituted a nation. Hindutva vision of the future lies in the past. It constructs a history and presents a loss that missionizes the Hindus to recover. Appropriating the religiosity of the people, Hindutva forces have elevated the nation to the status of a Goddess and led its worship. Nation, thus become a divine mother, Bharat Mata. Following the models from the Semitic religions, Hindutva ideologies counter posed Ram and Krishna to the Prophet and Jesus. Locations like Ayodhya and Mathura became the exact places where the new heroes of Hindutva were thought to be born. Popular epics like Ramayana and Mahabarata became the preferred texts than other sacred scriptures. The Hindutva Ideology was elaborated by Golwalkar. Like the Jews, he positioned India as the God given land of the Hindus. He taught that Hindus constituted a nation. He strongly believed that nothing can stop the divine destiny of the Hindu Nation / Rashtra. Thus, he successfully converted Hindutvas into a political theology with a triumphant eschatology. He presents five markers Hindu Nation as geography, race, religion, culture and language which are Hindustan, Hindu race, Hindu religion, Hindu culture, Hindu language.

9. Ram(s) of our Minds

The controversy over the number Ramayanas has seen violent resistance. Which of these Ramayanas get acceptance is obviously a matter of the one that enjoys hegemony. Lord Ram has inspired Indians in several ways. The story of Ram was already embedded in the consciousness of our people. Its impact on the minds of our masses is profound. Hence, Mahatma Gandhi made use of its presence to communicate with the people during the freedom struggle. The Hindutva ideologues presented Lord Ram as a warrior who will inspire to build an aggressive Hinduism that will annihilate Muslims/ minorities their demonized other.

---

20 Ibid, 26-28.

21 http://savarkar.org/en/encyc/2017/5/23/2_12_12_04_essentials_of_hindutva.v001.pdf_1.pdf accessed on 16/09/2019.

10. Ramayana and Ramayanas

There are many Ramayana traditions in South Asia. They are Hindu as well as Buddhist[22] and Jaina appropriation of the story of Ram. They varied as well as contradictory. What we notice is that the Hindu versions are privileged and the rest are largely marginalised. There is a clear politics over a plural tradition of the Ramayana as certain versions have become canonical while others are almost regarded as heretical. The very existence of the plural tradition of the story of Ramayana manifests the openness and democratic character of environment in which they emerged. Some scholars see them as counter Ramayanas because they do not belong to one moment of history but each has its own history and lies embedded in the values and concerns of the communities that embraced them. Indeed the person and the event of Lord Ram became a prism through which people interpreted the events of their lives. The tendency to mono-culture the Ramayanas is chiefly political and theological[23] and exhibits upper caste hegemony and enlightenment tendencies from the West. The singularization of the story of Rama does not recognize the tremendous impact that the event of Ram had on the people across south Asia and becomes an impoverishment and injustice to Lord Ram. Unfortunately, this impoverishment seems to be inflicted by those very forces who convert the noble name of Lord Ram into political capital.

11. Ramayana of the Television

The homogenisation of Ramayana got impetus with the telecasting of the story of Rama as a serial on national television in 1987. Observers estimate that about eighty million witnessed the re-enactment of Ramayana on the television. It captured the middle-class population of our country. The producer, Ramanand Sagar described it as a Ramyana written with a cambera.[24] The unique event emboldened the Hindutva brigade and only a single version of the story of Ram that of Tulsidas steadily begun to be regarded as canonical. This singualtization of Ramayana is used to build Hindu supramists view of India. The televised Ramayana captured the imagination of most people of India.

22 It is said that the Buddhist version of Ramayana is the earliest known version of Ramanyana. It is called Dasaratha Jataka. Dasratha is Ram's faather and Sita is his sister. Thier father Dasratha does not banish them but sends them away to protect them from their jealous step-mother. There is no mention of Laksman and even Ravana and his Lanka . see https://www.dailyo.in/variety/ram-mandir-ram-janmbhoomi-ayodhya-ramayana-bjp-rss-hindutva/story/1/23549.html accessed on 16/09/2019.

23 The theologization of Ramayana is a historical process that began in the Srivaisnava community of South India, 1250 to 1600. The Srivaisnavas, was the first religious order to worship the hero of the epic Ramayana. See Ajoy K. Rao, *The Theologization of Ramayana in South India, 1250-1600* (Chicago: Chicago University, 2006), 1.

24 See S. P. UdayaKumar, '*Presenting*' *Past*, 64.

This has steadily led to the closure of it's the heteroglossic character as well as its multiple tellings began to look illegitimate. Today there is a censoring of the Ramayanas to the extent that the voices of its plural versions are muzzled and silenced. This mono-culturing of the story of Lord Ram reinforces the Hindutva imagination of India. It has led to the consolidation of Hindu Identity formation and has emerged as a political reference point for right-wing politics. But there has been resistance to the monoframing of Ramayana among several scholars. They refuse to accept the centrality of Valmiki and Tulsidas tellings of Ramayana to the event of Lord Ram.

12. Ramayana of Hindutva

Ramayana of the Hindutva forces has acquired the power and force of a myth. Myth in Barthian[25] sense stands for an ideological narrative that is fictive but not quite a lie which naturalizes the power action of a particular group at the expense of another. This myth is successfully historisized and history is mythologized by the Hindutva forces. Lord Ram has been the primary deity of Sangh Parivar. Even Vedic gods are forgotten of in favour of Lord Ram. No other God in India has been made political relevant as Lord Ram. The quest for a grand Ram temple and its struggle with Babri Masjid in Ayodhya has put Lord Ram firmly on the political map of our country. This has almost Ramified our society. It led to the militarization of Hinduism and Hinduization of politics. This, in turn, resulted into the demolition of the Babri Masjid in an effort to re-claimed the supposed birthplace of Lord Ram. To Hindutva forces, Ram then emerged as an Icon and politics become enactment of Ramraj. The politics of Ramraj began to provide a cover of righteousness to the political actors as well as lead the Rambakts to daw the Laksman Rekha between them and others who then are demonised and fought to the point of annihilation.

13. Hinduism(s) of our Minds

The word Hindu has been was a geographical ascription used by the Arabs to name people who live across the river Indus. Later with the Islamic rulers, the term Hindu was used to offer the status of being subjects of their administration. It was a catch all term that caught into its semantics the large motley masses that were plural and diverse. With the coming of the British colonizers, birth, death and marriage records of their subject began in India. It was in the context of this recording exercise that subjects other than Muslims, Christians, Parsis, and Jews were all classified as Hindus. It was a matter of nomenclature but later under Indian Renaissance and reformist leaders this term steadily was

25 See Roland Barthes, *Mythologies*, Trans., Annete Lavers (New York: the Noonday press, 1991).

assimilated as self Identity and Santana dharma and its later evolution began to be viewed as Hinduism in hindsight.

14. Hinduism in Hindsight

The Sanatana Dharma is Hinduism only through a hermeneutics of hindsight.[26] The horizon of Hinduism becomes the prism through which the entire evolution of Sanatana Dharma is viewed. It does not mean that what started as Sanatana Dharma remains frozen only to be named as Hindu in hindsight. Sanatana Dharma was dynamic and not passive. Its entire journey is appropriated as Hinduism post 19th century. In fact, Hinduism has become a master signifier that captures the entire history of Sanatana Dharma. These evolutionary changes that occurred into it are imperceptible and lead to the formation of Hinduism which then becomes a totalising gaze through which its entire journey is appropriated. Scholars teach that it was in the nineteen century that a single notion of religion was constructed by the orientalists based upon a Judaeo-Christian understanding of what might constitute a religion. But this is just one side of the story that simply marks the native as passive and has no contribution to the evolution of Hinduism. Other scholars teach that the Hindu nationalist adopted it to push for their swaraj in response to British imperial rule over India.

15. Making of Hinduism as the Religion

The word Hindu bore no rebalance to the diverse religious belief and practice in India until the nineteenth century. The term Hindu is a Persian variant of the Sanskrit Sindhu which referred to the Indus River.[27] The Arabic Al-Hind was a term that denoted a geographical area.[28] The term does not acquire any religious connotation at that time. Even when the locals used it, they used it to assert their native character until the nineteenth century. We can even trace it alongside other religious terms like Hindoo Christians or Hindoo Muslims in the eighteenth century. Richard King teaches that the term Hinduism as religion firs came into use among the westerns in the 18th century. Earlier the westerners called the followers of non-abrahmic religions as heathens/ gentoos.[29] By the nineteenth century, the code of the Gentoos laws was replaced by the religion of the Hindoos.[30] It is only in the nineteenth century Hinduism was viewed as a

26 The term Hinduism was first used by Charles Grant in 1787. See Will Sweetman, Mapping Hinduism: Hinduism and the study of Indian Religions 1600-1776 (Verlag der Frankeschen Sfitungen Zu Halle: 2003), 56.

27 Richard King, "Orientalism and the Modern Myth of 'Hinduism', *Numen* , Vol. 46, No. 2, 162.

28 Ibid.

29 Ibid., 164.

30 Ibid., 165.

religion both in India and the west. The Indian religious thinkers and reformist embraced the term Hinduism and began to revive the Vedic and Upanisadic religion and steadily Brahminical texts and beliefs came to be thought to be foundational essence of Hinduism.[31] This why Hinduism has to be viewed both as a complex oriental and brahminical construct. Hinduism became a new espisteme and began to be viewed as the corrupt version of its former self.

16. Hinduism of Hindutva

Hinduism is a shift in espiteme[32] that happened to India. But it has not been viewed with Foucaultian eyes. The discontinuities from the golden Vedic era were seen as degradation of its pristine purity and it was therefore thought to be indeed of reformation. This gap between the ideal and the real of Hinduism was naturalized and normalised since we did not notice its development as a shift in episteme. The tripartite periodization of the History of India by James Mill[33] introduced impression that Hinduism was a single religion with Vedic origins which in the medieval period fell into decay and with the arrival of the West; it has taken the path of renewal. The gap between the original and fallen Hinduism was attempted to be filled by the growing Hindu reform movements of the nineteenth century. This loss and recovery impetus naturally among other things placed the blame on the Muslims. Hinduism which was formed on the same apriori assumption of religious unity of the Abrahmic religions undergoes further mimesis through Hindutva that sees Hinduism as having its holy land, fatherland. Thus, Hindutva creatively as well as craftily constructs a religious and cultural nationalism. With the coming of the Hindu Nation, Hindutva promises also restore Hinduism to restore its pristine glory. Thus, somehow Hindutva constructs an anxious present and promises a future of the past.

Conclusion

Hindutva has become the measure of everything that is regarded as Indian. Hindutva is reproducing the culture technology of power employed by the colonizers. Colonialism was among other things was a cultural project of control and we can notice that Hindutva continues this imperial legacy in several ways. The gaps introduced by colonial difference manufactured by the colonizer triggered a complex process of mimesis that borrowed the form(s) from the West and enfleshed them with matter that is distinct from the upper castes. This complex mimesis has led to the production of Caste, Hinduism

---

31 Ibid ., 170-172.

32 https://pdfs.semanticscholar.org/24f9/e80459e34355d3b5f5b83d40652230559b9e.pdf accessed on 16/09/2019.

33 https://www.outlookindia.com/magazine/story/the-colonial-roots-of-hindutva-nationalism/297420 accessed on 16/09/2019.

and HIndutva as we know them today. Unfortunately, Hindutva haunts all Indians. It has become siren that raises the alarm that a Hindu is not Hindu enough and challenges the Hindus to become sankari Hindus. The same logic marks the other minorities as not Indian enough. The purity/ pollution principle of casteism is embodied into Hindutva and it afflicts all Indians in different degree. The colonial difference of the colonizer and the colonized has become a Hindutva induced difference and its power is exercised over all Indians.

EPILOGUE

George Karuvelil:
A Philosopher, Brother and Friend

John Karuvelil SJ

Introduction

"Philosophy is written in this grand book, the universe, which stands continually open to our gaze. But the book cannot be understood unless one first learns to comprehend the language and read the letters in which it is composed," says Galileo Galilei. When I think of George, what comes to my mind first is this that he is one who constantly attempted and continues to attempt to comprehend the language of philosophy that is written in this grand book of the universe. I have no doubt and do not hesitate to say that he is one who has understood it to some extent and is a constant seeker to understand the real schema of this great book the author has in mind. It is true that he is my brother and a good friend too to me, yet what distinguishes him from my other brothers and friends is this particular strand of the deep thinker. This feeling and understanding of mine was reinforced in me recently, when one of my professors in the campus, Prof. Dr. Scaria Kuthirakattel, S.V.D., a scripture scholar and theologian, who knows George well said, "He is always thinking. He is a natural philosopher." I had to just nod and say 'yes'. Of course, all who know him would say that he is not just a philosopher but a good theologian too. This is very clear from his writings and publications. I don't need to write about the depth and breadth of his knowledge in the field of Western as well as Eastern philosophies, in theology, science and religions, etc. His publications in many national and international journals, like *Theological Studies*, *Zygon: Journal of Religion and Science*, *Heythrop Journal*, *Forum Philosophicum*, *Journal of Indian Council of Philosophical Research* (*JICPR*), *Vidyajyoti Journal of Theological Reflection*, etc. amply demonstrate this. He is an original thinker. His forth-coming book which,

I think, would be a real path-breaking one in the field of Philosophy and Fundamental Theology, and would establish his credentials beyond doubt.

In this short write-up I do not think, I need to concentrate on his intellectual and academic acumen. I am sure that there will be others who write on these aspects and, therefore, I shall not elaborate anything on them, unless they are related to some of the areas that I share about him at a personal level. What I would like to talk about here is about the person of George whom I have encountered as a brother, a Jesuit companion and also a good friend.

My Brother George

In fact, I knew little of George until I reached the end of my high school. Born in 1954 (September 21), almost ten years older to me, he had left home to become a Jesuit missionary in the province of Patna (Bihar) in July 1971 after his matriculation, when I was studying in the primary school, in the third standard. The only contact he had with the family those day was an Inland letter once in two or three months. When the family received it, it was read out to the whole family when the whole family came together (the family came together every evening for family prayers followed by supper) for everyone's hearing. The responsibility of responding to him was that of my eldest brother, older to George which too was read out to the whole family, to everyone's hearing, so that he did not miss any important piece of news from home. He came home those days once in three years or so, and in those visits what I remember is only the black and white family and other photos he would take and the printed copies he would show us.

Towards the end of my High School studies onwards, I remember his province sending us their quasi-newsletter in Malayalam which was primarily meant for vocation promotion from Kerala (although the original English version of it was meant for the benefactors, especially in the US, who supported the province). Those newsletters were very inspiring and eye-openers to persons like me (from completely different socio-religious, cultural and geographical backgrounds), especially with regard to the missionary works that were going on North India, especially among the Tribals (Adivasis), Scheduled Castes and other non-Christian groups. They were really eye-openers, because so far my understanding, especially of Tribals, was based on those Tribals of Idukki district, in the High Ranges and surrounding areas, of Kerala. My understanding was that they were people who lived far away from any civilization and, naturally, from education and who would hardly come out in the open, especially to towns and cities. When I read that these people in North India, especially in Bihar (of those days which is now Bihar and Jharkhand), were being educated and many of them get converted to Christianity, I was highly impressed. That was something beyond my imagination as a teenager from Kerala that they could be educated and even could become Christians. To confirm what I have been reading in these newsletters, at the end of my High School exams (Matriculation), during the summer holidays, George brought home on vacation two of his Tribal Jesuit companions who stayed at home for a few days. I used to accompany them, visiting places in and around our village and had ample time to converse with them in my broken English of those days. These were memorable days of interaction and learning.

I continued to read these newsletters till I finished my Pre-Degree course and got inspired by the missionary works described in them. (Of course, this is the beginning of my vocation story too.) I found the life of a missionary challenging and inspiring. Therefore, when I finished my pre-degree course, I decided to join the Jesuits to become a missionary in North India, primarily with the intention of educating the Tribals and if possible to bring them to my Christian faith. When I decided to join the Jesuits, naturally, I consulted George who recommended to me three provinces - Patna, Jamshedpur and Gujarat, of which I chose Jamshedpur.

From the time of my coming to North India we had more opportunities to interact with each other. My first year in North India was in Daltonganj for my Pre-Novitiate programme where for the first time I fell ill seriously with jaundice and was hospitalized. George came to meet me as soon as I returned from the hospital to the Pre-Novitiate, and after seeing me the first thing he noticed was a drastic change in me, in my expressions or responses in general. They were no more natural and spontaneous as he always used to see in me when I was at home. He was right in noticing that, because my life outlook and approaches, especially my spontaneous, jovial and free nature, had changed a little because of some initial interactions with my Pre-Novitiate director. George was not happy with that change and wanted me to keep my original dispositions and approaches to life. He was to a large extent responsible for my getting back to my original self of spontaneity and joviality or sociability.

Later on in the Novitiate he was a constant support to me in the face of continuous malarial attacks that had wrecked my health to a large extent. However, it was in Juniorate that we had the opportunity to associate with each other more closely. I was fortunate to have done my Juniorate in Xavier Teachers' Training Institute (XTTI) in Digha Ghat, Patna, while George himself was doing his Theological studies then at the Regional Theological Centre (RTC) at Danapur, a few kilometers away from XTTI. We had opportunities to come together, even for basketball matches between XTTI and RTC where we would play against each other. We also had the opportunity to go visiting places. One of those memorable journeys was when another brother of ours, older to me and just younger to George, Bro. Bastin Karuvelil, M.M.B., came visiting us. A beautiful and memorable experience we had there was that on our way to the railway station to send off Bastin, at George's initiative, we went into bar and restaurant to have our supper, a first experience for all three of us.

As times passed by our family ties became stronger. Of course, each one of the nine siblings played his or her role, but George as one of the seniors, the second in line and as a Jesuit and as a priest played a leading role in our coming together and in our sharings, outings, etc. that brought the family closer, not just as a family for which, naturally, parents played the biggest role, but as a close-knit 'family-friends' who are equals. In the decision making processes in the family too he played a leading role.

A Good Jesuit

George's commitment to his vocation to religious life as a Jesuit, in a very special way to the Society's intellectual tradition has not only made me wonder many times, but has inspired me. I often thought that he is one of those few people who still hold on to this tradition of the Society by mastering not only his own area of specialization, but a variety of subjects. He can speak with confidence and authority whether on Western Philosophy or Eastern Philosophy, whether on Science and Religion or Fundamental Theology, whether on political issues or on general knowledge. He keeps his interest varied and his insatiable interest in reading helps him to keep himself updated. For many people like me reading books lying on bed is like taking a sleeping pill to sleep, but often one can find a couple of books on his bed, all because of his habit of reading lying on bed, a quality I appreciated in him with envy.

His refusal to tread the beaten path is obvious in the courses he teaches and in the writings he has published. This is something his students have always appreciated in him, very notably the students who are doing Masters in Philosophy. It takes a person like Gerald O' Collins, S. J., the Australian theologian who was teaching in Gregorian University, Rome, to really recognize the originality in his thinking and writing. It only shows George's commitment to the *MAGIS*, the Ignatian motto, his refusal to stay with the ordinary and the minimum needed.

George is a very generous person. I am sure, the formation he received at home of committed, hard-working and devout parents with a large family and very modest means, and yet very generous and concerned about the needs of the less privileged around, helped him to imbibe many of those qualities which made him a good Jesuit with many of those qualities ingrained in him. While spending little on himself, I have found him to be very generous with those in need. His concern for the underprivileged has been very obvious even in the selection of his ministry throughout, especially visiting the sick and the disabled at the homes for destitutes, sick and orphanages run by the sisters of the Missionaries of Charity (MC) (founded by Mother Theresa), his association with poor co-workers, and so on. I have been very specifically noticing this from his days in RTC, Patna, where besides working with the Musahar community, the lowest among Dalits (Musahar, literally means rat eating people) in empowering them, he also used to visit the leprosariums and old-age homes run by the MC sisters. This, I think, is perfectly in tune with St. Ignatius asking the Jesuits at the Council of Trent (Diego Laínez, Alfonso Salmerón, and Pierre Favre), to find time also to teach catechism to children while the Council was still on.

An Authentic Human

One cannot think of George anything but as an authentic person, who is sincere to his commitments. He does not compromise on values and once he is convinced as to what is to be done, nothing detracts him from pursuing that goal. His priorities are clear to him. Even oppositions from all corners may not change him from his commitment. Of course, one may speak of a certain amount of rigidity in his approach, but I attribute it to his convictions in life and commitment to them which he thinks is the way to achieve the ultimate good. Of course, I need to acknowledge that this has got him a few people on the wrong side, which although he is not happy about, considers it a price that he has to pay for standing for certain values. He understands from experiences that to stand by convictions is costly. I am happy and thank God that he is able to withstand such pressures.

Another aspect of him is his genuine concern for others. I have experienced this at various times. He has been generous with his time, energy and other resources, again, I think, a quality he has learned from the parents and family. I remember a student of him telling me once that he once went to George and told him that he has not been able to understand what he has been teaching in the previous classes. The very next day he came to the class and revised the whole topics right from the beginning and made sure that the students understood what he was teaching before he proceeded.

At various occasions he has manifested his willingness even to go out of his way to help those in need, including people who are unknown to him but are recommended by others, even by requesting others to contribute if he cannot muster resources himself. Most of the times, it is done without letting anyone other than those who are involved know of it - literally not letting the right-hand know what the left is doing.

Another quality in him that I should not forget is his straightforwardness. Naturally, he would make a poor politician according to the present standards of politician. He speaks plain and without going roundabout. Of course, this is not considered one of the qualities needed for or appreciated in an effective leader. Political astuteness is considered an important quality among leaders now. It is hard to find this in George. He believes in leading by life.

A Good Friend

In general, among the siblings, he is considered the most introvert of all. Often he comes across as someone who spends most of his time with books and his computer – reading or writing. Even when we get together at home for holidays, while most of the other siblings, especially the religious in the family (four more besides him), get busy with all kinds of activities in or outside the house, or roaming around, he would be often found in the house with his books or computer. The general impression is that he has very few friends too. However, interacting with him one can immediately understand that this is not the case. I remember last summer (April-May 2019) while we were at home for holidays, one of his friends from their High School days, comes home with almost a dozen books. They were meeting for the first time after their High School days, that is, nearly 50 years. The two had developed a strong friendship then by sharing books taken out from the public library in the town. That friend of him had heard from someone that George had come home. And he comes home to visit George to revive their friendship, and he gifted George the books, something which very pleasantly surprised me.

Close association with George will make one realize that he is a very affectionate person and is very much committed to friends. He has a good circle of friends and is very much committed to them. Although my brother, I have been able to relate with him as a good friend, and today I would like to say that over and above being a brother we are good friends too. Although our interests and hobbies differ in more ways than one, we still can share a common ground in many areas. I found him a very supportive friend on whom I can rely on whenever needed. We have reached a stage where we have the freedom to share even the funny side of our lives and have a good laugh at ourselves. We share much, not only the nitty-gritties of life, our dreams and goals, but also a variety of subjects that affect our life as well as public life these days. We have our differences at times and we agree to disagree sometimes on issues, but that do not come on the way of our being open to share and hear the other side of the story from the other person. His support to me is irreplaceable, especially when it comes to clarifying concepts and correcting my expressions when I write. Today, I feel proud to have George, not just only as my brother, but also as a Jesuit companion and a good friend. It was God's special favour that even as Jesuits and, that too from two different provinces, we could be in the same place working in the same institution and, therefore, also as colleagues and companions on the same mission of the Lord. Now as he leaves the campus post-retirement, I wish him God's choicest blessings on all his endeavours. God bless!

Résumé and Publications of Dr. George Karuvelil

Date of birth: 21-09-1954

Joined the Jesuits: 01-07-1975

Studies:

1979-81: B. A. (Bachelor of Arts, University of Ranchi, Bihar).

1981-83: B. Ph. (Bachelor of Philosophy, Jnana-Deepa Vidyapeeth, Pune)

1984-86: M. A. (Master of Arts in Philosophy, University of Poona, Pune)

1986-89: B. Th. (Bachelor of Theology, Vidyajyoti College, Delhi)

1990-92: M. Phil. (Master of Philosophy, University of Delhi, Delhi)

1992-96: Ph. D. (University of Delhi, Delhi) on 'The Possibility of Religious Knowledge'.

Teaching:

1986: Jnana Deepa Vidyapeeth (JDV), Pune: taught courses in **Philosophy of Science, Symbolic Logic**

1991-93: JDV, Pune, taught **Religious Language** as a Visiting Staff.

1996—: Faculty of Philosophy, Jnana Deepa Vidyapeeth (JDV), Pune (resident). Besides regular courses on **Epistemology and Hermeneutics**, **Religious Language**, taught courses on **Philosophical Roots of Modern Atheism**, **Religious Experience**, **Metaphysics and God**, **Religious Pluralism**, **Faith and Reason**.

2002—: Jeevalaya Institute of Philosophy, Bangalore (visiting)

2008, 2014-16: Dharmaram Vidyakshetram, Bangalore (visiting)

Academic Administration: Served Jnana-Deepa Vidyapeeth (JDV) in various capacities:

Dean, Faculty of Philosophy (2006-09)

Head, Department of Systematic Philosophy, (2005-2006)

Co-ordinator, M.Ph. Program (1999-2004)

Member, Executive Committee (2001-09; 2012-)
Member, Doctoral Committee (2006-09)
Member, Jnana-Deepa Trust (1998-2008).

Honors and Fellowships:

1992-95: Junior Research Fellow, Indian Council of Philosophical Research.

1991—: Member, *Association of Christian Philosophers of India* (ACPI)

2000-01: Lonergan Fellow, Lonergan Centre, Boston College, USA.

2003-09: Elected Member, Executive Committee of the *Association of Christian Philosophers of India.*

2009-10: International Visiting Fellow, Woodstock Theological Center, Georgetown University, Washington D.C., U.S.A.

2011: Raised to the rank of professor by the Congregation for Catholic Education

2013—16: Chief Editor, *Jnanadeepa: Pune Journal of Religious Studies*

2015-16: Recipient of a Research Grant from the Indian Council of Philosophical Research for a project titled: "Realism and Relativism: Towards an Epistemology for the Postmodern World"

2017 —: member of the Scientific Board of *Gregorianum*

Publications:

Romancing the Sacred? Towards an Indian Christian Philosophy of Religion (Bangalore: Asian Trading Corporation, 2007). This is an edited volume of papers in the Philosophy of Religion.

Post-Hermeneutic Epistemology (New Delhi: Indira Gandhi National Open University, 2011). A series of lessons meant for the last part of the Course in Epistemology for the M.A. (Philosophy). It is my first attempt to look beyond the 'death of epistemology' movement. For details, see 11-14 below.

Faith, Reason, and Culture: An Essay in Fundamental Theology (Palgrave Macmillan, forthcoming)

Articles (discipline-wise):

A. Epistemology (General):

"Epistemic Justification and the Possibility of Empirical Evidence," *Journal of Indian Council of Philosophical Research (JICPR)*, XII (1994): 29-48.

"Re-Visioning Epistemology," *JICPR*, XVII (1999): 1-27.

"What Happened to Human Longings? A Reading of the History of Western Epistemology," *Disputatio philosophica: International Journal on Philosophy and Religion*, 3 (2001): 31-53.

"Reflective Equilibrium," in Johnson Puthenpurackal (ed.), *Philosophical Methods: Through the Prevalent to the Relevant*, Bangalore: ATC, 2004: 70-83.

"Thomistic Philosophy of Perception," in Goswami Shyam Manohar and Goswami Sharad (eds.), *Pratyaksha Prama*, Mandvi, Kach: Sri Vallabhacharya Trust, 2007: 232-46.

"Multiculturalism and Postmodernism," in E. P. Mathew (ed.), *Hermeneutics: Multicultural Perspectives*, Chennai: Satya Nilayam Publications, 2009: 87-107.

"Epistemology (Western)," in J. Puthenpurackal (ed.), *ACPI Encyclopedia of Philosophy*, Bangalore: ATC Publications, 2010: 452-58.

"Experience," in J. Puthenpurackal (ed.), *ACPI Encyclopedia of Philosophy*, Bangalore: ATC Publications, 2010: 515-20.

"Popperian Method and Naturalized Epistemology," lesson prepared for the B.A. (Philosophy) program of Indira Gandhi National Open University (IGNOU), 2010: 50-63

"Epistemology: Critical Appraisal and Synthesis," concluding lesson on epistemology prepared for the B.A. (Philosophy) program of Indira Gandhi National Open University (IGNOU), 2010: 46-58.

"Semantic Holism and Radical Interpretation," lesson prepared for the M.A. (Philosophy) program of Indira Gandhi National Open University (IGNOU), 2011: 5-16

"Epistemic Holism and Theory Laden Observations," lesson prepared for the M.A. (Philosophy) program of Indira Gandhi National Open University (IGNOU), 2011: 17-29

"Popperian Method and Naturalized Epistemology," lesson prepared for the M.A. (Philosophy) program of Indira Gandhi National Open University (IGNOU), 2011: 30-41

"Perception Naturalized," lesson prepared for the M.A. (Philosophy) program of Indira Gandhi National Open University (IGNOU), 2011: 42-54.

"Contextual Realism: Feminist Epistemology- 'Out of the Fly bottle'," *Journal of Dharma* 41, (2016): 249-72.

B. Epistemology of Religion

"Knowledge and Religious Consciousness," *Journal of Indian Council of Philosophical Research (JICPR)*, XI (1993): 37-58.

"Flew's Challenge: Logic to Universal Semantics," *The Journal of Religious Studies*, XXV, 1994: 83-112.

"Some Problems in the Epistemology of Religion," Job Kozhamthadom (ed.), in *Interrelations and Interpretation*, (New Delhi: Intercultural Publications, 1997: 109-40.

"Constructing God: A Contemporary Interpretation of Religion" *The Heythrop Journal*, 41 (2000): 25-46.

"Radical Hermeneutics or Pre-hermeneutic Nostalgia? A Critique of John Caputo's Philosophy of Religion," *Jnanadeepa: Pune Journal of Religious Studies*, 5 (2002): 63-80.

"Science-Religion Dialogue: The Cognitive Issues," *Vidyajyoti Journal of Theological Reflection*, 68 (2004): 799-812.

"Rationality of Mysticism: A Methodological Proposal," *Journal of Dharma*, Vol.30, 4 (2005): 423-44.

"Religious Pluralism: A Philosophical Critique," in Johnson Puthenpurackal (ed.), *Pluralism of Pluralism: A Pluralistic Probe into Philosophizing*, Bangalore: ATC, 2006: 207-28.

"Religious Experience and the Problem of Access," in George Karuvelil (ed.), *Romancing the Sacred? Towards an Indian Christian Philosophy of Religion*, Bangalore: ATC, 2007: 215-43.

"Missing the Wood for the Trees: A Critique of Proudfoot's Explanatory Reduction of Religious Experience," *The Heythrop Journal* L (2009): 31-43.

"Mysticism, Language and Truth," *Journal of Dharma* 35 (2010): 259-275.

"Absolutism to Ultimacy: Rhetoric and Reality of Religious 'Pluralism'," *Theological Studies* 73 (2012):55-81.

"Science of Religion and Theology: An Existential Approach," *Zygon: Journal of Religion & Science* 47 (2012):415-437.

"Epistemological Explorations in the Context of Religious Diversity," *Journal of Dharma* 40 (2015): 331-46.

"To Whom Am I Speaking? Communication, Culture, and Fundamental Theology," *Theological Studies* 76 (2015): 675-97.

C. Philosophy, Religion, Theology, and Culture

"Hierarchy, Equality, and Liberation: Some Reflections on Indian Culture," *Jnanadeepa: Pune Journal of Religious Studies*, (1999): 34-53.

"Gandhi on Religion in Public Life," in Kuruvilla Pandikattu (ed.) *Gandhi: the Meaning of the Mahatma for the Millennium*, Washington D.C.: The Council for Research in Values and Philosophy, 2001: 53-79.

"The Irrelevance of Subaltern Studies in India," in George Thadathil (ed.), *Subaltern Perspectives: Philosophizing in the Indian Context*, Bangalore: ATC, 2005: 119-36.

"The Contemporary Ecological Crisis: Tracing its Emergence," *Jnanadeepa: Pune Journal of Religious Studies*, 9 (2006): 5-19.

"Love and God-Talk," *Vidyajyoti Journal of Theological Reflection* 70 (2006): 326-41.

"Metatheology: Mediating Christianity in the Contemporary World," in Philippe Capelle (ed.), *La Filosofia Como Mediacion*, Mexico: COMUICAP and Univeridad Iberoamericana, 2007: 115-21

"Introduction," in George Karuvelil (ed.), *Romancing the Sacred? Towards an Indian Christian Philosophy of Religion*, Bangalore: ATC, 2007: 7-36.

"Religious Life in the Light of Deus Caritas," *Asian Journal for Priests & Religious* 53, (2008): 617-28.

"Transcendence-Immanence: An Essay in the Hermeneutics of Religion and Culture," in Keith D'Souza (ed.), *Culture as a Gift and a Task: Philosophical Reflections in the Indian Context*, Bangalore: ATC, 2008: 150-79.

"Secularism," in J. Puthenpurackal (ed.), *ACPI Encyclopedia of Philosophy*, Bangalore: ATC Publications, 2010: 1266-69.

"Religious Pluralists: What are They Upto?," *Journal of Dharma* 35 (2010): 3-22,

"Religious Experience," lesson written for the B.A. (Philosophy) program of Indira Gandhi National Open University (IGNOU), 2010: 18-29.

"Religious Experience: Reframing the Question," *Forum Philosophicum: International Journal for Philosophy* 16 (2011):139-155.

"The Vision of Fullness in Natural Mysticism," in M. Doss and A. Vonach (eds.), *Human and Cosmic Fullness: A Multidisciplinary Approach*, Innsbruck: iup - Conference Series, 2012: 9-24.

"Introduction to Atheism/A-theism," lesson written for the M.A. (Philosophy) program of Indira Gandhi National Open University (IGNOU), 2012.

"Philosophy and Theology," *Divyadaan: Journal of Philosophy and Education* 24 (2013): 217-238.

"Indian Secularism and Hinduism," *Vidyajyoti Journal of Theological Reflection* 78 (2014): 8-25.

"Christian Faith, Philosophy, and Culture: The Triumphs and Failures of Wisdom," *Jnanadeepa: Pune Journal of Religious Studies* 17 (2014): 101-18.

"Editorial" for the issue of *Jnanadeepa: Pune Journal of Religious Studies* 17 on "Faith, Reason, and Wisdom" (2014): 3-7.

"Afterward" for the issue of *Jnanadeepa: Pune Journal of Religious Studies* 17 on "Faith, Reason, and Wisdom" (2014): 197-200.

"The Mysticism of *Laudato Si*," *Vidyajyoti Journal of Theological Reflection* 79 (2015): 915-24.

"Dharma of Jesus: Exploring Its Philosophical Foundations," *Jnanadeepa: Pune Journal of Religious Studies* 18 (2015): 155-81.

"Mobocracy and Snobocracy: The Twin Temptations of Indian Democracy," in Jose Thayil and Andreas Vonach (eds.) *Democracy in an Age of Globalization*, Innsbruck: iup - Conference Series, 2015: 67-77.

"Philosophy and the Christian Experience," *Revue Roumaine de Philosophie* 60 (2016): 205-19.

"Neo-Gnosticism and Priestly Formation," Chap. 13, in Francis Gonsalves, Arjen Tete and Dinesh Braganza (eds.), *My Way or God's Way? Neo-Gnosticism and Neo-Pelagianism in Interdisciplinary Perspective*, Delhi; Pune: ISPCK; Jnana-Deepa Vidyapeeth, (2018): 214-41.

Contributors

Arun Philip SJ: Arun Philip is a Jesuit belonging to Bombay province. He finished his Licentiate in Philosophy from JDV, Pune. At present, he is pursuing his theological studies at Centre Sèvres, Paris. E-Mail: arunsimonjy@gmail.com

Clement Jesudoss Santhanam SJ: Clement Jesudoss pursues his PhD in the University of Innsbruck, Austria in the field of Social Epistemology. His areas of interest are epistemology, social epistemology, and philosophy of religion. He has his Licentiate in Philosophy from JDV, Pune. E-mail: clementsj@gmail.com

Dolichan Kollareth SJ: Dolichan Kollareth belongs to the Kerala province of the Jesuits. Fr. Kollareth holds Masters Degrees in Psychology and Philosophy and a PhD in Social Psychology. He is currently an assistant Professor of psychology at Jnana-Deepa Vidyapeeth, Pune and a Research Associate Professor at Boston College, USA. He does research in religion, culture, and cognition and has published research articles in international psychology journals. E-Mail: dollychank@gmail.com

Dolreich Pereira: Dolreich Pereira is a priest for Bombay Archdiocese for the last 20 years. At present, he is Dean of Philosophy at St Pius X College, Goregaon - the Archdiocesan Seminary and also Professor of Systematic Theology. Apart from his academic projects, he has been ministering to the French Catholics in Bombay since 2011. E-Mail: dolreichpereira@gmail.com

Doni Raja SJ: Doni Raja is a Jesuit belonging to the Jesuit Madurai Province. He has done his Masters in Philosophy at Jnana Deepa Vidyapeeth, Pune. The author is currently doing his theological studies at Vidyajyoti College, Delhi, and he is staff-recruit for the faculty of philosophy at Jnana Deepa Vidyapeeth. E-Mail: donirajasj@gmail.com

Gerald O'Collins SJ: After receiving a PhD at the University of Cambridge, Gerald O'Collins, SJ, taught theology for 33 years at the Gregorian University (Rome) and is now an adjunct Professor of the University of Divinity (Melbourne) and a research fellow of Australian Catholic University. As well as producing hundreds of articles, he has authored or co-authored 74 published books, including most recently the trilogy from Oxford University Press, Revelation, Inspiration, and Tradition. In early 2020, OUP will publish his The Beauty of Jesus Christ. E-mail: ocollins@unigre.it

Henry D'Almeida SJ: Henry D'Almeida teaches logic, Indian Philosophy, Sanskrit, Pali and Bhagavadgita at Jnana-deepa Vidyapeeth, Pune. He is also a visiting staff at Karnataka Regional Theology Centre, Anekal (Bangalore). His area of interest is logic, Indian Hermeneutics and Philosophy of Language. The Scriptural Hermeneutics of Madhvacharya was the area of his doctoral work. E-Mail: halmeida63@gmail.com

Isaac Parackal OIC: Isaac Parackal is a Professor of Philosophy who holds a doctorate in philosophy from the University of St. Thomas Aquinas in Rome. At Present, he is teaching at Jnana-Deepa Vidyapeeth in the faculty of Philosophy, Pune. He has authored a number of books and articles in philosophy and ecology and other secular subjects. He is a visiting faculty in different seminaries and secular institutions. E-mail: isaacparackal13@gmail.com

John Karuvelil SJ: John Karuvelil is Professor of Moral Theology at Jnana-Deepa Vidyapeeth (JDV) in Pune. He also teaches in other institutions and seminaries, besides taking classes for various lay and religious groups. He has a Licentiate from Alphonsianum, Rome, in Moral Theology and a Doctorate from Boston College (U.S.A) in Theology, and is specialized in Bio-Medical Ethics. His interests include Justice Issues in Health Care, Bio-medical Ethics, Ethics of Biotechnology, Social Teachings of the Church and Fundamental Moral Theology: E-mail: karusj@gmail.com

Jojo Joseph Varakukalayil CST: holds a PhD in Philosophy from Husserl Archives: Center for Phenomenology and Continental Philosophy from Higher Institute of Philosophy at Katholeike University Leuven, Belgium. He had his specialization in Phenomenology and Deconstructive Subjectivity of Emmanuel Levinas and Jacques Derrida. Currently he lectures in Philosophy at various Institutes and Faculties across India and serves as the President of the Little Flower Institute of Philosophy & Religion, Aluva, Kerala. E-mail: varakoocst@gmail.com

Jose Nandhikkara CMI: Jose Nandhikkara is a Professor of Philosophy, Dharmaram Vidya Kshetram and Christ (Deemed to be University), Bangalore, and the Chief Editor of the Journal of Dharma. He was a Visiting Fellow at University of Malaya, Kuala Lumpur; and Visiting Professor, KU University, Leuven; Adjunct Professor, ISM Dhanbad, and International Fellow of KAICIID, Vienna. He is also currently the Regional Director of Globethics.net India. He is a Wittgenstinian scholar who contributes in the fields of Philosophical Anthropology and Comparative Religion and promotes Faiths Seeking Harmony of Life and Fellowship in Religious Experience (FIRE), through visits, workshops, lectures and conferences. E-mail: nandhikkara@dvk.in

Joseph Kaipayil MCBS: Joseph Kaipayil is Professor of Philosophy at Jeevalaya Institute of Philosophy, Bengaluru. His research interests are ontology and metaphysics, Indian philosophy, comparative philosophy, and more particularly the relationalist theory of reality. E-mail: josephkaipayil@gmail.com

Keith D'Souza SJ: Keith D'Souza is Rector of St. Xavier's College, Mumbai. He has degrees in Science (Physics), Theology and Philosophy. His Ph.D. in Philosophy is from Marquette University in Wisconsin, USA, with a specialization in philosophical hermeneutics (Hans Georg Gadamer and Paul Ricoeur). He has edited two books and published around forty-five journal articles in the areas of hermeneutical theory, socio-political philosophy and religious studies. He is Vice President of the Bombay Philosophical Society (Dept. of Philosophy, Mumbai University), and is President of the Association of Christian Philosophers of India (ACPI). He is also on the faculty of a Leadership Programme called Power to Lead. E-mail: keith@jesuits.net

Maxim Pinto: Maxim Pinto is a priest of the Archdiocese of Delhi, ordained in the year 2000. He completed is Masters in Philosophy at Jnana-deepa Vidyapeeth, Pune and his Doctorate in Philosophy at Pontifical University of St. Thomas, Rome. Presently, he is the head of the Department of Philosophy at Holy Trinity Regional Major Seminary, Jalandhar, Punjab and visiting professor at St. Albert's College, Ranchi, Jharkhand. E-mail: maximdelhi@gmail.com

Michael Devin Coonghe IVD: Michael Devin is a Catholic priest from Sri Lanka, belonging to Institute Voluntas Dei, a secular Institute for Consecrated Life. He has received B. Ph and B. Th from the National Seminary of Our Lady of Lanka, Kandy, Sri Lanka which is affiliated to Urbania University, Rome. He has also received PGD in Philosophy from the Peradeniya University, Kandy, Sri Lanka. He has been teaching philosophy at National Seminary, Kandy from 2014-2019. E-Mail: devinivd@yahoo.com

Sathya Balan SJ: Sathya Balan is currently pursuing a Master's Degree in Philosophy at Jnana-Deepa Vidyapeeth, Pune. He is a Jesuit priest belonging to the Chennai Province of the Society of Jesus. He did his theological studies in Centre Sèvres, Jesuit Faculty of Philosophy and Theology, Paris, France. He also holds a Master's Degree in Physics St. Joseph's College, Tiruchirapalli in Tamil Nadu. Email: sathyabalansj@gmail.com

Savio Martires: Savio Martires is a seminarian of the Archdiocese of Goa and Daman. He was a student of philosophy at Jnana Deepa Vidyapeeth between 2012-2014. Currently, he is pursuing a Licentiate degree in Canon Law at the Pontifical Urban University, Rome, having obtained a Bachelors in Theology from the same university in 2018. Email: savio.martires@gmail.com

Subhash Anand: Subhash Anand retired as Professor, Indian Philosophy and Religions, Jnanadeep Vidyapeeth, Pune. Now his main interest is questions arising in the context of ecumenical and inter-religious dialogue. Among his books are Hindutva: A Christian Response (2001), Hindu Inspiration for Christian Reflection: Towards a Hindu-Christian Theology (2004), Major Hindu Celebrations: A Christian Appreciation (2008), A Preface for an Indian Christology (2010), May They All Be One: Towards an Ecumenical Theology of the Church (2012), The Divine Feminine: Towards A Biblical Gynaecology (2015), Postmodern Sage Premodern Wisdom: Some Gandhian Insights (2019). He has edited Wald-Bulcke Bible-Bhāṣya (Hindi, 2018), a work involving seventy scholars. He has published research articles in both national and international journals. Email: 43subhash@gmail.com

Thomas Kalary MSFS: Thomas Kalary obtained his PhD from Albert-Ludwig's University, Freiburg, Germany with a specialization on Martin Heidegger's philosophy. Besides having translated some of the key works of Heidegger into English, he has also authored a book in German and has published more than 30 scholarly articles in international journals. He is a professor at Suvidya College, Bangalore, and a visiting faculty at JDV, Pune and St. Joseph's Pontifical Seminary, Aluva. He is also an associate editor of Heidegger Studies, published from Germany. E-mail: kalary@gmail.com

Thomas Karimundackal SJ: Thomas Karimundackal teaches Old Testament at the Faculty of Theology, Jnana-Deepa Vidyapeeth, Pune, and currently serves as the head of the department of Scripture Studies, and coordinator of the Masters Programme in Biblical Studies at JDV. He is on the staff of Papal Seminary, Pune and involved in the laity formation in various dioceses in India. He has presented research papers in many national and international conferences, and published books, and articles in national and international Journals as well as in edited books. He is also a visiting faculty in many seminaries and colleges in India and abroad. E-mail: tomksj@gmail.com

V. Sebastian SJ: presently teaches philosophy and theology at Jnana-Deepa Vidyapeeth, Pune. He did his Post Graduate studies at the University of Louvain, Belgium and Doctoral studies at the Mysore University. He has published articles in books and journals and presented research papers in various universities. Apart from philosophy, his research interest areas include Sociology, Anthropology, Politics and history. E-mail: vvsaby@gmail.com

Victor Ferrao: Victor Ferrao is the Dean of Philosophy at Rachol Seminary, coordinator of Special study Centre of IGNOU, and columnist in the newspapers. He has Phd in Philosophy of Science, written six books and has several research papers in peer reviewed journals and edited books, co-founder and director of Science Religion Sangam Goa and actively involved in Science religion Dialogue, Active member of ACPI, organized / participated/ presented papers in several national and international conferences. He is also an external faculty at JDV and St. Pius College Mumbai. Email: victorferrao@yahoo.co.uk